# Rhode Island
## A Bibliography of Its History

*Volume Five of Bibliographies of New England History*

*Prepared by the*

COMMITTEE FOR A NEW ENGLAND BIBLIOGRAPHY
JOHN BORDEN ARMSTRONG
Boston University
*Chairman and Series Editor*

*Edited by*
ROGER PARKS
*Senior Research Associate*
*Boston University*

UNIVERSITY PRESS OF NEW ENGLAND
Hanover and London

University Press of New England

Brandeis University
Brown University
Clark University
Dartmouth College
University of New Hampshire
University of Rhode Island
Tufts University
University of Vermont

*This volume has been
made possible in part by a grant
from the Research Materials
Program of the National Endowment
for the Humanities*

Printed in the United States of America on permanent/durable acid-free paper.

LIBRARY OF CONGRESS CATALOGING IN PUBLICATION DATA
Main entry under title:

Rhode Island, a bibliography of its history.

   (Bibliographies of New England history; v. 5)
   Bibliography: p.
   Includes index.
   1. Rhode Island—History—Bibliography—Union lists.
2. Catalogs, Union—New England.   I. Parks, Roger N.
II. Committee for a New England Bibliography.   III. Series.
Z1331.R58   1983   [F79]        016.9745        83-50139
ISBN 0-87451-284-0

5    4    3    2

# Sponsors

A-Copy, Inc.
Acorn Club of Connecticut
American Antiquarian Society
Amherst College Library
Ella F. Anderson Trust
Association of Historical Societies of New Hampshire
Bangor Public Library
Bay State Historical League
Bennington Museum
Boston Athenaeum
Boston College
Boston Public Library
Boston University
Bowdoin College
Brown University Library
William F. Bryant Foundation
Helen P. Burns
Colonial Society of Massachusetts
Randolph P. Compton
Friends of Connecticut College Library

Connecticut Historical Society
Connecticut Library Association
Fred Harris Daniels Foundation, Inc.
Dartmouth College Library
Frederick P. Elwert
Essex Institute
Faust and Louisa Fiore Memorial
Historic Deerfield, Inc.
Cecil Howard Charitable Trust
Janet Wilson James
Maine Historical Society
Maine Library Association
Maine State American Revolution Bicentennial
Commission
Maine State Archives
Maine State Museum
Massachusetts Historical Society
Merrimack Valley Textile Museum
Middlebury College
Mount Holyoke College
Mount Madison Volunteer Ski Patrol Trust
Museum of Our National Heritage
National Society of the Colonial Dames of America in
the State of Vermont
New England Historic Genealogical Society
New England Library Association
New Hampshire American Revolution Bicentennial
Commission
New Hampshire Charitable Fund
New Hampshire Historical Society
New Hampshire State Library
Northeastern University
Norwich University
Old Sturbridge Village
Providence College

# *Officers*

## *Committee for a New England Bibliography*

# Contents

# Acknowledgments

A number of individuals provided assistance, and a number of institutions made resources available for the research phase of this project. I would like to thank in particular Marcus McCorison, Nancy Burkett, and other staff members of the American Antiquarian Society; Samuel Streit, Assistant University Librarian, Brown University; Richard B. Harrington, Curator of the Military Collection of Anne S. K. Brown, Brown University; James Agnew of the New England Historic Genealogical Society; Thomas Brennan of the Newport Historical Society; Fr. Robert Hayman of Providence College; Wayne Worcester, Editor of the Providence Journal Sunday Magazine; Jeanne Richardson of the Providence Public Library; Albert Klyberg, Paul Campbell, and other staff members of the Rhode Island Historical Society; Anthony S. Nicolosi and Evelyn M. Cherpak of the Naval Historical Collections, U.S. Naval War College; and David Maislyn of the University of Rhode Island Library.

Patrick T. Conley of Providence College several years ago prepared a selective bibliography of Rhode Island history that is available in typescript in the Rhode Island Historical Society Library. I found it useful as a reference point throughout the preparation of this volume.

Retiring editor T. D. Seymour Bassett helped to orient me to the procedures and editorial policies of the project. The members of the editorial board—James Findlay, William G. McLoughlin, Nancy Peace, and Richard K. Showman—offered valuable advice. Edward T. James, Editorial Vice Chairman, helped to solve many editorial problems and gave freely of his time in assisting with the preliminary proofreading and organization of the index.

This is the first computer-assisted volume in the series. William Marshall of the Boston University Academic Computer Center served as programmer and adviser for that phase of the work. Margaret Landy did much of the work of entering and correcting the data, with help from Boston University students Barry Greene, Vernon Yoshida, and others. Clair Dempsey, a graduate student at Boston University, checked bibliographical data against published listings in the *National Union Catalog* and assisted with the serials search. Webb Dordick did the final proofreading, as he had for the other volumes in the series.

Mary Brighthaupt, administrative assistant in Boston University's American and New England Studies Program, made sure that requests for supplies and payments got through the proper channels. Series Editor John B. Armstrong helped in many ways.

Roger Parks

# Preface

The purpose of the preface in the volumes of the Bibliographies of New England History is to explain the rationale and history of the project, and the means by which it is being accomplished. Both may be matters of interest to serious users of this bibliography and to the historical community. To the best knowledge of those of us on the Committee for a New England Bibliography, this series is the first regional historical bibliography with a reasonable claim to comprehensiveness to be compiled in this country. As such, it constitutes a landmark in American historical scholarship.

How the project came about and how it is being carried forward may be of equal significance. A more detailed account of the origins and history of the project down to 1981 appeared in the preface to the previous volume in the series, *Vermont: A Bibliography of Its History*. In brief, beginning in 1968 a group of college history teachers, librarians, and historical society and museum personnel concerned about the lack of bibliographical keys to the vast historical resources of the region formed a committee to compile and publish a multi-volume bibliography of New England history. The committee formulated a publication plan, editorial guidelines, and a strategy for securing financial support. In 1970 it was incorporated as a non-profit, tax exempt organization. In those beginning years, the cost and complexity of the project, and the lack of models, made for heavy going and slow progress. One of the thorniest problems concerned the scope of the bibliography, which loomed as potentially almost without limit. We wished to include as much historical material as we judged practicable to undertake, material that would be of the greatest use to the greatest number of researchers, and

to compile a bibliography that, though necessarily limited, would have a clear identity and be comprehensive within its defined limits. The result was a decision to limit the bibliography to printed works written as history or having an historical dimension or nature. Details of our editorial guidelines on inclusion are explained in the introduction to this volume.

By 1972, the committee had acquired funding that enabled it to obtain a full-time editor and begin work on the first volume. Two years later we signed a contract with G. K. Hall & Co. for publishing the series. Another two years and the volumes began to appear in print: Massachusetts in 1976 with 13,520 entries, Maine in 1977 with 5,355 entries, New Hampshire in 1979 with 6,542 entries, Vermont in 1981 with 6,413 entries, and now Rhode Island with 4,125 entries. Dr. John D. Haskell, Jr. edited the first two volumes. He also co-edited the New Hampshire volume with Dr. T. D. Seymour Bassett, who went on to edit the Vermont volume. Dr. Roger Parks began his labors as editor with the beginning of the work on the present volume. All three editors have been members of the committee since its early years.

In addition to moving the focus of the project from Northern to Southern New England (crossing what Jonathan Daniels thought of as New England's Mason-Dixon Line) we have since 1981 made several changes in how we are doing the project. Each of these was made to maintain or improve our performance and the quality, uniformity, and availability of the series. First, developments in the industry have now allowed us to do what we did not find practical at the beginning of the project, that is, to utilize the assistance of a computer. Although working out the necessary programing has taken time, the ability to call up, sort, and edit all or part of the file of entries as work on the volume progresses has expedited both the search and editorial phases. Secondly, after a decade of experience, the committee transferred the administration of its National Endowment for the Humanities grants to Boston University, where the editorial office has been located all along. This change has improved our administrative arrangements, and allowed the committee to make better use of the University's facilities, especially its Academic Computer Center. Dean Michael Mendillo of the Graduate School and Dr. David Berndt of the Office of Sponsored Programs were both particularly helpful during the rather complicated negotiations to make this change. Thirdly, the committee has secured a new publisher for its series, the University Press of New England. The committee made this change in order to ensure the continued availability of all its published volumes in the years ahead. Our editors at G. K. Hall & Co., Elizabeth Kubik and Meghan R. Wander, were understanding and helpful in the process of accomplishing this change. Despite all these changes, the essential guidelines, the standards, and the administrative and scholarly apparatus by which these bibliographies are being compiled and produced remain basically unchanged although, one should say, enhanced.

Since the first volume was published in 1976, the committee has been gratified by the favorable reception accorded its work. We have been particularly pleased by the amount of interest shown outside of New England, testifying as it does to the national importance of the series. Our admittedly primitive market analyses indicate that approximately three fourths of the published volumes held by research institutions are located outside New England. More concretely, last fall the committee was highly gratified to receive an Award of Merit for its series from the American Association for State and Local History.

Kudos notwithstanding, the committee has endeavored to heed criticisms and suggestions for improving its series. It is a constant challenge to the committee's editors and editorial board to interpret and apply our guidelines so as to make each of the volumes as comprehensive and useful as possible, and at the same time maintain the consistency that is essential to a series. As in the past, the committee very much wishes to have

errors and omissions in its volumes brought to its attention.

As suggested by the names already mentioned, none of our bibliographies could have been compiled and published without the cooperation and support of a host of individuals and institutions. This project was conceived of as an extensively cooperative effort, and so it has been and remains. The Committee for a New England Bibliography now numbers about 120 members, and possesses among them a fund of knowledge of New England history, research, bibliography, organization and publishing. In one way or another, a substantial majority of its members regularly assist the project, and some perform tasks that are prodigious. With good reason we have always tried to emphasize that the responsibility for and authorship of the Bibliographies of New England History belongs to the whole committee.

Consistent with this fact and policy, I have usually avoided mention of the contributions of individual members in these prefaces. Nonetheless, a few exceptions to this policy are justified. Dr. Edward T. James has served in the important capacity of Editorial Vice Chairman since 1976, and the four volumes, including the present one, published under his oversight have all benefited from, and reflect, his meticulous care and high editorial standards. The same four volumes have benefited from the design work of A. L. Morris, of Phoenix Publishing. In publishing matters, the committee has also profited greatly from the advice and guidance provided by William A. Frohlich, of Northeastern University Press. Albert T. Klyberg, of the Rhode Island Historical Society, has served the cause of the committee in many ways since 1969, not the least by the patient confidence he exhibited that the project would eventually reach Rhode Island. Essential to the success enjoyed by the committee to date has been the contribution of such members as these.

Underlying the success of the project has been the committee's ability to find its financial support. This was first sought from and demonstrated by the libraries and the academic and historical institutions of New England. The search for support was then widened to include foundations and private enterprise. In 1972, the National Endowment for the Humanities awarded the committee a two-year grant in support of the project. That grant, which made the Endowment the principal supporter of the project, has now been renewed four times. It is always a pleasure for me to find an occasion to express the committee's gratitude to the Endowment for its support, which has been crucial to the project, and our appreciation of the guidance and counsel provided by the Endowment's staff over the years.

The five grants received from the National Endowment for the Humanities have required that the committee raise matching funds that now approach fourteen thousand dollars a year. Raising these matching funds has always been a major challenge to the committee. Although all members are expected to assist in our fundraising efforts, much of the responsibility rests upon the State Vice Chairman whose state bibliography is currently being compiled. For the volume in hand, Samuel Streit, of Brown University, has had the principal responsibility. For his dedicated efforts, and for those of the other state vice chairmen, the committee is indeed fortunate. Without them, there is no reason to suppose that there would be any such bibliographies.

Early in the history of the project, on the basis of our estimated needs and possibilities for support, it was decided that a contribution of five hundred dollars or more would qualify the donor as a "sponsor" of the bibliographies. These sponsors now number ninety; except for those who wish to remain anonymous, they are listed herein. Some contributors have given much more than the amount stipulated for a sponsorship, others have given less. The total number of contributors now approaches four hundred. Large or small, all gifts have helped to demonstrate a local or regional commitment to the project, and thereby assisted the committee's efforts to secure major foundation support.

In this regard, on behalf of the committee, I would like to express our sincere gratitude for the generous support provided for this bibliography by the Merrimack Valley Textile Museum, the Rhode Island Committee for the Humanities, the Rhode Island Foundation, and the Providence Journal Company.

As for the future of the Bibliographies of New England History, even before this volume appears work will have begun in Connecticut. That state's volume is scheduled for publication in 1986. It will be one of the largest in the series, with perhaps 12,000 entries. The project will then conclude with the publication of the New England volume. This, which we expect to publish in 1988, will be the largest in the series, with perhaps 15,000 entries. It will list works that deal with New England as a whole, or with two or more states within the region. Our plans provide that the New England volume will also contain a section listing the accumulated additions and corrections for the state volumes in the series, and a section listing unpublished historical dissertations and theses on New England and on each of its six states. Clearly, the New England volume will be the crucial capstone of the Bibliographies of New England History.

The publication of the New England volume will round out twenty years' effort to bring this series into existence. We estimate the total direct cost of the project will be about three quarters of a million dollars. The voluntary contributions of time and labor rendered by members of the committee since 1969, if reckoned in monetary terms, would have to amount to considerably more. For that investment, the nation will have a seven-volume guide to the rich historical literature on New England, one listing between sixty and seventy thousand writings and containing much related information helpful to researchers, one that is already having a significant impact on the study and writing of New England history. As some reviewers have indicated, we shall also have a series that may serve as a model and inspiration for other areas of the country.

This projection of the future completion of the series rests upon certain assumptions. Great efforts must still be made to complete the Bibliographies of New England History, for the editorial challenges will continue to be formidable. The committee must soon address the difficult question of updating the volumes, and there will be other problems. One of our officers recently likened the history of the project to a soap opera. Nonetheless, I believe that the committee has clearly demonstrated that it has the resources of people and skills, the collective administrative and editorial experience and ability, and the determination to complete the project properly and on schedule. All the evidence indicates that the project is on a sounder basis at the present time than it has been in its fifteen year history. I believe that *if* the project continues to receive support from the National Endowment for the

Humanities and from new sources of matching funds, then it will unquestionably be successfully completed.

Finally, what can be said about the larger significance of the Bibliographies of New England History? I wrote in the preface to the first volume that the series should serve as an instructive example of how, even in times of social disorders and economic distress, scholarly projects of merit but with no special allure or modishness can still be accomplished by the voluntary, cooperative efforts of individuals and institutions. Perhaps I should have added that those cooperative efforts assume and depend upon the health and stability of the institutions in question. Two years ago, I wrote that the existence and fate of such efforts had acquired a new importance and urgency. Since then, the committee's experience confirms the continued existence of a very challenging atmosphere for a research project in the humanities, but it also suggests some of the possibilities for coping.

John Borden Armstrong
*Professor of History*
*Boston University*

*May 29, 1983*

# Foreword

## An Appraisal of Rhode Island Historiography

The focus of history writing can range from the global to the local—from Arnold Toynbee's civilizations to the history of a particular New England town. American scholars, drawn to national themes and new modes of analysis, have for the most part paid little attention to state and local history. Yet just as the best history is built upon a carefully researched set of particular details, so, in a sense, must national history rest ultimately upon local history. The assembling and recording of this grassroots history has so far been left largely to amateurs: individuals proud of their town, family, or group; history buffs fascinated by a particular era, place, or event. Though such writers sometimes lack perspective and sometimes stress the odd or colorful, they have served a wide nonscholarly audience eager to learn about the past of its own locality, and the information they have recorded has provided groundwork for broader scholarly studies. The New England Bibliography series, of which this volume is a part, seeks to make the whole range of published writing about the region's history available to interested readers, researchers, and scholars, amateur and professional alike.

The purpose of this Foreword is to appraise the present state of Rhode Island's published history and to suggest some needs and opportunities. One need, in some cases, would be a broader and more detached perspective. Local pride can lead to exaggerated claims. Rhode Islanders have been told that "the Revolution started here," or that Rhode Island was "the first colony to declare independence in 1776 and the last to ratify the U.S. Constitution in 1790, holding out until the Bill of Rights guaranteed individual liberties."

Another need is greater attention to the nineteenth and twentieth centuries as against the co-lonial years. State and local histories tend to emphasize a golden, mythic youth—pioneer days in the West and Midwest, the colonial era in the Atlantic states—rather than the complex, unglamorous more recent past. As the present bibliography attests, Rhode Island historiography has shared this imbalance. Such an emphasis has hindered an understanding of the state's present social, urban, and industrial situation. It has also led to exaggerated claims of the influence of the colonial period upon the state's subsequent character and development.

To be sure, the colonial experience did produce an individualistic, independent spirit which Rhode Islanders still hold dear, and which is symbolized by the statue of the "Independent Man" on top of the state capitol. The tumultuous beginnings of the original towns, established by determined individualists and refugees from more orderly societies elsewhere, produced an "other-mindedness" in Rhode Islanders. This independence manifested itself in an unwillingness to cooperate with each other, with other Rhode Island towns, with other colonies, with the British government, or with the United States government. Subsequent events and developments have served to reinforce this trait. Deep divisions emerged between the descendants of the original settlers and the waves of immigrants who began to arrive in the nineteenth century, and lesser ones separated the various immigrant groups. Attention to preserving one's place or to carving out a turf has perpetuated or recreated the independent-mindedness (that is, lack of cooperation) that characterized the seventeenth century founders. In the nineteenth century, the Yankee establishment fixed the governmental institutions to deny access and power to the immigrant, ethnic population. Then in the 1920s and 1930s came the "Bloodless Revolution" which over-threw the Yankee political power; but the once-deprived have spent much of the succeeding period indulging in the politics of gratification.

A clear continuity exists between the colonial era and the nineteenth century in political and constitutional matters. Many of the most contentious issues of the first half of the nineteenth century in Rhode Island involved problems and forces in place at the time of the American Revolution. Such problems as constitutional reform, taxation, broader suffrage, and competition between agrarian and commercial interests played themselves out in the new century, at least until the time of the Dorr War (1841).

Rhode Islanders, however, have tended to exaggerate the national importance of their colonial achievements. The state may claim certain distinctions and contributions, but the ones that mattered to the nation are probably not the ones which Rhode Islanders have traditionally asserted. Generations of Rhode Islanders have maintained that Roger Williams and Rhode Island blazed the way to religious and individual freedom in America. Rhode Island was certainly distinct in its colonial religious liberty and in being the freest, most independent of all of Great Britain's North American colonies, but whether these qualities exerted influence beyond its own borders is debatable. Indeed, they contributed to the colony's reputation among outsiders as the "licentious republic" and "Rogue's Island." The state's main impact on the rest of the nation came generally through oceanic commerce, and particularly through the African slave trade. Only in the last decade has the history of this trade received the attention it deserved, especially in Jay Coughtry's *The Notorious Triangle: Rhode Island and the American Slave Trade, 1700–1807* (1981).

Above all, emphasis upon the seventeenth and eighteenth centuries has tended to divert attention from the profound transformation of Rhode Island from a society based on agriculture and oceanic commerce into the nation's first urban, industrial society. Indeed, the state's entire economic history has been inadequately studied.

Rhode Island has undergone three economic transformations and is in the throes of a fourth. It began as an agricultural society in the seventeenth century and, according to Carl Bridenbaugh in *Fat Mutton and Liberty of Conscience: Society in Rhode Island, 1636–1690* (1974), created an exportable surplus in sheep, horses, and other such products. During the eighteenth century, as available farm land ran out, the focus of enterprise and fortune-building shifted to oceanic commerce. Newport, the principal beneficiary of the agricultural phase of Rhode Island history, used this advantage to dominate the second or oceanic phase. The "Providence Plantations" lagged behind as they were affected and afflicted by the persistent border disputes, Indian troubles, and a thin and stony soil.

The third phase of Rhode Island's history began with independence from Great Britain and the subsequent economic dislocation. The search for new sources of wealth pulled Rhode Islanders in many directions, including a reentry into the slave trade, new ventures in China trade, and a search for oceanic markets in every corner of the world. The future of Rhode Island, however, lay not on the seas but at home. Surrendering some of their independence in 1790 for the benefits of trade, tariffs, and national markets within the expanding United States of America, Rhode Islanders built turnpikes, bridges, stagecoach lines, canals, and railroads. In this new phase the economic and political center of Rhode Island shifted from water-bound Newport to Providence. The best present study of this shift is an increasingly outdated book by Peter Coleman, *The Transformation of Rhode Island, 1790–1860*, published twenty years ago (1963).

Providence leaders pressed to take advantage of the new opportunities. Samuel Slater's mill ushered in the industrial revolution which transformed Rhode Island from an agricultural, commercial state into the nation's first urban, industrial state. Over the course of the nineteenth century, Providence became the center of Rhode Island's industrial, commercial, financial, and institutional enterprise. Although the state had no hinterland, no natural resources, limited communications, and scarce capital, it became the home of some of the nation's leading industries; and Providence grew to be the nation's twentieth largest city in the 1890s. The city boasted of its "Five Industrial Wonders of the World," five factories that were the largest of their kind. These great plants stood among a myriad of smaller producers who fabricated everything from blackboards to door springs, automobiles, and electric light bulbs.

During the 1920s Rhode Island entered the fourth phase, which commentators today call "deindustrialization." First, its leading industry, textiles, began to dissolve, leaving the state with empty mills in nearly every corner. Later the rubber industry, once a powerful and prosperous element in the state, withdrew. Except for the emergency years of World War II, the industrial tide continued to flow out from the 1920s to the 1980s. Of the twenty-one companies that had employed 1,000 or more workers in 1940, only two remained in 1983; and of the forty-seven that had employed 500 workers, only seven remained—all of them subsidiaries of larger corporations. Between 1950 and 1983 the number of industrial workers declined 20 percent.

The foregoing is an outline of mainly economic forces, but nearly every detail needs further investigation. A political outline would produce a different division and other stages, but much political history remains to be written as well. Social and intellectual histories would produce still another landscape. All of these different approaches need to be made and their results worked into a multi-volume general history of Rhode Island. Two recent single-volume studies, William McLoughlin's *Rhode Island: A Bicentennial History* (1978) and George Kellner and Stanley Lemons's *Rhode Island: The Independent State* (1982), constrained as they were by space limits and the need to appeal to a general audience, could offer only a broad interpretation. Not since the larger works of Edward Field (1902), Thomas Bicknell (1920), and Charles Carroll (1932) has the state's history received an extensive treatment. The half-century that has elapsed since the most recent of these is one sixth of Rhode Island's entire history and includes the crucial era of deindustrialization, depression, World War II, and Democratic party dominance. Perhaps the Rhode Island Historical Society should undertake the production of a new multi-volume history with a particular scholar assigned to write each volume. In this way Rhode Island would fill a void and help attract professional historians to the field of state and local history.

Certainly Rhode Island's local history could use such attention. Scarcely any of the state's 39 cities and towns has a careful, scholarly history. The Bicentennial produced a few such efforts, but with the exception of Joseph Conforti's *Our Heritage: A History of East Providence* (1976) and Walter Nebiker's *History of North Smithfield* (1976), these were little more than sketches, picture books, or tour guides. The reports of the Rhode Island Historical Preservation Commission, which are primarily surveys of the architectural resources of the towns, have included historical sketches of at least thirty towns and sections of cities. But no substantial history has yet been written of Newport, once the fifth largest town in British America and co-capital of Rhode Island until 1899. If one were to judge by the existing publications, as listed in this bibliography, the "mystery" of the old Stone Mill (with 34 entries) is more important than the role of black slavery in Newport (10 entries).

Coverage of Afro-Americans is perhaps improved when one considers the history of the whole of Aquidneck Island, for there are an additional 25 items about the Battle of Rhode Island in 1778. Rhode Island's black regiment fought a successful rearguard action in the battle, which allowed the retreating colonials to escape capture by the British; but some accounts barely mention the black role. Black history fares little better in Providence: only now are scholarly studies being made of its black population in the early nineteenth century. In fact, the whole of Rhode Island history, from beginning to end, is almost untouched by the new social history. Only currently, in the work of Bruce Daniels and others, are the techniques of aggregate data being applied, using tax rolls, voting patterns, land and water use, census records, and social and class analysis. Daniels has characterized most local history so far written as being about "charming people living in charming towns." But the story must also include poverty and poor relief, land use and litigation, murders and migration. One still looks for studies of social stratification, institutional development, Yankee-immigrant accommodation, and inter- and intraethnic conflict for every group and period.

It is something of a cliché to say that the first wave of history-writing anywhere usually produces biographies of prominent persons, followed by political histories, institutional histories, and, later, social histories. Except for Erwin Levine's two volumes on Theodore Francis Green and the older biography of Nelson Aldrich by Nathaniel Stephenson, where are biographies of the major figures since the Civil War? Some political history is appearing, such as Jay Goodman's *The Democrats and Labor in Rhode Island, 1952–1962* (1967), as well as articles in *Rhode Island History*, but the field is wide open. One would like a sequel to Goodman's book to trace the changing relationship of the Democratic party and the labor unions from 1962 to the present. Indeed, we lack a good general history of either of the state's two parties.

Other aspects that need study are the sources of party leadership and the political influence of industrialists. Prior to Norman Case's becoming governor in 1928, rarely did a lawyer (unless a corporation lawyer) sit in the governor's chair; but since Case, all chief executives, save for the present incumbent, have been lawyers. Surely this is a sign of the growing importance of the legal profession, but we have little knowledge of that profession in Rhode Island. We lack a general legal history of the state and have only a few studies of its constitutional conventions. The rise of lawyers in party leadership did not necessarily mean a decline in the political power of industrialists. Only now are scholars beginning to examine the process by which business and industrial leaders sought to shape Rhode Island laws and influence court appointments in order to create a more favorable environment for their enterprises. How did Rhode Island reach the point that led Lincoln Steffens to declare it "a state for sale"?

The literature on Rhode Island's industrialists and industries is surprisingly thin. In a state so shaped and dominated by major industries and by a powerful business leadership, it is appalling that we do not have a history of that leadership. What would studies of town growth and development reveal about the role of industrialists in locating plants and factories and in exercising power and influence in town governments? Rhode Island is dotted with the mill villages created by the entrepreneurial and industrial leaders of the nineteenth century. We lack good studies of mill villages, the role of early paternalism in them, or the development of entire complexes based on industrial planning and good social relations, such as the predominantly English mill village of Greystone, in North Providence.

The story of Samuel Slater and the beginnings of the textile industry in America has been often told, but if one were to judge by much of the available literature one would think that Rhode Island's role in the industry ended with Slater. During one third of Rhode Island's history textile manufacturing was its leading industry, yet we still lack a good general history of that industry within the state. New Hampshire's Amoskeag may have been the largest single textile factory in the United States, and Fall River in Massachusetts may have become the city producing more textiles than any other, but no one surpassed the B. B. and R. Knight Company (Fruit of the Loom) as the largest textile company, with its nineteen mill villages and thousands of employees. Where are the histories of the giants of Rhode Island's textile industry, the Lippitts, Spragues, Sayleses, Knights, and Brown & Ives?

Many of these textile leaders deserve family histories as well as sound studies of their enterprises and their contributions to industry and marketing. James Hedges began the history of the Brown family, in *The Browns of Providence Plantations*, but died before completing the second volume. That story needs to be continued, for the Browns remain important to the economic and cultural history of the state. What about a study of the extended family networks of the Iveses, Goddards, Hazards, Robinsons, and other "first families" of Rhode Island?

Besides textile manufacturing itself, the related industries are waiting for their histories. Foundries, metal fabricators, makers of textile machinery, and stationary engine manufacturers, such as Sargeant, Harris & Green, and Corliss, are generally unstudied. Who could be more fascinating than George Corliss, the stubborn, eccentric, brilliant, and contentious inventor of the world's finest steam engine? We have little more than an occasional article, a philiopietistic sketch of his life by a descendant, and an unpublished dissertation.

Closely related were the metal trades and the successful machine tool industries. Of these, two of the world's largest enterprises, Nicholson File and Brown & Sharpe, have no histories even though each revolutionized its respective industry by inventions and mass production techniques. Rhode Island also has led the nation in the manufacture of jewelry and silverware, and such companies as Gorham are still in need of careful study and analysis. Although the rubber industry now barely exists in the state, some of the leading rubber manufacturers of Rhode Island shaped their respective communities, such as Bristol, and were influential in forming the United States Rubber Company, whose first two presidents, Joseph Banigan and Samuel P. Colt, were Rhode Islanders. The Colts were politically powerful; and LeBaron Colt served in the United States Senate, where he delayed the adoption of immigration restriction legislation until his death in the 1920s.

Rhode Island's industries were manned by thousands of immigrants. Articles in such journals as *Rhode Island History* and *Rhode Island Jewish Historical Notes* have thrown some light on the history of these immigrants, as have a few dissertations. But we still have only limited knowledge of their patterns of settlement, the structure of their communities and institutions, and their patterns of socialization with each other or with other groups, including those who controlled their employment. We have impressionistic information of immigrant economic mobility within the state, but no good studies of mobility across the generations in terms of occupations, housing patterns, and family patterns. Some immigrant groups, such as the English and Scots, entered the textile industry as "wet nurses" and skilled operatives; others worked as unskilled laborers and remained that way for several generations. Some, such as the French Canadians, are just beginning to break the textile-mill-village bond; others did so several generations ago. The Irish, the first immigrants, rose through political involvement and, after the 1935 Bloodless Revolution, through patronage employment. Some groups have been quite successful through close community ties and education; others succeeded by seizing the opportunities of catering to their own group's mercantile or service needs. We need to understand the process of immigrant economic involvement outside the mills and factories in order to understand the rise of ethnic businesses and industries.

The immigrants crowded into the mill villages and into the cities. Their arrival increased the demand for housing, and studies are needed to understand the role of mill owners, private developers, and real estate speculators involved in the process of housing the immigrants. The physical remains of the intense growth are visible everywhere: double- and triple-decker tenements, mill row housing, and some of the most densely congested communities in the nation; but what was the quality of life in these cities and towns? What is the rate of immigrant or ethnic ownership of housing?

One of the major problems of twentieth century Rhode Island has been the decay of the inner cities. Depopulation, which saw more people leave Providence than any other city in America except one, had a profound impact on city and state ability to provide essential services. The declining revenue base resulting from factory closings, decayed, abandoned, and devalued property, and a growing elderly and poor population seriously crippled urban reform, revitalization, and planning. These forces and their relationship to the political process need serious study. Suburban communities reaped the benefits of the exodus from the older industrial cities after World War II. But we know little of the process: the inducements, the kind of people who left, how they financed their homes, and the consequences of the migration for urban services, schools, and recreational needs on the receiving towns. The best studies available are Sidney and Alice Goldstein's *Metropolitanization and Population Change in Rhode Island* (1962) and Sidney Goldstein and Calvin Goldscheider's *Jewish Americans* (1968), a sound sociological study of the Providence Jewish community and its dispersal. In recent years the historical preservation movement, neighborhood revitalization, and redevelopment have revived and restored substantial sections of several cities and towns. The visible signs of change are everywhere, but understanding the process, the movers and shakers, financing, and alternatives would add greatly to the knowledge of our cities' transformation.

Nearly every aspect of employment in the state needs study. Providence, while it has lost its retail and commercial hold on southeast New England, remains a governmental and financial center. Who works there? Who trains them? What sort of effect did the rise of white collar female employment have on the ethnic family, marriage patterns, and mobility? Why was Rhode Island labor relatively docile, poorly organized, and ineffective throughout the nineteenth century; and why in the twentieth would the state become one of the most unionized in the nation? Did the rise of the Democratic party and its dependence upon the urban worker influence that change, or did a decline of nineteenth century ethnic conflicts and rivalries allow labor unity to develop? Ironically, unions became most active and militant at the time when the state's major employers were leaving the state. What role has organized labor played in the process of deindustrialization? It is known, for example, that Nicholson File Company elected to close its Rhode Island operations following a protracted strike. What accommodations have been made among labor, management, and government to retain the remaining elements of the state's industrial base?

If one longs for a study of the process of industrialization in Rhode Island, one must also crave an analysis of deindustrialization, and of organized efforts for economic development. What has been the effect of the costs of raw materials, transportation, and fuel; of declining markets, southern competition, conservative and unprofessional management and marketing, and external investment? Some have suggested that Rhode Island has plenty of investment capital, but that investors have sought higher yields in distant places, thus creating a capital scarcity that prevented bright young minds from developing their ideas. Rhode Island was tardy in establishing a professionally staffed, efficiently operated, and centralized economic development council, lagging as much as thirty years behind other New England states. The struggle to create such a council and its work and effect need to be told.

Rhode Island is surely the "Playground of New England." Although the story of High Society in Newport is widely known and ably told, the resorts of the not-so-rich, the working class, and day-trippers have not received adequate treatment. From Watch Hill on the western tip of Rhode Island, along the southern coast and up the Bay to Field's Point, Providence, and East Providence-Riverside, and down to Sakonnet in Little Compton, Rhode Island's shores have teemed with recreational sites and shore resorts for all levels of society. While the flamboyant rich of New York showed off in Newport, the more

discreet Philadelphians summered on Jamestown. New Yorkers engaged in the fine arts once had a visionary summer retreat near Westerly called Musicolony. Narragansett Pier and the southern beaches served the not-so-wealthy; the genteel middle class were entertained at places like Rocky Point. One historian described the East Providence-Riverside area of Narragansett Bay as the "Coney Island of New England" because of its large amusement parks, such as Crescent Park and Vanity Fair. Here working class families thronged and enjoyed the glitter and excitement of shows, games, and rides. Changes in taste and interest, hurricanes, and water pollution have eliminated nearly all of the shore resorts and amusement parks. An exacting study of their rise, decline, and fall remains to be written. One wonders also what relationship these summer communities, like Oakland Beach, had to the development of permanent settlements along the coast.

Resorts are part of economic as well as social history. Rhode Island today touts itself as the Ocean State and emphasizes recreation and tourism as a form of industry. But the history of that industry remains to be traced. Neither the efforts of businesses, such as steamship lines in the nineteenth century, nor those of the Automobile Association, nor those of the state itself have been told. Such a study would have to examine the building of roads, highways, interstate freeways, and bridges as well as the active promotion of tourism by the state government. Finally, Narragansett Bay is not only a recreational resource; it is also the workshop of the clam and oystermen, fishermen, and ship builders. These activities have been secondary to the recreational uses of Rhode Island waters, but they are not insignificant. Water pollution, of such intense current concern, is not new; eighty years ago it was already destroying the clam and oyster industry as well as the dining halls that served those world-famous Rhode Island shore dinners.

If Rhode Island's fisheries have been largely ignored by historians, so has its agriculture. Rhode Island may be densely populated, but it is now mostly a forested state. When one considers that by the late eighteenth century nearly 80 percent of the land was cleared farmland, one realizes that the story of land use is as little studied as the use of Rhode Island's waters. Of particular merit would be a study of suburban development, the filling in of rural spaces between mill villages in the Providence metropolitan area. The impact of the automobile on life styles and the growth of shopping malls and their impact on main streets and downtowns offer related possibilities for study.

State and local history helps to shape a state's self-image and to mold perspectives on contemporary life. As Richard Wohl and Theodore Brown wrote of Kansas City, "What people believe about the history of their locale may shape their notions of how they ought to live in it and of the values they may hope to realize in the community." What Rhode Islanders think of themselves and their state has been fashioned and is being molded by what is written about their past. If those writings are incomplete or unbalanced, one must not be surprised at unsatisfactory undertakings or inappropriate responses. Much has been written, as the pages of this bibliography attest, but much remains to be done.

George H. Kellner
J. Stanley Lemons

*Rhode Island College*
*March 1983*

# Introduction

This volume lists published writings—books, pamphlets, magazine and journal articles—about the history of Rhode Island, its cities, towns, and counties, its people and their institutions. Within editorial guidelines that will be described shortly, we have tried to compile as complete a list of published historical writings as possible.

The varied works cited here were written by academic scholars, professional writers, and amateur historians. Some of the subjects dealt with are of broad, current interest to students, scholars, or general readers; others are of more local concern or reflect the interests of earlier generations of Rhode Island historians and their readers. In bringing these materials together, we make no qualitative judgment. Our purpose is to identify and make accessible the many scattered references and to suggest the kinds of information that can be extracted from them through careful use of this bibliography and its index of authors, subjects, and places.

This is the fifth in a projected seven-volume series of bibliographies of New England history. It was compiled under guidelines established by the Committee for a New England Bibliography in its early years and refined through experience with the four previous volumes.

To be included in this series, published writings must have been produced as works of history or include a significant historical dimension. They must have been written at least a year after the events they describe, and they must deal mainly with events within the state. Accounts of the 1938 hurricane and 1978 blizzard that appeared soon after the fact are thus excluded from this volume, as are combat histories of Rhode Island units in the Civil War and World War I. Certain classes of materials—with exceptions to be described below—are also excluded: almanacs, directories, and guidebooks, for example; biographies and autobiographies; government documents; historical articles published in newspapers; genealogies; maps and atlases; works of fiction; juvenile literature.

"These exclusions, however," as former editor T. D. Seymour Bassett explained in his introduction to an earlier bibliography in this series, "are not absolute. . . . We try to go beyond the form and determine the substance." Each volume thus includes both collected biographies and a substantial number of individual biographies that in our opinion have something significant to say about some aspect of state or local history. We also include published documents that are accompanied by an historical introduction or scholarly annotations. While we make no attempt to search the many files of newspapers that might contain historical articles, we include a certain number of such articles—especially articles in a series—that have come to the editor's attention.

In compiling this volume, the strategy once again was to start with large research collections within the state, then work outward to local libraries around the state and large collections elsewhere in New England. Rhode Island's small size and small number of communities made it possible for perhaps the only time in the series to survey the holdings of at least one public library in every city and town. This local search turned up some materials that had not been found elsewhere. Most of the books and pamphlets cited here, however, are available in one or more of the major Rhode Island collections surveyed during the initial phases of the project: the Rhode Island Historical Society, Providence Public Library, and Brown University Libraries, in Providence; the Newport Historical Society and the Redwood Library and Athenaeum, in Newport; and the University of Rhode Island Library, in Kingston.

Elsewhere in Rhode Island, sizeable state and local history collections were found in a number of public libraries, especially those of Central Falls, Cranston, East Greenwich, Johnston, Newport, North Kingstown, North Providence, Pawtucket, South Kingstown, Warwick, Westerly, and Woonsocket. Noteworthy special collections are those of the Bristol Historical and Preservation Society; the U.S. Naval Historical Collections and U.S. Naval War College Library, in Newport; the Military Collection of Anne S. K. Brown, in the Hay Library, Brown University; the Rhode Island Jewish Historical Association, in Providence; the Chancery Office of the Diocese of Providence (Roman Catholic); and the Union Saint-Jean-Baptiste, in Woonsocket, which specializes in Franco-American history and culture. Two useful private collections are the architectural history holdings of Richard B. Harrington of Providence and the Roman Catholic parish histories collected by Fr. Robert Hayman, unofficial historian of the Diocese of Providence.

Outside of Rhode Island, some additional entries were found in the American Antiquarian Society, Worcester, Mass.; the Boston Public Library, Massachusetts State Library, and New England Historic Genealogical Society, in Boston; and the Harvard University Libraries, in Cambridge, Mass. Finally, a search of the Library of Congress shelflist for Rhode Island yielded a few titles not found in Rhode Island or other New England libraries.

Almost without exception, the libraries surveyed for this volume granted us stack privileges. This made it possible to conduct the search volume-by-volume and shelf-by-shelf, examining each item before recording the bibliographical data and assigning index headings. Extensive use also was made of the card catalogs in most of the institutions.

As in earlier volumes, magazine and journal articles account for more than half of the Rhode Island entries. At the beginning of the Bibliographies of New England History project, a core list of national, regional, and state periodicals was thoroughly searched for titles pertaining to New England and each of its states. Titles were briefly noted at that time. Since then, as each state volume has been researched in turn, the core list has

been updated and the briefly noted articles pertaining to the state in question have been found and carefully examined before being cited. For this volume, a number of Rhode Island periodicals also were thoroughly searched. These included the publications of various historical societies, colleges and schools, professional societies, and trade organizations. Also searched was the *Rhode Islander*, Sunday magazine of the *Providence Journal*, which for a number of years published frequent articles about Rhode Island history. Abbreviations or initials have been used for the titles of periodicals frequently cited; for the full titles, see the list of Serial Abbreviations elsewhere in the introductory matter to this volume.

Work on the Rhode Island volume began in late 1981, and we have attempted to compile a complete list of relevant works published up to the end of that year. Although this is our official cut-off date, we have also included, as opportunity offered, a number of 1982 titles and a few published in early 1983.

As in the rest of the series, entries in this volume are organized geographically, with separate sections for state, county, and local listings. Works pertaining to more than one town appear under the appropriate county; those relating to more than one county are included in the state section. The "see also" references at the end of many county, city, and town listings are a guide to these boundary-spanning materials.

Under each geographical heading, entries are arranged alphabetically. Works by the same author are listed in alphabetical order by title, followed by any titles written by that author and a collaborator. A dash at the beginning of an entry means that the work was written by the author of the preceding entry. Where an author's name has been determined from information other than the title page, it is enclosed in brackets.

Author and corporate-author entries have been preferred in most cases. Edited and compiled works are given a title entry, unless it is evident from the text that the "compiler" should instead be regarded as an author. Otherwise, the editor's or compiler's name follows the title.

Titles or imprints, when not shown on the title page or verso, appear in brackets. Where there is more than one edition, the most recent or best one is cited, and the date of the first edition, if known, appears in parentheses after the title.

Pagination indicates the last numbered page, with substantial unnumbered pages shown in brackets.

The index lists authors, editors, and compilers, and also provides access to scores of different subjects. As in previous volumes, we also have identified a number of place names in the index, whether or not those places are subjects of works cited in the bibliography.

Starting with this volume, we give one library location for each book and pamphlet entry. Previously, we provided locations only for titles not listed in the various editions of the *National Union Catalog* (NUC). That series, however, is not readily accessible to some of our readers; it has become increasingly cumbersome to search; and it sometimes fails to list a location that most readers would find useful. We compared Rhode Island titles with the NUC listings and have provided a plus sign (+) to identify titles found in the NUC. Readers who wish to consult that source for additional locations may find the effort rewarding.

Library locations are indicated by standard library symbols. For a list of those used in this volume, see the section of Location Symbols. The locations cited in this volume reflect the order in which libraries were surveyed. Since the Rhode Island Historical Society has the largest collection of books and pamphlets on Rhode Island history and was the first library searched, the majority of book and pamphlet entries carry its symbol

(RHi). Many titles, of course, are also available in other libraries. Readers should refer especially to the Rhode Island and New England collections mentioned above. A local-library symbol at the end of an entry means that it is less likely that the title also will be found in one of the major collections. Readers outside of Rhode Island may also wish to refer to the published lists of the local history holdings of the Harvard University Library, Library of Congress, and New York Public Library. These lists are cited under Supplementary Bibliographies and Guides, the section immediately preceding the index.

In searching for the journal and magazine articles listed here, readers should also be familiar with the *Union List of Serials*. This work lists libraries that own runs of a particular periodical.

This, as we have mentioned, is the fifth in a projected seven-volume series. Volume seven, which will deal with New England as a whole, will include some works not cited here that relate jointly to Rhode Island and another New England state. As planned, volume seven will also include additions and corrections to each of the state volumes and will list unpublished doctoral dissertations relating to each New England state. Readers of this volume should also be aware that the Rhode Island Historical Society plans to publish a listing of dissertations on that state's history in its journal, *Rhode Island History*, probably in 1984.

Roger Parks

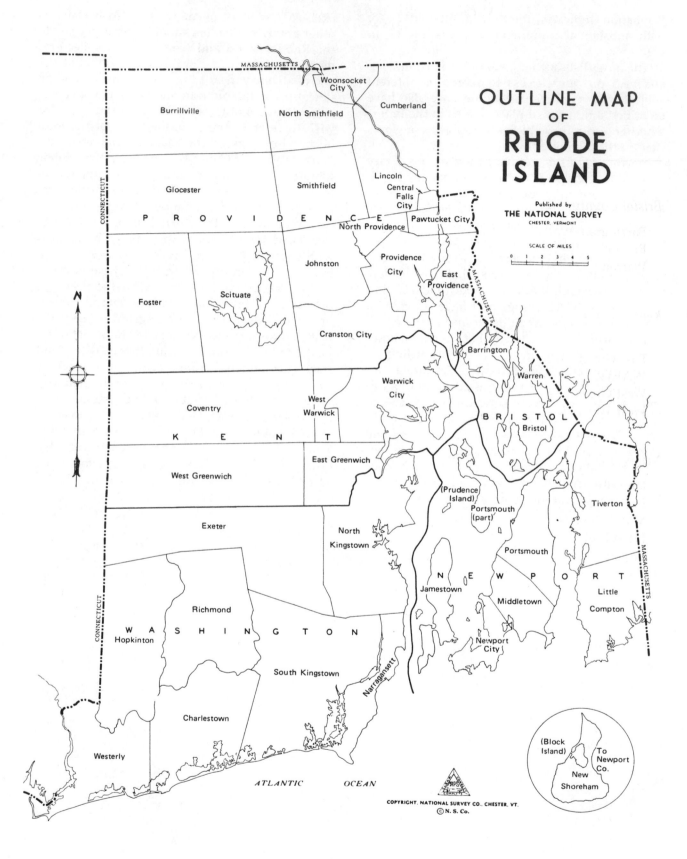

# OUTLINE MAP
## OF
# RHODE
# ISLAND

Published by
**THE NATIONAL SURVEY**
CHESTER, VERMONT

SCALE OF MILES
0  1  2  3  4  5

MASSACHUSETTS

Woonsocket City
Burrillville
North Smithfield
Cumberland

CONNECTICUT

Glocester
Smithfield
Lincoln
Central Falls City

P R O V I D E N C E
North Providence
Pawtucket City

Johnston
Providence City
East Providence

Foster
Scituate

Cranston City
Barrington
Warren

N

Warwick City

B R I S T O L
Bristol

Coventry
West Warwick

K    E    N    T

East Greenwich
(Prudence Island)
Portsmouth (part)
Tiverton

West Greenwich

Exeter
North Kingstown
Portsmouth

N    E    W    P    O    R    T

Jamestown
Little Compton

MASSACHUSETTS

Richmond
Middletown

W A S H I N G T O N
Hopkinton

South Kingstown
Newport City

CONNECTICUT

Charlestown

Narragansett

Westerly

*ATLANTIC        OCEAN*

COPYRIGHT, NATIONAL SURVEY CO., CHESTER, VT.
Ⓒ N. S. Co.

(Block Island)
To Newport Co.
New Shoreham

# Cities and Towns, by Counties

*The eight cities are in capital letters.*

*Bristol County*

Barrington
Bristol
Warren

*Kent County*

Coventry
East Greenwich
WARWICK
West Greenwich
West Warwick

*Newport County*

Jamestown
Little Compton
Middletown
NEWPORT
Portsmouth
Tiverton

*Providence County*

Burrillville
CENTRAL FALLS
CRANSTON
Cumberland
EAST PROVIDENCE
Foster
Glocester
Johnston
Lincoln
North Providence
North Smithfield
PAWTUCKET
PROVIDENCE
Scituate
Smithfield
WOONSOCKET

*Washington County*

Charlestown
Exeter
Hopkinton
Narragansett
New Shoreham
North Kingstown
Richmond
South Kingstown
Westerly

# Serial Abbreviations

| | |
|---|---|
| BN | *Book Notes* |
| BrAlumMo | *Brown Alumni Monthly* |
| BTJ | *Board of Trade Journal (Providence)* |
| CHSN | *Cranston Historical Society, Newsletter* |
| JHSB | *Jamestown Historical Society, Bulletin* |
| NEM | *New England Magazine* |
| NG | *Preservation Society of Newport County, Newport Gazette* |
| NH | *Newport History* |
| NHM | *Newport Historical Magazine* |
| NHR | *Narragansett Historical Register* |
| NHSB | *Newport Historical Society, Bulletin* |
| PBTJ | *Providence Board of Trade, Journal* |
| PJC | *Providence Journal of Commerce* |
| PM | *Providence Magazine* |
| PMJ | *Providence Medical Journal* |
| PR | *Pettaquamscutt Historical Society, Pettaquamscutt Reporter* |
| RIer | *Rhode Islander (Sunday magazine, Providence Journal)* |
| RIH | *Rhode Island History* |
| RIHM | *Rhode Island Historical Magazine* |
| RIHSC | *Rhode Island Historical Society, Collections* |
| RIHSPr | *Rhode Island Historical Society, Proceedings* |
| RIHSPubs | *Rhode Island Historical Society, Publications* |
| RIJHN | *Rhode Island Jewish Historical Notes* |
| RIMJ | *Rhode Island Medical Journal* |
| RIY | *Rhode Island Yearbook* |
| WHSR | *Westerly Historical Society, Records* |
| WRICHSH | *Western Rhode Island Civic Historical Society, Hinterlander* |
| WRICHSP | *Western Rhode Island Civic Historical Society, Proceedings* |

# Location Symbols

+ Listings in the National Union Catalog *for books and pamphlets marked with this symbol may include additional library locations.*

| | |
|---|---|
| DLC | *Library of Congress, Washington* |
| M | *Massachusetts State Library, Boston* |
| MBNEH | *New England Historic Genealogical Society, Boston* |
| MH | *Harvard University Libraries, Cambridge, Mass.* |
| MWA | *American Antiquarian Society, Worcester, Mass.* |
| R | *Rhode Island State Library, Providence* |
| RBr | *Rogers Free Library, Bristol* |
| RBrHi | *Bristol Historical and Preservation Society* |
| RBuH | *Jesse M. Smith Memorial Library, Harrisville (Burrillville)* |
| RCe | *Central Falls Public Library* |
| RCo | *Coventry Public Library* |
| RCr | *William H. Hall Free Library, Cranston* |
| REaG | *East Greenwich Free Library* |
| RFo | *Foster Public Library* |
| RGl | *Glocester Manton Free Library, Chepachet* |
| RHi | *Rhode Island Historical Society, Providence* |
| RJa | *Jamestown Public Library* |
| RJo | *Marian J. Mohr Memorial Library, Johnston* |
| RLit | *Brownell Library, Little Compton* |
| RMi | *Middletown Public Library* |
| RNHi | *Newport Historical Society* |
| RNR | *Redwood Library and Athenaeum, Newport* |
| RNW | *U.S. Naval War College Library, Newport* |
| RNW-Hi | *Naval Historical Collection, U.S. Naval War College, Newport* |
| RNeS | *Island Free Library, New Shoreham* |
| RNoK | *North Kingstown Free Library, Wickford* |
| RNoP | *North Providence Union Free Library, Centerdale* |
| RP | *Providence Public Library* |
| RP-Harrington | *Richard B. Harrington, Providence* |
| RP-K | *Providence Public Library, Knight Memorial Branch* |
| RPB | *Brown University Libraries, Providence* |
| RPB-ASKB | *Military Collection of Anne S. K. Brown, Brown University* |
| RPC | *Providence College Library* |
| RPD | *Archives, Diocese of Providence (Roman Catholic), Chancery Office, Providence* |
| RPD-H | *Archives, Diocese of Providence. Collection of Fr. Robert Hayman, unofficial historian of the diocese* |
| RPJ | *Rhode Island Jewish Historical Association and Bureau of Jewish Education libraries, Providence* |

# Entries for Rhode Island

Works on the state as a
whole or touching upon
more than one county

---

1  ACHTERMIER, WILLIAM O.  Rhode Island arms makers & gunsmiths, 1643-1883.  Providence: Man at Arms, 1980.  xiii, 108p.  RHi. +

2  ADAMS, JAMES P.  "Our common heritage." RIJHN, 1 (1955), 165-172.
   Jews and Christians in R.I.

3  ADAMS, JAMES TRUSLOW.  Rhode Island's part in making America:  an address delivered at Rhode Island College of Education. [Providence:]  State of R.I., Public Education Service, 1923.  12p.  RHi. +

4  ADELMAN, DAVID C.  "Roger Williams and the Jews."  RIJHN, 1 (1955), 149-157.

5  _____.  "Strangers:  civil rights of Jews in the colony of Rhode Island."  RIJHN, 1 (1954), 104-118.
      Another version appeared in RIH, 13 (1954), 65-77.

6  "THE ADJUSTMENT of Rhode Island into the Union in 1790."  RIHSPubs, 8 (1900), 104-135.

7  ADLAM, SAMUEL.  The First Church in Providence, not the oldest of the Baptists in America, attempted to be shown.... Newport:  Cranston & Norman's Power Pr., 1850.  28p.  RHi. +
      First Baptist Church, Providence; and First Baptist Church, Newport.  See also entry 2314.

8  _____.  Origin of the institutions of Rhode Island:  a lecture delivered...before the Newport Historical Society, January 19th, 1871.  Providence:  John F. Greene, 1871. 25p.  RHi. +

9  ADVENTURE (sloop).  A Rhode Island slaver: trade book of the sloop Adventure, 1773-1774; from original manuscript in the library of George L. Shepley, with notes and introduction by...Verner W. Crane.... Providence:  Shepley Library, 1922.  10p. RHi. +

10  AHMAT, SHAROM.  "The Rhode Island Java trade, 1799-1836."  RIH, 24 (1965), 1-10.

11  AN ALBUM of the attorneys of Rhode Island, with a portrait and brief record of the life of each.  (1904)  E. C. Bowler, comp. Newton Highlands, Mass., 1942.  208p. RHi. +

12  ALDERMAN, CLIFFORD LINDSEY.  The Rhode Island colony.  [N.Y.:]  Crowell-Collier Pr., 1969.  134p.  RHi. +

13  ALGEO, SARA M.  The story of a sub-pioneer. Providence:  Snow & Farnham, 1925.  318p. RHi. +
      Woman suffrage movement in R.I.

14  "ALL aboard on the good ship 'Reminiscence.'"  RIer (July 28, 1957), 10-12.
      Narragansett Bay steamboats.

15  ALLEN, DEVERE.  "Those shift-y marriages." RIer (Apr. 10, 1955), 7.
      Marriage customs.

16  ALLEN, R. W.  "Roger Williams."  Methodist Quarterly Review, 4 ser. 4 (Apr. 1852), 199-212.

17  ALLEN, SAMUEL H.  "The Federal ascendency of 1812."  NHR, 7 (1889), 381-394.
      Federalist Party.

18  _____.  "Rhode Island judiciary."  NHR, 7 (1889), 57-63.

+ Listings in the National Union Catalog for books and pamphlets marked
  with this symbol may include additional library locations.

19   ALLEN, ZACHARIAH.  Defence of the Rhode
     Island system of treatment of the Indians,
     and of civil and religious liberty:  an
     address before the Rhode Island Historical
     Society, April 10th, 1876.  Providence:
     Providence Pr., 1876.  34p.  RHi. +
       Occasioned by 200th anniversary of the
     burning of Providence during King Philip's
     War.

20   _____.  Memorial of Roger Williams:  paper
     read before the Rhode Island Historical
     Society, May 18, 1860.  n.p., n.d.  10p.
     RHi. +

21   "ALONG the Queen Anne Highway."  PM, 28
     (1916), 23-25.
       Colonial route between Westerly and
     Warwick.

22   ANDERSON, JAMES.  "Rhode Island & the
     Revolution."  Rhode Island Review, 2
     (Nov./Dec. 1981), 6-7.

23   _____.  "The Rhode Island homefront in World
     War II."  Rhode Island Review, 3 (Jan./Feb.
     1982), 16-17.

24   ANDREWS, ELISHA BENJAMIN.  "Rhode Island."
     NEM, n.s. 7 (1892), 63-85.

25   ANDREWS, NEIL.  The development of the
     nominating convention in Rhode Island.
     Providence, 1894.  14p.  RHi. +
       Reprinted from RIHSPr, n.s. 1 (1893),
     258-269.

26   ANGELL, WALTER F.  "Rhode Island's
     Declaration of Independence:  address
     delivered before the Rhode Island Historical
     Society on May 4th, 1926."  RIHSC, 19
     (1926), 65-80.

27   "AN ANNOTATED critical bibliography of
     materials relating to the history of the
     Jews in Rhode Island, located in Rhode
     Island depositories (1678-1966)."  RIJHN,
     4 (1966), 305-506.
       Freda Egnal, comp.

28   APPLETON, MARGUERITE.  A portrait album of
     four great Rhode Island leaders.
     Providence:  R.I. Historical Society, 1978.
     xi, 125p.  RHi.
       Biographical sketches of Roger Williams,
     Stephen Hopkins, John Howland, Elizabeth
     Buffum Chace.

29   _____.  "Rhode Island's first court of
     admiralty."  NEQ, 5 (1932), 148-158.

30   ARNOLD, JAMES N.  "The causes of the
     popularity of the Revolutionary movement in
     Rhode Island."  NHR, 4 (1885), 81-99.

31   _____.  "The first commission at sea from
     Rhode Island."  Magazine of History, 7
     (1908), 197-207, 259-270.
       For the capture of Dutch fort and ships
     (1653).  See also BN, 25 (1908), 137-142,
     145-150, 153-158.

32   _____.  The life and times of Benedict
     Arnold, first governor of Rhode Island under
     the charter....  Newport:  Mercury
     Publishing, 1901.  [10]p.  RHi. +

33   _____.  "Pre-historic Rhode Island."  NHR,
     6 (1888), 97-110.

34   _____.  The reasons why Rhode Island
     declared her independence of Great Britain,
     May 4, 1776.  [Wickford, 1907.]  20p.
     RHi. +

35   _____.  "Rebel treatment of Tories during
     the Revolution."  NHR, 3 (1884-1885), 52-58,
     132-136, 202-204, 263-267; 4 (1885), 77-78.

36   _____.  "The stone worshippers."  NHR, 6
     (1888), 317-330.
       Speculations on Indian worship practices.

37   ARNOLD, JOHN NELSON.  Art and artists in
     Rhode Island.  Providence, 1905.  47p.
     RHi. +
       Author published an article under same
     title in PM, 26 (1914), 133-135.

38   ARNOLD, NOAH J.  "Biographical reminiscences
     of the Pawtuxet Valley."  NHR, 8 (1890),
     97-118; 9 (1891), 153-194.

39   _____.  "Further reminiscences of the valley
     of the Pawtuxet River and its branches."
     NHR, 7 (1889), 233-280.

40   _____.  "The history of suffrage in Rhode
     Island."  NHR, 8 (1890), 305-331.

41   _____.  "The valley of the Pawtuxet."  NHR,
     6 (1888), 222-259.

42   ARNOLD, SAMUEL GREENE.  History of the State
     of Rhode Island and Providence Plantations.
     (1859-1860)  4th ed.  Providence:  Preston
     & Rounds, 1894.  2v.  RHi. +

43   _____.  The spirit of Rhode-Island history:
     a discourse, delivered before the Rhode
     Island Historical Society, on the evening of
     Monday, January 17, 1853.  Providence:
     George H. Whitney, 1853.  32p.  RHi. +

44   "ARRIVAL of the Quakers in Rhode Island."
     PM, 32 (1920), 499, 501, 503, 505, 507.

45   ASHLEY, GEORGE H.   Rhode Island coal.
Washington:  Government Printing Office,
1915.  62p.  RHi. +
     Includes historical sketch.

46   ASPINWALL, THOMAS.  Remarks on the
Narragansett Patent, read before the
Massachusetts Historical Society, June,
1862.  2d ed.  Providence:  Sidney S. Rider
& Brother, 1865.  40p.  RHi. +
     "...An instrument...which purports to be
a grant, dated Dec. 10, 1643, from...the
colony of Massachusetts, of the territory
which substantially at present constitutes
the State of Rhode Island."  This entry was
first published in Massachusetts Historical
Society, Proceedings, 6 (1862), 41-77.

47   "ASSIZE of bread."  NHR, 6 (1888), 261-268.
     Colonial price regulation.  Article signed
F.C.C.

48   BABIN, NEHAMA ELLA.  "A study of residential
mobility of Jews in Rhode Island,
1963-1972."  RIJHN, 6 (1973), 390-453.

49   BACON, EDGAR MAYHEW.  Narragansett Bay:  its
historic and romantic associations and
picturesque setting.  N.Y.: Putnam, 1904.
xii, 367p.  RHi. +

50   BAILEY, ARNOLD C.  "Stouthearted men."  RIY
(1965-1966), 67-75.
     State Police.

51   _____.  "Whatever happened to Miss Rhode
Island?"  RIY (1968), 82-88.
     Beauty contest winners.

52   BAIR, BARBARA.  "'The full light of this
dawn':  Congressman John Fogarty and the
historical cycle of community mental health
policy in Rhode Island."  RIH, 41 (1982),
127-138.
     R.I. Congressman John E. Fogarty "based
his career on a faith that national
legislative reforms like the
deinstitutionalization policies of the 1960s
could bring about meaningful change at the
local level."

53   _____.  "The Parents Council for Retarded
Children and social change in Rhode Island,
1951-1970."  RIH, 40 (1981), 145-159.

54   BAKER, HARRY.  "Preparing for the worst."
RIer (June 9, 1974), 12.
     Preparations for war in Revolutionary-era
R.I.

55   BANNING, H. E.  "The story of Roger Williams
retold."  Magazine of American History, 24
(1890), 312-318.

56   "A BAPTIST semi-centennial:  fiftieth
anniversary of the Rhode Island Baptist
State Convention...the history of the
convention."  Providence Daily Journal (May
13, 1875).
     Lengthy article includes historical
discourse by A. H. Granger.

57   BARNARD, HENRY.  Report on documents
relating to the public schools of Rhode
Island, for 1848.  Providence, 1849.  560p.
RHi. +
     Report of the Commissioner for Public
Schools.  Includes "Reports and documents
relating to the history and condition of
public schools of the several
towns," 33-175.

58   BARROWS, COMFORT EDWIN.  The development of
Baptist principles in Rhode Island,            •
1636-1875:  a discourse delivered on the
occasion of the semi-centennial anniversary
of the Rhode Island Baptist State
Convention, at Providence, May 12, 1875.
Providence:  J. A. & R. A. Reid, 1875.  46p.
RHi. +

59   BARTLETT, IRVING H.  From slave to citizen:
the story of the Negro in Rhode Island.
(1954)  Providence:  Urban League of Greater
Providence, 1972.  76p.  RHi. +

60   [BARTLETT, JOHN RUSSELL.]  "History of
lotteries and the lottery system in Rhode
Island."  Providence Journal (1856).
     Series of five articles found in Rider
Collection, Brown Univ.  Last two articles
in series dated Nov. 17 and Dec. 8, 1856.

61   _____.  A history of the destruction of His
Britannic Majesty's Schooner Gaspee, in
Narragansett Bay, on the 10th June, 1772;
accompanied by the correspondence connected
therewith; the action of the General
Assembly of Rhode Island thereon, and the
official journal of the proceedings of the
commission of inquiry appointed by King
George the Third, on the same.  Providence:
A. Crawford Greene, 1861.  140p.  RHi. +

62   _____.  Memoirs of Rhode Island officers who
were engaged in the service of their country
during the Great Rebellion of the South.
Providence:  Sidney S. Rider & Brother,
1867.  viii, 452p.  RHi. +

63   BATES, FRANK GREENE.  Rhode Island and the
formation of the Union.  N.Y., 1898.  ix,
221p.  RHi. +

64   _____.  "Rhode Island and the impost of
1781."  American Historical Association,
Annual Report (1894), 351-359.

65 Rhode Island

65    BATES, W. LINCOLN. "Slavery days in Rhode Island." JHSB, No. 2 (1921), 1-14.

66    BEALS, CARLETON. Colonial Rhode Island. Camden, N.J.: Thomas Nelson, 1970. 160p. RHi. +

67    BEAMAN, CHARLES C. "The Hopkins family in Rhode Island, to which Stephen Hopkins, one of the signers of the Declaration of Independence, July 4, 1776, belonged." Essex Institute, Historical Collections, 2 (1860), 115-123.

68    BELCHER, HORACE G. "In old Pawtuxet." RIH, 11 (1952), 125-127.
      Folklore about local witchcraft. Pawtuxet is in Cranston and Warwick.

69    ____. "Mr. Tambo and Mr. Bones: Rhode Island in Negro minstrelsy." RIH, 8 (1949), 97-111.

70    ____. "Pawtuxet and the Rhodes family." RIHSC, 32 (1939), 97-115.
      Textile manufacturers.

71    BIBLIOGRAPHY of Rhode Island: a catalogue of books and other publications relating to the State of Rhode Island, with notes, historical, bibliographical and critical. John Russell Bartlett, comp. Providence: Alfred Anthony, 1864. iv, 287p. RHi. +

72    BIBLIOGRAPHY of Rhode Island history. Clarence Saunders Brigham, comp. n.p., 1902. [29]p. RHi. +
      Reprinted from entry 1027.

73    BICKNELL, THOMAS WILLIAMS. The history of the State of Rhode Island and Providence Plantations. N.Y.: American Historical Society, 1920. 5v. RHi. +
      Vols. 4-5 biographical.

74    THE BIOGRAPHICAL cyclopedia of representative men of Rhode Island. Providence: National Biographical Publishing, 1881. 589p. RHi. +

75    BIOGRAPHICAL history of the manufacturers and business men of Rhode Island at the opening of the twentieth century. Joseph Davis Hall, ed. Providence: J. D. Hall, 1901. 336p. RHi. +

76    BISHOP, HILLMAN METCALF. Why Rhode Island opposed the federal Constitution. Providence: Roger Williams Pr., 1950. 47p. RHi. +
      Reprinted from RIH, 8 (1949), 1-10, 33-44, 85-95, 115-126.

77    BOBICK, JAMES E. "Medical periodicals of Rhode Island: Part I, transactions of the Rhode Island Medical Society." RIMJ, 56 (1973), 500-506, 532.
      Published 1859-1912.

78    BOISVERT, DONALD J. "Rhode Island's battle of the stamp." New-England Galaxy, 18 (Winter 1977), 44-51.
      Gilbert Stuart commemorative stamp (1940).

79    "'BORN out of strikes': an interview with Luigi Nardella." Radical History Review, No. 17 (1978), 153-160.
      Paul Buhle and James Celenza, eds.
      Textile strike of 1922.

80    BOURGAIZE, EIDOLA JEAN. "Witches, devils roamed Rhode Island." R.I. Alumni Bulletin, 36 (July-Aug. 1956), 8-10.
      Witchcraft.

81    BOUVIER, LEON F., and INGE B. CORLESS. An ethnic profile of the State of Rhode Island. Kingston: Univ. of R.I., 1968. 34, [5]p. RWa. +

82    BOUVIER, LEON F., and S. L. N. RAO. Socioreligious factors in fertility decline. Cambridge, Mass.: Ballinger Publishing, 1975. xvi, 204p. M. +
      R.I. study (1967-1971).

83    BOWDITCH, JOSIAH B. "Child labor in Rhode Island." PBTJ, 20 (1908), 289-291.

84    [BOWEN, FRANCIS.] The recent contest in Rhode Island: an article from the North American Review, for April, 1844. Boston: Otis, Broaders, 1844. 69p. RHi. +
      Dorr Rebellion.

85    BOWEN, RICHARD LeBARON. Rhode Island colonial money and its counterfeiting, 1647-1726. Providence: Society of Colonial Wars, R.I., 1942. x, 112p. RHi. +

86    BOWEN, RICHARD M. The origin of the Rhode Island Greening apple. n.p.: R.I. Fruit Growers' Association, 1922. 15p. RHi. +

87    BOY SCOUTS OF AMERICA. NARRAGANSETT COUNCIL, PROVIDENCE. 25 years of Scouting in Rhode Island, 1910-1935. Providence: [E. A. Johnson,] 1935. 30p. RHi.

88    BOYDEN, BEN. A brief history of Rhode Island Italians, 1880-1924. [Providence: Providence County Times,] 1924. 29p. RHi.

89    BOYNTON, RACHAEL CHASE. "Some teachers don't need degrees." RIY (1970), 101-102.
      30 years in R.I. schools.

90   BOZEMAN, THEODORE DWIGHT.  "Religious liberty and the problem of order in early Rhode Island." NEQ, 45 (1972), 44-64.

91   BRAYTON, GLADYS W.  "The circus is coming!" CHSN [June 1981, 3-6].
     Circuses in R.I.

92   _____.  "Old Pawtuxet."  CHSN (Dec. 1969).
     Place in Cranston and Warwick.

93   _____.  "A rocking chair trip to some of Rhode Island's historic rocks."  CHSN [Sept. 1981, 3-5].

94   _____.  "Strange visitors in Narragansett Bay."  CHSN [Jan. 1981, 4-5].
     Seals, sharks, etc.

95   _____.  "What's in a name?"  CHSN [May 1980, 4-6].
     Place names in Pawtuxet.

96   BRAYTON, SUSAN STANTON.  "The library of an eighteenth-century gentleman of Rhode Island."  NEQ, 8 (1935), 277-283.
     Henry Marchant, of Newport and South Kingstown.

97   BRENNAN, JOSEPH.  Social conditions in industrial Rhode Island, 1820-1860. Washington:  Catholic Univ. of America, 1940.  ix, 178p.  RHi. +

98   BRIDENBAUGH, CARL.  Fat mutton and liberty of conscience:  society in Rhode Island, 1636-1690.  Providence:  Brown Univ. Pr., 1974.  xxiv, 157p.  RHi. +

99   _____.  Silas Downer:  forgotten patriot; his life and writings.  Providence:  R.I. Bicentennial Foundation, 1974.  118p. RHi. +
     "...First colonial to openly proclaim that the authority of the British Parliament did not extend to the colonies."

100  _____.  "Silas Who?"  RIer (June 4, 1972), 16-17.
     Silas Downer's contributions to the Revolutionary cause.  See also preceding entry.

101  BRIGHAM, CLARENCE SAUNDERS.  History of the State of Rhode Island and Providence Plantations.  [Boston:  Mason Publishing,] 1902.  392p.  RHi. +
     Reprinted from entry 1027.

102  _____.  "The Indians of Rhode Island." Apertyx, 1 (1905), 29-36.

103  _____.  "A portrait of Stephen Hopkins." RIHSC, 11 (1918), 44-47.
     Likeness of the Revolutionary-era political leader in a painting by Robert Edge Pine, believed to have been done ca. 1784-1785.

104  BRINLEY, FRANCIS.  "A brief account of the several settlements and governments in and about the lands of the Narragansett-Bay, in New England."  Massachusetts Historical Society, Collections, 5 (1798), 216-220.

105  BROCHES, S.  Jewish merchants in colonial Rhode Island.  N.Y.:  Bloch Publishing, 1942.  80p.  RHi. +

106  BROCK, EDMUND J.  The background and recent status of collective bargaining in the cotton industry in Rhode Island. Washington:  Catholic Univ. of America Pr., 1942.  xiv, 252p.  RHi. +

107  BROCKUNIER, SAMUEL HUGH.  The irrepressible democrat:  Roger Williams.  N.Y.:  Ronald Pr., 1940.  xii, 305p.  RHi. +

108  BROWN, ARTHUR W.  Rhode Island's tercentenary miscellanies.  Volume I. Providence:  Wm. R. Brown Printing, 1937. 224p.  RHi. +

109  BROWN, CHARLES W.  "Hurricanes and shore-line changes in Rhode Island." Geographical Review, 29 (1939), 416-430.

110  BROWN, MADELAINE R.  "Rhode Island pewterers."  RIHSC, 31 (1938), 1-8.

111  BROWN, WALLACE.  "The Loyalists had a rough time of it."  RIer (June 4, 1972), 34-36.
     American Revolution.

112  BRUNKOW, ROBERT DeV.  "Love and order in Roger Williams' writings."  RIH, 35 (1976), 115-126.
     Ideas on an orderly society and examples of their applicability to conditions in early R.I.

113  BRYANT, SAMUEL W.  "Rhode Island justice: 1772 vintage."  RIH, 26 (1967), 65-71.
     Burning of the British schooner Gaspee.

114  BUENKER, JOHN D.  "Urban liberalism in Rhode Island, 1909-1919."  RIH, 30 (1971), 35-50.

115  BUHLE, PAUL.  "Italian-American radicals and labor in Rhode Island, 1905-1930."  Radical History Review, No. 17 (1978), 121-151.

116  _____.  "The Knights of Labor in Rhode Island."  Radical History Review, No. 17 (1978), 39-73.

117  BULLOCK, EMMA WESCOTT. "Journalism in Rhode Island during the Revolution." American Monthly Magazine, 6 (1895), 677-681.

118  BURBANK, CALEF M. "The noble experiment." RIY (1969), H162-H164.
    Prohibition in R.I.

119  [BURGES, TRISTRAM.] The plough and the sickle: or, Rhode Island in the War of the Revolution of 1776. Providence: B. T. Albro, 1846. 28p. RHi. +

120  BURKE, GEORGE E. "Education then and now." RIY (1963), 58-62.

121  BUTMAN, DEAN P. "His murder changed Rhode Island law." RIY (1968), H108-H114.
    Amesa Sprague's murder (1843) and the abolition of capital punishment.

122  BUTTERFIELD, BRUCE D. [Series of articles on Rhode Island's jewelry industry.] Providence Journal-Bulletin (June 21-26, 1981).
    Includes historical information. Articles were reprinted and brought together in a special section of the newspaper (n.d., 24p.). Copy in RHi collection.

123  BYRNES, GARRETT D. "After all these years, she's yours." RIer (Sept. 22, 1968), 22-23.
    Rhode Islander Anne Fairchild Bowler, whose portrait by John Singleton Copley had recently been acquired by the National Gallery of Art.

124  _____. "The America's Cup." RIer (Sept. 13, 1970), 14-15, 19-20, 22-24.
    R.I. and the cup races. See additional entries on this subject under Newport.

125  _____. "And then the trolleys stopped, alas." RIer (May 6, 1973), 2, 4, 6.
    Trolley-car era in R.I.

126  _____. "Call it disaster." RIer (Aug. 18, 1968), 6-8.
    1938 hurricane.

127  _____. "Cape Fear sank like the stone she was." RIer (Oct. 11, 1970), 14-15, 17.
    The sinking of a concrete ship in R.I. waters (1920).

128  _____. "A confidential dispatch from Newport (June 10, 1772)*. *Written in May, 1972." RIer (June 4, 1972), 6-7, 9-12, 14.
    Gaspee affair; conditions in R.I. shortly before the Revolution.

129  _____. "February is the hottest month." RIer (Jan. 31, 1971), 6-7.
    February fire disasters.

130  _____. "Narragansett steamboats." Providence Evening Bulletin (July 12-15, 17-22, 24-29, 31; Aug. 1, 1933).
    Series of 18 articles. Scrapbook, MWA.

131  _____. "The Navy in Rhode Island: America owes a lot to Narragansett Bay." RIer (July 1, 1973), 12, 15-19.

132  _____. "Radio: the noisy baby grew quickly." RIer (Dec. 8, 1968), 4-5, 7-8, 10.
    Early days of broadcasting in R.I.

133  _____. "Rhode Island early birds and their flying machines." RIer (Dec. 7, 1969), 66, 69, 71-72, 75-76, 78, 80-84.
    Early days of aviation.

134  _____. "The silver perfectos." RIer (Nov. 24, 1968), 12-13, 15.
    1920s zeppelin flights over R.I.

135  _____. "The steam trains don't stop here anymore." RIer (Feb. 28, 1971), 12-13, 16, 18, 20; (Mar. 7, 1971), 16-20, 22.
    Railroading in the 1920s. Concluding article deals with Union Station, Providence.

136  _____. "Suddenly there was a lot of noise from seaward...." RIer (July 23, 1972), 6-8.
    1924 collision in R.I. waters involving the steamboat Boston.

137  _____. "Uncle Henri Schonhardt is still remembered--here and there." RIer (Nov. 17, 1968), 4-8, 10.
    R.I. sculptor and his works around the state.

138  _____. "When the bubble burst." RIer (Oct. 26, 1969), 29-31, 33-35.
    R.I. and the 1929 stock market crash.

139  CADY, JOHN HUTCHINS. Rhode Island boundaries, 1636-1936. [Providence:] R.I. Tercentenary Commission, 1936. 31p. RHi. +

140  _____. "The stone-ender--from Sussex to R.I." RIer (Oct. 9, 1949), 27-29.
    English origins of an early R.I. house type.

141  CALDER, CHARLES A. Rhode Island pewterers and their work; together with a list of American pewterers. Providence: E. A. Johnson, 1924. 38p. RHi. +
    See also this author's article on same subject in RIHSC, 17 (1924), 65-87.

142  _____. "Some additional notes on Rhode Island pewterers." RIHSC, 19 (1926), 37-45.

143  CALLENDER, JOHN. An historical discourse, on the civil and religious affairs of the colony of Rhode-Island...with a memoir of the author; biographical notices of some of his distinguished contemporaries; and annotations and original documents, illustrative of the history of Rhode-Island and Providence Plantations, from the first settlement to the end of the first century, by Romeo Elton. (1739) 3d ed. Boston: T. H. Webb, 1843. viii, 270p. RHi. +
Also published as RIHSC, 4 (1838).

144  CAMP, LEON R. "Roger Williams vs. 'the upstarts': the Rhode Island debates of 1672." Quaker History, 52 (1963), 69-76.
Williams's debates with Quaker spokesmen.

145  CANNON, JOSEPH E. "Rhode Island's health: yesterday, today, tomorrow." RIMJ, 62 (1979), 297-301, 304-306.

146  CARLSON, JOYCE MANGLER. "Early music in Rhode Island. V: Oliver Shaw and the Psallonian Society." RIH, 23 (1964), 35-50.
See also entries 2898-2899 and 3205-3206.

147  CARPENTER, DANIEL H. "Rhode Island families who went to Long Island, 1676, during King Philip's War." NHM, 6 (1886), 213-216.

148  CARPENTER, EDMUND J. Roger Williams: a study of the life, times and character of a political pioneer. N.Y.: Grafton Pr., 1909. xxxiv, 253p. RHi. +

149  CARPENTER, RICHARD B. "James Mitchell Varnum, Esq." Rhode Island Bar Journal, 24, No. 6 (Mar. 1976), 2-3, 14-17.
Includes his role as defense lawyer in the historic case, Trevett v. Weeden (1786).

150  CARROLL, CHARLES. Constitution of the State of Rhode Island and Providence Plantations as amended, with a condensed outline of the constitution and history of the constitution. [Providence:] Commissioner of Education, 1924. 32p. RHi. +

151  _____. Public education in Rhode Island. Providence: E. L. Freeman, 1918. 500p. RHi. +

152  _____. Rhode Island: three centuries of a democracy. N.Y.: Lewis Historical Publishing, 1932. 4v. RHi. +
Vols. 3-4 biographical.

153  _____. School law of Rhode Island. Providence: E. L. Freeman, 1914. 109p. RHi. +
Includes historical background.

154  CASE, NORMAN STANLEY. Address of His Excellency Norman S. Case, governor of Rhode Island, broadcast at Chicago, Illinois, September 28, 1929.... Providence: State Bureau of Information, 1929. 20p. RHi. +
R.I. history.

155  CASEY, DOROTHY NEEDHAM. "Rhode Island silversmiths." RIHSC, 33 (1940), 49-64.

156  CASEY, THOMAS B., EARL F. KELLY, MICHAEL DiMAIO, and JOHN C. MYRICK. "Medical licensure in Rhode Island: a review of the history and current status of the regulation by statute of the practice of medicine." RIMJ, 45 (1962), 625-629.

157  CASTIGLIONI, LUIGI. "Voyage in the State of Rhode Island." RIer (Apr. 30, 1967), 36-40.
"An Italian count's memoirs of R.I. in the 1780s." Translated by Samuel J. Hough. See also next entry.

158  "CASTIGLIONI'S visit to Rhode Island." RIH, 26 (1967), 53-64.
See also preceding entry.

159  "CAUSES and extent of the Dorr War." PM, 31 (1919), 65-68, 75, 79.

160  CHACE, ELIZABETH BUFFUM. "Old Quaker days in Rhode Island." NEM, n.s. 16 (1897), 655-663.

161  CHAFEE, ZECHARIAH, JR. The constitutional convention that never met: first part, 1935. Providence: The Booke Shop, 1938. xv, 88p. RHi. +

162  _____. "Records of the Rhode Island Court of Equity, 1741-1743." Colonial Society of Massachusetts, Publications, 35 (1942-1946), 91-118.

163  _____. Weathering the panic of '73: an episode in Rhode Island business history. Providence: The Book Shop, n.d. [24]p. RHi. +
Reprinted from Massachusetts Historical Society, Proceedings, 66 (1936-1941), 270-293.

164  CHAMPLIN, RICHARD L. "The ins and outs of twig and turf." NH, 45 (1972), 45-50.
Antiquated legal terms, used in colonial R.I.

165  _____. "The silk craze in Rhode Island." NH, 42 (1969), 97-109.
Sericulture.

166  _____. "Some guardians of the East Bay." NH, 44 (1971), 29-62.
Narragansett Bay lighthouses.

167 CHAPIN, ANNA AUGUSTA, and CHARLES V. CHAPIN. A history of Rhode Island ferries, 1640-1923. Providence: Oxford Pr., 1925. viii, 293p. RHi. +

168 CHAPIN, CHARLES V. "Epidemics and medical institutions." PM, 28 (1916), 74-76.

169 CHAPIN, HOWARD M. Cartography of Rhode Island. Providence: Preston & Rounds, 1915. [11]p. RHi. +

170 _____. "Colonial heraldry." RIHSC, 20 (1927), 91-100, 125-132; 21 (1928), 33-40, 69-76, 101-108, 133-144; 22 (1929), 21-32, 59-64, 87-96.
  R.I. Also published separately (1929).

171 _____. Early American signboards. Providence, 1926. 24p. RHi. +
  Tavern signs, mainly R.I.

172 _____. Early Rhode Island flags. [Providence:] Society of the Cincinnati in the State of R.I., [1925]. 14p. RHi. +
  Military. Reprinted from RIHSC, 18 (1925), 129-140.

173 _____. "Indian graves: a survey of the Indian graves that have been discovered in Rhode Island." RIHSC, 20 (1927), 14-32.

174 _____. Indian implements found in Rhode Island. Providence: R.I. Historical Society, 1925. 32p. RHi. +
  Reprinted, with additions, from RIHSC, 17 (1924), 105-124; 18 (1925), 22-32.

175 _____. Rhode Island privateers in King George's War, 1739-1748. Providence: R.I. Historical Society, 1926. 225p. RHi. +

176 _____. "Rhode Island signboards." RIHSC, 19 (1926), 20-32, 53-64.
  Early.

177 _____. The Tartar: the armed sloop of the Colony of Rhode Island in King George's War.... Providence: Society of Colonial Wars, R.I., 1922. 67, viii p. RHi. +

178 _____. "Unusual Indian implements found in Rhode Island." RIHSC, 19 (1926), 117-128.

179 CHAPPLE, BENNETT. "'What cheer' in Rhode Island." National Magazine, 14 (1911), 79-137.
  Historical accounts of Pawtucket, Providence, Westerly, and Woonsocket.

180 CHARTERS and legislative documents, illustrative of Rhode-Island history, showing that the people of Rhode Island, from the foundation of the state, until their constitution of 1842, possessed and exercised the rights of self-government; and in what manner and under what form of government they declared their independence, in 1776, became a member of the Confederation of the United States, in 1778, and adopted the constitution of the United States in 1790. Providence: Knowles & Vose, 1844. 68p. RHi. +

181 [CHASE, FRED D., JR.] Newport, Block Island and Narragansett Pier, illustrated: a brief history, and tourist's guide to points of interest.... Boston: Botolph Pr., 1895. 111p. RHi. +

182 CHASSE, PAUL P. Rhode Island's Franco-Americans in our pluralistic society.... n.p.: Editions de l'Abbaye de Theleme, [1973]. 12p. RPRIC.

183 "CHECK list of Rhode Island almanacs, 1643-1850." Howard M. Chapin, comp. American Antiquarian Society, Proceedings, n.s. 25 (1915), 19-54.
  Includes historical introduction.

184 CHRIST'S own: a descriptive story of the forty religious orders for women in the Diocese of Providence. Barbara C. Jencks, ed. Providence: Visitor Printing, 1949. 60p. RHi. +
  Roman Catholic.

185 CHUPACK, HENRY. Roger Williams. N.Y.: Twayne Publishers, 1969. 168p. RHi. +

186 "CHURCHES of the Pawtuxet Valley: historical sketches of many of the different religious denominations." Pawtuxet Valley Gleaner (Apr. 14, 1905), 2-6.
  Lengthy newspaper article.

187 CHURCHILL, DONALD. "The early history of medicine in Rhode Island." PMJ, 3 (1902), 54-67.

188 _____. "The history of smallpox in Rhode Island." PMJ, 3 (1902), 131-136.

189 CHURCHWARD, LLOYD G. "Rhode Island and the Australian trade, 1792-1812." RIH, 7 (1948), 97-104.

190 CIABURRI, ROBERT L. "The Dorr Rebellion in Rhode Island: the moderate phase." RIH, 26 (1967), 73-90.

191   [CLAPP, ROGER TILLINGHAST.]  Duelling in
      Rhode Island (and elsewhere).  [Providence:
      Society of Colonial Wars, R.I., 1978.]  30p.
      RHi. +

192   CLARK, F. C.  "The game laws of Rhode
      Island."  NHR, 8 (1890), 345-350.

193   CLARK, JANE.  "Metcalf Bowler as a British
      spy."  RIHSC, 23 (1930), 101-117.
         During American Revolution in R.I.

194   CLARK, THOMAS MARCH.  ...Centennial
      discourse...at the 100th annual session of
      the Diocese of Rhode Island, June 10th,
      1890.  [Providence, 1890.]  24p.  RHi. +
         Episcopal.

195   CLARK, WILLIAM RICHARD.  Emergency
      education:  a social study of the W.P.A.
      education project in Rhode Island.
      Washington:  Catholic Univ. of America Pr.,
      1940.  xii, 184p.  RHi. +

196   CLARKE, PRESCOTT O.  Rhode Island and
      Providence Plantations:  a short historical
      sketch and statistical compilation....
      Providence:  E. A. Johnson, 1885.  56p.
      RHi. +

197   CLARKE, RICHARD H.  "Maryland or Rhode
      Island--Lord Baltimore or Roger
      Williams--which was first?"  American
      Catholic Quarterly Review, 20 (1895),
      289-312.
         Religious liberty.

198   "CLARKSON A. Collins III (1911-1972):  a
      bibliography."  RIH, 31 (1972), 126-127.
         Writings on R.I. history by librarian of
      R.I. Historical Society.  Noel P. Conlon,
      comp.

199   CLAUSON, JAMES EARL.  These plantations....
      Providence:  E. A. Johnson, 1937.  120p.
      RHi. +
         Collected articles about R.I. history.

200   COGGESHALL, MRS. CHARLES P.  "Some old Rhode
      Island grist mills."  NHSB, No. 39 (1922),
      1-21.

201   COHEN, JOEL A.  "Democracy in Revolutionary
      Rhode Island:  a statistical analysis."
      RIH, 29 (1970), 3-16.

202   _____.  "Lexington and Concord:  Rhode
      Island reacts."  RIH, 26 (1967), 97-102.
         Responses to first battles of American
      Revolution.

203   _____.  "Molasses to muskets:  Rhode Island,
      1763-1775."  RIH, 34 (1975), 99-103.
         Events leading up to the Revolution.

204   _____.  "Rhode Island loyalism and the
      American Revolution."  RIH, 27 (1968),
      97-112.

205   _____.  "When they burned the Gaspee."  RIer
      (June 4, 1972), 19, 22.
         1772.

206   COLE, J. R.  History of Washington and Kent
      Counties, Rhode Island, including their
      early settlement and progress to the present
      time; a description of their historic and
      interesting localities; sketches of their
      towns and villages....  N.Y.:  W. W.
      Preston, 1889.  xiv, 1344p.  RHi. +

207   COLEMAN, PETER J.  "The entrepreneurial
      spirit in Rhode Island history."  Business
      History Review, 37 (1963), 319-344.

208   _____.  "The industrial revolution."  RIY
      (1967), H70-H74.
         In R.I.

209   _____.  "The insolvent debtor in Rhode
      Island, 1745-1828."  William and Mary
      Quarterly, 3 ser. 22 (1965), 413-434.

210   _____.  "Rhode Island cotton manufacturing:
      a study in economic conservatism."  RIH, 23
      (1964), 65-80.

211   _____.  The transformation of Rhode Island,
      1790-1860.  Providence:  Brown Univ. Pr.,
      1963.  xiv, 314p.  RHi.
         Economic change.

212   _____, and PENELOPE K. MAJESKE.  "British
      immigrants in Rhode Island during the War of
      1812."  RIH, 34 (1975), 66-75.

213   COLLINS, CLARKSON A. III.  "Rhode Island
      state houses."  RIY (1970), H166-H172.

214   "THE COLONIZATION of Rhode Island."
      American Monthly Magazine, 3 (1893),
      512-523.

215   COLT, LeBARON BRADFORD.  The contributions
      of Rhode Island to the American Union:
      address...delivered at the Louisiana
      Purchase Exposition, St. Louis, Missouri,
      Rhode Island Day, October 5, 1904.
      Providence:  R.I. Printing, n.d.  18p.
      RHi. +

216   COMMERCE of Rhode Island, 1726-1800.
      Boston:  [Massachusetts Historical Society,]
      1914-1915.  2v.  RHi. +
         Edited documents.  Vols. 69-70 of Mass.
      Historical Society Collections.

Rhode Island: A Bibliography of Its History

217 Rhode Island

217 CONLEY, PATRICK T. The constitutional
significance of Trevett v. Weeden....
Bicentennial Law Day address, May 3, 1976,
Colony House, Newport, Rhode Island.
Providence: R.I. Bicentennial Commission,
n.d. [12]p. RHi.
  1786 case that helped establish principle
of judicial review. See also this author's
article under similar title in R.I. Bar
Journal, 24, No. 8 (May 1976), 2-4, 14.

218 _____. Democracy in decline: Rhode
Island's constitutional development,
1776-1841. Providence: R.I. Historical
Society, 1977. xvi, 433p. RHi. +
  Bibliography, 381-415.

219 _____. "The Dorr Rebellion of 1842." RIY
(1967), H80-H88.
  See also next entry.

220 _____. The Dorr Rebellion: Rhode Island's
crisis in constitutional government.
Providence: R.I. Bicentennial Foundation,
1976. 13p. RHi.
  See also preceding entry.

221 _____. "Revolution's impact on Rhode
Island." RIH, 34 (1975), 121-128.

222 _____. Rhode Island constitutional
development, 1636-1775: a survey.
Providence, 1968. 35p. RHi. +
  Reprinted from RIH, 27 (1968), 49-63,
74-94.

223 _____. "Rhode Island in disunion,
1787-1790." RIH, 31 (1972), 99-115.

224 _____. Rhode Island profile. Providence:
R.I. Publications Society, 1982. 60p.
RHi. +
  Includes brief sketch of state history.

225 _____. "Rhode Island's paper money issue
and Trevett v. Weeden (1786)." RIH, 30
(1971), 95-108.
  See note, entry 217.

226 _____, and FERNANDO CUNHA. "State aid to
Rhode Island's private schools: a case
study of DiCenso v. Robinson." Catholic
Lawyer, 22 (1976), 329-343.

227 CONLEY, PATRICK T., and JOHN CARPENTER.
"Rhode Island's Latin Americans: an
historical profile." Providence Visitor
(Aug. 9, 16, 23, 1974).

228 CONLEY, PATRICK T., and MATTHEW J. SMITH.
Catholicism in Rhode Island: the formative
era. [Providence]: Diocese of Providence,
1976. xiv, 173p. RHi. +
  Bibliography, 153-162.

229 CONROY, VIRGINIA. "From the Gibson girl to
the flapper." RIY (1969), H160-H161.
  Changes in women's clothing in R.I.

230 THE CONSECRATION: a souvenir order of
service to the consecration of Bishop
Harkins, with historical sketches of the
Catholic Church in Rhode Island, the city of
churches, the orders connected with the
church, and short biographical sketches of
the lives of former bishops and the newly
elected bishop of the diocese. Providence:
J. A. & R. A. Reid, 1887. 16p. RHi.
  Roman Catholic.

231 COOK, CHARLES D. "Early Rhode Island
pottery." RIHSC, 18 (1925), 81-83.

232 COOK, FRANK ATWOOD. Customs of the service:
a paper read before the officers of the
Brigade, Rhode Island Militia, Dec. 5, 1887.
Providence: E. L. Freeman, 1888. 14p.
RHi.

233 COOL, ROBERT N. "Rhode Island and the War
of 1812." RIY (1968), H102-H107.

234 CORBETT, SCOTT. Rhode Island. N.Y.:
Coward-McCann, 1969. 124p. RHi. +

235 CORNWELL, ELMER E., JR. "Colonial politics:
was anarchy ever this complicated?" RIer
(June 4, 1972), 24-25, 27-28, 30.

236 _____. "15 minutes that changed Rhode
Island." RIer (Mar. 12, 1972), 24-28.
  "Revolution of 1935" in the General
Assembly.

237 _____. "Inauguration was at noon, but who
was governor?" RIer (Dec. 31, 1972), 12,
14-15.
  "Long count" election of 1956, in which
Dennis J. Roberts was finally declared the
winner.

238 _____. "The ordeal of Governor Joseph
Wanton." RIer (June 9, 1974), 32, 34-35,
37, 39.
  Revolutionary-era governor.

239 _____, and JAY S. GOODMAN. The politics of
the Rhode Island Constitutional Convention.
N.Y.: National Municipal League, 1969. vi,
96p. RHi. +
  1964-1968.

240 _____, WILLIAM J. DeNUCCIO, and ANGELO A.
MOSCA, JR. The Rhode Island General
Assembly. Washington: American Political
Science Association, 1970. 174p. RHi. +
  Includes historical information.

10

241   THE CORRESPONDENCE of the colonial governors of Rhode Island, 1723-1775. Gertrude Selwyn Kimball, ed. Boston: Houghton, Mifflin, 1902-1903. 2v. RHi. +

242   COSGROVE, JOHN J. "The Irish in Rhode Island, to and including the Revolution." American Irish Historical Society, Journal, 9 (1910), 365-385.

243   "COTTON in Rhode Island: development of the industry from insignificant beginnings; natural advantages for manufacturing in the river valleys; accounts of some of the early mills and manufacturers." BTJ (Nov.-Dec. 1890), 20, 22, 23-26, 28-30, 32, 34.

244   "COTTON manufacturing in Rhode Island, 1788-1911." PBTJ, 23 (1911), 242-244, 246, 248-249.

245   COUGHTRY, JAY. The notorious triangle: Rhode Island and the African slave trade, 1700-1807. Philadelphia: Temple Univ. Pr., 1981. xiii, 361p. RHi. +

246   COVELL, ELIZABETH GREENE. "Newport Harbor and lower Narragansett Bay, Rhode Island, during the American Revolution." NHSB, No. 86 (1933), 3-37.
      Based on diary of a British officer, Frederick Mackenzie.

247   COVELL, WILLIAM KING. "The age of steamboats." RIY (1968), H115-H121.

248   _____. "Steamboats on Narragansett Bay." NHSB, No. 90 (1934), 2-57.

249   _____. "Steamship exhibition." RIH, 5 (1946), 73-81.
      Exhibit at R.I. Historical Society relating to R.I. steamship history.

250   COVEY, CYCLONE. The gentle radical: a biography of Roger Williams. N.Y.: Macmillan, [1966]. viii, 273p. RHi. +

251   COWELL, BENJAMIN. Spirit of '76 in Rhode Island: or, sketches of the efforts of the government and people in the War of the Revolution; together with names of those who belonged to Rhode Island regiments in the army.... Boston: A. J. Wright, 1850. 352p. RHi. +

252   CRAIG, CLARA E. Roger Williams: the founder of Providence, the pioneer of religious liberty; with suggestions for study in the schools. [Providence:] State of R.I., Dept. of Education, 1908. 19p. RHi. +

253   CRAWFORD, WALTER FREEMAN. "The commerce of Rhode Island with the southern continental colonies in the eighteenth century." RIHSC, 14 (1921), 99-110, 124-129.

254   CREECH, MARGARET. Three centuries of poor law administration: a study of legislation in Rhode Island. Chicago: Univ. of Chicago Libraries, 1936. xxii, 331p. RHi. +

255   CREPEAU, HENRY J. Rhode Island: a history of child welfare planning. Washington: Catholic Univ. of America Pr., 1941. xii, 340p. RHi. +

256   CROWE, CHARLES R. "Utopian Socialism in Rhode Island, 1845-1850." RIH, 18 (1959), 20-26.

257   CULLEN, THOMAS F. The Catholic Church in Rhode Island. North Providence: Franciscan Missionaries of Mary, 1936. 482p. RHi. +

258   CULLUM, GEORGE WASHINGTON. Historical sketch of the fortification defenses of Narragansett Bay since the founding, in 1638, of the colony of Rhode Island. Washington, 1884. 32p. RHi. +
      Reprinted from Magazine of American History, 11 (1884), 465-496.

259   DAIGNAULT, ELPHEGE-J. Le vrai Mouvement Sentinelliste en Nouvelle Angleterre, 1923-1929, et l'affaire du Rhode Island. Montreal: Les Editions du Zodiaque, n.d. 246p. RHi. +
      Sentinelle Affair, a French-nationalist movement within the Roman Catholic Church. Text in French.

260   DANIELS, BRUCE C. "The 'particular courts' of local government: town councils in eighteenth-century Rhode Island." RIH, 41 (1982), 54-65.

261   _____. "Poor relief, local finance, and town government in eighteenth-century Rhode Island." RIH, 40 (1981), 75-87.

262   DAVIS, ARTHUR W. Yachting in Narragansett Bay, 1921-1945. Providence: Providence Journal, 1946. 127p. RHi. +

263   DAVIS, DAVID. "The first republican form of government in America." Ohio Archaeological & Historical Quarterly, 41 (1932), 108-114.
      In colonial R.I.

264   DAVIS, HADASSAH F. An account of Roger Williams and the Narragansett Indians. Providence: Pafnuty Publishers, [1977?]. 18p. RHi.

265    DEANE, CHARLES. "Notice of Samuel Gorton."
New England Historical and Genealogical
Register, 4 (1850), 201-221.
    Prominent in the early years of the R.I.
colony and one of the first settlers of
Warwick.

266    DeJONG, DAVID CORNEL. "Rhode Island."
New-England Galaxy, 1 (Winter 1960), 11-19.

267    DeJONG, HELEN M. "Rhode Island's health and
medical landmarks." RIer (Apr. 8, 1962),
6-7.

268    DELABARRE, EDMUND B. "Alleged runic
inscriptions in Rhode Island." RIHSC, 28
(1935), 49-57.

269    _____. "The inscribed rocks of Narragansett
Bay." RIHSC, 13 (1920), 1-28, 73-93; 14
(1921), 10-22; 15 (1922), 1-15, 65-76; 16
(1923), 46-64; 18 (1925), 51-79.

270    _____. "Miguel Cortereal: the first
European to enter Narragansett Bay." RIHSC,
29 (1936), 97-119.

271    DENISON, FREDERIC. "The Israelites in Rhode
Island." NHR, 4 (1886), 301-327.
    Jewish history.

272    DENNISON, GEORGE M. "The Dorr War and
political questions." Supreme Court
Historical Society, Year Book (1979), 45-62.
    See also next entry.

273    _____. The Dorr War: republicanism on
trial, 1831-1861. Lexington, Ky.: Univ.
Pr. of Kentucky, 1976. xiv, 250p. RHi. +
    Bibliographical essay, 235-244.

274    DeVARO, LAWRENCE J., JR. "The Gaspee affair
as conspiracy." RIH, 32 (1973), 107-121.
    1772.

275    DEXTER, THEODORE EVERETT. "Early education
in the towns of western Rhode Island."
WRICHSP, 2, No. 1 (1953), [2-11].

276    DiNUNZIO, MARIO R., and JAN T. GALKOWSKI.
"Political loyalty in Rhode Island: a
computer study of the 1850s." RIH, 36
(1977), 93-95.

277    DOCUMENTARY history of Rhode Island....
Howard M. Chapin, comp. Providence:
Preston & Rounds, 1916-1919. 2v. RHi. +
    To mid-17th century. Includes materials
relating to the early history of Newport,
Portsmouth, Providence, and Warwick.

278    THE DOCUMENTARY history of the destruction
of the Gaspee; compiled for the Providence
Journal. William R. Staples, comp.
Providence: Knowles, Vose, and Anthony,
1845. 56p. RHi. +
    British naval schooner, burned by Rhode
Islanders in 1772 in a famous incident
preceding the American Revolution.

279    "DOCUMENTS relating to the Ray, Greene, and
Turner families." RIH, 6 (1947), 65-85.
    G. Andrews Moriarty, ed.

280    DODD, MARION E. "Along New England's book
trails: IV. Rhode Island." Yankee, 5
(Jan. 1939), 25-28, 39.
    R.I. authors and publishers.

281    "THE DORR War: complete account of that
episode." Providence Press (Nov. 5, 1869).
    Lengthy historical article.

282    "DORR War flags." RIHSC, 25 (1932), 53-60.

283    DOWNING, ANTOINETTE FORRESTER. Early homes
of Rhode Island. Richmond, Va.: Garrett
and Massie, 1937. xviii, 480p. RHi. +

284    _____. "Historic preservation in Rhode
Island." RIH, 35 (1976), 3-28.

285    DUCKWORTH, ED. "How R.I. got in on the
ground floor." RIer (Apr. 6, 1969), 6-9.
    R.I. and the early history of golf in the
U.S.

286    "DUELLING in Rhode Island." WRICHSH, 16
(June 1972), [2]; (July 1972), [2].

287    DUNNIGAN, KATE, HELEN KEBABIAN, LAURA B.
ROBERTS, and MAUREEN TAYLOR. "Working
women: images of women at work in Rhode
Island, 1880-1925." RIH, 38 (1979), 3-23.
    Also printed separately.

288    DUNWELL, STEVE. "The fabric of our lives
was woven here." RIer (Dec. 3, 1978),
30-35.
    R.I. textile industry.

289    DURAND, ROGER H. Obsolete notes and scrip
of Rhode Island and the Providence
Plantations. n.p.: Society of Paper Money
Collectors, 1981. 276p. RHi. +
    Includes bank notes.

290    DURANT, CHARLES H. III, SORAYA MOORE, ARLINE
RUTH KIVEN, and BRADFORD FULLER SWAN. "The
Negro in Rhode Island: from slavery to
community." RIer (Oct. 12, 1969), 16-17,
19-20, 22-23.

Entries for Rhode Island

291  [DURFEE, JOB.]  Charge of the Hon. Chief Justice Durfee, delivered to the Grand Jury at the March term of the Supreme Judicial Court, at Bristol, Rhode-Island, A.D. 1842.... n.p., n.d. 16p. RHi. +
History of R.I. criminal law.

292  _____.  A discourse, delivered before the Rhode-Island Historical Society, on the evening of Wednesday, January 13, 1847. Providence:  Charles Burnett, Jr., 1847. 32p. RHi. +
On R.I. history.

293  DURFEE, THOMAS.  Gleanings from the judicial history of Rhode Island.  Providence: Sidney S. Rider, 1883.  164p.  RHi. +

294  _____.  Oration delivered at the dedication of the Providence County Court House, December 18, 1877.  Providence:  E. L. Freeman, 1879.  38p.  RHi. +
Legal history.

295  DYER, ELISHA.  "Reminiscences of Rhode Island in 1842 as connected with the Dorr Rebellion."  NHR, 6 (1888), 145-197.

296  _____.  "The state fairs."  NHR, 8 (1890), 27-31.

297  EARLE, RALPH.  The value of Narragansett Bay to the Navy.  n.p., 1924.  10p.  RNW.

298  "EARLY attempts at Rhode Island history, comprising those of Stephen Hopkins and Theodore Foster."  RIHSC, 7 (1885), 5-134.
William E. Foster, ed.

299  "THE EARLY commerce of Rhode Island."  PBTJ, 27 (1915), 745-748.

300  EARLY homes of Rhode Island:  from material originally published as the White Pine Series of Architectural Monographs....  Robert G. Miner, ed.  [N.Y.:]  Arno Pr., 1977.  223p.  RHi. +

301  "EARLY steamboating on Narragansett Bay."  PM, 26 (1914), 503-506.

302  "AN EARLY suggestion for the care of the insane in Rhode Island."  American Journal of Psychiatry, 104 (1952), 40-45.
Petition to General Assembly (1724).

303  EASTON, EMILY.  Roger Williams:  prophet and pioneer.  Boston: Houghton Mifflin, 1930. ix, 399p.  RHi. +

304  EATON, AMASA M.  The development of the judicial system in Rhode Island.  [New Haven, Conn., 1904.]  [23]p.  RHi. +
Reprinted from Yale Law Journal (Jan. 1904).

305  _____.  The French spoliation claims and Rhode Island claimants:  a paper read before the Rhode Island Historical Society, December 1, 1885.  Providence:  E. L. Freeman, 1885.  33p.  RHi. +
Legal claims that resulted from French seizure of American ships during French Revolution.  See also this author's article on same subject in NHR, 4 (1886), 202-234; 5 (1887), 286-288.

306  _____.  "Roger Williams:  the pioneer of religious liberty."  BrAlumMo, 8 (1907), 51-56.

307  _____.  Thomas Wilson Dorr and the Dorr War: a paper read...at the fifteenth annual convention, Bedford Springs, Pennsylvania, June 29, 1909.  n.p.:  [Pennsylvania Bar Association,] n.d.  43p.  RHi. +

308  EATON, ARTHUR WENTWORTH HAMILTON.  "Rhode Island settlers on the French lands in Nova Scotia."  Americana, 10 (1915), 1-43, 83-104, 179-197.

309  EDWARDS, KNIGHT.  "Burnside:  a Rhode Island hero."  RIH, 16 (1957), 1-23.
Ambrose E. Burnside, the Civil War general, who in later life was one of R.I.'s most prominent citizens.

310  EDWARDS, MORGAN.  "Materials for a history of the Baptists in Rhode Island."  RIHSC, 6 (1867), 302-370.

311  EDWARDS, WILLIAM H.  "My five senators."  RIY (1970), H179-H181.
Efforts to call a constitutional convention (1924).

312  EGNAL, FREDA.  "A catalogue of all Rhode Island Jews mentioned in materials relating to the history of the Jews in Rhode Island, located in Rhode Island depositories (1678-1966)."  RIJHN, 5 (1967), 7-79.

313  _____.  "A guide to the more important printed sources concerning the history of the Jews in Rhode Island based on materials in the Brown University Library."  RIJHN, 4 (1963), 79-99.

314  "EIGHTEENTH century governors of Rhode Island."  RIY (1965-1966), 66-68.

315  ELTON, ROMEO.  Life of Roger Williams, the earliest legislator and true champion for a full and absolute liberty of conscience. (1852)  Providence:  George H. Whitney, 1853.  viii, 173p.  RHi. +

316  ELY, J. W. C.  "The Rhode Island Medical Society of fifty years ago."  R.I. Medical Society, Transactions, 5 (1898), 570-576.

Rhode Island: A Bibliography of Its History

317 Rhode Island

317  EMLEN, ROBERT P. "A masterful William
Claggett clock: a short story in a tall
case." Antiques, 118 (1980), 502-507.
Newport-made clock belonging to the R.I.
Historical Society.

318  ENO, JOEL N. "The expansion of Rhode Island
--chronological--based on official
records." American, 24 (1930), 515-526.
Expansion of R.I.'s jurisdiction during
colonial times; establishment of local units
of government. Includes historical
commentary.

319  ENRIGHT, ROSEMARY. A dictionary of Rhode
Island biography, 1636-1800: written...for
the libraries of Johnston, North Providence
and Smithfield. n.p., 1976. [247]p. RHi.

320  ERNST, JAMES E. The political thought of
Roger Williams. Seattle: Univ. of
Washington Pr., 1929. iii, 229p. RPB. +

321  _____. Roger Williams: New England
firebrand. N.Y.: Macmillan, 1932. xiv,
538p. RHi. +

322  FARNHAM, CHARLES W. "Rhode Island colonial
records." RIH, 29 (1970), 36-44.

323  _____. "Rhode Island genealogy." R.I.
Roots, 4, No. 1 (Spring 1978), 6-8.

324  FARNUM, ALEXANDER. Visits of the Northmen
to Rhode Island. Providence: Sidney S.
Rider, 1877. 41p. RHi. +

325  FARRELL, JOHN T. "The early history of
Rhode Island's court system." RIH, 9
(1950), 65-71, 103-117; 10 (1951), 14-25.

326  FEDERAL Rhode Island: the age of the China
trade, 1790-1820; lectures presented at the
Second Annual Forum on Rhode Island History,
January, 1976, Providence, R.I., sponsored
by the Rhode Island Historical Society and
the Providence Preservation Society. Linda
Lotridge Levin, ed. [Providence:] R.I.
Historical Society, 1978. ix, 166p. RHi. +
Lectures on various aspects of R.I.
history during that period.

327  FEDERAL WRITERS' PROJECT. RHODE ISLAND.
Rhode Island: a guide to the smallest
state. Boston: Houghton Mifflin, 1937.
xxvi, 500p. RHi. +

328  FEINBERG, BANICE. "Thirty-five year review
of rheumatic fever and rheumatic heart
disease in Rhode Island (1925-1960)." RIMJ,
45 (1962), 145-148.

329  FIELD, EDWARD. Revolutionary defences in
Rhode Island: an historical account of the
fortifications and beacons erected during
the American Revolution, with muster rolls
of the companies stationed along the shores
of Narragansett Bay. Providence: Preston
and Rounds, 1896. xvi, 161p. RHi. +
See also his State of Rhode Island and
Providence Plantations at the turn of the
century (entry 1027).

330  FINDLAY, JAMES F. "The great textile strike
of 1934: illuminating Rhode Island history
in the thirties." RIH, 42 (1983), 17-29.

331  "THE FIRST real estate trust of Rhode
Island." PM, 23 (1924), 185, 187, 189.
The Atherton Company, involved in buying
and selling Indian lands.

332  FISKE, JANE FLETCHER. "Genealogical
research in Rhode Island." New England
Historical and Genealogical Register, 136
(1982), 173-219.
A guide for the genealogist that includes
a brief historical sketch of the settlement
of R.I., a bibliographical overview of books
on R.I. history, and information about the
history of record keeping in R.I.

333  FITZPATRICK, EDWARD J. "Eben Tourjée's
Rhode Island roots." RIH, 36 (1977), 81-91.
Founder of Boston's New England
Conservatory of Music.

334  FLATHER, M. RANDOLPH. "Don't bank on it."
RIY (1971), H198-H203.
Bank holiday of 1933.

335  _____. "Four hundred dollars for a hat when
inflation raged in Rhode Island." RIH, 1
(1942), 134-141.
Fluctuating value of paper money (18th
century).

336  FLATHER, RANDOLPH. "Things are not always
what they seem." CHSN [Jan., Feb. 1977].
Counterfeiting.

337  FLETCHER, GRACE ABBOTT. "The servant
problem in 1845." RIY (1968), H131-H132.

338  FLYNN, WILLIAM S. "Working on the Bay
boats." RIer (July 31, 1960), 4-6.
Steamboats.

339  FOISY, J. ALBERT. The Sentinellist
agitation in New England, 1925-1928.
[Providence: Providence Visitor Pr., 1930.]
234p. RHi. +
French-nationalist movement within the
Roman Catholic Church, centered in
R.I. This title was also published in
French.

340   FOSTER, ETHAN.  The conscript Quakers: being a narrative of the distress and relief of four young men from the draft for the war in 1863.  (1883)  2d ed.  Cambridge, Mass.: Riverside Pr., 1885.  16p.  RHi. +

341   FOSTER, HOWARD.  "Whatever happened to Hopkins Hollow?"  Univ. of R.I. Alumni Bulletin, 58 (Summer 1977), 5-9.
        Land-use case studies of four rural centers:  Hopkins Hollow, an extinct village in Coventry; Greene, also in Coventry; Foster Center; and Kingston.

342   FOSTER, THEODORE.  Foster's minutes of the convention held at South Kingstown, Rhode Island, in March, 1790, which failed to adopt the Constitution of the United States.  Robert C. Cotner, ed.  Providence:  R.I. Historical Society, 1929.  vi, 99p.  RHi. +

343   FOSTER, WILLIAM E.  Some Rhode Island contributions to the intellectual life of the last century.  Worcester, Mass.: Charles Hamilton, 1892.  32p.  RHi. +
        Reprinted from American Antiquarian Society, Proceedings, n.s. 8 (1892), 103-132.

344   _____.  Stephen Hopkins, a Rhode Island statesman: a study in the political history of the eighteenth century.  Providence: Sidney S. Rider, 1884.  2v.  RHi. +

345   _____.  Town government in Rhode Island. Baltimore:  N. Murray, Publications Agent, Johns Hopkins Univ., 1886.  36p.  RHi. +

346   14 Rhode Island militia flags.  Providence: R.I. Development Council, n.d.  [4]p.  RHi.

347   FOWLER, A. N.  "Rhode Island mill towns." Pencil Points, 17 (1936), 271-286.
        Architectural.

348   FOWLER, WILLIAM M.  William Ellery: a Rhode Island politico and Lord of Admiralty. Metuchen, N.J.:  Scarecrow Pr., 1973.  vi, 231p.  RHi. +

349   _____.  "William Ellery:  making of a Rhode Island politician."  RIH, 30 (1971), 125-135.
        Politics in the pre-Revolutionary era.

350   FOWLER, WILLIAM S.  "Man's early arrival in Rhode Island."  Narragansett Archaeological Society of R.I., Report (June 1982), 1-5.

351   FRANKLIN, SUSAN BRALEY.  "A short history of the west ferries of Jamestown."  JHSB, No. 8 (1941), 3-16.

352   _____.  "William Ellery, signer of the Declaration of Independence."  RIH, 12 (1953), 110-119; 13 (1954), 11-17, 44-52.

353   FRANKOVICH, GEORGE R.  "History of the Rhode Island jewelry and silverware industry." RIY (1971), 83-88.

354   FREEDMAN, STANLEY S.  "The early practice of allergy in Rhode Island."  RIMJ, 59 (1976), 531-532.

355   FREEMASONS.  PAWTUXET.  HARMONY LODGE, NO. 9.  The centennial celebration of Harmony Lodge, No. 9, A.F. & A.M., Pawtuxet, Rhode Island, Sunday, May 7, and Monday, May 8, 1905.  [Providence:]  Providence Pr., 1906. 139p.  RHi.
        Pawtuxet is a village in Cranston and Warwick.

356   FREEMASONS.  RHODE ISLAND.  GRAND LODGE. A bicentennial review of Rhode Island Freemasonry.  n.p.:  Grand Lodge of the Most Ancient and Honorable Society of Free and Accepted Masons for the State of R.I. and Providence Plantations, [1976?].  104p. RHi. +

357   "THE FRENCH in Rhode Island."  Magazine of American History, 3 (1879), 385-436.
        During the American Revolution.

358   THE FRENCH in Rhode Island:  a history. Albert K. Aubin, ed.  Providence:  R.I. Heritage Commission, 1981.  iii, 52p.  RHi.
        Franco-Americans.

359   "FRENCH occupation of Rhode Island during the Revolution."  PM, 32 (1920), 395-400.

360   FREUND, MICHAEL.  "Roger Williams:  apostle of complete religious liberty."  RIHSC, 26 (1933), 101-133.

361   FRIEDMAN, LEE M.  "Jews in the vice-admiralty court of colonial Rhode Island."  American Jewish Historical Society, Publications, 37 (1947), 391-418.

362   FRIENDS, SOCIETY OF.  PROVIDENCE MONTHLY MEETING.  BICENTENNIAL COMMITTEE.  Rhode Island Quakers in the American Revolution, 1775-1790.  [Providence,] 1976.  64p. RHi. +

363   FRIEZE, JACOB.  A concise history of the efforts to obtain an extension of suffrage in Rhode Island; from the year 1811 to 1842. (1842)  2d ed.  Providence:  Benjamin F. Moore, 1842.  179p.  RHi. +
        3d ed., 1912.

364 FROST, J. WILLIAM. "Quaker versus Baptist: a religious and political squabble in Rhode Island three hundred years ago." Quaker History, 63 (1974), 39-52.

365 GABRIEL, RICHARD A. The Irish and Italians: ethnics in city and suburb. N.Y.: Arno Pr., 1980. xix, 289p. RPC. +
Voting patterns in Providence and Warwick. See also entry 2978.

366 _____. The political machine in Rhode Island. Kingston: Univ. of R.I., Bureau of Government Research, 1970. 16p. RHi. +

367 _____. "The political machine is still alive and well in Rhode Island." RIer (Mar. 21, 1971), 9-13, 16, 18.
Article sketches the historical background.

368 GALPIN, W. FREEMAN. Early peace efforts in Rhode Island; reprinted from Advocate of Peace, August 1930. n.p., n.d. 11p. RHi.
R.I. Peace Society.

369 GAMMELL, WILLIAM. Address delivered before the Rhode-Island Historical Society, at the opening of their cabinet, on Wednesday, Nov. 20, 1844. Providence: B. Cranston, 1844. 30p. RHi. +
On the R.I. Historical Society and its relationship to the history of R.I.

370 _____. Life of Roger Williams, founder of the State of Rhode Island. Boston: Gould, Kendall & Lincoln, 1846. ix, 221p. RHi. +

371 GANO, STEPHEN. "Sketch of a missionary tour in the State of Rhode-Island...." Massachusetts Baptist Missionary Magazine, 2 (1809), 155-158.

372 GARDINER, ASA BIRD. The Rhode Island line in the Continental Army, and its Society of the Cincinnati: a paper read before the Rhode Island Historical Society, April 30, 1878. Providence: Providence Pr., 1878. 12p. RHi. +

373 GARDINER, GEORGE W. Roger Williams, peacemaker: an address delivered...at the North Kingstown celebration of the founding of Rhode Island, held at Cocumscussoc, North Kingstown, August 29, 1936.... n.p., n.d. 8p. RHi.

374 GARRETT, JOHN. Roger Williams: witness beyond Christendom, 1603-1683. N.Y.: Macmillan, 1970. x, 306p. RHi. +

375 GARRETT, WENDELL D. "Speculations on the Rhode Island block-front in 1928." Antiques, 99 (1971), 887-891.
Furniture.

376 GERLACH, LARRY R. "Charles Dudley and the customs quandary in pre-Revolutionary Rhode Island." RIH, 30 (1971), 53-59.

377 GERSUNY, CARL. "Seth Luther: the road from Chepachet." RIH, 33 (1974), 47-55.
Luther (1795-1863), an early labor leader and supporter of Thomas Wilson Dorr, was imprisoned for his role in the Dorr Rebellion. See also entry 508.

378 _____. "Uphill battle: Lucius F. C. Garvin's crusade for political reform." RIH, 39 (1980), 57-75.
Late 19th and early 20th centuries.

379 GETTLEMAN, MARVIN E. The Dorr Rebellion: a study in American radicalism, 1833-1849. N.Y.: Random House, 1973. xxii, 257p. RHi. +
Bibliographical references, 239-250.

380 GIBBS, JAMES W. "Horologic Rhode Island visited." Bulletin of the National Association of Watch and Clock Collectors, Inc., 14 (1970), 801-811.
R.I. clock makers and their patents.

381 GIFFORD, WILLIAM L. R. "The Dorr Rebellion in Rhode Island in 1842." New Princeton Review, n.s. 4 (1887), 213-226.

382 GILMAN, JOHN F. W. "Aesculapius comes to the colonies." RIMJ, 59 (1976), 328-332, 342-344.
Physicians in early R.I.

383 GLEESON, ALICE COLLINS. Colonial Rhode Island. Pawtucket: Automobile Journal Publishing, 1926. 260p. RHi. +

384 GLEESON, PAUL F. Rhode Island: the development of a democracy. Providence: R.I. State Board of Education, 1957. xx, 332p. RHi. +

385 GODDARD, WILLIAM GILES. An address to the people of Rhode-Island, delivered in Newport, on Wednesday, May 3, 1843, in presence of the General Assembly, on the occasion of the change in the civil government of Rhode-Island, by the adoption of the constitution, which superseded the charter of 1663. Providence: Knowles & Vose, 1843. 80p. RHi. +

386 GOLDOWSKY, SEEBERT J. "The beginnings of medical education in Rhode Island." RIMJ, 38 (1955), 496-502, 515, 555-560, 590, 592-593, 632-634, 638, 640, 650-651, 660-661.

387 _____. "Jews in medicine in Rhode Island." RIJHN, 2 (1957), 151-191.

388   GOLDOWSKY, SEEBERT J.  "Local Jewish
history:  the Rhode Island experience."
RIJHN, 6 (1974), 622-628.
R.I. Jewish Historical Associaton.

389   _____.  "Rhode Island's first woman
physician."  RIMJ, 54 (1971), 546-549.
Dr. Martha Mowry (1818-1899).

390   _____.  "Some Rhode Island pioneers in
cancer surgery."  RIMJ, 41 (1958), 492-497,
512.

391   [_____.]  The story of private hospitals in
Rhode Island.  [Providence:]  R.I. Dept. of
Health, 1979.  69p.  R. +

392   GOLDSTEIN, ALICE.  "Mobility of natives and
Jews in Providence, 1900-1920."  RIJHN, 8
(1979), 62-93.

393   GOLDSTEIN, SIDNEY.  The Greater Providence
Jewish community:  a population survey.
Providence:  General Jewish Committee of
Providence, 1964.  xix, 256p.  RHi. +
Includes historical information.

394   _____, and ALICE GOLDSTEIN.  "The declining
use of Yiddish in Rhode Island."  RIJHN, 7
(1977), 401-409.

395   GOLDSTEIN, SIDNEY, and KURT B. MAYER.
Metropolitanization and population change in
Rhode Island.  [Providence:]  Planning
Division, R.I. Development Council, [1962].
vii, 60p.  RHi. +

396   GOODELL, WILLIAM.  The rights and wrongs of
Rhode Island:  comprising views of liberty
and law, of religion and rights, as
exhibited in the recent and existing
difficulties in that state.  Whitesboro,
N.Y.:  Pr. of the Oneida Institute, 1842.
120p.  RHi. +
Includes historical background of Dorr
Rebellion.

397   GOODMAN, JAY S.  The Democrats and labor in
Rhode Island, 1952-1962:  changes in the old
alliance.  Providence:  Brown Univ. Pr.,
1967.  xi, 154p.  RHi. +

398   GOODRICH, JOSEPH L.  "Six businesses under
one label:  Bostitch."  RIer (Aug. 28,
1966), 4-7, 9.

399   GOODWIN, DANIEL.  "The counties of Rhode
Island."  Magazine of History, 16 (1913),
66-73.

400   GOODWIN, WILLIAM B.  "The Dee River of 1583
(now called Narragansett Bay) and its
relation to Norumbega."  RIHSC, 27 (1934),
38-50.
See also entry 688.

401   GOODYEAR, FRANK H., JR.  American paintings
in the Rhode Island Historical Society.
Providence:  R.I. Historical Society, 1974.
x, 116p.  RHi. +
Mostly "of Rhode Island faces, events and
places."

402   GORMAN, CHARLES E.  An historical statement
of the elective franchise in Rhode Island.
[Providence, 1879.]  37p.  RHi. +

403   GORTON, ADELOS.  The life and times of
Samuel Gorton:  the founders and the
founding of the republic, a section of early
United States history, and a history of the
Colony of Rhode Island and Providence
Plantations in the Narragansett Indian
country, now the State of Rhode Island,
1592-1636-1677-1687.  Philadelphia, 1907.
x, 154p.  RHi. +
One of the important figures in the early
years of the R.I. colony, Gorton was also
one of the first settlers of Warwick.

404   GORTON, SAMUEL.  Simplicity's defence
against seven-headed policy.  With notes
explanatory of the text, and appendixes
containing original documents referred to in
the work, by William R. Staples.
Providence:  Marshall, Brown, 1835.  [7],
278p.  RHi. +
Vol. 2 of RIHSC.  Includes information on
Gorton's role in the early history of
Warwick and R.I.  See note, preceding entry.

405   GOUGH, ROBERT E.  Apples from Rhode Island.
Kingston:  Univ. of R.I., College of
Resource Development, n.d.  28p.  RHi.

406   GOULDING, STUART D.  "Roger Williams of
Rhode Island."  History Today, 25 (1975),
741-748.

407   GRANT, PHILIP A.  "Party chaos embroils
Rhode Island."  RIH, 26 (1967), 113-125; 27
(1968), 24-33.
1833-1835.

408   GRAY, CHANNING.  "Louise Herreshoff
rediscovered."  RIer (Nov. 14, 1976), 22,
24, 26, 29-30.
R.I. artist.

409   GREAVES, RICHARD L.  "A colonial fifth
monarchist?:  John Clarke of Rhode Island."
RIH, 40 (1981), 41-47.

410   GREEN, FRANCES.  "Growing up in Rhode Island
mill villages."  New-England Galaxy, 13
(Winter 1972), 36-44.

411 GREENE, FRANCIS VINTON. General Greene. (1893) N.Y.: D. Appleton, 1913. 332p. RHi. +
Nathanael Greene. Includes early years and military service in R.I. during the American Revolution.

412 GREENE, GEORGE WASHINGTON. The life of Nathanael Greene, Major-general in the Army of the Revolution. (1846, 1848) N.Y.: Hurd and Houghton, 1871. 3v. RHi. +
Includes early years and military service in R.I.

413 _____. A short history of Rhode Island. Providence: J. A. & R. A. Reid, 1877. xxvi, 356p. RHi. +

414 GREENE, LORENZO J. "Some observations on the Black Regiment of Rhode Island in the American Revolution." Journal of Negro History, 37 (1952), 142-172.
1st R.I. Regt.

415 GREENE, MARY A. "General Nathanael Greene." NEM, n.s. 17 (1898), 558-570.
Includes his early years in R.I.

416 GREENE, MELINDA, and SHIRLEY GREENE. "Early Seventh-Day Baptists in Rhode Island." R.I. Roots, 4, No. 3 (Fall 1978), 1, 4-7.

417 GREENE, NATHANAEL. "Nathanael Greene's letters to 'Friend Sammy' Ward." RIH, 15 (1956), 1-10, 46-54; 16 (1957), 53-57, 79-80, 119-121; 17 (1958), 14-21.
When both were young Rhode Islanders. Clifford P. Monahon and Clarkson A. Collins III, eds.

418 _____. The papers of General Nathanael Greene.... Richard K. Showman, ed. Chapel Hill, N.C.: Univ. of North Carolina Pr., 1976-1980. 2v. RHi. +
A continuing series. Vol. 1 includes correspondence relating to Greene's early years in R.I.; vol. 2 includes correspondence relating to the Battle of R.I. (1778).

419 GREENE, SHIRLEY M. "The Warwick Railway." RIY (1970), 19-20.
Originally (1878) a steam-engine railroad; later a street railroad that provided excursions from Providence to Rocky Point and Oakland Beach.

420 GREENE, WELCOME ARNOLD. "Some of the 'whys and wherefores' of the issues of the Rhode Island colonial paper currency." NHR, 4 (1885), 6-26.

421 GRIEVE, ROBERT. The sea trade and its development in Rhode Island and Providence Plantations; with an account of the evolution of travel and transportaton by land and water. Providence, [1919]. [173]p. RHi. +
Republished from entry 1027.

422 GRIFFITHS, LUCY W. One hundred years of Rhode Island agriculture (statistics and trends). Kingston: Univ. of R.I., Agricultural Experiment Station, 1965. v, 107p. RHi. +

423 GROSSMAN, LAWRENCE. "George T. Downing and desegregation of Rhode Island public schools, 1855-1866." RIH, 36 (1977), 99-105.

424 "GROWING in affluence as the town developed." PM, 26 (1914), 793-795.
"Architectural transitions of the colonial house in Rhode Island."

425 "THE GROWTH of the jewelry industry in Rhode Island." PBTJ, 20 (1908), 442-446.

426 GUILD, REUBEN ALDRIDGE. Footprints of Roger Williams. Providence: Tibbitts & Preston, 1886. 48p. RHi. +

427 _____. Historical address delivered in the First Baptist Meeting House, Providence, June 4, 1890, at the fiftieth anniversary of the Rhode Island Baptist Sunday School Convention. [Providence:] Snow & Farnham, 1890. 15p. RHi. +
History of the Sunday school organization.

428 HABERMAN, IAN S. "The Rhode Island business elite, 1895-1905: a collective portrait." RIH, 26 (1967), 33-48.

429 HADCOCK, EDITHA. "Labor problems in the Rhode Island cotton mills, 1790-1940." RIH, 14 (1955), 82-85, 88-93, 110-119.

430 HAFFENREFFER, CAROLYN. "Our beautiful gardens." RIY (1964-1965), 43-48.
Historical and contemporary.

431 HALE, STUART O. Narragansett Bay: a friend's perspective. [Narragansett:] Marine Advisory Service, Univ. of R.I., [1980]. ix, 122p. RHi. +

432   [HALEY, JOHN WILLIAMS.]  Before Gilbert
Stuart.  Providence:  "Old Stone
Bank," 1931.  10p.  RHi.
      Painters John Smibert and Robert Feke in
R.I.  This entry and others by the same
author under the imprint of "Old Stone
Bank" (i.e., Providence Institution for
Savings) were part of that institution's
historical pamphlet series.  The pamphlets
were reprints of scripts of a long-running
radio series.  Many of the scripts, together
with some that were not published and others
that are not cited here, were later brought
together in somewhat condensed form in the
four-volume "Old Stone Bank" history of
Rhode Island (entry 465).

433   [_____.]  Benjamin Church.  Providence:
"Old Stone Bank," 1930.  10p.  RHi.
      Resident of Little Compton and later of
Bristol; best known as a military leader in
R.I. and elsewhere during King Philip's War.

434   [_____.]  The blizzard of '88.  Providence:
"Old Stone Bank," 1933.  10p.  RHi.

435   [_____.]  By coach and six.  Providence:
"Old Stone Bank," 1931.  10p.  RHi.
      Stagecoaching in R.I.

436   [_____.]  "The call to arms."  Providence:
"Old Stone Bank," 1932.  10p.  RHi.
      Colonial militia in R.I.

437   [_____.]  Catherine Littlefield Greene and
other stories.  Providence:  "Old Stone
Bank," n.d.  40p.  RHi. +
      Wife of Gen. Nathanael Greene.  Other
subjects dealt with in this pamphlet include
Jemima Wilkinson, the "Universal Friend";
the history of Block Island; and R.I.
lotteries.

438   [_____.]  Civil and religious liberty.
Providence:  "Old Stone Bank," 1932.  10p.
RHi.
      Samuel Gorton's contributions.

439   [_____.]  Colonial law and order.
Providence:  "Old Stone Bank," 1932.  10p.
RHi.
      In R.I.

440   [_____.]  Colonial schools and schooldays.
Providence:  "Old Stone Bank," 1931.  10p.
RHi.
      In R.I.

441   _____.  Corn husking days.  Providence:
"Old Stone Bank," 1932.  10p.  RHi.
      In R.I.

442   [_____.]  The country auction.  Providence:
"Old Stone Bank," 1931.  10p.  RHi.
      In R.I.

443   _____.  Curfew.  Providence:  "Old Stone
Bank," 1931.  10p.  RHi.
      Sketch of its history in R.I.

444   [_____.]  Duelling in Rhode Island.
Providence:  "Old Stone Bank," 1932.  10p.
RHi.

445   [_____.]  The early Catholic Church in Rhode
Island.  Providence:  "Old Stone
Bank," 1932.  10p.  RHi.

446   [_____.]  Early Rhode Island libraries.
Providence:  "Old Stone Bank," 1933.  10p.
RHi.

447   [_____.]  "Epics of land and sea."
Providence:  "Old Stone Bank," n.d.  29p.
RHi. +
      Privateering; fires in Providence, etc.

448   [_____.]  The Episcopal Church in Rhode
Island.  Providence:  "Old Stone
Bank," 1933.  10p.  RHi.

449   [_____.]  The first Rhode Island elections.
Providence:  "Old Stone Bank," 1932.  10p.
RHi.

450   [_____.]  Fish and fisheries of Rhode
Island.  Providence:  "Old Stone
Bank," 1930.  10p.  RHi.

451   [_____.]  A forgotten art.  Providence:
"Old Stone Bank," 1931.  10p.  RHi.
      The making of R.I. jonny-cake.

452   [_____.]  "Genius and renown."  Providence:
Old Stone Bank, n.d.  28p.  RHi. +
      Vignettes of the capture of British
General Richard Prescott (1777) in
Middletown; the "first steamboat"; and the
lives of Moses Brown and Governors John and
Samuel Cranston.

453   _____.  George Washington and Rhode Island.
[Providence:]  Commissioner of Education,
State of R.I., 1932.  40p.  RHi. +

454   [_____.]  "Glances backward"....
Providence:  "Old Stone Bank," n.d.  26p.
RHi. +
      Vignettes about two early R.I.
balloonists; election "torchlights and
transparencies"; "Indian athletics";
"Prehistoric Rhode Island."

455   [_____.]  "Huguenots in Rhode Island."
Providence:  "Old Stone Bank," 1930.  10p.
RHi.
      French Huguenots.

456   [_____.]  Indian traits and customs.
Providence:  "Old Stone Bank," 1930.  10p.
RHi.

457 [HALEY, JOHN WILLIAMS.] James S. Slater. Providence: "Old Stone Bank," 1932. 10p. RHi.
His efforts in securing official recognition of May 4 as R.I. Independence Day.

458 [_____.] The Kentish Guards. Providence: "Old Stone Bank," n.d. 44p. RHi.
East Greenwich militia organization. Pamphlet also contains historical vignettes about William Blackstone, of what is now Cumberland, one of the first white settlers in R.I.; about Newport architect Peter Harrison; and about the Rev. James MacSparran, of North Kingstown.

459 [_____.] King Philip and other stories. Providence: "Old Stone Bank," n.d. 32p. RHi. +
This pamphlet also contains historical vignettes about Point Judith; the British raid on Warren during the Revolution; and visits of the Northmen to R.I.

460 [_____.] "Legends and facts": Rhode Island history; the early Rhode Island stage; Providence in 1819; a saga of Rhode Island; Providence's commercial beginnings. Providence: "Old Stone Bank," n.d. [28]p. RHi. +
"Saga" pertains to visits of the Northmen to R.I.

461 [_____.] Maritime Rhode Island. Providence: "Old Stone Bank," n.d. 40p. RHi. +

462 [_____.] News from Lexington. Providence: "Old Stone Bank," 1933. 10p. RHi.
How R.I. reacted to news of the first battle of the American Revolution.

463 [_____.] Old Rhode Island prisons. Providence: "Old Stone Bank," 1930. 10p. RHi.

464 [_____.] Old stagecoach days. Providence: "Old Stone Bank," n.d. 10p. RHi.
R.I. stagecoaching and stagecoach taverns.

465 _____. "The Old Stone Bank" history of Rhode Island. Providence: Providence Institution for Savings, 1929-1944. 4v. RHi. +
A series of historical vignettes, originally presented as radio broadcasts. Many of the vignettes were previously published in somewhat expanded, pamphlet form. A number of the pamphlets are cited elsewhere in this bibliography. See note, entry 432.

466 [_____.] The old stone chimney house and other stories. Providence: "Old Stone Bank," n.d. 32p. RHi. +
Eleazer Arnold House, Lincoln, R.I. Also included in this pamphlet: "Cocumcussoc" (historic house in North Kingstown); "History of lighting in Providence"; "East Greenwich pottery."

467 [_____.] Patriots and pioneers of Rhode Island: Rhode Island in the World War; the Providence stage after the Revolution;...the Wantons of Rhode Island. Providence: "Old Stone Bank," n.d. 32p. RHi. +
I.e., World War I; Wanton family.

468 [_____.] The political saviour of Rhode Island. [Providence:] "Old Stone Bank," n.d. 10p. RHi.
Samuel Gorton in the early history of the R.I. colony.

469 [_____.] Post roads and the mails. Providence: "Old Stone Bank," 1933. 10p. RHi.
In R.I.

470 [_____.] A Quaker martyr and other stories. Providence: "Old Stone Bank," n.d. 40p. RHi. +
Rhode Islander Mary Dyer, hanged in Boston (1660). Other vignettes in this pamphlet deal with a South County ex-slave and with Moses Brown.

471 [_____.] The return home. Providence: "Old Stone Bank," 1932. 10p. RHi.
Return of the 2d R.I. Regt. from Civil War service in 1865.

472 [_____.] Rhode Island and the telephone. Providence: "Old Stone Bank," 1931. 10p. RHi.

473 [_____.] The Rhode Island clambake. Providence: "Old Stone Bank," 1931. 10p. RHi.
Historical sketch of the custom.

474 [_____.] Rhode Island ferries. Providence: "Old Stone Bank," n.d. 10p. RHi.

475 [_____.] The Rhode Island flag, together with accounts of Captain Stephen Olney, Captain Michael Pierce, General Ambrose E. Burnside. Providence: "Old Stone Bank," n.d. [22]p. RHi. +
Olney was a R.I. military hero in the American Revolution; Pierce and most of his men were killed in "Pierce's Fight" during King Philip's War; Burnside was a Civil War general.

476    [HALEY, JOHN WILLIAMS.]   "Rhode
Island recollections."  Providence: "Old
Stone Bank," n.d.  31p.  RHi. +
    Rochambeau and his French troops in R.I.
during the American Revolution; Simeon
Potter, Bristol sea captain; Edgar Allen Poe
in Providence; Mowry & Goff's School,
Providence (founded 1860s).

477    [_____.]  The Rhode Island turkey.
Providence: "Old Stone Bank," 1931.  10p.
RHi.
    R.I. Thanksgiving traditions and the
former tradition of a R.I.-raised turkey
being served each Thanksgiving in the White
House.

478    [_____.]  Rhode Island women.  Providence:
"Old Stone Bank," n.d.  38p.  RHi. +
    The historical vignettes in this pamphlet
include the story of Hannah Robinson and
Hannah's Rock in South Kingstown; social
conditions in Newport during the Revolution;
and the bombardment of Bristol during the
Revolution.

479    [_____.]  Rhode Island's just claim.
Providence: "Old Stone Bank," 1933.  10p.
RHi.
    "...Her leadership in the cause of
independence."

480    [_____.]  Rocks of Rhode Island.
Providence: "Old Stone Bank," 1931.  10p.
RHi.
    Historic and inscribed rocks.

481    [_____.]  Roger Williams and other famous
Rhode Islanders.  Providence:  Old Stone
Bank, n.d.  29p.  RHi. +
    Nathanael Greene, Esek Hopkins, Gilbert
Stuart.

482    [_____.]  Sheriff Robinson and other
stories.  Providence: "Old Stone
Bank," n.d.  32p.  RHi.
    Rowland Robinson, "Sheriff of King's
[Washington] County" in the 18th century.
Also the Carter-Jackson murder in South
Kingstown (1751); "The shipping firm of
Brown & Ives" of Providence; America's Cup
races in Newport.

483    [_____.]  The slave trade.  Providence:
"Old Stone Bank," 1933.  10p.  RHi.
    R.I. slave trade.

484    [_____.]  Stirring moments of Rhode Island
history:  the Great Swamp Fight; the Gaspee
affair; the Great Gale of 1815....
[Providence:]  "Old Stone Bank," n.d.
[22]p.  RHi. +
    Great Swamp Fight occurred in 1675; Gaspee
affair (the burning of the British schooner
Gaspee) in 1772.

485    [_____.]  Thomas Wilson Dorr.  Providence:
"Old Stone Bank," n.d.  10p.  RHi.
    Dorr Rebellion (1842).

486    [_____.]  "Treasures of Rhode Island...."
Providence: "Old Stone Bank," 1928.  [20]p.
RHi.
    Stone Mill, Newport; also First Baptist
Church, Betsy Williams's home, and the
Arcade, all in Providence.

487    [_____.]  The turnpike era.  Providence:
"Old Stone Bank," 1933.  10p.  RHi.
    R.I.'s early toll roads.

488    [_____.]  'Twas Christmas Eve and other
stories.  Providence: "Old Stone
Bank," n.d.  32p.  RHi. +
    "Other stories" include capital punishment
in R.I.; the Tartar, R.I. colony's sloop in
King George's War.

489    [_____.]  Washington's first visit to Rhode
Island.  Providence: "Old Stone
Bank," 1932.  10p.  RHi.
    George Washington first traveled through
R.I. in 1756.  See also next three entries
and entry 453.

490    [_____.]  Washington's fourth visit to Rhode
Island.  Providence: "Old Stone
Bank," 1932.  10p.  RHi.
    As U.S. President (1790).  See also the
preceding entry, the next two entries, and
entry 453.

491    [_____.]  Washington's second visit to Rhode
Island.  Providence: "Old Stone
Bank," 1932.  10p.  RHi.
    In 1776, during the Revolution.  See also
the two preceding entries, the next entry,
and entry 453.

492    [_____.]  Washington's third visit to Rhode
Island.  Providence: "Old Stone
Bank," 1932.  10p.  RHi.
    1781.  See also the three preceding
entries and entry 453.

493    [_____.]  Whaling days in Rhode Island.
Providence: "Old Stone Bank," 1933.  10p.
RHi.

494    HALL, EDWARD B.  A discourse delivered
before the Rhode Island Historical
Society...on the life and times of John
Howland, late president of the society.
Providence: G. H. Whitney, 1855.  36p.
RHi. +
    Providence community leader, who played an
important role in the campaign for free
schools in R.I.

495    HALL, MAY EMERY.  Roger Williams.  Boston:
Pilgrim Pr., 1917.  xviii, 212p.  RHi. +

496 HAMMETT, CATHERINE T. "Fifty golden years of Girl Scouting in Rhode Island." RIY (1971), 73-78.

497 HAMMILL, OLIVIA D. Thirty-five years of accomplishment: the story of the Rhode Island Council of Women from 1889 to 1924. n.p.: R.I. Council of Women, 1925. 16p. RHi.

498 HANLON, JOHN. "Mrs. Clara Dimond Holland: for 50 years, she turned mavericks into little ladies and gentlemen." RIer (Nov. 7, 1965), 4-6.
    Ballroom dancing classes.

499 "HARBOR and Bay improvements since 1852." PBTJ, 27 (1915), 159-162.
    Providence Harbor.

500 HARKNESS, R. E. E. "Principles established in Rhode Island." Church History, 5 (1936), 216-226.
    Roger Williams and "free rights in religion; separation of church and state; representative government or government derived from the people; and public ownership of land or the natural resources."

501 HARNEY, GILBERT L. "How Rhode Island received the Constitution." NEM, n.s. 2 (1890), 272-276.
    U.S. Constitution.

502 HARPIN, MATHIAS P. The high road to Zion. n.p.: Harpin's American Heritage Foundation, 1976. 240p. RHi.
    Historical sketches of Warwick, the Pawtuxet Valley, and other parts of the state.

503 _____. Patterns on the river. West Warwick: Pilot Publishing, 1946. 81p. RHi.
    Pawtuxet River Valley.

504 _____. "The rebel flame." WRICHSH, 4 (July 1961), [2]; 5 (Aug. 1961), [2]; (Sept. 1961), [2]; (Oct. 1961), [2].
    R.I. in the American Revolution.

505 _____. "They heeded the call: 'go ye and teach.'" RIer (Apr. 2, 1961), 6-8.
    Louis and Elise Samson, who taught children of Franco-American immigrants in a number of Roman Catholic schools.

506 HARRIS, WILLIAM. Harris papers: with an introduction by Irving B. Richman and a calendar and notes by Clarence S. Brigham. Providence: [R.I. Historical Society,] 1902. 416p. RHi. +
    Harris was a 17th-century claimant to lands in Pawtuxet Purchase. This entry was published as RIHSC, 10 (1902).

507 HARTOGENSIS, BENJAMIN H. "Rhode Island and consanguineous Jewish marriages." American Jewish Historical Society, Publications, 20 (1911), 137-146.
    I.e., marriages between kin permitted under Mosaic law.

508 HARTZ, LOUIS. "Seth Luther: the story of a working-class rebel." NEQ, 13 (1940), 401-418.
    Early labor leader. See also entry 377.

509 HASLAM, CHARLES B. "'Two score years and ten' (in retrospect)." Rhode Island Bar Journal, 5, No. 4 (Jan. 1957), 1, 3, 6.
    Changes in legal practices and court procedures.

510 HASSE, ADELAIDE ROSALIA. Index of economic material in documents of states of the United States: Rhode Island, 1789-1904. [Washington:] Carnegie Institution of Washington, 1908. 95p. RHi. +

511 HAVHOLM, BONNIE. "A unique Rhode Island entity: the election prox." NH, 41 (1968), 118-121.
    Printed list of candidates, usable as a ballot (colonial period and later).

512 HAYMAN, ROBERT W. Catholicism in Rhode Island and the Diocese of Providence. [Providence: Diocese of Providence, 1982.] 353p. RHi.
    A study of the early history of the diocese, which covers all of R.I. Includes bibliography.

513 HAZARD, CAROLINE. "Records of Narragansett weather, 1797 to 1802; with additional notes from Newport to 1804." RIHSC, 30 (1937), 1-9.

514 [HAZARD, EDWARD H.] "Reminiscences of the Dorr War." Providence Daily Journal (Jan. 1885).
    Series of five articles, the first three dated Jan. 15, 16, 17, 1885. Rider Collection, Brown Univ.

515 HAZELTINE, HAROLD DEXTER. Appeals from colonial courts to the King in Council, with especial reference to Rhode Island. n.p., 1896. [52]p. RPB. +
    Reprinted from American Historical Association, Annual Report (1894), 299-350.

516 HELLERICH, MAHLON H. "The Luther cases in the lower courts." RIH, 11 (1952), 33-45.
    Antecedents of Luther v. Borden (1849).

517  HENSHAW, J. P. K.  A discourse delivered in Grace Church, Providence, on the occasion of the third jubilee, or one hundred and fiftieth anniversary of the Society for the Propagation of the Gospel in Foreign Parts, on the first Sunday after Trinity, June 22d, 1851.  Providence:  John F. Moore, 1851.  36p.  RHi. +
Includes early history of Episcopal churches in R.I.

518  HIGGINS, JOHN SEVILLE.  The Episcopal bishops of Rhode Island, 1790-1980.  n.p., n.d.  55p.  RHi. +

519  HIIRONEN, REINO.  "Why Finnish people came to western Rhode Island."  WRICHSP, 2, No. 2 (1955), [2-6].

520  HINCKLEY, ANITA W.  "Sea chanteys."  RIer (June 29, 1969), 12-13.
Narragansett Bay ships and their owners.

521  HISTOIRE des Canadiens-francais du Rhode Island, nos sociétés et nos bienfaiteur.  Souvenir d'une fête nationale, le 24 juin, 1895, Woonsocket, R.I.  Woonsocket: [Société Saint Jean Baptiste de Woonsocket, R.I., 1895.]  124p.  RWoU. +
Franco-Americans.  Text in French.

522  HISTORICAL RECORDS SURVEY.  RHODE ISLAND.  Inventory of the church archives of Rhode Island:  Baptist.  Providence, 1941.  231p.  RHi. +
Includes brief historical sketches of many churches.

523  ____.  Inventory of the church archives of Rhode Island:  Society of Friends.  Providence, 1939.  iii, 80p.  RHi. +
Includes brief historical sketches of the various meetings.

524  ____.  Summary of legislation concerning vital statistics in Rhode Island.  Providence, 1937.  15, 3p.  RHi. +

525  "HISTORICAL sketch."  BTJ, 1 (Sept. 1890), iii-iv, vi-vii, ix-x, xii.
R.I. Society for the Encouragement of Domestic Industry.

526  HISTORY and roster of Rhode Island Masonry in World War Two.  Winfield Scott Solomon, comp.  n.p.:  E. L. Freeman, n.d.  166p.  RHi. +

527  THE HISTORY of the State of Rhode Island and Providence Plantations:  biographical.  N.Y.:  American Historical Society, 1920.  2v.  RHi. +

528  HISTORY of the State of Rhode Island; with illustrations.  Philadelphia:  Hoag, Wade, 1878.  iv, 370p.  RHi. +

529  HITCHCOCK, HENRY-RUSSELL.  Rhode Island architecture.  (1939) N.Y.:  Da Capo, 1968.  ix, 69p.  RHi. +

530  HOBERMAN, HARRY, and WENDY YONDORF.  Changing conceptions of public health:  a centennial history of the Rhode Island Department of Health, 1878-1978.  Providence:  R.I. Department of Health, 1978.  iii, 72p.  R.

531  HOLMAN, WINIFRED LOVERING.  "Roger Williams."  American Genealogist, 28 (1952), 197-209.
Biographical sketch.

532  HOLST, ANNE CRAWFORD ALLEN.  "The old town pounds of Rhode Island."  RIH, 3 (1944), 13-17.
Animal pounds.

533  HOPKINS, JANET W.  History of Rhode Island State Grange, with biographies of past state masters and annals of subordinate, Pomona and juvenile granges.  n.p.:  R.I. State Grange, 1939.  120p.  RU.

534  HOPKINS, STEPHEN.  The rights of colonies examined.  Introduced and edited by Paul Campbell.  Providence:  R.I. Bicentennial Foundation, 1974.  vii, 53p.  RHi. +
Pamphlet, first published in 1765, argued against taxation by Parliament.

535  HORR, GEORGE G.  "Rhode Island in World War I."  RIY (1969), H146-H159.

536  HORVITZ, ELEANOR F.  "Jews and the Boy Scout movement in Rhode Island."  RIJHN, 7 (1977), 341-384.

537  ____.  "The Outlet story and the Samuels brothers."  RIJHN, 6 (1974), 488-531.
Outlet Department Stores.

538  ____.  "The years of the Jewish woman."  RIJHN, 7 (1975), 152-170.
Jewish women's charitable organizations in R.I.

539  HOWIESON, MARION LILLIAN.  "Portrait of Rhode Island."  Daughters of the American Revolution Magazine, 107 (1973), 675-678, 754.

540  ____.  "The thick and the thin of it:  or the great jonnycake conflict."  Daughters of the American Revolution Magazine, 112 (Jan. 1978), 14-17.
Different R.I. recipes.

541 Rhode Island

541 HOWLAND, JOHN. "John Howland's address."
NH, 41 (1968), 74-84.
On the importance of preserving papers and
artifacts relating to R.I's history (1839).

542 _____. Notices of the military services
rendered by the Militia, as well as by the
enlisted troops, of the State of Rhode
Island, during the Revolutionary War. n.p.,
[1832?]. 11p. RHi. +

543 HOYT, DAVID W. The influence of physical
features upon the history of Rhode Island.
[Providence:] State of R.I., Dept. of
Education, 1910. 20p. RHi. +

544 HULING, RAY GREENE. "The Rhode Island
emigration to Nova Scotia." NHR, 7 (1889),
89-136.

545 HUMPHRY, JOHN A. Library cooperation: the
Brown University study of university-
school-community coordination in the State
of Rhode Island. Providence: Brown Univ.
Pr., 1963. x, 213p. RHi. +
Includes chapter on "The library tradition
in R.I."

546 HUNTER, WILLIAM. "Rhode Island and
religious liberty." Magazine of New England
History, 3 (1893), 246-249.
From an address delivered July 4, 1826.

547 HUNTSMAN, JUDITH. "In the beginning were
the Indians." RIY (1964-1965), H17-H21.

548 HUSTON, JAMES L. "The threat of radicalism:
Seward's candidacy and the Rhode Island
gubernatorial election of 1860." RIH, 41
(1982), 87-99.
William H. Seward and Republican Party
radicalism.

549 ILLUSTRATIONS of the seals, arms and flags
of Rhode Island; with historical notes by
Howard M. Chapin and an introduction by
Norman M. Isham. Providence: R.I.
Historical Society, 1930. ii, 77p. RHi. +

550 "IN perspective: how Jewish settlers fared
in colonial Rhode Island." RIJHN, 1 (1954),
102-103.
Signed B.F.S.

551 IN the wake of '38: oral history interviews
with Rhode Island survivors of the
devastating hurricane of September 21,
1938...project of South Kingstown High
School and the Rhode Island Committee for
the Humanities, spring 1977. [Providence:]
R.I. Committee for the Humanities, 1977.
254p. RHi.

552 "INDIAN slaves of King Philip's War."
RIHSPubs, 1 (1893-1894), 234-240.
Signed J.G.V. (James Gardiner Vose).
Article is followed by his "Note on the
transaction of Roger Williams and others, in
selling Indians into slavery," 239-240.

553 "INDUSTRIAL conditions, past and present."
PM, 28 (1916), 357-359.

554 INDUSTRIES and wealth of the principal
points in Rhode Island: being city of
Providence, Pawtucket, Central Falls,
Woonsocket, Newport, Narragansett Pier,
Bristol and Westerly. N.Y.: A. F. Parsons
Publishing, 1892. x, 282p. RHi. +

555 ISHAM, NORMAN MORRISON, and ALBERT F. BROWN.
Early Rhode Island houses: an historic and
architectural study. Providence: Preston
& Rounds, 1895. 100p. RHi. +

556 JACKMAN, SYDNEY W. "A Tory's claim to the
Wanton estates." RIH, 19 (1960), 1-7,
50-61, 79-88.
William Browne, who held unpaid debts from
Joseph and William Wanton.

557 JACKSON, E. P. "Early uses of land in Rhode
Island." Geographical Society of
Philadelphia, Bulletin, 19 (1923), 69-87.

558 JACKSON, HENRY. An account of the churches
in Rhode-Island: presented at an adjourned
session of the twenty-eighth annual meeting
of the Rhode-Island Baptist State Convention, Providence, November 8, 1853.
Providence: G. H. Whitney, 1854. 134p.
RHi. +

559 JAMES, SYDNEY V. Colonial Rhode Island:
a history. N.Y.: Scribner's, 1975. xviii,
423p. RHi. +

560 _____. "The worlds of Roger Williams."
RIH, 37 (1978), 99-109.

561 JANES, LEWIS G. "Samuel Gorton of Rhode
Island.: NEM, n.s. 18 (1898), 287-305.
Prominent in the early years of the R.I.
colony and one of the first settlers of
Warwick.

562 JERNEGAN, MARCUS W. The Tammany Societies
of Rhode Island. Providence: Preston &
Rounds, 1897. 39p. RHi. +
Political.

563 "JEWISH cemeteries (Beth Chayim)." RIJHN,
3 (1958), 55-74.

564 JOHNSON, KATHARINE W. Rhode Island
Baptists: their zeal, their times. Valley
Forge, Pa.: Judson Pr., 1970. 128p.
RHi. +

565  JOHNSON, LUCIAN.  Religious liberty in Maryland and Rhode Island.  Brooklyn, N.Y.: International Catholic Truth Society, 1903. 56p.  RHi. +

566  JOHNSTON, WILLIAM D.  Slavery in Rhode Island, 1755-1776.  Providence:  Standard Printing, 1894.  56p.  RHi. +

567  JONES, PETER E.  "Grant us commission to make reprisals upon any enemies shipping."  RIH, 34 (1975), 105-119.
  Privateering during the Revolution.

568  JORDY, WILLIAM H., and CHRISTOPHER P. MONKHOUSE.  Buildings on paper:  Rhode Island architectural drawings, 1825-1945....  Providence:  Brown Univ., 1982.  xiii, 243p.  RHi.
  Text to accompany an exhibition at Brown Univ., R.I. Historical Society, and R.I. School of Design.  Includes biographical sketches of R.I. architects and other major architects who designed buildings in the state.  Bibliography, 241-243.

569  "JOURNAL of the committee who built the ships Providence and Warren for the United States in 1776."  Magazine of History, 8 (1908), 249-254, 312-323; 9 (1909), 1-6, 63-79, 133-140, 195-202.
  Edited by James N. Arnold.

570  JUDD, FRANCES.  "Little Rhody covered bridges."  Connecticut River Valley Covered Bridge Society, Bulletin, 17 (Spring 1971), 3-5.

571  KAISER, MRS. KARL W.  Musical expressions of early Rhode Island Indians,...as told by Princess Red Wing....  [Providence,] n.d. 15p.  RPB.

572  KAMINSKI, JOHN P.  "Political sacrifice and demise:  John Collins and Jonathan J. Hazard."  RIH, 35 (1976), 91-98.
  R.I. politics during the Confederation period (1783-1789).

573  KARR, KATHLEEN.  "Flicks produced in Rhode Island."  RIer (Feb. 7, 1971), 10-14, 16, 18.
  Early years of motion-picture making.

574  KEEFE, JOHN W.  "Traditions of medicine in Rhode Island."  Boston Medical and Surgical Journal, 193 (1925), 899-905.

575  KELLNER, GEORGE H., and J. STANLEY LEMONS. Rhode Island:  the independent state. Woodland Hills, Calif.:  Windsor Publications for the R.I. Historical Society, 1982.  224p.  RHi. +

576  KENNEDY, HAZEL WADE.  A guide to historic Pawtuxet.  Providence: Oxford Pr., 1972. 31p.  RHi. +

577  KENNY, ROBERT W.  "The beginnings of the Rhode Island train bands."  RIHSC, 33 (1940), 25-38.
  Forerunners of the militia.

578  KINDER, NANCY.  "The 'vampires' of Rhode Island."  Yankee, 34 (Oct. 1970), 114-115, 166-167.
  Instances of belief in vampires.

579  KING, DAN.  The life and times of Thomas Wilson Dorr, with outlines of the political history of Rhode Island.  Boston:  Priv. Print., 1859.  368p.  RHi. +

580  KING, HENRY MELVILLE.  The baptism of Roger Williams:  a review of Dr. W. H. Whitsitt's influence.  Providence:  Preston & Rounds, 1897.  143p.  RHi. +

581  _____.  A brief picture of the historic background of our freedom of worship in Rhode Island.  n.p., [1901?].  7p.  RHi. +

582  _____.  Historical discourse delivered at the one hundredth anniversary of the Rhode Island Bible Society in the First Baptist Meeting House, Providence, Sept. 29, 1913. Providence, 1913.  24p.  RHi. +

583  _____.  The true Roger Williams:  an address delivered by request in the First Baptist Meeting House, Providence, R.I....July 28, 1907; Roger Williams Sunday, Old Home Week. Providence:  Townsend, F. H., [1907?].  32p. RHi. +

584  KIVEN, ARLINE RUTH.  Then why the Negroes: the nature and course of the anti-slavery movement in Rhode Island, 1637-1861. [Providence:]  Urban League of R.I., 1973. 91p.  RHi. +

585  KLEIN, MAURY.  "'Rebellion hangs in the very air of this colony.'"  RIer (June 9, 1974), 6, 9-11.
  Events of 1774 in R.I.

586  _____.  "Rhode Island in the Civil War." RIY (1967), H89-H96.

587  KLYBERG, ALBERT T.  "'Some of the king's horses and some of the king's men.'"  NH, 45 (1972), 69-82.
  Needs and opportunities for preserving and writing R.I. history.

588  _____.  "Toward a Rhode Island history." RIH, 34 (1975), 23-32.
  Strengths and weaknesses of the state's historiography.

589 Rhode Island

589 KLYBERG, ALBERT T., and NANCY GREY OSTERUD.
The lay of the land. Providence: R.I.
Historical Society, 1979. 48p. RHi.
Publication relating to R.I. Historical
Society exhibition on how Rhode Islanders
have shaped their state's landscape.

590 KNIGHT, BENJAMIN, SR. History of the
Sprague families, of Rhode Island, cotton
manufacturers and calico printers, from
William I to William IV, with an account of
the murder of the late Amasa Sprague, father
of Hon. Wm. Sprague, ex-U.S. Senator from
Rhode Island. Santa Cruz: H. Coffin, 1881.
ii, 74p. RHi. +

591 KNOWLES, JAMES DAVIS. Memoir of Roger
Williams, the founder of the State of
Rhode-Island. Boston: Lincoln, Edmands,
1834. xx, 437p. RHi. +

592 KNOX, HORATIO B. The destruction of the
Gaspee. [Providence:] Dept. of Education,
State of R.I., 1908. 15p. RHi. +
British schooner, burned by Rhode
Islanders in 1772.

593 KOOPMAN, HARRY LYMAN. "Libraries of Rhode
Island." PM, 28 (1916), 201-207.

594 _____. Library progress in Rhode Island.
n.p., n.d. 7p. RHi. +

595 LaFANTASIE, GLENN W. "Act for all reasons:
Revolutionary politics and May 4, 1776."
RIH, 35 (1976), 39-47.
R.I. Declaration of Independence.

596 LAMBERT, D. J. History of the Rhode Island
Reds. [Providence:] R.I. State Board of
Agriculture, 1920. 8p. RNoP.
Breed of chicken.

597 "LAND titles in Rhode Island: their origin
and evolution." Netopian, 3 (Sept. 1922),
13-16.

598 "LAST of the old johnny cake mills."
Johnnycake Journal, 1 (June-July 1978),
[1-2].
Gristmills. First published in Providence
Sunday Journal (Sept. 10, 1911).

599 LASWELL, GEORGE D. "Corners and characters
of Rhode Island." Providence: Oxford Pr.,
1924. 103p. RHi.
Drawings and historical vignettes.

600 LEACH, DOUGLAS EDWARD. "Away to Rhode
Island from their cellars." RIH, 18 (1959),
43-55.
Flight of Warwick settlers to Aquidneck
Island during King Philip's War. See also
this author's Flintlock and tomahawk: New
England in King Philip's War (1958), for a
detailed account of R.I.'s role in the war.

601 LEADING manufacturers and merchants of Rhode
Island: historical and descriptive review
of the industrial enterprises of the city of
Providence, Pawtucket, Central Falls,
Woonsocket, Westerly and Newport. N.Y.:
International Publishing, 1886. viii, 213p.
RHi. +

602 LEE, THOMAS ZANSLAUR. "The Irish of the
Rhode Island colony in peace and war."
Journal of the American-Irish Historical
Society, 15 (1916), 156-167.

603 LEGISLATIVE history and souvenir of Rhode
Island, 1899 and 1900.... William Harrison
Taylor, comp. Providence: E. L. Freeman,
1900. 224p. RHi. +
Includes biographical sketches of
then-current legislators; also Josiah
Bowditch, "Legislative history of Rhode
Island," 173-221.

604 LEIGHTON, ETTA V. The story of Roger
Williams and the founding of Rhode Island.
Dansville, N.Y.: F. A. Owen Publishing,
1912. 32p. RHi. +

605 LEMONS, J. STANLEY, and MICHAEL A. McKENNA.
"Re-enfranchisement of Rhode Island
Negroes." RIH, 30 (1971), 3-13.

606 LERCHE, CHARLES O., JR. "The Dorr Rebellion
and the federal Constitution." RIH, 9
(1950), 1-10.

607 LESLIE, WILLIAM R. "The Gaspee affair: a
study of its constitutional significance."
Mississippi Valley Historical Review, 39
(1952), 233-256.
1772.

608 "LETTERS from the Pawtuxet." Providence
Journal, Jan. 18, Feb. 1, Mar. 17, 18, Apr.
1, 8, 22, May 3, 11, 18, 31, July 26, Aug.
16, 23, Sept. 6, 1859; Sept. 27, Oct. 2, 15,
22, 29, 1860.
Historical sketches of Pawtuxet Valley
villages.

609 LeVEQUE, ANN. "Made to order: familiar
scenes on Rhode Island bank notes." RIH, 40
(1981), 89-97.

610 LEVINE, ERWIN L. "The Rhode Island Lincoln
Party and the 1906 election." RIH, 21
(1962), 8-15.

611   LEVINE, ERWIN L.  Theodore Francis Green: the Rhode Island years, 1906-1936. Providence: Brown Univ. Pr., 1963. ix, 222p. RHi. +
      Green's career in state politics.  A 2d vol., entitled, Theodore Francis Greene: the Washington years, 1937-1960 (1971), deals with his service in the U.S. Senate.

612   "LIFE on relief in Rhode Island, 1934: a contemporary view from the field."  RIH, 39 (1980), 79-93.
      James T. Patterson, ed.

613   LINCOLN, CHARLES E.  "The making of Rhode Island's railroad system."  PM, 29 (1917), 457-465.

614   _____.  "Philanthropy and charity."  PM, 28 (1916), 569-576.
      Public and private philanthropic institutions.

615   _____.  "Rhode Island always foremost in preparedness."  PM, 29 (1917), 397-411.
      R.I.'s participation in colonial and U.S. wars.

616   _____.  "Rhode Island's turkey coming into its own."  PM, 39 (1928), 460-463.
      Narragansett breed of turkey.  Article includes historical sketch of Thanksgiving Day customs in R.I.

617   LIPPINCOTT, BERTRAM.  Indians, privateers and high society: a Rhode Island sampler. Philadelphia: Lippincott, 1961. 301p. RHi. +

618   LIPPITT, CHARLES WARREN.  The Rhode Island Declaration of Independence: an address delivered before the Rhode Island Citizens' Historical Association on the 130th anniversary of the declaration of independence by the Colony of Rhode Island, May 4, 1906. Providence: E. L. Freeman, 1907. 38, xxx p. RHi. +

619   _____.  Rhode Island's early efforts in the Revolution: an address delivered before the Rhode Island Society of the Cincinnati in the State House at Newport, R.I., on July fourth, 1896. Central Falls: E. L. Freeman, n.d. 19p. RHi. +

620   LIST of books upon Rhode Island history. Clarence Saunders Brigham, comp. [Providence:] State of R.I., Dept. of Education, 1908. 8p. RHi. +

621   A LIST of Rhode Island literary women (1726-1892), with some account of their work. Fanny Purdy Palmer, comp. (1892) Providence, 1893. 24p. RHi. +

622   A LIST of Rhode Island soldiers and sailors in the old French and Indian War, 1755-1762. Howard M. Chapin, comp. Providence: R.I. Historical Society, 1918. 155p. RHi. +
      Includes historical introduction.

623   LONGACRE, CHARLES SMULL.  Roger Williams: his life, work, and ideals. Washington: Review and Herald Publishing Association, 1939. 191p. RHi. +

624   LOUGHREY, MARY ELLEN.  France and Rhode Island, 1686-1800. N.Y.: King's Crown Pr., 1944. vii, 186p. RHi. +

625   LOVEJOY, DAVID S.  "A Rhode Island election broadside, 1767."  Books at Brown, 18 (1960), 187-193.

626   _____.  Rhode Island politics and the American Revolution, 1760-1776. Providence: Brown Univ. Pr., 1958. 256p. RHi. +

627   LOWENHERZ, ROBERT J.  "Roger Williams and the great Quaker debate."  American Quarterly, 11 (1959), 157-165.

628   LOWTHER, LAWRENCE L.  "Town and colony in early eighteenth-century Rhode Island."  NH, 37 (1964), 81-92.

629   LUTI, VINCENT F.  "Seth Luther: stone carver of the Narragansett basin."  RIH, 39 (1980), 3-13.
      Gravestones.

630   McCANNA, FRANCIS I.  "Study of the history and jurisdiction of Rhode Island courts." American Irish Historical Society, Journal, 22 (1923), 170-195.

631   McCARTHY, LAWRENCE T.  "Palmy days of the Consolidated."  RIer (Dec. 26, 1954), 2-5.
      Street railroad.

632   McCARTHY, PETE.  "The lively pursuit of par."  RIY (1964-1965), 64-66.
      Golf in R.I.

633   M'CARTY, J. H.  "Roger Williams."  Ladies' Repository, 26 (1866), 513-517, 593-597.

634   McCLELLAND, THOMAS CALVIN.  Historical address delivered before the Rhode Island Home Missionary Society.... [Newport: Milne Printery, 1903?] 25p. RHi. +

635   McGRATH, J. HOWARD.  "The constitutional convention of 1944."  RIH, 4 (1945), 1-6.

636  MacGUNIGLE, BRUCE CAMPBELL.  "Rhode Island town names:  an etymological study.  The meanings and origins of the names of Rhode Island's 39 cities and towns."  R.I. Roots, 8, No. 3 (Sept. 1982), 45-50.
     Part 1 of a series.

637  MacINTOSH, MILTON R.  150 years of Harmony: a history of the first 150 years of Harmony Lodge, No. 9, F. & A.M., of Pawtuxet, Rhode Island.  n.p., 1955.  138p.  RCr.

638  MACKEY, PHILIP ENGLISH.  "'The results may be glorious':  anti-gallows movement in Rhode Island, 1838-1852."  RIH, 33 (1974), 19-31.

639  McLAUGHLIN, BERNARD ALOYSIUS.  Some financial trends of commercial banks of Rhode Island, 1915-1937....  Washington: Catholic Univ. of America Pr., 1941.  xi, 106p.  RHi. +

640  McLOUGHLIN, WILLIAM G.  Rhode Island:  a bicentennial history.  N.Y.:  Norton, 1978.  xi, 240p.  RHi. +

641  MacMANUS, EILEEN M.  "Rhode Island's contribution to California."  Americana, 26 (1932), 232-246.
     R.I. residents who went there during the Gold Rush of 1849.

642  McMURTRIE, DOUGLAS C.  The beginning of printing in Rhode Island.  Somerville, N.J., 1935.  [23]p.  RHi. +
     Reprinted from Americana, 39 (1935).

643  ____.  "Pioneer printing in Rhode Island."  National Printer Journalist (Sept. 1932), 18-19, 72-73.

644  MAGRATH, C. PETER.  "Optimistic democrat: Thomas W. Dorr and the case of Luther vs. Borden."  RIH, 29 (1970), 94-112.

645  ____.  "Samuel Ames:  the great chief justice of Rhode Island."  RIH, 24 (1965), 65-76.

646  MANCHESTER, ANNA B.  "Rhode Island in the American Revolution."  American Monthly Magazine, 34 (1909), 157-162.

647  MANGLER, JOYCE ELLEN.  Rhode Island music and musicians, 1733-1850.  Detroit: Information Service, 1965.  90p.  RHi. +
     Bibliography, 85-90.

648  "MANUFACTURING progress in Rhode Island."  PM, 28 (1916), 349-353.
     Industrial history.

649  MARSIS, JAMES L.  "Agrarian politics in Rhode Island, 1800-1860."  RIH, 34 (1975), 13-21.

650  MASON, GEORGE CHAMPLIN.  "The British fleet in Rhode Island."  RIHSC, 7 (1885), 301-325.
     American Revolution.

651  MASONIC WAR BOARD OF RHODE ISLAND.  Honor roll:  Rhode Island Masons who served in the World War, 1914-1918.  Central Falls:  E. L. Freeman, 1921.  123p.  RHi. +

652  MAYER, KURT B.  Economic development and population growth in Rhode Island.  Providence:  Brown Univ. Library, 1953.  70p.  RHi. +

653  ____, and SIDNEY GOLDSTEIN.  Migration and economic development in Rhode Island.  Providence:  Brown Univ. Pr., 1958.  64p.  RHi. +

654  "THE MEANING of Indian place names:  an interview with William B. Cabot."  RIHSC, 22 (1929), 33-38.

655  MEHTA, SURINDER KUMAR.  Population redistribution and business structure and location patterns:  Rhode Island, 1929-1958....  [Providence,] 1963.  xiii, 172p.  RPB. +

656  "MEMOIR of Mr. Roger Williams."  American Baptist Magazine and Missionary Intelligencer, 1 (Jan. 1817), 7-14.

657  MEN of progress:  biographical sketches and portraits of leaders in business and professional life in the State of Rhode Island and Providence Plantations.  Richard Herndon, comp.  Boston:  NEM, 1896.  282p.  RHi. +

658  MENSEL, KAREN D.  The Victorian heritage: nineteenth century architecture in Rhode Island.  Photographs by Tess Hoffman.  Providence:  Office of Publications, R.I. College, 1980.  32p.  RHi.

659  METZ, WILLIAM D.  "The road to rebellion."  RIY (1965-1966), 37-43.
     Incidents in R.I. leading up to the Revolution.

660  MICHEL, SONYA.  "Family and community networks among Rhode Island Jews:  a study based on oral histories."  RIJHN, 7 (1978), 513-533.

661   MIGHT and right; by a Rhode Islander.
Providence: A. H. Stillwell, 1844. xii,
345p. RHi. +
Events leading to the Dorr Rebellion.
Authorship has been attributed to Frances
Harriet Greene McDougall.  But this has been
disputed in entry 3643.

662   MILLAR, JOHN FITZHUGH.  "The black
privateersman."  NH, 54 (1981), 51-52.
Revolutionary-era portrait.

663   _____.  "The French in Rhode Island."  RIY
(1974), 32-37.
Troops in Newport and elsewhere during the
Revolution.

664   _____.  "The Gaspee."  RIY (1972), 22-25.
British schooner, destroyed by Rhode
Islanders in 1772.

665   _____.  Rhode Island:  forgotten leader of
the Revolutionary era.  Providence: Journal
Bulletin, 1975. 64p. RHi. +

666   _____.  "Stephen Hopkins:  an architect of
independence, 1705-1785."  NH, 53 (1980),
24-36; 54 (1981), 53.
Revolutionary politics.

667   _____.  "'Truly a solid nest of rebels.'"
RIer (June 8, 1975), 8-9, 11.
R.I. on the eve of the American
Revolution.

668   MILLARD, CHARLES E.  "Rhode Island medicine
in the Revolution."  RIMJ, 59 (1976),
299-316, 334, 338-339.

669   MILLER, ALBERT H.  "Anesthesia in Rhode
Island."  RIMJ, 31 (1948), 37-41.

670   MILLER, PERRY.  Roger Williams:  his
contribution to the American tradition.
Indianapolis: Bobbs-Merrill, 1953. xviii,
273p. RHi. +

671   MILLER, THEODORE A., and FRANCIS J. MAGUIRE.
"R.I. Supreme Court surveys (1972-1974) and
precis (74-75)."  Rhode Island Bar Journal,
24, No. 3 (Dec. 1975), 6-14.

672   MILLER, WILLIAM DAVIS.  Ancient paths to
Pequot.... Providence: Society of Colonial
Wars, R.I., 1936. 16p. RHi. +
Indian paths between Providence and
Westerly.

673   _____.  "Fox hunting in colonial Rhode
Island."  RIHSC, 27 (1934), 33-38.
Finds no evidence of it.

674   _____.  "The Kay bequest."  RIHSC, 34
(1941), 1-4.
Silver left by Nathaniel Kay to the
Anglican churches of R.I. (1734).

675   MILLER, WILLIAM J.  King Philip and the
Wampanoags of Rhode Island, with some
account of a rock picture on the shore of
Mount Hope Bay, in Bristol. 2d ed.
Providence: Sidney S. Rider, 1885. 148p.
RHi. +
Originally published as Notes concerning
the Wampanoag tribe of Indians (1880).

676   MILLWARD, CELIA M.  "Language of colonial
Rhode Island."  RIH, 34 (1975), 35-42.
English language as used during that era.

677   MINCHINTON, W. E.  "Shipbuilding in colonial
Rhode Island."  RIH, 20 (1961), 119-124.

678   MINER, GEORGE L.  "Rhode Island samplers."
RIHSC, 13 (1920), 41-51.
Needlework.

679   MINER, LILIAN BURLEIGH.  Our state:  Rhode
Island.  Providence: Oxford Pr., 1925. xi,
248p. RHi. +

680   MOHR, RALPH S.  Governors for three hundred
years, 1638-1959:  Rhode Island and
Providence Plantations.  (1954)
[Providence:] Oxford Pr., 1959. 339p.
RHi. +

681   _____.  Rhode Island footprints on the sands
of time:  a bicentennial remembrance.
Providence: Oxford Pr., 1975. 142p.
RHi. +

682   MOLLOY, SCOTT.  Division 618:  streetcar
employees fight for a union in Rhode Island.
n.p., 1977. 58p. RHi.

683   _____.  "Rhode Island communities and the
1902 carmen's strike."  Radical History
Review, No. 17 (1978), 75-98.

684   _____.  Rhode Island transit album.
Cambridge, Mass.: Boston Street Railway
Association, 1978. 64p. RHi.
Mass transit, from trolley cars to buses.

685   MONAHON, CLIFFORD P.  "Our historic
landmarks."  RIY (1963), 46-47.

686   _____.  Rhode Island: a students' guide to
localized history.  N.Y.: Teachers College
Pr., Columbia Univ., 1965. x, 36p. RHi. +

687   MONTGOMERY, FLORENCE M.  "'Fortunes to be
acquired':  textiles in 18th-century Rhode
Island."  RIH, 31 (1972), 53-63.
Imported fabrics.

688 MOOD, FULMER. "Narragansett Bay and Dee River, 1582." RIHSC, 28 (1935), 97-100.
See also entry 400.

689 MOORE, LeROY, JR. "Roger Williams and the historians." Church History, 32 (1963), 432-451.

690 MOORE, SORAYA. "A gallery of notables." RIer (Oct. 12, 1969), 24-25.
Notable R.I. blacks.

691 MORGAN, EDMUND SEARS. Roger Williams: the church and the state. N.Y.: Harcourt, Brace & World, 1967. 170p. RHi. +

692 MORRIS, MAXWELL H. "Roger Williams and the Jews." American Jewish Archives, 3 (Jan. 1951), 24-27.

693 MORSE, JEDIDIAH. An account of Rhode Island and the people therein: extracted from the writings of Dr. Jedidiah Morse; published in the years 1792 and 1796. n.p., n.d. [16]p. RPB.

694 MOWRY, ARTHUR MAY. The constitutional controversy in Rhode Island in 1841. Washington: Government Printing Office, 1896. [10]p. RHi. +
Reprinted from American Historical Association, Annual Report (1894), 361-370.

695 _____. The Dorr War: or the constitutional struggle in Rhode Island. Providence: Preston & Rounds, 1901. xvi, 420p. RHi. +

696 MOWRY, WILLIAM A. Concerning Roger Williams: an address delivered before the Hyde Park Historical Society, October 25, 1909. n.p., n.d. 16p. RHi. +

697 _____. Thomas Wilson Dorr: an address...before the Rhode Island Citizens' Historical Association on its twenty-fifth anniversary, 1908. n.p., 1908. 39p. RHi. +

698 MUDGE, ZACHARIAH ATWELL. Footprints of Roger Williams: a biography, with sketches of important events in early New England history, with which he was connected. N.Y.: Carlton & Lanahan, 1871. 285p. RHi. +

699 MUNRO, WALTER LEE. Early medical history in Rhode Island and the Rhode Island Medical Society: read before the Friday Night Club, May 17th, 1935. n.p., 1935. 38p. RHi. +

700 MUNRO, WILFRED HAROLD. Memorial encyclopedia of the State of Rhode Island. N.Y.: American Historical Society, 1916. 428p. RHi. +
Biographical.

701 _____. "Notes on William Harris." RIHSPr, n.s. 1 (1893), 214-229.
Includes material on Pawtuxet Purchase.

702 _____. Picturesque Rhode Island: pen and pencil sketches of the scenery and history of its cities, towns, and hamlets, and of the men who have made them famous. Providence: J. A. & R. A. Reid, 1881. 304p. RHi. +

703 MURRAY, THOMAS HAMILTON. "Commerce between Ireland and Rhode Island." American-Irish Historical Society, Journal, 6 (1906), 31-36.

704 _____. Irish Rhode Islanders in the American Revolution.... Providence: American-Irish Historical Society, 1903. 90p. RHi. +

705 _____. The Irish vanguard of Rhode Island. Boston, 1904. 27p. RHi. +
Irish settlers during colonial period. Rerpinted from American-Irish Historical Society, Journal, 4 (1904), 109-133.

706 MUSSELLS, CONSTANCE. "Angels, skulls and hourglasses." RIer (Jan. 25, 1976), 4-9.
R.I. gravestones.

707 MYERS, JOHN L. "Antislavery agencies in Rhode Island, 1832-1835." RIH, 29 (1970), 82-93.
See also next entry.

708 _____. "Antislavery agents in Rhode Island, 1835-1837." RIH, 30 (1971), 21-31.
See also preceding entry.

709 NATIONAL SOCIETY OF THE COLONIAL DAMES OF AMERICA. RHODE ISLAND. Addresses delivered before the Society of the Colonial Dames in Rhode Island at their third annual celebration, held in the rooms of the Newport Historical Society, August 31, 1894. Newport, 1894. 40p. RHi. +
Various aspects of early R.I. history.

710 "NAVAL history of Rhode Island." Providence Daily Journal (1860-1861).
Series of articles pertaining to colonial period, beginning Nov. 20, 1860. Rider Collection, Brown Univ.

711 NEEL, JOANNE L. "Some interesting transactions in Rhode Island." RIH, 19 (1960), 97-118.
The stopping and search of an American ship by a British naval vessel (1795).

712 "NEIGHBORS, once a part of Providence." PM, 28 (1916), 442-445.
Neighboring towns.

713 NERNEY, HELEN. "An Italian painter comes to Rhode Island." RIH, 1 (1942), 65-71.
Michele Felice Corne.

714 NEWMAN, A. H. "Roger Williams." Magazine of Christian Literature, 5 (1892), 271-282.

715 NEWPORT, Block Island and Narragansett Pier, illustrated: a brief history and tourists' guide to points of interest.... Boston: Botolph Pr., 1895. 111p. RHi. +

716 NICHOLAS, HERBERT NEWELL. A survey of legislation concerning town boundaries in Rhode Island, 1639-1914 inclusive. [Providence:] Legislative Reference Bureau, R.I. State Library, 1916. [30]p. R.

717 NICHOLS, L. NELSON. "The Rhode Island cavaliers." Journal of American History, 7 (1913), 1023-1040.
Royalists during Oliver Cromwell's rule in England.

718 NICOLOSI, ANTHONY S. "Foundations of the Naval presence in Narragansett Bay: an overview." NH, 52 (1979), 61-82.

719 [NOYES, ISAAC PITMAN.] Reminiscences of Rhode Island and ye Providence Plantations. [Washington, 1905.] 47p. RHi. +
Also five supplements (1905-1906).

720 O'BRIEN, FRANCIS J. "Early days." Rhode Island Bar Journal, 20, No. 3 (Dec. 1971), 12-14.
R.I. lawyers of Irish extraction.

721 O'BRIEN, JOHN J. "The valley that was." RIY (1973), 110-117.
Pawtuxet River Valley.

722 ODD FELLOWS, INDEPENDENT ORDER OF. RHODE ISLAND. RIGHT WORTHY GRAND ENCAMPMENT. Journal of proceedings of the Right Worthy Grand Encampment of the Independent Order of Odd Fellows of the State of Rhode Island, from its institution, June 11, 1849, to its annual session, August, 1870, inclusive.... Vol. 1. Providence: Providence Pr., 1872. xxiv, 406p. RHi. +
Includes historical sketch of Odd Fellows in R.I.

723 OLSEN, STEPHEN, DONALD D. ROBADUE, JR., and VIRGINIA LEE. An interpretive atlas of Narragansett Bay. [Narragansett:] Univ. of R.I., Coastal Resources Center, 1980. 82p. RHi. +
Includes historical maps and text.

724 OSTERBERG, J. S. Svenskarna i Rhode Island: en historik öffrer Svenskarnas uti Rhode Island.... Worcester, Mass.: Svea Publishing, 1915. 360, [6]p. RHi. +
Swedish-language history of Swedes in R.I.

725 OTT, JOSEPH K. "Exports of furniture, chaises, and other wooden forms from Providence and Newport, 1783-1795." Antiques, 107 (1975), 135-141.

726 _____. "Lesser-known Rhode Island cabinetmakers: the Carliles, Holmes Weaver, Judson Blake, the Rawsons, and Thomas Davenport." Antiques, 121 (1982), 1156-1163.

727 _____. "More notes on Rhode Island cabinetmakers and their work." RIH, 28 (1969), 49-52.

728 _____. "Recent discoveries among Rhode Island cabinetmakers and their work." RIH, 28 (1969), 3-25.

729 _____. "Rhode Island furniture exports, 1783-1800: including information on chaises, buildings, other woodenwork and trade practices." RIH, 36 (1977), 3-13.

730 _____. "Rhode Island housewrights, shipwrights, and related craftsmen." RIH, 31 (1972), 65-79.

731 _____. "Some Rhode Island furniture." Antiques, 107 (1975), 940-951.

732 _____. "Still more notes on Rhode Island cabinetmakers and allied craftsmen." RIH, 28 (1969), 111-121.

733 "OUR steamboats: a claim for Rhode Island; history of steam navigation on Narragansett Bay...." Providence Journal (1867).
Series of newspaper articles beginning Apr. 23, 1867. Rider Collection, Brown Univ.

734 "OUR textile history: Samuel Slater made Rhode Island the busiest state in the Union." PBTJ, 25 (1913), 501-503.

735 "OUR town names." WRICHSH, 13 (Sept. 1969), [2]; (Oct. 1969), [2].
Towns and villages represented in Western R.I. Civic Historical Society.

736 OUTLINE history of the 243rd Coast Artillery (HD). East Greenwich: Greenwich Pr., 1928. 64p. RHi. +
Militia and National Guard unit.

737 "OVER the hill to the poorhouse." RIer (June 9, 1957), 12, 14, 16.
The last days of a once-important institution in R.I.

738 PABODIE, W. H. "Rhode Island: a survey of her titles to distinction and honor." BrAlumMo, 13 (1912), 115-117.

739 PALMER, HENRY ROBINSON. "The libraries of Rhode Island." NEM, n.s. 22 (1900), 478-500.

740 _____. "Population tendencies in Rhode Island." NEM, n.s. 14 (1896), 159-162.

741 PARRINGTON, VERNON L. Roger Williams, seeker. n.p., n.d. [14]p. RHi. +
Reprinted from author's Main currents in American thought (1927).

742 PARSONS, CHARLES W. "Early votaries of natural science in Rhode Island." RIHSC, 7 (1885), 241-263.

743 _____. Notice of the history of population in the State of Rhode Island. n.p., n.d. 8p. RHi. +
Ca. 1850s.

744 _____. Report on the medical topography and epidemic diseases of Rhode Island. Philadelphia: Collins, Printer, 1864. 27p. RHi. +

745 _____. "Town names in Rhode Island." RIHSPr (1886-1887), 42-51.

746 PARSONS, USHER. "A brief account of the early physicians and of the Medical Society of Rhode Island." American Quarterly Register, 12 (1840), 254-260.

747 _____. Indian names of places in Rhode-Island. Providence: Knowles, Anthony, 1861. iv, 32p. RHi. +

748 _____. "Indian relics of R.I., with notices of the Nyantic Indians." Dawson's Historical Magazine, 7 (1863), 41-44.

749 _____. Sketches of Rhode Island physicians deceased prior to 1850. Providence: Knowles, Anthony, 1859. 64p. RHi. +
Published as R.I. Medical Society, Transactions, 1.

750 PARSONS, WILLIAM T. "'Journey to Rhoad Island.'" Pennsylvania Magazine of History and Biography, 85 (1961), 411-422.
Account of Isaac Norris II's journey from Philadelphia in 1725.

751 PATTEN, DAVID. Rhode Island story: recollections of 35 years on the staff of the Providence Journal and the Evening Bulletin. [Providence:] Providence Journal, 1954. 119p. RHi.
Collection of newspaper articles.

752 PAULHUS, DAVID L. "Rhode Island and the Mexican War." RIH, 37 (1978), 89-96.

753 PAYNE, ABRAHAM. Reminiscences of the Rhode Island bar. Providence: Tibbitts & Preston, 1885. x, 277p. RHi. +
See also RISHPr (1875-1876), 39-42.

754 PAYNE, CHARLES H. "The great Dorr War." NEM, n.s. 2 (1890), 389-402.

755 PEACE, NANCY E. "Roger Williams: a historiographical essay." RIH, 35 (1976), 103-113.

756 PEATTIE, DONALD CULROSS. "Roger Williams: first modern American." Reader's Digest, 49 (Dec. 1946), 65-69.

757 PECK, GEORGE B. Historical sketch of the Narragansett Baptist Association, Rhode Island, 1860-1884. Providence: Providence Pr., 1884. 15p. RHi. +

758 PELL, CLAIBORNE De B. Rochambeau and Rhode Island. [Providence]: State of R.I., General Rochambeau Commission, [1954]. 16p. RHi. +
French participation in American Revolution.

759 PENNINGTON, EDGAR LEGARE. The first hundred years of the Church of England in Rhode Island. Hartford, Conn.: Church Missions Publishing, [1935]. 20p. RPB. +

760 PERRY, AMOS. "New England almanacs, with special mention of those published in Rhode Island." NHR, 4 (1885), 27-39.

761 _____. "Rhode Island Revolutionary debt." RIHSPubs, n.s. 4 (1897), 234-243.

762 _____. Some New England almanacs, with special mention of the almanacs of Rhode Island. Providence: E. L. Freeman, 1885. 13p. RHi. +

763 PERRY, CALBRAITH BOURN. The Perrys of Rhode Island and tales of Silver Creek, the Bosworth-Bourn-Perry homestead. N.Y.: Tobias A. Wright, 1913. 115p. RHi. +
Silver Creek was in Bristol.

764 PERRY, CHARLES M. "Cranston and Warwick railroads." WRICHSH, 2 (Oct. 1958), [2].

765  PERRY, THOMAS, JR.  "Surgery in Rhode Island after the American Revolution."  RIMJ, 59 (1976), 105-108, 138.

766  PESATURO, UBALDO U. M.  Italo-Americans of Rhode Island:  an historical and biographical survey of the origin, rise and progress of Rhode Islanders of Italian birth or descent.  2d ed.  Providence:  Visitor Printing, 1940.  193p.  RHi. +
     1st ed. (1936) contains information not included in the later work.

767  PHELPS, HAROLD A.  "Frequency of crime and punishment."  Journal of the American Institute of Criminal Law and Criminology, 19, No. 2 (Aug. 1928), 165-180.
     Article based on a study of the Superior Court records of Providence and Bristol Counties (1897-1927).

768  PHENIX NATIONAL BANK.  The bank holiday of 1933 and its place in the romance of Rhode Island industry.  Providence, 1945.  10p.  RHi.
     This entry and those that follow under the heading of Phenix National Bank were part of the Romance of R.I. Industry pamphlet series, published in 1945-1946 from scripts for a weekly radio series.  The pamphlets include historical sketches as well as contemporary descriptions of a number of R.I. companies and institutions.

769  _____.  ..."The hen or the egg?" [Providence,] 1945.  10p.  RHi.
     New Haven Railroad.

770  _____.  ...Narragansett Electric Company. [Providence,] 1945.  10p.  RHi.
     Utility.

771  _____.  ...New England Telephone & Telegraph Co.  [Providence,] 1946.  10p.  RHi.
     One of two telephone companies then serving the state.

772  _____.  ...Rhode Island agriculture. [Providence,] 1946.  10p.  RHi.

773  _____.  ...The Outlet Company. [Providence,] 1945.  10p.  RHi.
     Dept. store chain.

774  _____.  ...U.S. Bobbin & Shuttle Company. [Providence,] 1946.  10p.  RHi.
     A R.I. corporation.

775  PHILLIPS, MARY SCHUYLER.  Colonial Rhode Island.  n.p.:  Ebbert & Richardson, 1916.  36p.  RP. +

776  PICTURES of Rhode Island in the past, 1642-1833, by travellers and observers.  Gertrude Selwyn Kimball, ed.  Providence:  Preston and Rounds, 1900.  xiii, 175p.  RHi. +

777  PIERCE, EDWIN C.  Rhode Island, its making and its meaning:  speech of...Democratic and Lincoln Party candidate for representative from Cranston at Hamilton, R.I., October 19, 1906.  [Providence:  Industrial Printing,] n.d.  [16]p.  RHi. +

778  PITTERMAN, MARVIN.  "Martin Chase: grandfather of discounts."  RIJHN, 7 (1972), 191-202.
     Ann and Hope Stores.

779  THE PLOUGH and the sickle; or, Rhode-Island in the War of the Revolution of 1776.  Providence:  B. T. Albro, 1846.  28p.  RHi. +

780  POINTS of historical interest in the State of Rhode Island; prepared with the cooperation of the Rhode Island Historical Society.  [Providence:]  Dept. of Education, State of R.I., 1911.  84p.  RHi.

781  POLISHOOK, IRWIN H.  "The Collins-Richardson fracas of 1787:  a problem in state and federal relations during the Confederation era."  RIH, 22 (1963), 117-121.
     Gov. John Collins and Jacob Richardson, postmaster at Newport.

782  _____.  "Peter Edes's report of the proceedings of the Rhode Island General Assembly, 1787-1790."  RIH, 25 (1966), 33-42, 87-97, 117-129; 26 (1967), 15-31.
     In his newspaper, the Newport Herald.

783  _____.  Rhode Island and the Union, 1774-1795.  Evanston, Ill.:  Northwestern Univ. Pr., 1969.  x, 268p.  RHi. +

784  _____.  "Trevett v. Weeden and the case of the judges."  NH, 38 (1965), 45-69.
     Set precedent for principle of judicial review.

785  POPE, THOMAS E. B.  Historical review of the Pawtuxet Baptist Church.  Providence, 1955.  16p.  RHi.

786  POPKIN, GEORGE.  "The Italian heritage in Rhode Island."  RIer (Aug. 30, 1967), 22-23, 25, 28, 30, 32, 34-35.

787  POTEAT, EDWIN McNEIL.  Roger Williams redivivus:  an attempt to interpret the mind of Roger Williams in the light of the present concerning the separation of church and state.  N.Y.:  Northern Baptist Convention, 1940.  36p.  RHi. +

788 POTTER, ELISHA R. An address delivered before the Rhode-Island Historical Society, on the evening of February nineteenth, 1851. Providence, 1851. 27p. RHi. +
History of education in R.I.

789 [_____.] A brief account of emissions of paper money, made by the Colony of Rhode-Island. Providence: John E. Brown, 1837. 48p. RHi. +

790 _____, and SIDNEY S. RIDER. Some account of the bills of credit or paper money of Rhode Island, from the first issue in 1710, to the final issue, 1786. Providence: Sidney S. Rider, 1880. xii, 229p. RHi. +

791 POWERS, WILLIAM F. In the service of the state: the Rhode Island State Police, 1925-1975. Providence: R.I. Bicentennial Commission Foundation, 1975. x, 196p. RHi. +

792 PRESTON, HOWARD WILLIS. "Lafayette's visits to Rhode Island." RIHSC, 19 (1926), 1-10.

793 _____. "Rhode Island and the Loyalists." RIHSC, 21 (1928), 109-116; 22 (1929), 5-10.

794 _____. Rhode Island and the sea. Providence: State of R.I., State Bureau of Information, 1932. 140p. RHi. +

795 _____. Rhode Island's historic background. (1930) [Providence:] R.I. Tercentenary Commission, 1936. 62p. RHi. +

796 _____. Washington's visits to Rhode Island; gathered from contemporary accounts. Providence: State of R.I., State Bureau of Information, 1932. 28p. RHi. +

797 "PRIMOGENITURE in Rhode Island." RIHSC, 31 (1938), 76-78.

798 PRITCHARD, FRANK C. "Rhode Island's chartered commands." RIY (1970), 13-16.
Militia.

799 PROVIDENCE, R.I. TERCENTENARY COMMITTEE. Official chronicle and tribute book of Rhode Island and Providence Plantations.... Lucia Hammond Wheeler, comp. n.p.: George D. Hall, 1936. 159p. RHi. +

800 PROVIDENCE COUNTY COURTHOUSE. COMMISSIONERS ON DECORATIONS AND IMPROVEMENTS. Report...and proceedings of the legislative visit, February 4, 1885. Providence: E. L. Freeman, 1885. 85p. RHi. +
Addresses by John H. Stiness on "The return of Roger Williams with the first charter of the Colony, in 1644," 13-58; and Horatio Rogers on "The importance of the Charter of 1643-4," 59-73.

801 PROVIDENCE JOURNAL (newspaper). RHODE ISLANDER (Sunday magazine). Journal of a Rhode Island tour, 1776: a special bicentennial issue (May 2, 1976). 72p. RHi. +
Histical account of the Revolutionary era in R.I., written as a first-person, contemporary narrative. Text by Elmer E. Cornwell, Jr.

802 PROVIDENCE VISITOR (newspaper). [History of Roman Catholic parishes in Diocese of Providence] (Mar. 14, 1935-May 27, 1937).
A series of more than 100 articles, sketching the histories of nearly all the then-existing parishes in R.I.

803 _____. Special souvenir supplement (Apr. 26, 1968). 56p. RPD-H.
Includes histories of "all 157 parishes" in Diocese of Providence, biographies of bishops and auxiliary bishops in the diocese, historical description of Cathedral of SS. Peter and Paul in Providence, history of Providence Visitor.

804 _____. Special 20th anniversary edition, honoring the Most Reverend Russell J. McVinney, Bishop of Providence (Nov. 29, 1968). 24p. RPD-H.
Includes sketches of various Catholic organizations and institutions in R.I.

805 PUCKREIN, GARY ALEXANDER. The Black Regiment in the American Revolution. Providence: R.I. Black Heritage Society, 1978. xvi, 38p. RHi.
1st R.I. Regt.

806 PURCELL, RICHARD JOSEPH. "Irish builders of colonial Rhode Island." Studies, (June 1935), 289-300.
Early Irish settlers.

807 _____. "Rhode Island's early schools and Irish teachers." Catholic Educational Review, 32 (1934), 402-415.

808 RAE, JOHN BELL. "The issues of the Dorr War." RIH, 1 (1942), 33-44.
1842.

809 _____. "Rhode Island pioneers in regulation of banking." RIH, 2 (1943), 105-109.
Bank Act of 1836.

810 RAND, LARRY ANTHONY. "The Know-nothing Party in Rhode Island: religious bigotry and political success." RIH, 23 (1964), 102-116.

811 RANDALL, DEXTER. Democracy vindicated and Dorrism unveiled. Providence: H. H. Brown, 1846. 100p. RHi. +

812   RANSOME, DAVID R.   "Rhode Island 'observes' the siege of Boston."  RIY (1965-1966), 44-50.
    1775-1776.

813   RAVITZ, ABE C.   "Anarch in Rhode Island." RIH, 10 (1952), 117-124.
    Background of The Anarchiad (poem).

814   RAY, JOHN MICHAEL.   "Anti-Catholicism and Know-Nothingism in Rhode Island."  American Ecclesiastical Review, 148 (1963), 27-36.

815   _____.   "Rhode Island's reactions to John Brown's Raid."  RIH, 20 (1961), 97-108.
    1859.

816   "REMEMBER Sept. 21, 1938? Three who remember it well."  RIer (Aug. 18, 1968), 10-13.
    1938 hurricane.  Signed G.D.B. (Garrett D. Byrnes).

817   RENZULLI, MERCEDES.   "The fate of the old 508."  Yankee, 28 (Mar. 1964) 62-63, 100-102.
    Long-time commuter train between South County and Providence.

818   "REPORT on the settlement of Warwick, 1642; and the seal of the Rhode Island Historical Society."  RIHSPr (1887-1888), 40-60.

819   REPRESENTATIVE men and old families of Rhode Island:  genealogical records and historical sketches of prominent and representative citizens and of many of the old families. Chicago:  J. H. Beers, 1908.  3v.  RHi. +

820   "RESPONSES to the Rhode Island workingmen's reform agitation of 1833."  RIH, 28 (1969), 74-94.
    Marvin E. Gettleman and Noel P. Conlon, eds.  Efforts to extend the suffrage and secure a new constitution.

821   RETSINAS, JOAN.   "Smallpox vaccination:  a leap of faith."  RIH, 38 (1979), 113-124.
    In R.I.

822   REYNOLDS, BILL.   "Beneath the waves, a silent, cold tomb."  RIer (Oct. 10, 1982), 6, 8, 10-11.
    German submarine, sunk off R.I. coast in 1945.

823   REYNOLDS, POLLY.   "Big politics in little ole Rhode Island."  Rhode Island, 1 (Oct. 1980), 25-28.
    Historical anecdotes about state politics.

824   RHODE ISLAND (COLONY).   The earliest laws of the colony of Rhode Island and Providence Plantations, 1647-1719.  John D. Cushing, ed.  Wilmington, Del.:  Michael Glazier, 1977.  239p.  RHi. +

825   _____.   Records of the Colony of Rhode Island and Providence Plantations, in New England.  Printed by order of the General Assembly.  John Russell Bartlett, ed.  Providence:  A. C. Greene et al., 1856-1863.  10v.  RHi. +
    Vols. 8-10 entitled Records of the State of R.I.

826   RHODE ISLAND (COLONY).  GENERAL ASSEMBLY. The proceedings of the first General Assembly of "the incorporation of Providence Plantations," and the code of laws adopted by that assembly, in 1647; with notes historical and explanatory, by William R. Staples.  Providence:  Charles Burnett, Jr., 1847.  x, 64p.  RHi. +

827   RHODE ISLAND (COLONY).  VICE-ADMIRALTY COURT.  Records of the Vice-admiralty Court of Rhode Island, 1716-1752.  Dorothy S. Towle, ed.  Washington:  American Historical Association, 1936.  595p.  RHi. +

828   RHODE ISLAND.  BOARD OF EDUCATION. ...Commemoration of public education in recognition of the fiftieth anniversary of the creation of the State Board of Education and of the seventy-fifth anniversary of the appointment of the Commissioner of Education....  Providence:  E. L. Freeman, 1920.  24p.  RHi. +

829   RHODE ISLAND.  BOARD OF INSPECTORS OF THE STATE PRISON.  Report...for the year 1876. Providence:  Angell, Burlingame, 1877.  81p. RHi.
    Cover title:  A historical sketch of the jails and prisons of Rhode Island, 1638-1877.

830   RHODE ISLAND.  CIVIL WAR CENTENNIAL COMMISSION.  Rhode Island Civil War chronicles:  a presentation of articles and photographs recalling Rhode Island's part in the Civil War, 1861-1865.  Providence, 1960. 32p.  RHi.
    Includes Leonard J. Panaggio, "The Naval Academy at Newport," 17-19.

831   RHODE ISLAND.  COMMITTEE ON MARKING HISTORICAL SITES.  Report...made to the General Assembly at its January session, 1913.  Providence:  E. L. Freeman, 1914. 183p.  RHi. +
    Includes historical information on a number of sites.

832   RHODE ISLAND.  DEPARTMENT OF PUBLIC SCHOOLS. Handbook of historical sites in Rhode Island; published in connection with the tercentenary celebration of the founding of Providence.  Providence, 1936.  96p.  RHi.

833  RHODE ISLAND. EXECUTIVE DEPARTMENT. Rhode Island in the war with Spain: compiled from the official records of the Executive Department of the State of Rhode Island; presented to the General Assembly at its January session, 1900. Providence: E. L. Freeman, 1900. viii, 417p. RHi.

834  RHODE ISLAND. GENERAL ASSEMBLY. Proceedings in Congress, attending the reception of the statue of Roger Williams, founder of the State of Rhode Island, presented by the State of Rhode Island. [Providence:] A. Crawford Greene, [1872?]. 31p. RHi. +
    Includes historical address by Benjamin T. Eames, 12-31.

835  RHODE ISLAND. GENERAL ASSEMBLY. JOINT SPECIAL COMMITTEE. The remains of Major-general Nathanael Greene: a report of the...committee...appointed to take into consideration the desirability of securing within the state a permanent resting-place for the remains of General Nathanael Greene. Providence: E. L. Freeman & Sons, 1903. 257p. RHi. +
    Includes sketch of his years in R.I.

836  RHODE ISLAND. HISTORICAL PRESERVATION COMMISSION. An historical survey of United States Navy property in Rhode Island. [Providence,] 1974. 11p. RNW-Hi.

837  _____. Pawtuxet Village, Cranston and Warwick, Rhode Island: statewide preservation report PK-P-1. Providence, 1973. v, 27, [13]p. RHi. +

838  RHODE ISLAND. NATIONAL GUARD. Historical and pictorial review: National Guard of the State of Rhode Island, 1940. Baton Rouge, La.: Army and Navy Publishing, 1940. xxxvi, 145p. RHi.

839  [RHODE ISLAND. PUBLIC WELFARE COMMISSION.] Rhode Island State Prison and Providence County Jail, 1638-1924. n.p.: Prison Pr., 1924. [7]p. RHi.

840  RHODE ISLAND. SPECIAL COMMISSION TO STUDY THE ENTIRE FIELD OF EDUCATION. Financing public education in Rhode Island: Part I, historical and fiscal trends, 1947-1966. Providence, 1967. 49, [29]p. R.

841  RHODE ISLAND. STATE BUREAU OF INFORMATION. The book of Rhode Island: an illustrated description of the advantages and opportunities of the State of Rhode Island and the progress that has been achieved, with historical sketches of many leading industries and a biographical record of citizens who have helped to produce the superb structure--historical, commercial, industrial, agricultural and recreational-- which comprises the strength of this charming state. [Providence], 1930. 299p. RHi. +

842  RHODE ISLAND. STATEWIDE PLANNING PROGRAM. Historic preservation plan. [Providence,] 1970. x, 132, [18]p. RHi.
    Co-published by R.I. Historical Preservation Commission. See also the latter agency's planning reports for individual cities and towns, which, like this entry, contain significant historical information.

843  RHODE ISLAND. SUPREME JUDICIAL COURT. History of the criminal law of Rhode Island: charge of Hon. William R. Staples, delivered to the grand jury of the Court of Common Pleas in Newport and Providence. (Published by order of the General Assembly.) [Providence, 1853.] 29p. RHi. +

844  RHODE ISLAND. TERCENTENARY COMMISSION. Rhode Island tercentenary, 1636-1936.... [Providence,] 1937. 158p. RHi. +

845  RHODE ISLAND. TERCENTENARY COMMITTEE. Commemorating three hundred years.... [Providence,] 1936. 80p. RHi. +

846  RHODE ISLAND ASSOCIATION OF FREE BAPTIST CHURCHES. Centennial minutes of the Rhode Island Association of Free Baptist Churches, held with the Pawtucket Church, May 19, 20 and 21, 1880. Dover, N.H.: Morning Star Job Printing House, 1880. 58p. RHi.
    Includes sermon by J. M. Brewster on "The Free Baptists of Rhode Island and vicinity." Freewill Baptists.

847  RHODE ISLAND BAPTIST STATE CONVENTION. Hymns, ode and discourses delivered at the fiftieth anniversary of the formation of the Rhode Island Baptist State Convention, May 12, 1875. Providence: J. A. & R. A. Reid, 1875. 135p. RHi. +
    Includes historical discourse by A. H. Granger.

848  RHODE ISLAND BUSINESS MEN'S ASSOCIATION. Manual...1890-1907. Providence: Standard Printing, [1907]. 190p. RHi. +
    Includes sketches of R.I. and Providence history; also early manufacturing history.

849   RHODE ISLAND CENTRAL TRADES AND LABOR UNION,
PROVIDENCE.  20th century illustrated
history of Rhode Island and the Rhode Island
Central Trades and Labor Union and its
affiliated organizations....  (1899)
Providence, 1901.  557p.  RHi. +
      Includes histories of a number of
different unions.

850   RHODE ISLAND CHRISTIAN ENDEAVOR UNION.
Official souvenir of the Rhode Island
Christian Endeavor Union, containing a
complete history of the Christian Endeavor
movement since its inception in Rhode
Island....  Cora A. Wells, ed.  Providence,
1895-1896.  128p.  RHi.

851   RHODE ISLAND CITIZENS HISTORICAL
ASSOCIATION.  Addresses and poems at the one
hundred and thirty-second anniversary of the
independence of Rhode Island and the
twenty-fifth anniversary of the Rhode Island
Citizens Historical Association at
Providence, Rhode Island, 1909.  Thomas
Williams Bicknell, ed.  n.p., n.d.  83p.
RHi. +

852   _____.  The Rhode Island Declaration of
Independence, May 4, 1776:  addresses
delivered before the Rhode Island Citizens
Historical Association on the 131st
anniversary of the Declaration of
Independence by the Colony of Rhode Island
in the Old State House, Providence, R.I.,
May 4, 1907.  n.p., n.d.  35p.  RHi. +

853   _____.  Rhode Island Independence Day
addresses, May 4, 1910....  n.p., 1910.
64p.  RHi. +
      Historical addresses by Thomas Williams
Bicknell, Edward Holyoke, Ellen Ryan Jolly.

854   _____.  Rhode Island Independence Day
addresses; one hundred & fiftieth
anniversary of governorship of Hon. Samuel
Ward, 1762, addresses; two hundred &
fiftieth anniversary of the presidency of
Hon. Benedict Arnold, 1662, addresses; the
seventieth anniversary of the Dorr War and
erection of monument and tablet, addresses.
Thomas Williams Bicknell, ed.  n.p., 1912.
121p.  RHi. +

855   "THE RHODE Island Company."  PM, 28 (1916),
792-793.
      Street railroad company.

856   RHODE ISLAND DIGEST COMMISSION.  West's
Rhode Island Digest, 1783 to date.  Volume
I:  descriptive-word index, A-K.  Boston:
Boston Law Book Co., 1952.  xxxii, 923p.
R. +
      Includes "Judicial history of Rhode
Island," by Edmund W. Flynn, xiii-xxii.

857   RHODE ISLAND FEDERATION OF MUSIC CLUBS.  250
years of music in Providence, Rhode Island,
1636-1806, by Herbert Chandler Thrasher;
Rhode Island composers, native and adopted,
Dorothy Joslin Pearce, comp.  n.p., 1942.
31p.  RHi. +

858   RHODE ISLAND HISTORICAL SOCIETY.  The John
Brown House loan exhibition of Rhode Island
furniture, including some notable portraits,
Chinese export porcelain & other items, May
16 - June 20, 1965.  Providence, 1965.  xxv,
178p.  RHi. +

859   "RHODE Island in last two centuries."  PM,
28 (1916), 9-15.

860   RHODE Island local government:  past,
present, future.  Robert W. Sutton, Jr., ed.
[Kingston:]  Univ. of R.I., Bureau of
Government Research, 1974.  166p.  RP. +

861   RHODE ISLAND MEDICAL SOCIETY.  The history
of the Rhode Island Medical Society and its
component societies, 1812-1962.  [East
Providence:  Roger Williams Pr., 1966.]  xi,
276p.  RHi. +

862   "RHODE Island Negroes in the Revolution:
a bibliography."  RIH, 29 (1970), 52-53.
Noel P. Conlon, ed.

863   RHODE ISLAND PHARMACEUTICAL ASSOCIATION.
Official souvenir book, fiftieth anniversary
of Rhode Island Pharmaceutical Association,
July 24th and 25th, 1924.  n.p., n.d.  111p.
RHi.
      Includes "Old time druggists and drug
stores of R.I.," 44-70; "Fifty years with
the R.I. Board of Pharmacy," 74-88; "History
of R.I. College of Pharmacy," 92-100.

864   RHODE ISLAND RED CENTENNIAL COMMITTEE.  A
history of the Rhode Island Red, 1854-1954:
a presentation of documentary articles and
photographs describing the Rhode Island Red,
the breed of fowl which helped to begin the
poultry industry in America.  Providence,
1954.  24p.  RHi. +

865   RHODE ISLAND SANITARY AND RELIEF
ASSOCIATION.  History and work of the Rhode
Island Sanitary and Relief Association
during the Spanish-American War, 1898-1899.
Providence:  Snow & Farnham, 1900.  103p.
RHi. +

866   RHODE ISLAND SCHOOL OF DESIGN.  MUSEUM OF
ART.  Early portraits in Rhode Island,
1700-1850:  an exhibition to honor the
seventy-fifth anniversary of the National
Society of the Colonial Dames of America in
the State of Rhode Island and Providence
Plantations, 8 March - 9 April, 1967.
[Providence, 1967.]  29p.  RHi. +

867  RHODE ISLAND SCHOOL OF DESIGN. MUSEUM OF ART. Rhode Island tercentenary celebration: a catalog of an exhibition of paintings by Gilbert Stuart, furniture by the Goddards and Townsends, silver by Rhode Island silversmiths. Providence, 1936. 48p. RHi.

868  RHODE ISLAND SHORT STORY CLUB. Revolutionary portraits: people, places and events from Rhode Island's historic past. Providence: R.I. Bicentennial Foundation, 1976. i, 80p. RHi. +

869  "RHODE Island signboards." RIHSC, 22 (1929), 1-3.

870  THE RHODE Island signers of the Declaration of Independence: Stephen Hopkins, by Robert Perkins Brown; William Ellery, by Henry Robinson Palmer. Providence: Sons of the American Revolution, R.I. Society, 1913. [36]p. RHi. +

871  RHODE Island, 1636-1896: small in area, unlimited in her resources, unsurpassed in the activity, intelligence and patriotism of her people; a brief sketch of the state from foundation until the present time, together with sketches of many mercantile and manufacturing concerns which contribute to her progress and prosperity. N.Y.: Consolidated Illustrating, 1896. xxxiii, 219p. RHi. +

872  RHODE ISLAND STATE DENTAL SOCIETY. The history of the Rhode Island State Dental Society. Diamond jubilee celebration, January 18, 19, 20, 21, 1951.... n.p., n.d. 54p. RHi. +

873  RHODE Island tales: depicting social life during the colonial, Revolutionary and post-Revolutionary era. Henrietta R. Palmer, ed. N.Y.: Purdy Pr., 1928. 181p. RHi. +

874  "RHODE Island's gift to the world." PBTJ, 27 (1915), 617-624.
     "First to recognize religious liberty... first in war and first in peace."

875  "RHODE Island's own Declaration of Independence." PM, 32 (1920), 165-169.

876  "RHODE Island's part in the development of the telephone." PM, 34 (1922), 253, 255, 257, 259, 261.

877  "RHODE Island's place in the history of naval signal flags." RIHSC, 22 (1929), 39-41.
     Signed H.M.C. (Howard M. Chapin).

878  RICHARDS, J. J. Rhode Island's early defenders and their successors. East Greenwich: R.I. Pendulum, 1937. 103p. RHi. +
     Militia.

879  RICHMAN, IRVING BERDINE. Rhode Island: a study in separatism. Boston: Houghton, Mifflin, 1905. x, 395p. RHi. +

880  _____. Rhode Island: its making and its meaning; a study of the annals of the commonwealth from its settlement to the death of Roger Williams, 1636-1683. (1902) 2d ed. N.Y.: Putnam's, 1908. xv, 560p. RHi. +
     1st ed. 2 vols.

881  RICHMOND, JOHN W. Rhode Island repudiation: or the history of the Revolutionary debt of Rhode Island, in three chapters. (1848) 2d ed. Providence: Sayles, Miller & Simons, 1855. xvi, 208p. RHi. +
     First ed. entitled History of the registered state debt of R.I....

882  RIDER, HOPE S. "The little sloop that first challenged Britannia's rule." RIer (June 8, 1975), 4-6.
     The Katy, flagship of the R.I. Navy. See also next entry.

883  _____. Valour fore & aft: being the adventures of the Continental Sloop Providence, formerly Flagship Katy of Rhode Island's Navy. Annapolis, Md.: Naval Institute Pr., 1977. xiv, 259p. RHi. +

884  RIDER, SIDNEY S. "Aboriginal remains in Rhode Island and the exhumation of Weunquash, daughter of Ninigret, and queen of the Niantics." BN, 29 (1912), 17-31.

885  _____. "An account of wampum-peague, the Indian money of the Narragansetts." BN, 29 (1912), 33-39.
     See also BN, 33 (1916), 49-55.

886  _____. "The belief in vampires in Rhode Island." BN, 5 (1888), 37-39.

887  _____. Bibliographical memoirs of three Rhode Island authors: Joseph K. Angell, Frances H. (Whipple) McDougall, Catherine R. Williams...to which is added the nine lawyers' opinion on the right of the people of Rhode Island to form a constitution. Providence: Sidney S. Rider, 1880. vi, 90p. RHi. +

888  [_____.] "Brigade muster of the olden time and the trial by court martial of Col. Leonard Blodgett in 1821." Providence Daily Journal (Nov. 12, 1873).
     Lengthy historical article.

889 RIDER, SIDNEY S. "A century of banks and banking in Rhode Island." BN, 16 (1899), 145-148, 153-156, 161-164, 169-171, 177-179.

890 _____. "The charge of treason against William Harris: did Roger Williams make it?" BN, 24 (1907), 193-197, 201-206.
See also next entry.

891 _____. "The complete destruction of the charge that Roger Williams charged William Harris with treason; nevertheless Harris was legally guilty of the crime." BN, 25 (1908), 1-6.
See also previous entry.

892 _____. "A consideration of the land tenure clauses as they exist in the charter of Maryland in 1632, and in the charter of Rhode Island, 1663." BN, 22 (1905), 25-31.

893 _____. "Development of commerce in Narragansett Bay." PJC, 2 (Apr. 1894), 3-6.

894 _____. "Does the fabrication of a statute take from the people the fundamental title to land beneath tide waters, and land beneath rivers?" BN, 23 (1906), 9-12.
Claims colonial law on this subject was fraudulently altered when the original documents were transcribed by the secretary of state in 1827.

895 _____. "Duels and dueling in Rhode Island: an account of four duels fought in or near Providence between the years 1827-35." BN, 21 (1904), 73-78.

896 _____. "The earliest colonial Rhode Island printing press." BN, 11 (1894), 301-302.

897 _____. "The early marriage laws of Rhode Island." BN, 12 (1895), 241-145.

898 _____. "The end of a great political struggle in Rhode Island." BN, 5 (1888), 53-58.
Broadening of voting rights.

899 _____. "The giving of constitutional power to the R.I. General Assembly, to exempt corporations from taxation by the R.I. Supreme Court, on the 20th July, 1900, and what has resulted from that decision." BN, 26 (1909), 81-83.

900 _____. "The great land conspiracy of the 17th century in Rhode Island: the William Harris lawsuit." BN, 7 (1890), 157-162, 165-170, 173-177.
Relating to lands in the Pawtuxet Purchase.

901 _____. An historical inquiry concerning the attempt to raise a regiment of slaves during the War of the Revolution. Providence: Sidney S. Rider, 1880. xxii, 86p. RHi. +

902 _____. The history of denization and naturalization in the colony of Rhode Island, 1636-1790. n.p., n.d. 14p. RHi. +

903 _____. "The history of the construction of two bronze statues of Roger Williams by Rhode Island in years 1871-1877, both by Franklin Simmons of Maine. He died at Rome, Dec. 8, 1913." BN, 31 (1914), 33-35.
In Providence and Washington, D.C.

904 _____. "History of the law books of Rhode Island." BN, 33 (1916), 201-202, 204-206, 207.

905 _____. "The history of the Rhode Island 'bank process' and of the terrible work of the General Assembly in connection with it." BN, 22 (1905), 74-77, 89-93.
1818 resolution to "'secure the estates of debtors attached by bank process from sale until after judgment upon such process shall have been rendered by the court to which such process is made returnable.'"

906 _____. "How Rhode Island came by two capitals." BN, 8 (1891), 113-115.
Providence and Newport.

907 _____. "How Stephen Hopkins destroyed a century of political rottenness in Rhode Island, 1755-1767." BN, 27 (1910), 145-152.

908 _____. "How the people in Rhode Island towns held the power to levy, assess, fix the valuation and name the things which should be taxed; these people can fix the single tax." BN, 25 (1908), 49-52.

909 _____. "How the U.S. Senate forced Rhode Island to ratify the U.S. Constitution." BN, 11 (1894), 73-75, 85-86.

910 _____. An inquiry concerning the authenticity of an alleged portrait of Roger Williams. Providence, 1891. 31p. RHi. +

911 _____. An inquiry concerning the origin of the clause in the laws of Rhode Island (1719-1783) disfranchising Roman Catholics. Providence, 1889. 72p. RHi. +

912 _____. The lands of Rhode Island as they were known to Caunounicus and Miantunnomu when Roger Williams came in 1636; an Indian map of the principal locations known to the Nahigansets, and elaborate historical notes. Providence: Sidney S. Rider, 1904. 297p. RHi. +

913 RIDER, SIDNEY S. "Liberty of conscience in matters of religion, traced from the charter of Charles the Second, 1663, back to its sources." BN, [24] (1907), 49-52.
Identifies source as Roger Williams.

914 _____. "The measure of punishment for crime in Rhode Island." BN, 16 (1898), 25-27.

915 _____. "The mental development of Rhode Island, as shown in the publication of books." BN, 30 (1913), 193-199, 201-207.

916 _____. "The name Narragansett: its origin and history." BN, 27 (1910), 9-14.

917 _____. "The nobility of Roger Williams in opposing the land conspiracy of Arnold and Harris." BN, 12 (1895), 289-290.

918 _____. "The origin, meaning and duration of existence in Rhode Island of the political word prox." BN, 25 (1908), 201-204.
List of candidates, which could be used as a ballot. Use discontinued after 1842. See also BN, 26 (1909), 1-5.

919 _____. "The origin of a stumbling block in the Rhode Island constitution." BN, 9 (1892), 277-281.
Pertaining to the jurisdiction of the Supreme Judicial Court.

920 _____. "The origin of the colonial seal of Rhode Island." BN, 20 (1903), 25-31.

921 _____. "Origin of the first three sections of Article X of the constitution--on the judiciary." BN, 19 (1902), 49-53.
R.I. Constitution.

922 _____. "Origin of the name Rhode-Island." BN, 7 (1890), 29-33.
See also BN, 33 (1916), 57-58.

923 _____. "Pocasset." BN, 33 (1916), 185, 188.
Place name, used in several different ways in R.I. history.

924 _____. "The political results of the banishment of Williams." BN, 8 (1891), 129-133.
I.e., Roger Williams's banishment from Massachusetts and emigration to R.I.

925 _____. "The position of the Supreme Court of Rhode Island in the matter of a prescriptive right to poison running streams." BN, 14 (1897), 25-26.
Water-rights.

926 _____. "The punishment for contempt by the General Assembly." BN, 4 (1887), 97-102.
History of the practice.

927 _____. "The real history of the finding and the publication of the tract written by Roger Williams, 'Christenings make not Christians,' in 1881." BN, 26 (1909), 161-164.

928 _____. "The referendum in colonial Rhode Island." BN, 11 (1894), 97-99.

929 _____. "The Rhode Island copyright law of 1783." BN, 9 (1892), 25-27.

930 _____. "The Rhode Island Jews in history." BN, 22 (1905), 153-158, 161-166.

931 _____. "Roger Williams on the origin of the name Rhode Island." BN, 20 (1903), 210-202.

932 [_____.] [Series of articles on Rhode Island local history.] Providence Daily Journal (1872-1882).
Scrapbooks, Rider Collection, Brown Univ.

933 _____. "Silas Downer: an educated Rhode Island lawyer of the Revolution." BN, 9 (1892), 110-111.

934 _____. "The silly story of the exercise of Masonic rites by Jews, at Newport, R.I., in 1656, exploded; the unlawful naturalization of a Jew, and his election to the Rhode Island Senate in June, 1800." BN, 22 (1905), 94-103.
The naturalized Jew was Samuel Elam.

935 _____. Soul liberty: Rhode Island's gift to the nation; an inquiry concerning the validity of the claims made by Roman Catholics that Maryland was settled upon that basis before Roger Williams planted the Colony of Rhode Island. Providence: Sidney S. Rider, 1897. viii, 87p. RHi. +

936 _____. "The Sunday laws of Rhode Island." BN, 12 (1895), 168-169.

937 _____. "The terrible work of the General Assembly of Rhode Island of June 15, 1898, carefully set forth." BN, 25 (1908), 9-16.
Tax on street railroads, which, Rider claims, gave Sen. Nelson Aldrich control "for his private gain, [over] all streets, or roads, or highways in the northern half of the state."

938 _____. "The text of the commission supposed to have been given...to William Coddington in 1651." BN, 24 (1907), 185-189.
For government of the colony.

939 _____. "The titles given to the chief executive in Rhode Island." BN, 27 (1910), 121-122.

940  RIDER, SIDNEY S.  "The true place in Rhode
Island history of Roger Williams."  BN, 24
(1907), [1]-21, 25-32, 41-42.

941  ____.  "Was ever a woman hanged in Rhode
Island for witchcraft."  BN, 5 (1888), 9-10.

942  ____.  "The water nectar and the rocks pure
gold."  BN, 8 (1891), 145-148.
     Polluted Pawtuxet River drinking water and
the Providence typhoid epidemic of 1888.
See also BN, 8 (1891), 161-164.

943  ____.  "Wawaloam, the Indian queen of the
Narragansetts."  BN, 13 (1896), 84-88.
     17th century.

944  ____.  "The word gavel and its Rhode Island
origin."  BN, 22 (1905), 65-69.
     See also BN, 24 (1907), 121-122.

945  RIVARD, PAUL E.  "Textile experiments in
Rhode Island, 1788-1789."  RIH, 33 (1974),
35-45.

946  ROBERTNIER, LOUIS JEAN BAPTISTE SYLVESTRE
DE.  "Rhode Island in 1780."  RIHSC, 16
(1923), 65-78.
     Edited extracts from a French lieutenant's
Revolutionary War journal.

947  ROBERTS, KENNETH B.  "When Lincoln visited
Rhode Island."  RIer (Feb. 10, 1957), 2-5.
     Abraham Lincoln (1848 and 1860).

948  ROBINSON, CAROLINE E.  The Hazard family of
Rhode Island, 1635-1894....  Boston:
Printed for the Author, 1895.  vi, 293p.
RHi. +

949  ROBINSON, JOHN R.  "Rhode Island Reports,
1828-1885."  Rhode Island Bar Journal, 24,
No. 8 (May 1976), 5-7.
     I.e., published reports of court cases.

950  ROCHE, JOHN P.  "Convicts, bartenders, and
New York radicals: a Quaker view of Dorr's
Rebellion."  Quaker History, 42 (1953),
41-44.

951  ROCHEFORT, DAVID A.  "Three centuries of
care of the mentally disabled in Rhode
Island and the nation, 1650-1950."  RIH, 40
(1981), 111-132.

952  ROELKER, WILLIAM GREENE.  "General Nathanael
Greene's contributions to the War of
American Independence."  RIH, 1 (1942),
118-125.

953  ____.  "Samuel Gorton's master stroke."
RIH, 2 (1943), 1-10.
     Treaty with Narragansett Indians (1644),
subjecting them to royal authority.

954  ____, and CLARKSON A. COLLINS III.  "The
patrol of Narragansett Bay (1774-76) by
H.M.S. Rose, Captain James Wallace."  RIH,
7 (1948), 12-19, 90-95; 8 (1949), 45-63,
77-83; 9 (1950), 11-23, 52-58.

955  ROGERS, HORATIO.  Discourse before the Rhode
Island Historical Society at its centennial
celebration of Rhode Island's adoption of
the federal constitution, in Providence, May
29, 1890....  [Providence:]  Providence Pr.,
1890.  44p.  RHi. +
     Cover title:  Rhode Island's adoption of
the federal constitution, 1790-1890.

956  "THE ROMAN Catholic Church in Rhode Island."
PM, 26 (1914), 568-570.

957  ROOT, JAMES PIERCE.  "Contributions to the
history of the Waterman family of
Providence, Warwick, etc."  NHM, 5
(1884-1885), 85-91, 193-204.

958  ROSEN, BENTON H.  "The Gemiloth Chasodim of
Rhode Island:  the Hebrew Free Loan
Associations."  RIJHN, 5 (1969), 275-288.

959  ____.  "Some outstanding Jewish athletes
and sportsmen in Rhode Island (1916-1964)."
RIJHN, 5 (1968), 153-167.

960  ROSSITER, CLINTON.  "Roger Williams on the
anvil of experience."  American Quarterly,
3 (1951), 14-21.

961  RUGG, HENRY W.  History of Freemasonry in
Rhode Island...together with a full account
of the celebration of the one hundredth
anniversary of the Grand Lodge of Rhode
Island, held June 24, 1891.  Providence:  E.
L. Freeman, 1895.  xx, 869p.  RHi. +

962  RUSSELL, C. ALLYN.  "Rhode Island Baptists,
1825-1931."  RIH, 28 (1969), 35-48.
     See also this author's article of same
title in Foundations, 14 (1971), 33-49.

963  RUSSO, FRANCIS X.  "John Howland:  pioneer
in the free school movement."  RIH, 37
(1978), 111-122.
     Beginning of public schools in R.I.

964  SAINSBURY, JOHN A.  "Indian labor in early
Rhode Island."  NEQ, 48 (1975), 378-393.

965  SAKLAD, SARAH M.  "Psychiatry in Rhode
Island:  1725-1980."  RIMJ, 63 (1980),
207-216.

966  SALTER, EDWIN.  "Rhode Islanders who settled
in Monmouth County, New Jersey."  NHM, 3
(1883), 201-210.

967 SANDE, THEODORE ANTON. "The textile factory in pre-Civil War Rhode Island." Old-time New England, 66, Nos. 1-2 (1975), 13-31.

968 SANDLER, S. GERALD. "Doctors afield: John Clarke (1609-1676)." New England Journal of Medicine, 269 (1963), 1026-1029.
Includes his role in securing the R.I. colonial charter.

969 SARGENT, FRANCIS B. "History of otolaryngology in Rhode Island." RIMJ, 60 (1977), 433-435, 458.
Branch of medicine dealing with the ear, nose, and throat.

970 SAUNDERS, LAURA SMITH. "Early nineteenth-century merchant sail in Rhode Island." RIH, 35 (1976), 63-66.

971 SCHRODER, WALTER K. Defenses of Narragansett Bay in World War II. Providence: R.I. Bicentennial Foundation, 1980. xiii, 131p. RHi.

972 SCHUCHMAN, JOHN S. "The political background of the political-question doctrine: the judges and the Dorr War." American Journal of Legal History, 16 (1972), 111-125.
"...Conduct of the R.I. bench during the early 1840s."

973 SCOTT, KENNETH. Counterfeiting in colonial Rhode Island. Providence: R.I. Historical Society, 1960. ix, 74p. RHi. +

974 _____. "A half sheet of stolen Rhode Island bills." RIH, 17 (1958), 86-89.
Theft of recently printed money (1776).

975 "SCRAPS of local history." PBTJ, 27 (1915), 749-757.

976 SEELEY, RICHARD A. "The Reverend James Manning: first pastor, first president." Foundations, 16 (1973), 255-260.
First pastor of the Baptist Church in Warren; first president of Brown Univ.

977 SEGAL, BERYL. "The General Jewish Committee: the first quarter-century, 1945-1970." RIJHN, 6 (1971), 5-35.
Jewish Federation of R.I.

978 _____. "The year 1905 in Rhode Island." RIJHN, 5 (1968), 147-152.
Efforts to aid Russian Jews.

979 SHEA, WALTER. "Seventy-five years of water-works progress in Rhode Island, 1871-1957." New England Water Works Association, Journal, 72 (Jan. 1958), 134-137.

980 SHEFFIELD, WILLIAM P. An address delivered...before the Rhode Island Historical Society, in Providence, February 7, A.D. 1882; with notes. Newport: John P. Sanborn, 1883. 67p. RHi. +
Cover title: Rhode Island privateers and privateersmen.

981 _____. John Clarke: physician, philanthropist, preacher and patriot. Chicago: [American Medical Association,] 1889. 16p. RPB. +
Includes his role in securing colonial charter.

982 _____. Random notes on the government of Rhode Island. Newport: Daily News Job Print, 1897. 63p. RHi. +

983 SHEPARD, THOMAS. "A brief history of the Congregational churches and ministers in...Rhode Island...." American Quarterly Register, 12 (1840), 261-273.

984 SHERER, ROBERT GLENN. "Negro churches in Rhode Island before 1860." RIH, 25 (1966), 9-25.

985 SHERMAN, CONSTANCE D. "The Isle of Rhodes: a French vignette." RIH, 17 (1958), 65-72.
Artist Jacques Gérard Milbert in R.I.

986 _____. "The theatre in Rhode Island before the Revolution." RIH, 17 (1958), 10-14.

987 SHIPPEE, LESTER BURRELL. Exercise of the sanitary police powers in Rhode Island. Providence: E. L. Freeman, 1916. 36p. RHi. +

988 "SHIPS' protests." RIHSC, 28 (1935), 70-79, 110-111; 29 (1936), 30-31; 32 (1939), 84-86.
For damages (1697-1700).

989 SIMISTER, FLORENCE PARKER. "Famous Rhode Island men and women of the seventeenth century." RIY (1964-1965), H2-H10.

990 _____. The fire's center: Rhode Island in the Revolutionary era, 1763-1790. Providence: R.I. Bicentennial Foundation, 1979. xiv, 258p. RHi. +

991 _____. "Life in these plantations in the eighteenth century." RIY (1965-1966), 30-33.
See also article of same title by this author in RIY (1974), 119-122.

992 _____. "Rhode Island and the First Continental Congress." RIY (1974), 39-42.

993 _____. "Rhode Island exodus." RIY (1968), 71-74.
18th-century emigration to Nova Scotia.

994 SIMISTER, FLORENCE PARKER. "Rhode Island exodus, III: San Francisco, 1849--the forty-niners." RIY (1970), 77-81.
The second article in the series (RIY, 1969, 77-81), deals with emigration from R.I. to western Massachusetts.

995 _____. "Rhode Island exodus, IV: New York State, 1797--John Brown's Tract." RIY (1971), 12-16.
In the Adirondacks.

996 _____. "Some prominent figures of the nineteenth century." RIY (1967), H75-H79.
In R.I.

997 SIMON, ABRAHAM. "Roger Williams, the prophet of soul liberty: Sunday discourse before the Reform Congregation Keneseth Israel, Philadelphia, Pa." Reform Congregation Keneseth Israel, Sunday Doscourses, Ser. 26, No. 4 (Nov. 24, 1912), 1-12.

998 SIMPSON, ALAN. "How democratic was Roger Williams?" William and Mary Quarterly, 3 ser. 13 (1956), 53-67.

999 SIMPSON, ROBERT V. "King Philip's War." RIY (1964-1965), H11-H16.

1000 SIMS, W. GILMORE. The life of Nathanael Greene, Major-general in the Army of the Revolution. (1856) N.Y.: Derby & Jackson, 1861. 393p. RHi. +
Includes early years and military service in R.I.

1001 SISTERS OF MERCY. PROVIDENCE. Mercy marks the century. Providence, 1951. 161p. RHi.
History of the work of the Sisters of Mercy in the Diocese of Providence, which includes all of R.I. See also entries 3615-3617.

1002 "SKETCH of the life of Roger Williams." RIHSC, 1 (1827), 2-16.

1003 "SLAVERY days in Rhode Island." PM, 33 (1921), 101, 103, 105.

1004 SMELSER, MARSHALL. "Roger Williams." American History Illustrated, 10 (Aug. 1975), 30-38.

1005 SMITH, EDWARD P. "The Rhode Island Bar Association: a short history." Rhode Island Bar Association Journal, 26, No. 8 (May 1978), 4-5.

1006 SMITH, FRED J. "Improved Order of Red Men." NHR, 4 (1885), 186-189.
In R.I.

1007 SMITH, HENRY H. "Davy was here!" RIer (May 22, 1955), 12-13.
Davy Crockett's 1834 visit to R.I.

1008 SMITH, JUDITH E. "Our own kind: family and community networks." Radical History Review, No. 17 (1978), 99-120.
"...The reshaping of southern Italian and eastern European Jewish family traditions in a fast-paced, urban, industrial environment."

1009 SMITH, MATTHEW J. "The real McCoy in the bloodless revolution of 1935." RIH, 32 (1973), 67-85.
Thomas P. McCoy, of Pawtucket, and Democratic state politics.

1010 _____. "Rhode Island politics, 1956-1964: party realignment." RIH, 35 (1976), 49-61.

1011 SMITH, NORMAN W. "The Ku Klux Klan in Rhode Island." RIH, 37 (1978), 35-45.

1012 SMYTH, CLIFFORD. Roger Williams and the fight for religious freedom. N.Y.: Funk & Wagnalls, 1931. 171p. DLC. +

1013 SOCIETY OF COLONIAL WARS. RHODE ISLAND. Further letters on King Philip's War, written by Mr. Richard Smith, Jr., Mr. John Paine, the Commissioners of the United colonies, Mrs. Mary Pray. Providence: E. L. Freeman, 1923. 31p. RHi. +

1014 [_____.] Intercourse and non-intercourse with the Narragansett Indians: based on original manuscripts in the collection of the R.I. Historical Society and assembled at a time when there is still much controversy in New England and elsewhere as to the ownership of lands occupied by various tribes of Indians.... [Providence, 1979.] [16]p. RHi. +

1015 _____. The Narragansett Mortgage: the documents concerning the alien purchases in southern Rhode Island.... Providence: E. L. Freeman, 1925. 45p. RHi. +
Land claims by other colonies.

1016 _____. Nine muster rolls of Rhode Island troops enlisted during the old French War; to which is added the journal of Captain William Rice in the expedition of 1746. Providence: Standard Printing, 1915. 54p. RHi. +

1017 Rhode Island

1017 SOCIETY OF COLONIAL WARS. RHODE ISLAND. Samuel Gorton's letter to Lord Hyde in behalf of the Narragansett sachems.... Providence: E. L. Freeman, 1930. 20p. RHi. +
Concerning conflicting claims to lands on west side of Narragansett Bay. Includes historical introduction.

1018 ____. Some further papers relating to King Philip's War.... Providence: E. L. Freeman, 1931. 14p. RHi. +
Documents, with historical introduction.

1019 SONS OF THE AMERICAN REVOLUTION. RHODE ISLAND SOCIETY. Manual of the Rhode Island Society of the Sons of the American Revolution for the years from eighteen hundred and ninety-three to eighteen hundred and ninety-nine, both inclusive. Central Falls: E. L. Freeman, 1900. xviii, 328p. RHi. +
Includes historical articles relating to R.I. and the Revolution.

1020 SOUVENIR bulletin of Friends Meeting, Newport, R.I. n.p., n.d. 16p. RNHi.
Includes historical sketch of Quakers in R.I.

1021 SOUVENIR program: dedication of the Jamestown Bridge, replacing centuries-old ferries crossing the west passage of lower Narragansett Bay...August 2-3-4, nineteen hundred forty. Jamestown, 1940. [32]p. RHi.
Includes article on "The Jamestown ferries," signed W.L.W. (Walter Leon Watson).

1022 SPENCER, WILLIAM B. "A history of the north branch of the Pawtuxet Valley." NHR, 6 (1888), 122-135.

1023 STACHIW, MYRON O. "For the sake of commerce": Rhode Island, slavery, and the textile industry. An essay...to accompany the exhibit "The loom and the lash: northern industry and southern slavery." [Providence: R.I. Historical Society, 1982.] 12p. RHi.
1982-1983 exhibition at R.I. Historical Society.

1024 STACKHOUSE, DAVID LUDLOW. "First blow for freedom." RIY (1969), 13-16, 19-21.
Gaspee affair (1772).

1025 "STAGE-coach routes." RIHSC, 31 (1938), 68-71.
In R.I.

1026 STAPLES, WILLIAM R. Rhode Island in the Continental Congress, with the journal of the convention that adopted the constitution; 1765-1790. Reuben Aldridge Guild, ed. Providence: Providence Pr., 1870. xlviii, 725p. RHi. +

1027 STATE of Rhode Island and Providence Plantations at the end of the century: a history. Edward Field, ed. Boston: Mason Publishing, 1902. 3v. RHi. +
Usually known as Field's history of R.I.

1028 "STATISTICS of women at work, Rhode Island, 1875-1905." PBTJ, 20 (1908), 361-365.

1029 STEDMAN, MURRAY S., JR., and SUSAN W. STEDMAN. "The rise of the Democratic Party of Rhode Island." NEQ, 24 (1951), 329-341.

1030 [STEERE, THOMAS.] "The manufacturing and mechanical industry of Rhode Island." Providence Daily Journal (Feb. 28, 1870-June 24, 1871).
42-part series. Rider Collection, Brown Univ. Articles pertain to the history of local textile mills as well as other industries.

1031 STEGEMAN, JOHN F., and JANET A. STEGEMAN. Caty: a biography of Catherine Littlefield Greene. Providence: R.I. Bicentennial Foundation, 1977. ix, 235p. RHi. +
Wife of Gen. Nathanael Greene. Includes early life in R.I.

1032 STEVENS, JOHN AUSTIN. "The French in Rhode Island." Magazine of American History, 3 (1879), 385-436.
American Revolution.

1033 STEWART, RANDALL. "Rhode Island literature." RIH, 12 (1953), 97-105; 13 (1954), 1-10.

1034 STEWART, ROWENA. A heritage discovered: Blacks in Rhode Island. Providence: R.I. Black Heritage Society, [197_]. 39p. RHi. +

1035 STICKNEY, CHARLES. Know-nothingism in Rhode Island. Providence, 1894. 17p. RHi. +
Reprinted from RIHSPr, n.s. 1 (1893), 243-257.

1036 STILLMAN, KARL G. "Extending the Seventh Day Baptist horizons." NHSB, No. 101 (1940), 61-64.
The church in R.I.

1037 STINESS, JOHN H. A century of lotteries in Rhode Island. Providence: Sidney S. Rider, 1896. xi, 123p. RHi. +

1038 STINESS, JOHN H. Civil changes in the state: address at the seventy-fifth anniversary of the Rhode Island Historical Society, April 19, 1897. Providence: Standard Printing, 1897. 33p. RHi. +
Civil rights of R.I. citizens.

1039 _____. A sketch of Rhode Island legislation against strong drink: a paper presented to the Legislative Committee on a Prohibitory Law, January session, 1881. Providence: Sidney S. Rider, 1882. 50p. RHi. +

1040 STOCKWELL, THOMAS B. A history of public education in Rhode Island, from 1636 to 1876; embracing an account of the rise and progress of the present school system of the state; the various city and town systems; together with sketches of Brown University and many of the academies, libraries and literary associations of Rhode Island. Providence: Providence Pr., 1876. 458p. RHi. +

1041 STOKES, HOWARD KEMBLE. Public and private finance: a history of the finances of Rhode Island, 1636-1900, and of chartered banking in Rhode Island, 1791-1900. Providence: Mason Publishing, 1901. 154p. RHi. +
Reprinted from entry 1027.

1042 STONE, EDWIN MARTIN. The life and recollections of John Howland. Providence: G. H. Whitney, 1857. 348p. RHi. +
Providence community leader, who played an important role in the campaign for free schools in R.I.

1043 _____. Manual of education: a brief history of the Rhode Island Institute of Instruction, including a synopsis of annual and other meetings, list of officers and members, together with the constitution and charter. Providence: Providence Pr., 1874. 144p. RHi. +
Teachers' institute. Reprinted from RIHSPr (1873-1874), 75-216.

1044 STONE, EDWIN WINCHESTER. Rhode Island in the Rebellion. Providence: George H. Whitney, 1864. xxxviii, 398p. RHi. +
Civil War.

1045 STONE, THOMAS T. Roger Williams, the prophetic legislator: a paper read before the Rhode Island Historical Society, November 8, 1871. Providence: A. Crawford Greene, 1872. 16p. RHi. +

1046 STORER, HORATIO ROGERS. The medals and tokens of Rhode Island.... n.p.: Priv. Print., 1895. 14p. RHi. +

1047 STOUT, NEIL R. "The Gaspee affair." Mankind, 1 (1967), 48-51.
1772.

1048 STRAUS, OSCAR S. Roger Williams, the pioneer of religious liberty. N.Y.: Century, 1894. xvii, 257p. RHi. +

1049 "STRENUOUS financing in colony days." PM, 34 (1922), 429, 431.
Money and other media of exchange.

1050 STRICKLAND, ARTHUR B. Roger Williams: prophet and pioneer of soul liberty. Boston: Judson Pr., 1919. xx, 152p. RHi. +

1051 STROM, SHARON HARTMAN. "Old barriers and new opportunities: working women in Rhode Island, 1900-1940." RIH, 39 (1980), 43-56.

1052 _____. Rhode Island women: profiles of changing social values. n.p.: Permanent Advisory Commission on Women in Rhode Island, 1976. 14p. RHi. +

1053 SUTCLIFFE, DORIS K. "Rhode Island clambake." New-England Galaxy, 10 (Summer 1968), 41-50.
Clambakes of the past.

1054 SWAN, BRADFORD FULLER. The case of Richard Chasmore, alias Long Dick. Providence: Society of Colonial Wars, R.I., 1944. 26p. RHi. +
Pawtuxet man, charged in 1656 with sodomy in a case that helped solidify R.I.'s claim to jurisdiction over the area.

1055 _____. "G. Washington slept here." RIer (Feb. 14, 1971), 6-8, 11.
His visits to R.I.

1056 _____. "Our history flows with the tide." RIer (Apr. 28, 1968), 21, 23.
Narragansett Bay in R.I. history.

1057 _____. "Roger Williams and the insane." RIH, 5 (1946), 65-70.
His views on treatment of the insane.

1058 _____. "Roger Williams' most persistent metaphor." RIH, 35 (1976), 127-129.
His use of nautical metaphors.

1059 _____. "Stephen Hopkins said it first." RIer (June 9, 1974), 22, 24-25, 27.
In his Rights of colonies examined (1764), Hopkins argued for colonial representation in the British Parliament.

1060 _____. "They go to join the Larkin." RIer (Sept. 4, 1966), 4-6.
R.I.'s old summer hotels.

1061 Rhode Island

1061 SWAN, JAMES C. "The Newport Artillery in 1842: Federal Hill and Chepachet." NHR, 7 (1889), 25-35.
Dorr Rebellion.

1062 SWASEY, JEANETTE H. "Some Rhode Island almanacs of long ago." NHSB, No. 92 (1934), 3-11.

1063 TANNER, EARL C. "International wars and the Revolution." RIY (1965-1966), 51-59.
R.I.'s involvements in the various colonial wars and the American Revolution.

1064 _____. Rhode Island: a brief history. [Providence:] R.I. State Board of Education, 1954. xxi, 172p. RHi. +

1065 TANNER, MARY C. N. "Bridges across the chasm of despair: the depression years in Rhode Island." RIY (1971), H204-H208.

1066 _____. "European invasion." RIY (1968), H122-H125.
Immigration to R.I.

1067 TANNER, MARY NELSON. "The middle years of the Anthony-Brayton alliance; or politics in the Post Office, 1874-1880." RIH, 22 (1963), 65-76.
Henry B. Anthony and Charles R. Brayton.

1068 TASHJIAN, DICKRAN, and ANN TASHJIAN. "Gravestones of Rhode Island." RIH, 27 (1968), 33-44.

1069 [TERRY, RODERICK.] "The commission of Governor Coddington and the early charters of Rhode Island." NHSB, No. 44 (1923), 1-22.
William Coddington.

1070 _____. "The first European visitors to Narragansett Bay." NHSB, No. 22 (1917), 1-30.

1071 TEUNISSEN, JOHN J., and EVELYN J. HINZ. "Roger Williams, Thomas More, and the Narragansett utopia." Early American Literature, 11 (1976-1977), 281-295.
I.e., European views of Narragansett Indian culture.

1072 THOMPSON, ELMER J. A study of the constitution of Rhode Island and Providence Plantations. n.p., 1954. 76p. RHi. +

1073 THOMPSON, MACK E. "The Ward-Hopkins controversy and the American Revolution in Rhode Island: an interpretation." William and Mary Quarterly, 3 ser. 16 (1959), 363-375.
Samuel Ward, Stephen Hopkins, and Revolutionary-era politics.

1074 TILLEY, MILDRED C. "A picture in search of a title." RIY (1967), 76-78.
R.I.'s 1892 Woman's World's Fair Advisory Board.

1075 _____. "Rhode Island wheelmen: pavement pioneers." RIY (1968), H126-H129.
Early bicycling.

1076 TITLE GUARANTEE COMPANY OF RHODE ISLAND. The great great grandfather of your land title. Providence: Edward S. Jones Sons, 1925. 23p. RHi.
History of land titles in R.I.

1077 TOLMAN, WILLIAM HOWE. History of higher education in Rhode Island. Washington: Government Printing Office, 1894. 210p. RHi. +

1078 TOMPKINS, HAMILTON B. "Benedict Arnold: first governor of Rhode Island." NHSB, No. 30 (1919), 1-18.

1079 TOOKER, WILLIAM WALLACE. "Indian geographic names, and why we should study them; illustrated by some Rhode Island examples." RIHSPubs, n.s. 5 (1897), 203-215.

1080 TOWLES, JOHN KER. Factory legislation of Rhode Island. n.p.: American Economic Association, 1908. vi, 119p. RHi. +

1081 TRAVELERS PROTECTIVE ASSOCIATION OF AMERICA. RHODE ISLAND DIVISION. Commercial history of the State of Rhode Island...representing the manufacturing, wholesale, banking and commercial interests and resources of the state in general, 1898. T. Edgar Harvey, ed. Providence: Snow & Farnham, 1898. 163p. RHi.

1082 TUCKER, KATHERINE PATRICIA. "The Block Islander who captured a general." RIY (1974), 108-112.
Catherine Littlefield Greene and Nathanael Greene.

1083 _____. "The Short Story Club: a history." RIY (1974), 9-12.
R.I. Short Story Club.

1084 TURNER, HENRY E. "The two governors Cranston." NHR, 7 (1889), 305-342.
John and Samuel, colonial governors.

1085 "TWO early Rhode Island steam-boats." NHR, 6 (1888), 373-390.

1086 TYNG, DUDLEY. Rhode Island Episcopalians, 1653-1953.... Providence: Little Rhody Pr., [1954]. 100, [29]p. RHi. +

1087 ULLMAN, EDWARD L. "The historical geography of the eastern boundary of Rhode Island." Washington State College, Research Studies, 4 (1936), 67-87.

1088 UNITED BROTHERHOOD OF CARPENTERS & JOINERS OF AMERICA. CARPENTERS LOCAL UNION, NO. 94. 100th anniversary dinner dance, Rocky Point Palladium, Warwick, R.I., Saturday, August 15, 1981.... n.p., 1981. 15p. RNoP.
    Includes historical sketch of Council 94, by Susan Chapdelaine and Richard Slaney.

1089 U.S. CONGRESS. HOUSE OF REPRESENTATIVES. Rhode Island: interference of the executive in the affairs of. U.S., 28th Congress, 1st Session, House of Representatives, Report No. 546. [Washington, 1845.] 1070p. RHi. +
    Includes historical information pertaining to the Dorr Rebellion and its aftermath.

1090 U.S. DEPARTMENT OF THE INTERIOR. HISTORIC AMERICAN ENGINEERING RECORD. Rhode Island: an inventory of historic engineering and industrial sites.... Written by Gary Kulik and Julia C. Bonham. [Washington,] 1978. xv, 296p. RHi. +

1091 U.S. DEPARTMENT OF TRANSPORTATION. FEDERAL RAILROAD ADMINISTRATION. NORTHEAST CORRIDOR IMPROVEMENT PROJECT. Cultural resources inventory and evaluation of effect. Historic sites: Rhode Island. Washington, 1978. xi, 270p. RHi.

1092 UPDIKE, WILKINS. History of the alleged state debt of Rhode-Island. n.p., [1846]. 12p. RHi. +
    Revolutionary War debt.

1093 _____. Memoirs of the Rhode Island bar. Boston: Thomas H. Webb, 1842. 311p. RHi. +

1094 UTTER, G. BENJAMIN. "Seventh Day Baptists in Newport and Westerly." NHSB, No. 101 (1940), 58-61.

1095 VICTOR, STEPHEN. "Lewis Hine's photography and reform in Rhode Island." RIH, 41 (1982), 35-49.
    Ca. 1912.

1096 VINTON, FRANCIS. An oration on the annals of Rhode Island and Providence Plantations ... and a rhyme of Rhode Island and the times, by George William Curtis, delivered before the Sons of Rhode Island in New York, May 29, 1863. N.Y.: C. A. Alvord, 1864. 80p. RHi. +

1097 VOLPE, FRED S. "Rhode Island advisory opinions: ghosts that slay?" Rhode Island Bar Journal, 25, No. 5 (Feb. 1977), 2-3, 8, 13, 15-17, 19-21.
    History of advisory opinions by R.I. Supreme Court.

1098 WADE, HERBERT T. "Colonel Wade and his Massachusetts State Troops in Rhode Island, 1777-1778." Essex Institute, Historical Collections, 89 (1953), 357-375.

1099 WALSH, EVELYN M. "Crisis, 1780-1790: to ratify or not to ratify." RIY (1965-1966), 60-63.
    R.I. and the Articles of Confederation and U.S. Constitution.

1100 "THE WAR in Rhode Island." New Englander, 1 (Jan. 1843), 85-102.
    Dorr Rebellion.

1101 "THE WAR of the Revolution: centennial commemorations." RIHSPr (1877-1878), 83-93.
    Events of the war in R.I.

1102 WARD, JOHN. "The ice harvest is no more." RIer (Feb. 9, 1964), 16-17.

1103 WARD, SAMUEL. Correspondence of Governor Samuel Ward, May 1775-March 1776, with a biographical introduction based chiefly on the Ward papers covering the period 1725-1776, edited by Bernhard Knollenberg; and genealogy of the Ward family...compiled by Clifford P. Monahon. Providence: R.I. Historical Society, 1952. ix, 254p. RHi. +

1104 WARREN, WILFRED E. The Jamestown ferry boats, 1873-1969. Jamestown, 1976. [141]p. RHi. +
    Pictorial study, with some historical text.

1105 _____. A short history of transportation on Narragansett Bay and its environs. Jamestown, 1979. 36p. RHi.

1106 "WATERMARKS on early Rhode Island paper." RIHSC, 23 (1930), 117-119.

1107 "'WE want integrity': an interview with Al Sisti." Radical History Review, No. 17 (1978), 181-190.
    Paul Buhle, ed. Unionization and working conditions in the textile industry.

1108 WEBB, ROBERT N. The colony of Rhode Island. N.Y.: Watts, 1972. 89p. RHi. +

1109 WEEDEN, WILLIAM BABCOCK. Early Rhode Island: a social history of the people. N.Y.: Grafton Pr., 1910. x, 381p. RHi. +

1110 Rhode Island

1110  WEEDEN, WILLIAM WAGER. "Roger Williams' contribution to world civilization." JHSB, No. 9 (June 1942), 3-12. RHi.
Founding of R.I.

1111  ____. "Samuel Gorton: a forgotten founder of our liberties." NHSB, No. 102 (1942), 1-15.

1112  WESTON, FRANK. The passing years, 1791-1966. [Providence:] Industrial National Bank of R.I., 1966. 142p. RHi. +
Events in R.I. during the bank's history.

1113  WHEELER, ROBERT L. "Grave hunters: finding the resting places of some of our governors took a lot of sleuthing." RIer (June 27, 1954), 3-4, 6-7, 9.

1114  ____. "Named for a plowman." RIer (July 3, 1955), 3-4.
Society of the Cincinnati in R.I.

1115  ____. "The strange and cryptic picture diary of Charles DeWolf Brownell." RIer (June 8, 1947), 8-10.
R.I. artist.

1116  "WHEN people commuted by boat." Netopian, 1, No. 12 (Mar. 1921), 7, 10-11.
Steamboats on Narragansett Bay.

1117  WHITE, ELIZABETH NICHOLSON. Mary Barnard, wife of Roger Williams. n.p.: [Watchemoket Pr., 1956?]. [35]p. RHi.
Includes R.I. years.

1118  WHITE, JOHN K. "Alfred E. Smith's Rhode Island revolution: the election of 1928." RIH, 42 (1983), 57-66.
Contends that the 1928 presidential campaign laid the groundwork for the Democratic Party's long-term domination of politics in R.I. Shows how various thnic and religious groups altered their party loyalties at this time.

1119  WHYTE, J. BRUCE. "'The Public Universal Friend.'" RIH, 26 (1967), 103-112; 27 (1968), 18-24.
Part 1 deals with prophetess Jemima Wilkinson's years in R.I., before departing with her followers for N.Y. State in 1788.

1120  WIECEK, WILLIAM M. "'A peculiar conservatism' and the Dorr Rebellion: constitutional clash in Jacksonian America." American Journal of Legal History, 22 (1978), 237-253.

1121  ____. "Popular sovereignty in the Dorr War: conservative counterblast." RIH, 32 (1973), 35-51.

1122  WIENER, FREDERICK BERNAYS. "Notes on the Rhode-Island Admiralty, 1727-1790." Harvard Law Review, 46 (1932), 44-90.

1123  ____. "The Rhode Island merchants and the Sugar Act." NEQ, 3 (1930), 464-500.
1764.

1124  ____. "Roger Williams' contribution to modern thought." RIHSC, 28 (1935), 1-20.
Includes ideas on religious liberty, as developed in R.I.

1125  WILBOUR, BELINDA O. The destruction of the Gaspee and the reasons therefor. Providence: Standard Printing, 1892. 16p. RHi. +
British schooner, burned by Rhode Islanders in 1772. See also her article on this subject in American Monthly Magazine, 7 (1896), 131-138.

1126  WILCOX, WILLIAM B. "Rhode Island in British strategy, 1780-1781." Journal of Modern History, 17 (1945), 304-331.

1127  WILLIAMS, ALVIN DIGHTON. The Rhode Island Freewill Baptist pulpit. Boston: Gould and Lincoln, 1852. 398p. RHi. +

1128  WILLIAMS, CATHERINE READ (ARNOLD). Annals of the aristocracy: being a series of anecdotes of some of the principal families of Rhode-Island. Providence: B. T. Albro, 1845. 2v. in 1. RHi. +

1129  WILLIAMS, J. HAROLD. Scout trail, 1910-1962: history of the Boy Scout movement in Rhode Island. Providence: Rhode Island Boy Scouts, 1964. 72p. RHi. +

1130  WILLIAMS, ROGER. Complete writings. (1866-1874) N.Y.: Russell & Russell, 1963. 7v. RPB. +
1963 ed. was edited by Perry Miller.

1131  WILLIAMS, THOMAS. A sermon, on the conclusion of the second century from the settlement of the State of Rhode-Island and Providence Plantations. Providence: Knowles, Vose, 1837. 32p. RHi. +
Cover title: Rhode-Island Protestantism, stated and condemned. Historical.

1132  WILLIAMSON, CHILTON. "The disenchantment of Thomas W. Dorr." RIH, 17 (1958), 97-108.
Dorr Rebellion.

1133  ____. "Rhode Island suffrage since the Dorr War." NEQ, 28 (1955), 34-50.

1134  WINDSOR, RICHARD D. "I remember the queen of the Bay and her king." RIer (Aug. 17, 1958), 18, 20-21.
Steamboat Mount Hope.

1135   WINSLOW, JOHN.  The trial of the Rhode
Island judges:  an episode touching currency
and constitutional law....  Brooklyn, N.Y.:
Geo. Tremlett, 1887.  24p.  RHi.
     1786 trial, an outcome of the case Trevett
v. Weeden.

1136   WINSLOW, OLA ELIZABETH.  Master Roger
Williams:  a biography.  N.Y.:  Macmillan,
1957.  xi, 328p.  RHi. +
     Reprinted 1973.

1137   _____.  "The religion of Roger Williams."
Bulletin of the Congregational Library, 8
(May 1957), 5-13.

1138   WITHEY, LYNNE E.  "Household structure in
urban and rural areas:  the case of Rhode
Island, 1774-1800."  Journal of Family
History, 3 (1978), 37-50.

1139   WOMEN'S Liberation Union of Rhode Island:
a history.  n.p., [1976].  28p.  RHi.

1140   WONSON, RICHARD L., and PAUL W. FRAZIER.
The Rhode Island Company:  part I, equipment
roster.  Short Beach, Conn.:  Branford
Electric Railway Association, n.d.  96p.
RHi. +
     Street railroad company.

1141   WOODWARD, CARL RAYMOND.  "Pacers, chickens,
stone walls and plantations."  RIer (Nov.
19, 1967), 8-14.
     Agriculture in R.I.

1142   "WOOLEN manufacturing in Rhode Island."
PBTJ, 23 (1911), 280, 282, 284.

1143   WORCESTER, WAYNE.  "It's time to
rehabilitate the Greening."  RIer (Oct. 19,
1975), 6-7.
     R.I. apple variety.

1144   WRIGHT, MARION I., and ROBERT J. SULLIVAN.
The Rhode Island atlas.  Providence:
R.I. Publications Society, 1982.  xvi, 239p.
RHi. +
     Includes historical maps and text.

1145   WRIGHT, T.  The Navy in Narragansett Bay,
past and present.  n.p., 1957.  13p.
RNW-Hi.

1146   WROTH, LAWRENCE COUNSELMAN.  Roger Williams:
Marshall Woods Lecture, in Sayles Hall,
October 26, 1936.  Providence:  Brown Univ.,
1937.  41p.  RHi. +

1147   WULSIN, EUGENE.  "Political consequences of
the burning of the Gaspee."  RIH, 3 (1944),
1-11, 55-64.
     1772.

1148   WYMAN, LILLIE B. C., and ARTHUR CRAWFORD
WYMAN.  Elizabeth Buffum Chace, 1806-1899:
her life and its environment.  Boston:  W.
B. Clarke, 1914.  2v.  RHi. +
     R.I. antislavery and woman suffrage
leader.

1149   YOUNG, HAROLD H.  "Clang! clang! clang! went
the trolley."  RIY (1972), H236-H244.
     Interurban lines.

1150   ZURIER, MELVIN L.  "How Jewish parties fared
in the Rhode Island Supreme Court:
1870-1912."  RIJHN, 7 (1972), 203-208.
     See also next entry.

1151   _____.  "How Jewish parties fared in the
Rhode Island Supreme Court:  1913-1924."
RIJHN, 7 (1973), 385-389.
     See also preceding entry.

# Entries for Counties

## BRISTOL COUNTY

1152 BRISTOL County, Rhode Island and Providence
Plantations. Bristol: Bristol County Water
Company, [1951?]. 18p. RHi.
  Historical sketch of the county, reprinted
from the magazine H2O, 26 (1951).

1153 BULLOCK, EMMA WESCOTT. "A Revolutionary
reminiscence." American Monthly Magazine,
2 (1893), 369-371.
  British raid on Warren and Bristol (1778).

1154 SLADE, WILLIAM ADAMS. "The King Philip
country." NEM, n.s. 18 (1898), 605-629.

1155 STETSON, OSCAR F. "Foreclosure of mortgage
by suit of trespass and ejectment." RIHSC,
23 (1930), 1-4.
  Bristol County, 18th century.

  SEE ALSO entry 767.

## KENT COUNTY

1156 ELDREDGE, JAMES HENRY. "Early medical
history of Kent County, Rhode Island."
RIMJ, 23 (1940), 135-139.

1157 PERRY, CHARLES M. "The southwest corner of
the Shawomet Purchase." RIH, 10 (1951),
65-68, 80-85.
  "The point where Coventry, West Greenwich
and Connecticut join."

  SEE ALSO entry 206.

## NEWPORT COUNTY

1158 BATTLE, CHARLES A. Negroes on the island of
Rhode Island. n.p., [1932]. 39p. RHi. +
  I.e., Aquidneck Island.

1159 "BATTLE of Rhode Island." RIHSPr
(1877-1878), 88-93.
  1778.

1160 BATTLE of Rhode Island, Tiverton, 1778-1970.
n.p., n.d. [52]p. +
  Program for colonial muster. Includes
historical sketches of the Revolutionary War
battle and of Tiverton. 1971, 1972 and 1973
eds. contain other historical sketches.

1161 BICKNELL, THOMAS WILLIAMS. Story of Dr.
John Clarke, the founder of the first free
commonwealth of the world on the basis of
"full liberty in religious concernments."
Providence: Priv. Print., 1915. 212, [4]p.
RHi. +
  On Aquidneck Island.

1162 BILLIAS, GEORGE A. "General Glover's role
in the Battle of Rhode Island." RIH, 18
(1959), 33-42.
  Gen. John Glover (1778).

1163 BIRCHHEAD, SARAH K. "Governor William
Coddington." NHSB, No. 5 (1913), 1-20.

1164 BOISVERT, DONALD J. "The storm that changed
the course of history." Yankee, 34 (Aug.
1970), 62-65, 160, 162, 164.
  The Great Storm of Aug. 1778 and its
effects on the Battle of R.I.

1165 BOLHOUSE, GLADYS E. "Women and the battle
for Rhode Island." NH, 41 (1968), 34-41.
  Revolutionary War years.

1166 BRADBY, MARIE A. "In 1778, former slaves
saved the day." RIer (Aug. 24, 1975),
14-16.
  Black troops of the 1st R.I. Regt. in the
Battle of R.I.

1167 A BRIEF history of St. Mary's Church, South
Portsmouth, & Holy Cross Chapel, Middletown,
Rhode Island, 1843-1916. n.p.: Priv.
Print., 1916. 23p. RHi. +
  Episcopal.

---

+ Listings in the National Union Catalog for books and pamphlets marked
  with this symbol may include additional library locations.

1168 "A BRITISH account of the Siege of Rhode Island, 1778." RIH, 38 (1979), 79-85.
John Fitzhugh Millar, ed.

1169 BUELL, WILLIAM ACKERMAN. "Maker of schools and Benedictine monk: the life of John Byron Diman." NH, 43 (1970), 85-130.
Portsmouth Abbey School, Portsmouth; St. George's School, Middletown. Born John Byron Diman, he was known in later life as John Hugh Diman.

1170 BULL, HENRY. "Memoirs of Rhode Island: republished from the Rhode Island Republican, 1832-7, with additions and corrections." NHM, 6 (1886), 174-188, 241-264; 7 (1886-1887), 1-18, 145-151, 185-192, 241-257.
Articles relating to history of Aquidneck Island.

1171 CHAMPLIN, RICHARD L. "In the wake of the ferries: introduction to a ferry exhibition." NH, 42 (1969), 61-73.
With catalog of 1969 exhibit at Redwood Library, Newport, 74-84. Newport-Jamestown ferries.

1172 _____. "We'll all miss the boat." RIer (Apr. 13, 1969), 6-10.
Ferries between Jamestown and Newport.

1173 CHAPIN, CHARLES V., and ANNA AUGUSTA CHAPIN. The Jamestown and Newport ferries. Providence, 1921. 10p. RHi. +

1174 COGGESHALL, HENRY T. "Address delivered at the Coggeshall family reunion, Newport, R.I., Sept. 9, 1884." NHM, 5 (1884), 144-172.
The Coggeshalls in the early history of Aquidneck Island.

1175 COHEN, JOEL A. "The battle nobody won." RIer (June 8, 1975), 16-18.
Battle of Rhode Island (1778).

1176 COVELL, ELIZABETH GREENE. "Military events on Rhode Island: from the diary of a British officer." NHSB, No. 93 (1934), 3-29.
Frederick Mackenzie (American Revolution).

1177 DAVIS, ALBERT P., FOSTER H. MIDDLETON, and BRADLEY M. ALTON. University of Rhode Island underwater bicentennial expedition: a report on past achievements and future objectives. Kingston: Univ. of R.I., Dept. of Ocean Engineering, 1976. 26p. RHi.
Report on underwater recovery work on three British ships sunk off Aquidneck Island in 1778. Includes historical background of sinkings.

1178 DEARDEN, PAUL F. The Rhode Island campaign of 1778: inauspicious dawn of alliance. Providence: R.I. Bicentennial Foundation, 1980. xv, 169p. RHi. +
American Revolution. See also entry 1994.

1179 FISKE, JOHN. "The Monmouth and Newport campaigns." Century, 64 (1889), 463-476.
American Revolution. Includes events leading up to Battle of R.I. (1778).

1180 GARDINER, ASA BIRD. The Battle of Rhode Island, August 29, 1778: impromptu remarks...June 23, 1911. n.p., n.d. 10p. RHi. +

1181 HALDEN, JOHN C. "Little Compton and Tiverton Four Corners." Pencil Points, 17 (1936), 707-722.
Domestic architecture.

1182 HISTORY of Newport County, Rhode Island, from the year 1638 to the year 1887, including the settlement of its towns, and their subsequent progress. Richard M. Bayles, ed. N.Y.: L. E. Preston, 1888. x, 1060p. RHi. +

1183 "I ran rum." Providence Evening Bulletin and Sunday Journal (July 23, 1934 - Aug. 16, 1934).
Series of 25 articles detailing Prohibition-era bootlegging operations in southeastern R.I. (1920-1933).

1184 KAULL, JAMES T. "Hello, Newport...Hello, Jamestown!" RIer (June 23, 1969), 8-10, 12, 17, 19.
History of the project to link the two places by bridge.

1185 KING, DAVID. Discourse on the life and character of William Coddington. n.p., [1912?]. 22p. RHi. +
A founder of the colony on Aquidneck Island and first governor.

1186 LIPPITT, CHARLES WARREN. The Battle of Rhode Island. Newport: Mercury Publishing, 1915. 17p. RHi. +
Reprinted from NHSB, No. 18 (1915), 1-14.

1187 LITTLE, P. F. Fragmentary sketches & incidents in Little Compton & Tiverton, during the Revolution, and the War of 1812. Little Compton, 1880. 32p. RHi. +

1188 MAYER, LLOYD M. "The Battle of Rhode Island." NHSB, No. 4 (1912), 1-6.
1778.

1189 MORRIS, ANNA WHARTON. "A trip across the Bay." NHSB, No. 96 (1936), 3-12.
Summer life in Newport and Jamestown.

1190 MURRAY, THOMAS HAMILTON. Gen. John Sullivan and the Battle of Rhode Island: a sketch of the former and a description of the latter. [Providence: American-Irish Historical Society, 1902.] 32p. RHi. +

1191 NELSON, WILBUR. The hero of Aquidneck: a life of Dr. John Clarke. N.Y.: Fleming H. Revell, 1938. 95p. RHi. +
Physician, minister, and a leading figure in the early history of the R.I. Colony.

1192 PATYKEWICH, VICTORIA H. C. "This organ wandered all over Aquidneck." RIer (Apr. 24, 1960), 12-13.
19th-century church organ.

1193 PETERSON, EDWARD. History of Rhode Island and Newport. N.Y.: John S. Taylor, 1853. xvi, 370p. RHi. +
I.e., Aquidneck Island.

1194 PRESERVATION SOCIETY OF NEWPORT COUNTY. The first twenty-five years. Newport, 1972. Unp. RNR.
History of the society.

1195 PRESTON, HOWARD WILLIS. The Battle of Rhode Island, August 29th, 1778. Providence: State of R.I., State Bureau of Information, 1928. 56p. RHi. +

1196 "THE RELATIVE importance of Coddington and Clarke from 1637 to 1648." RIHSC, 21 (1928), 119-123.
William Coddington and John Clarke.

1197 RIDER, HOPE S. "'The enemy have full possession of the island.'" RIer (May 30, 1976), B27-B30, B32-B41.
British occupation of Aquidneck Island (1776-1779).

1198 RIDER, SIDNEY S. "The secret work of William Coddington in attempting individual possession of Aquidnec Island and making a kingdom of it for his family and descendants." BN, 30 (1913), 33-38.

1199 ROSS, ARTHUR A. A discourse, embracing the civil and religious history of Rhode-Island; delivered April 4, A.D. 1838, at the close of the second century from the first settlement of the island. Providence: H. H. Brown, 1838. 161p. RHi. +
Aquidneck Island.

1200 "THE SETTLEMENT of Aquidnick Island." PM, 34 (1922), 97, 99.

1201 SHERMAN, CONSTANCE D. "Curious crimes in colonial Newport County." RIH, 18 (1959), 116-118.

1202 SHERMAN, WILLIAM S. "Some notes on early medicine and surgery in Newport County, the cradle of American medicine." RIMJ, 14 (1931), 76-82.
See also this author's article on same subject in RIMJ, 24 (1941), 93-96.

1203 SOCIETY OF COLONIAL WARS. RHODE ISLAND. John Albro's deposition of 1705 as to the purchase of Aquidnick, with Coddington's deposition of 1687.... Providence: E. L. Freeman, 1938. 11p. RHi. +

1204 SPRANGER, GEOFFREY. "The three-fold legacy of Father Diman." RIY (1967), 34-38.
John Hugh Diman and Portsmouth Abbey School, in Portsmouth; St. George's School, Middletown.

1205 STEVENS, MAUD LYMAN. "Early inhabitants of Rhode Island." NHSB, No. 7 (1913), 1-13.
I.e., Aquidneck Island.

1206 STONE, EDWIN MARTIN. The Battle of Rhode Island.... (1884) Tiverton: Sentinel Pr., 1930. 12p. RHi. +

1207 TAYLOR, ERICH A. O'D. Campaign on Rhode Island, MDCCLXXVIII. n.p., n.d. [31]p. RHi. +
Battle of Rhode Island (1778).

1208 TOMPKINS, HAMILTON B. "Newport County lotteries." NHSB, No. 1 (1912), 1-16; No. 2 (1912), 1-18.

1209 TURNER, HENRY E. Settlers of Aquidneck, and liberty of conscience: read before the Rhode Island Historical Society, February, 1880. [Newport:] Newport, R.I., Historical Publishing, 1880. 55p. RHi. +

1210 _____. William Coddington in Rhode Island colonial affairs. Providence: Sidney S. Rider, 1878. 60p. RHi. +

1211 WALDEN, GEORGE F. "The Battle of Rhode Island." RIY (1974), 24-27.
1778.

1212 "WASHINGTON decorations in household articles in the vicinity of Newport." NHM, 5 (1885), 282-290.
Signed X. Y. Z.

1213 WATSON, WILLIAM ARGYLE. "History of the Rhode Island Bridge Company." NHM, 3 (1882), 170-172.
Between Portsmouth and Tiverton.

1214 WEST, EDWARD H. "New interpretations of the records of the island of Rhode Island." RIHSC, 32 (1939), 107-115.
I.e., Aquidneck Island. See also next entry.

1215   WEST, EDWARD H.  "The records of Rhode
Island."  RIHSC, 32 (1930), 16-26.
     Aquidneck Island.  See also preceding
entry.

1216   _____.  "The signing of the Compact and the
purchase of Aquidneck."  RIHSC, 32 (1939),
66-78.
     Portsmouth Compact.

1217   WHEELER, ROBERT L.  "Battle of Rhode
Island."  RIer (Dec. 13, 1953), 3-5, 8.
     1778.

1218   WHITE, ELIZABETH NICHOLSON.  "A record of
William Coddington, Esquire."  NHSB, No. 100
(1939), 1-21.
     One of the founders of the colony on
Aquidneck Island, and its first governor.

1219   WHYTE, J. BRUCE.  "The Battle of Rhode
Island."  WRICHSH, 8 (May 1965), [2]; (June
1965), [2].
     1778.

1220   WILBOUR, BELINDA O.  The Battle of Rhode
Island and some of the events preceding.
Providence:  Standard Printing, 1893.  20p.
RHi. +
     1778.  See also her article of same title
in American Monthly Magazine, 3 (1893),
228-234.

1221   WILLIAMS, EMILY CODDINGTON.  William
Coddington of Rhode Island: a sketch.
Newport: Priv. Print., 1941.  RHi. +
     One of the founders of the colony on
Aquidneck Island, and its first governor.

1222   WOOLSEY, SARAH CHAUNCEY.  "The isle of
peace."  Scribner's, 22 (1881), 481-497.
     Aquidneck Island.

1223   YARNALL, JAMES L.  "John La Farge's 'New
England Pasture Land.'"  NH, 55 (1982),
79-91.
     Part of a series on La Farge, one of the
19th-century landscape "painters who drew
upon the Newport County scenery for a great
many of their paintings."  See also next two
entries.

1224   _____.  "John La Farge's 'Paradise Valley'
Period."  NH, 55 (1982), 6-26.
     See also the preceding and the following
entry.

1225   _____.  "John La Farge's 'The Last Valley.'"
NH, 5 (1982), 130-142.
     Part of a series of articles on the
19th-century landscape painter.  See also
the two preceding entries.

     SEE ALSO entries 418, 600, 1069, 1098, 2656,
2667.

PROVIDENCE COUNTY

1226   "AUG. Johnston and Wm. Smith."  RIY (1963),
74-75.
     Men for whom the towns of Johnston and
Smithfield were named.

1227   BLACKSTONE CANAL NATIONAL BANK.  The
hundredth milestone: a few pages of Rhode
Island history suggested by the coming of
the one hundredth anniversary of the
Blackstone Canal National Bank of
Providence, Rhode Island, 1831-1931.
[Providence:  Edward S. Jones Sons,] n.d.
19p.  RHi. +
     Includes historical information about the
Blackstone Canal and the bank.

1228   "BLACKSTONE Valley sketches."  Providence
Journal (Sept. 13, 1853; Dec. 5, 21, 1854).
     Blackstone River Valley.

1229   BRAYTON, GLADYS W.  "Prisons and punishment
in these Providence Plantations."  CHSN
[Jan. 1980, 3-7.]

1230   BROWN, FRANK CHOUTEAU.  "Rhode Island houses
along the Blackstone River Valley."  Pencil
Points, 16 (1935), 197-211.

1231   BYRNES, GARRETT D.  "A hospital where kids
had fun."  RIer (Sept. 26, 1971), 18-21.
     Article about the Floating Hospital, a
summertime facility for children on Starve
Goat Island in Providence; and also about
Edgewood Beach, in Cranston.  See also next
entry.

1232   _____.  "How it all ended, a long time ago."
RIer (Oct. 3, 1971), 18-20.
     The end of Field's Point (Providence),
Starve Goat Island (Providence), and
Edgewood Beach (Cranston), as locally
popular summer resorts.  See also previous
entry and 2803.

1233   "CENTENARY of Rhode Island's only inland
waterway project."  PM, 35 (1923), 307, 309,
311.
     Blackstone Canal.

1234   CLEMENCE, CLARA E.  "The Ponaganset River."
WRICHSP, 2, No. 2 (1955), [10-12].

1235   _____.  "The Roger Williams School
District."  WRICHSP, No. 4 (1950), 24-26.
     In Foster and Glocester.

1236   CLOUGH, BEN C.  "The corpse and the beaver
hat."  BrAlumMo, 61 (May 1961), 10-13.
     Political and legal consequences of the
medical dissection in Providence of a
Scituate suicide's body.

1237 CONLEY, PATRICK T. A sketch of the Blackstone Valley: its river, its canal and its people. Providence: R.I. Publications Society, 1982. [19]p. RHi. +
Includes information on a number of ethnic groups.

1238 FOSTER, THEODORE G. "The minutes of the Westconnaug Purchase." RIHSC, 25 (1932), 121-128; 26 (1933), 26-36, 94-98; 27 (1934), 24-32, 57-61, 127-128.
Tract in Foster and Scituate.

1239 GREENE, WELCOME ARNOLD. "The history of a ferry." NHR, 8 (1890), 274-301.
Across Seekonk River, between Providence and East Providence.

1240 GRIEVE, ROBERT. An illustrated history of Pawtucket, Central Falls and vicinity: a narrative of the growth and evolution of the community. Pawtucket: Pawtucket Gazette and Chronicle, 1897. 509p. RHi. +

1241 [HALEY, JOHN WILLIAMS.] The Blackstone Canal. Providence: "Old Stone Bank," 1931. 10p. RHi.
Mainly about the R.I. section of the canal, which linked Providence with Worcester, Mass. This and entry 1243 were part of the "Old Stone Bank" historical series. See note, entry 432.

1242 _____. The lower Blackstone River Valley: the story of Pawtucket, Central Falls, Lincoln, and Cumberland, Rhode Island; an historical narrative. Pawtucket: E. L. Freeman, 1936. 169p. RHi. +

1243 [_____.] The Providence Purchase. Providence: "Old Stone Bank," 1933. 10p. RHi.
Roger Williams's land grant from the Indians in 1637.

1244 HISTORY of Providence County, Rhode Island. Richard M. Bayles, ed. N.Y.: W. W. Preston, 1891. 2v. RHi. +

1245 JENKS, GROVER L. "Dwellings in northeastern Rhode Island and the Smithfields." Pencil Points, 16 (1935), 317-332.

1246 KENNEDY, AMBROSE. Quebec to New England: the life of Monsignor Charles Dauray. Boston: Bruce Humphries, 1948. 242p. RHi. +
Built Franco-American churches in Central Falls and Woonsocket.

1247 LEACH, CHARLES H., and EDITH H. NOBREGA. "The Great Road." RIY (1970), 47-56.
R.I. portion of colonial highway between Providence and Boston.

1248 NORTHERN INTERRELATED LIBRARY SYSTEM. The history of northern Rhode Island: a booklist. Pawtucket, 1971. 20p. RPRIC.

1249 OUTLINE history of Pawtucket Fire Department and an outline history of Central Falls Fire Department. H. H. Easterbrook, ed. Taken from the Firemans Standard, published Nov. 1, 1916 and Oct. 16, 1916 respectively. n.p., 1916. Unp. RPa.

1250 "THE PLAINFIELD Pike." WRICHSH, 13 (Apr. 1970), [2].
Once a toll road; now Route 14.

1251 RHODE ISLAND. GENERAL ASSEMBLY. JOINT SPECIAL COMMITTEE ON TITLE OF STATE TO LANDS IN WOONASQUATUCKET VALLEY. Reports relating to the title of the state to certain lands in the Woonasquatucket Valley, and establishing boundary line between the city of Providence and the town of North Providence. Providence: Public Park Association, 1884. 44p. RHi. +

1252 RIDER, SIDNEY S. "Quinsniket, and 'Nine Men's Misery.'" BN, 33 (1916), 41-47.
Includes the story of Pierce's Fight (1676), during King Philip's War, and "Nine Men's Misery," where the English survivors were tortured and killed.

1253 RIVARD, PAUL E. "Seventeenth century Blackstone Valley houses." Old Slater Mill, The Flyer, 1 (Aug. 1970), 4-5, 11.

1254 ROELKER, WILLIAM GREENE. "The Providence Plantations Canal." RIH, 5 (1946), 19-25, 54-56.
Projected canal from Providence to Worcester County, Mass. (1790s).

1255 SAUNDERS, C. ERNEST, and EARL BROWN. The street railway strike of Providence and Pawtucket: a complete history of the cause and effect of the strike, showing the difference between the organization of capital and labor. Providence: Franklin Pr., n.d. 107p. RHi.

1256 SEVENTEENTH century place-names of Providence Plantations, 1636-1700. Clarence Saunders Brigham, comp. Providence, 1903. 28p. RHi. +
Reprinted from RIHSC, 10 (1902), 373-400.

1257 SMITH, HOWARD BUCKLIN. "The Westconnaug Purchase." WRICHSP, 2, No. 2 (1955), [21-33].
In present-day Foster and Scituate.

1258 STREICKER, PAUL W. "Gold mines? In Rhode Island?" RIer (Jan. 24, 1971), 18-20.
Mining attempts in Foster and Glocester.

1259 TOWNSEND, ELIZABETH JANE. "Teaching the three r's: Eliza Smith, schoolmistress." RIH, 37 (1978), 47-51.
In Providence and Johnston (late 19th century).

1260 WHEELER, ROBERT L. "General Carrington's ditch." RIer (Jan. 9, 1949), 12-15.
Blackstone Canal in R.I.

1261 YOUNG, HAROLD G. "A short history of the Providence and Danielson Railroad." WRICHSP, 1, No. 4 (1949), 22-23.
Street railroad.

SEE ALSO entry 767.

## WASHINGTON COUNTY

1262 ALLEN, ZACHARIAH. "Narragansett's place in Rhode Island history." NHR, 1 (1882), 12-27.
Narragansett Country.

1263 ARNOLD, JAMES N. "The evidences of the mound builders in Narragansett." NHR, 6 (1888), 205-222.
Places sacred to the Narragansett Indians.

1264 _____. "The great secret: an historical enquiry into the causes of the contention, for the possession of the Narragansett Country, by the colonies of New England." NHR, 6 (1888), 1-24.

1265 _____. Pen pictures of Narragansett history. n.p., n.d. 31p. RHi. +
Narrangansett Country.

1266 _____. A statement of the case of the Narragansett tribe of Indians.... Newport, 1896. 70p. RHi. +

1267 "THE BIG flood in the Wood River Valley." Hopkinton Historical Association, Hopkinton Notes, 2, No. 2 (Mar. 1979), 1-3.

1268 BOISSEVAIN, ETHEL. "Detribalization and group identity: the Narragansett Indian case." N.Y. Academy of Sciences, Transactions, 25 (1963), 493-502.

1269 _____. "The detribalization of the Narragansett Indians: a case study." Ethnohistory, 3 (1956), 225-245.

1270 _____. The Narragansett people. Phoenix, Ariz.: Indian Tribal Series, 1975. vi, 104p. RPB. +

1271 _____. "Narragansett survival: a study of group persistence through adopted traits." Ethnohistory, 6 (1959), 347-362.
Narragansett Indians.

1272 BRAMAN, HENRY THEODORE. Reminiscences of men and events of long-ago years in the old South County and elsewhere. n.p., 1930. [52]p. RHi. +

1273 "A BRIEF narrative of that part of New England called the Nanhiganset Country." NHR, 8 (1890), 176-199.
I.e., Narragansett Country. Attributed to Francis Brinley.

1274 [BRIGGS, M. E.] Pettaquamscutt region: legends of the South County, Rhode Island. [Allenton, 1922.] [12]p. RHi. +

1275 CAMPBELL, JACQUELYN. "When is an Indian not an Indian? In South County, it's when he's a Negro." RIer (Feb. 22, 1970), 12-14, 16, 18.
Includes historical information about the county's Narragansett Indian and black populations.

1276 CAMPBELL, PAUL R., and GLENN W. LaFANTASIE. "Scattered to the winds of heaven: Narragansett Indians, 1676-1880." RIH, 37 (1978), 67-83.

1277 CARLSON, ERIC T., and MERIBETH M. SIMPSON. "Tarantism or hysteria? an American case of 1801." Journal of the History of Medicine and Allied Sciences, 26 (1971), 293-302.
Nancy Hazard, of North Kingstown, treated by Drs. Joshua Perry and Joseph Comstock, of South Kingstown.

1278 CARPENTER, ESTHER BERNON. South-County neighbors. Boston: Roberts Brothers, 1887. vii, 272p. RHi. +

1279 _____. South County studies of some eighteenth century persons, places & conditions in that portion of Rhode Island called Narragansett.... Boston: Priv. Print., 1924. xv, 296p. RHi. +

1280 CHANNING, EDWARD. The Narragansett planters: a study of causes. Baltimore: N. Murray, Publication Agent, Johns Hopkins Univ., 1886. 23p. RHi. +

1281 CHAPIN, HOWARD M. "Queen's Fort." RIHSC, 24 (1931), 141-156.
17th-century Indian fortification near the Exeter-North Kingstown line. Site of a battle during King Philip's War.

1282 _____. Sachems of the Narragansetts. Providence: R.I. Historical Society, 1931. 117p. RHi. +

1283 COOK, BENJAMIN LADD. "The Narragansett Pacer." RIY (1965-1966), 56-58.
Breed of horse.

1284 COWAN, WILLIAM. "Narragansett 126 years after." International Journal of American Linguistics, 39 (1973), 7-13.
Changes in the Narragansett Indian language between 1643, when Roger Williams published his Key into the language of America; and 1769, when Ezra Stiles compiled a list of Narragansett words and phrases.

1285 DAVIS, JACK L. "Roger Williams among the Narragansett Indians." NEQ, 43 (1970), 593-604.

1286 DENISON, FREDERIC. Westerly (Rhode Island) and its witnesses, for two hundred and fifty years, 1626-1876. Including Charlestown, Hopkinton, and Richmond, until their separate organization, with the principal points of their subsequent history. Providence: J. A. & R. A. Reid, 1878. 314p. RHi. +

1287 DORR, HENRY C. "The Narragansetts." RIHSC, 7 (1885), 135-237.
Narragansett Indians.

1288 DUNN, RICHARD S. "John Winthrop, Jr., and the Narragansett Country." William and Mary Quarterly, 3 ser. 13 (1956), 68-86.
Conflicting land claims.

1289 EARLE, ALICE MORSE. In old Narragansett: romances and realities. N.Y.: Scribner's, 1898. vii, 196p. RHi. +

1290 _____. "Narragansett Pacers." NEM, n.s. 2 (1890), 39-42.
Breed of horse.

1291 EATON, WALTER PRICHARD. "In old South County." Outing Magazine, 60 (1912), 259-275.

1292 ENRIGHT, ROSEMARY. South County authors: a continuing project of the libraries of the South County Interrelated Library System.... n.p., 1979. Unp. RNoP.
"50 original sketches."

1293 FOLSOM, ALBERT A. "The Duke of Hamilton and Brandon's power of attorney." New-England Historical and Genealogical Register, 45 (1891), 71-74.
Claim to lands in the Narragansett Country.

1294 FOSTER, GEORGE. "The Foster family." NHR, 1 (1883), 222-225.

1295 GOODWIN, DANIEL. "Social life in old Narragansett." Magazine of History, 4 (1906), 166-170, 209-215.
Narragansett Country.

1296 GOULDING, STUART D. "Deep in the Rhode Island forest." Yankee, 33 (Mar. 1969), 42-44, 46, 48.
Queen's Fort, near the Exeter-North Kingstown line, where more than 200 Narragansett Indians were killed in 1676 during King Philip's War.

1297 [HALEY, JOHN WILLIAMS.] Christmas in Narragansett. Providence: "Old Stone Bank," 1930. [10]p. RHi.
"...A holiday season that has long since passed, and that was never equalled in other parts of R.I." This entry and those that follow by the same author were part of the "Old Stone Bank" historical pamphlet series. See note, entry 432.

1298 [_____.] The Narragansetts. Providence: "Old Stone Bank," 1932. 10p. RHi.
Narragansett Indians.

1299 [_____.] Odd characters of old Narragansett. Providence: "Old Stone Bank," 1930. 10p. RHi.
South County eccentrics.

1300 [_____.] Open pages of Narragansett history. Providence: "Old Stone Bank," 1932. 10p. RHi.

1301 [_____.] The Queen's Fort. Providence: "Old Stone Bank," n.d. 9p. RHi.
Indian fort near Exeter-North Kingstown line, the "last stronghold of the Narragansetts" in King Philip's War.

1302 HARRIS, MARY A. "Life in old Narragansett." RIHSC, 19 (1926), 33-36.

1303 HAZARD, CAROLINE. Anchors of tradition: a presentment of some little known facts and persons in a small corner of colonial New England, to which are added certain weavings of fancy from the thread of life upon the loom of time. New Haven, Conn.: Yale Univ. Pr., 1924. viii, 242p. RHi. +

1304 _____. Judge Sewall's gifts in the Narragansett Country. (1898) [Providence: Roger Williams Pr.,] 1936. [16]p. RHi. +
Samuel Sewall's absentee land holdings.

1305 _____. The Narragansett Friends Meeting in the XVIII century, with a chapter on Quaker beginnings in Rhode Island. (1899) Boston: Houghton, Mifflin, 1900. vi, 191p. RHi. +

1306 Washington County

1306 HAZARD, JOSEPH PEACE. "Notes on Narragansett." NHR, 1 (1882-1883), 225-228, 291-300.
Narragansett Country.

1307 _____. "Shipbuilding in Narragansett." NHR, 2 (1883), 61-77.
Record of ships built by Capt. John Aldrich Saunders in various places in Washington County.

1308 HAZARD, THOMAS R. Folklore of the Narragansett Country in Rhode Island: the jonny-cake letters of "Shepherd Tom." 2d ed. Providence: Sidney S. Rider, 1888. 448p. RHi. +

1309 HENWOOD, JAMES N. J. A short haul to the Bay: a history of the Narragansett Pier Railroad. Brattleboro, Vt.: Stephen Greene Pr., 1969. 48p. RHi. +

1310 HINCHLIFFE, EVA. "The Pawcatuck River story." Richmond Historical Society, Richmond History, 1, No. 10 (Dec. 1968), 48-50.

1311 JOY, ROBERT J. T. "The natural bonesetters, with special reference to the Sweet family of Rhode Island." Bulletin of the History of Medicine, 28, No. 5 (1954), 416-441.
South County family. See also entry 1320.

1312 KELLEY, LEONA McELROY. "Early history of South (Washington) County." R.I. Roots, 4, No. 4 (Winter 1978), 1, 3-7.

1313 KENYON, ESTHER L. "Usquepaug." Richmond Historical Society, Richmond History, 1, No. 8 (Oct. 1968), 36-37.
Village in Richmond and South Kingstown.

1314 KNOWLES, HARRY. "Famous farm houses in the Narragansett Country." NEM, n.s. 26 (1902), 387-398.

1315 KOOPMAN, HARRY LYMAN. The Narragansett Country: glimpses of the past....
Providence: Society of Colonial Wars, R.I., 1926. 55p. RHi. +

1316 LAMPHEAR, N. HENRY. "The Providence and New London Turnpike." WHSR (1915-1916), 17-26.

1317 LEES, SIDNEY. "Hunting and trapping." Hopkinton Historical Association, Hopkinton Notes, 2, No. 3 (May 1979), 3-5; No. 4 (July 1979), 1-3.
In Washington County.

1318 LEWIS, NATHAN B. "The last of the Narragansetts." Worcester Society of Antiquity, Collections, 16 (1899), 27-51.
A brief overview of Narragansett Indian history since the 17th century.

1319 LOWNES, ALBERT E. "Cheese making in old South County." RIHSC, 28 (1935), 21-24.
Author published another article under same title in Old-time New England, 27 (1936), 67-69.

1320 McPARTLAND, MARTHA R. "The bonesetter Sweets of South County, Rhode Island." Yankee, 32 (Jan. 1968), 80, 98-101.
Family who practiced the medical art of bonesetting. See also entry 1311.

1321 MASON, GEORGE CHAMPLIN. "Old plantation life in Rhode Island." NEM, n.s. 21 (1899), 735-740.
Narragansett planters.

1322 MILLER, WILLIAM DAVIS. A brief account of the William Withington plat of Boston Neck, with a description of the shares of the proprietors.... Providence: Society of Colonial Wars, R.I., 1924. 29p. RHi. +
1675 plat of part of "alien purchases" in what is now Narragansett and North Kingstown.

1323 _____. "Narragansett." RIHSC, 34 (1941), 44-46.
Historical uses of the name in reference to both the Narragansett Country and the present-day town of Narragansett.

1324 _____. "The Narragansett Pacer." South County (1950), [21-23].
Breed of horse.

1325 _____. The Narragansett planters. Worcester, Mass.: American Antiquarian Society, 1934. 69p. RHi. +
Reprinted from American Antiquarian Society, Proceedings, n.s. 43 (1933), 49-115.

1326 _____. "Volumes from book shelves in old South County." RIHSC, 31 (1938), 8-17.

1327 NATIONAL SOCIETY OF THE COLONIAL DAMES OF AMERICA. RHODE ISLAND. Old houses in the South County of Rhode Island. Providence: The Society, 1932. ix, 68p. RHi. +

1328 PETTAQUAMSCUTT HISTORICAL SOCIETY, KINGSTON. Historic buildings of South County. [Kingston, 1973?] 65p. RHi. +

1329 _____. Ships, sailors and seaports. Kingston, 1963. 51p. RHi. +
Articles about Washington County communities and the sea.

1330 POTTER, ELISHA R., JR. The early history of Narragansett; with an appendix of original documents, many of which are now for the first time published. (1835) 2d ed. Providence: Marshall, Brown, [1886]. xix, 423p. RHi. +
  Reprinted, with 166p. of additional notes, from RIHSC, 3 (1835).

1331 PRINCE, MATLACK. "Narragansett manors." NEM, n.s. 44 (1911), 54-64.
  Domestic architecture.

1332 RANDOLPH, NORRIS. "Only 19 lived." Yankee, 24 (Feb. 1960), 54-57, 88-89, 94-95.
  Wreck of the steamboat Larchmont in Block Island Sound (1907).

1333 RHODE ISLAND. GENERAL ASSEMBLY. HOUSE OF REPRESENTATIVES. Narragansett tribe of Indians: report of the Committee of Investigation; a historical sketch, and evidence taken, made to the House of Representatives, at its January session, A.D. 1880. Providence: E. L. Freeman, 1880. 92p. RHi. +

1334 RIDER, SIDNEY S. "The King's Province." BN, 12 (1895), 265-268.
  In the Narragansett Country; given this designation in 1665.

1335 RIDGEWAY, GEORGE D. "Six miles of fun!" Yankee, 29 (Sept. 1965), 46-48, 50, 52.
  Narragansett Pier Railroad.

1336 SIMMONS, WILLIAM SCRANTON, and GEORGE F. AUBIN. "Narragansett kinship." Man in the Northeast, No. 9 (Spring 1975), 21-31.
  Narragansett Indians.

1337 "THE SIX Principle Baptists in the Narragansett Country." NHR, 1 (1882-1883), 203-208.

1338 SMITH, ELEANOR HOUSE. "Carolina village." Richmond Historical Society, Richmond History, 4, No. 3 (Oct. 1971), 16-17.
  Carolina is in Charlestown and Richmond.

1339 SMITH, HENRY H. "The end of the line." RIer (Oct. 26, 1947), 4-6, 8.
  Wood River Valley Branch Railroad, which ran between Hope Valley and Wood River Junction.

1340 STEDMAN, OLIVER H. A stroll through memory lane: stories of South County's past. West Kingston: Kingston Pr., 1978. 2v. RHi.

1341 _____. Usquepaugh: biography of a New England mill community; the history of the Kenyon Corn Meal Company and a quiet mill village. Usquepaugh: Queen's River Books, 1976. 20p. RHi.
  In Richmond and South Kingstown.

1342 TOOTELL, LUCY RAWLINGS. "Rhode Island's last frontier." South County (1965), 5-11.
  Narragansett Indian history.

1343 [TRUMBULL, JAMES H.] "Lineal and collateral descent of the Narragansett sachems." Massachusetts Historical Society, Collections, 5 ser. 9 (1885), 104-108.

1344 UTTER, GEORGE B. Old "Westerle," Rhode Island: now constituting the towns of Charlestown, Hopkinton, Richmond and Westerly. Rhode Island's jubilee year, 1636-1936. [Westerly:] Westerly Chamber of Commerce, n.d. 55p. RHi. +

1345 WATER power revisited: a circle of dam sites along the Wood and Pawcatuck Rivers. Gladys Segar and Betty Salomon, project directors. n.p., 1980. RHi.

SEE ALSO entries 206, 948.

# Entries for Cities and Towns

## BARRINGTON (BRISTOL CO.)

1346    BARRINGTON, R.I.  CHURCH OF THE HOLY ANGELS.
Golden jubilee and dedication of the new
church.  n.p., [1963?].  [70]p.  RHi.
    Roman Catholic.

1347    BARRINGTON, R.I.  FIRST CONGREGATIONAL
CHURCH.  The articles of faith, the
covenant, and the standing rules of the
Congregational Church, Barrington, R.I.;
with a list of the pastors, officers, and
members of the church.....  (1853) Central
Falls: E. L. Freeman, 1874.  51p.  RHi.
    Thomas Williams Bicknell, comp.  Includes
historical notes.

1348    BARRINGTON, R.I.  SAINT LUKE'S CHURCH.
Saint Luke's Parish, silver jubilee,
1942-1967.  n.p., n.d.  40p.  RHi.
    Roman Catholic.

1349    BARRINGTON BICENTENNIAL COMMITTEE.
Barrington:  two hundredth anniversary.
Robert E. Anderson, Judith A. Hurst, and
Martha F. Patten, eds.  n.p., [1970?].  68p.
RHi.

1350    BICKNELL, THOMAS WILLIAMS.  Barrington
soldiers in the War of the Revolution, the
Dorr War and in the War of the Rebellion.
Providence:  Snow & Farnham, 1898.  109p.
RHi. +

1351    _____.  An historical address and poem,
delivered at the centennial celebration of
the incorporation of the town of Barrington,
June 17, 1870; with an historical appendix.
Providence: Providence Pr., 1870.  192p.
RHi. +

1352    _____.  A history of Barrington, Rhode
Island.  Providence:  Snow & Farnham, 1898.
viii, 620p.  RHi. +

1353    _____.  Sowams:  with ancient records of
Sowams and parts adjacent, illustrated.  New
Haven, Conn.:  Associated Publishers of
American Records, 1908.  vi, 195p.  RHi. +
    Title refers to name of an Indian village,
the site of which has been disputed.  See
index for other references to Sowams.

1354    McLOUGHLIN, WILLIAM G.  "The relevance of
Congregational Christianity:  Barrington
Congregational Church, 1717-1967."  RIH, 29
(1970), 63-81.

1355    OFFICIAL program, 53rd Women's Amateur
Championship of the United States Golf
Association, August 24-29, 1953; Rhode
Island Country Club, West Barrington, Rhode
Island.  n.p., [1953].  63, [103]p.  RHi.
    Includes history of the R.I. Country Club.

1356    RIGGS, DOUGLAS R.  "Still relevant after 75
years."  RIer (Feb. 18, 1968), 24-25, 27-33.
    Saint Andrew's School.

1357    SAINT ANDREW'S SCHOOL, BARRINGTON.  The
story of a vision fulfilled:  St. Andrew's
School.  Barrington:  Board of Trustees,
1930.  29p.  RHi.
    Cover title:  "All my life I shall
remember St. Andrew's."  Includes historical
sketch.

1358    VARE, GLENNA COLLETT.  "A champ recalls an
old battle."  RIer (Aug. 23, 1953), 12, 14.
    1924 women's national golf championship at
R.I. Country Club, Barrington.

1359    WARD, JOHN.  "Barrington's white church:
after 250 years, it's still young."  RIer
(Nov. 12, 1967), 7, 9-12, 14.
    Barrington Congregational Church.

+ Listings in the National Union Catalog for books and pamphlets marked
  with this symbol may include additional library locations.

## BRISTOL (BRISTOL CO.)

1360   AN ACCOUNT of the settlement of the town of Bristol, in the State of Rhode Island, and of the Congregational Church therein, with the succession of pastors, from its origin to the present time; together with the act of incorporation of the Catholic Congregational Society, and the rules established in said society. Providence: Bennett Wheeler, 1785. 16p. RHi.
       Catholic Congregational Church later became First Congregational Church.

1361   ARCHITECTURAL and historical Bristol, Rhode Island. n.p.: [Halladay,] n.d. [12]p. RHi. +

1362   BECK, BUSHNELL PEARCE. "Yankee of 1812." NH, 43 (1970), 1-7.
       Privateer.

1363   THE BOOK of Bristol: published as an official souvenir of the celebration of the 250th anniversary of the settlement of the town, 1680-1930. [Bristol:] Bristol Phoenix Publishing, [1930]. [68]p. RHi. +
       Includes historical sketches.

1364   THE BOOK of Bristol, Rhode Island: published as an official souvenir of the celebration of the 275th anniversary of the settlement of the town. Edward P. Travers, ed. Bristol: Franklin Publishing, 1955. [128]p. RHi.
       Includes historical sketches.

1365   BRISTOL, R.I. CATHOLIC CONGREGATIONAL CHURCH. The Catholic Congregational Church, Bristol, R.I., organized May 3d, 1687. Providence: Hammond, Angell, 1867. 15p. RHi. +
       Became First Congregational Church. Cover title: The church debt paid....

1366   BRISTOL, R.I. FIRST CONGREGATIONAL CHURCH. The Memorial Chapel of the First Congregational Church, Bristol, R.I. Providence: Providence Pr., 1870. 19p. RHi. +

1367   BRISTOL, R.I. OUR LADY OF MOUNT CARMEL CHURCH. 1966, the golden jubilee year: a history of the Church of Our Lady of Mount Carmel, Bristol, Rhode Island. n.p., [1967]. 126p. RHi. +
       Roman Catholic. Italian parish.

1368   BRISTOL, R.I. SAINT ELIZABETH CHURCH. St. Elizabeth Church: golden jubilee, 1913-1964; Bodas de Ouro, Bristol, Rhode-Island, U.S.A. [Bristol, 1964.] [71]p. RBrHi.
       Roman Catholic. Portuguese parish.

1369   BRISTOL, R.I. SAINT MARY'S CHURCH. One hundredth anniversary, St. Mary's Church, Bristol, Rhode Island, May 11, 1869 - May 11, 1969. [Bristol: Franklin Printing, 1969.] [80]p. RPD.
       Roman Catholic. Includes historical sketch by Frederick T. Goff.

1370   BRISTOL PHOENIX (newspaper). The 4th in Bristol, R.I., July 4, 1953. Bristol, 1953. 14, [6]p. RBrHi.
       The town's famous Fourth of July celebrations.

1371   BRISTOL: three hundred years. Susan E. Cirillo, ed. Providence: Franklin Graphics, 1980. 263p. RHi.

1372   BULLOCK, EMMA WESCOTT. "Bombardment of Bristol, Rhode Island." American Monthly Magazine, 1 (1892), 207-211.
       During American Revolution.

1373   BURLEIGH, WILLIAM J. "The houses of Bristol, Rhode Island." Pencil Points, 17 (1936), 335-350, 447-462.

1374   BURNETT, CONSTANCE BUEL. Let the best boat win: the story of America's greatest yacht designer. Boston: Houghton Mifflin, 1957. 266p. RPB. +
       Nathanael Greene Herreshoff.

1375   CARTER, SAMUEL III. The boatbuilders of Bristol: the story of the amazing Herreshoff family of Bristol, Rhode Island--inventors, individualists, yacht designers, and America's Cup defenders. Garden City, N.Y.: Doubleday, 1970. xvii, 215p. RHi. +

1376   _____. "The Herreshoff story." Yankee, 28 (June 1964), 64-70, 109-113.
       See also preceding entry.

1377   "CATHOLIC Congregational Church, Bristol, R.I." Congregational Quarterly, 7 (1865), 236-237.
       Became First Congregational Church.

1378   CELEBRATION of the two-hundredth anniversary of the settlement of the town of Bristol, Rhode Island, September 24th, A.D. 1880. William J. Miller, comp. Providence: Providence Pr., [1881]. viii, 194p. RHi. +

1379   CRANSTON WORSTED MILLS. As the yarn is spun: the story of a lively experiment. Bristol, 1927. 31p. RBrHi.
       Includes brief history of the company in Bristol.

1380 DEMOS, JOHN. "Families in colonial Bristol, Rhode Island: an exercise in historical demography." William and Mary Quarterly, 3 ser. 25 (1968), 40-57.

1381 DIMAN, J. LEWIS. The settlement of Mount Hope: an address delivered September 24, 1880. n.p., n.d. 23p. RHi. +

1382 DOW, JOY WHEELER. "The Bristol renaissance." White Pine Series of Architectural Monographs, 3 (Oct. 1917), 3-13.
      Early-19th-century architecture. See also his article of same title in House Beautiful, 10 (1901), 263-270.

1383 DeWOLF, LOUISE HENRY. "A boy's will is the wind's will." RIY (1969), 93-95.
      John Brown Herreshoff, yacht-builder.

1384 EDELSTEIN, ELEANOR ROCKWELL. A casual history of Point Pleasant Farm in Bristol, Rhode Island. [Los Angeles: Wm. M. Cheney, 1963.] 21p. RHi.

1385 [HALEY, JOHN WILLIAMS.] Captain John DeWolf. Providence: "Old Stone Bank," n.d. 10p. RHi.
      Bristol sea captain (19th century). This entry and those that follow by the same author were part of the "Old Stone Bank" historical pamphlet series. See note, entry 432.

1386 _____. "King Philip of Mount Hope." BrAlumMo, 56 (Feb. 1956), 5-7.

1387 _____. "Mount Hope." Daughters of the American Revolution Magazine, 71 (1937), 198-200.

1388 _____. Mount Hope: a radio address...Station WJAR, Providence, Wednesday, May 29, 1946, 7:30 p.m. Bristol: Haffenreffer family, n.d. 14p. RHi.

1389 [_____.] Origin of "Mount Hope." Providence: "Old Stone Bank," 1932. 10p. RHi.

1390 [_____.] Original proprietors of Bristol. Providence: "Old Stone Bank," 1930. 10p. RHi.

1391 HERRESHOFF, JEANETTE BROWN. The early founding and development of the Herreshoff Manufacturing Company. Tampa, Fla.: Rinaldi Printing, 1949. [47]p. RHi. +
      Yacht builders.

1392 HERRESHOFF, LEWIS FRANCIS. Capt. Nat Herreshoff, the wizard of Bristol: the life and achievements of Nathanael Greene Herreshoff, together with an account of some of the yachts he designed. N.Y.: Sheridan House, 1953. 349p. RHi. +
      Herreshoff Mfg. Co.

1393 _____. Nathanael Greene Herreshoff, 1848-1938: a life and an appreciation of his work.... Hartford, Conn., 1944. 31p. RHi. +

1394 HERRESHOFF MANUFACTURING COMPANY. Herreshoff yachts. Providence: Haley & Sykes, n.d. 58p. RHi.
      Includes historical sketch to ca. 1930.

1395 HOWE, GEORGE. "The Bristol story." RIY (1967), 51-61.

1396 _____. "The glorious Fourth, Bristol fashion: the Bristol story, part II." RIY (1968), 25-33.
      Fourth of July celebrations.

1397 _____. Mount Hope: a New England chronicle. N.Y.: Viking Pr., 1959. viii, 312p. RHi. +

1398 _____. "There's never been a Fourth like Bristol's." RIer (Feb. 15, 1959), 14-16.
      Fourth of July celebrations.

1399 HOWE, GEORGE LOCKE. "A love letter to Bristol." RIer (Dec. 2, 1951), 12-15.

1400 HOWE, MARK ANTONY DeWOLFE. Bristol, Rhode Island: a town biography. Cambridge, Mass.: Harvard Univ. Pr., 1930. 172p. RHi. +

1401 HUBBARD, H. G. A historical discourse, delivered on the fiftieth anniversary of the First Baptist Church, in Bristol, R.I. Providence: A. Crawford Greene, 1861. 18p. RHi. +

1402 HYDRAULION ENGINE & HOSE COMPANY, NO. 1, BRISTOL. 100th anniversary program of the Hydraulion Engine & Hose Co., No. 1, Bristol, R.I., July 22, 1943; organized July 22, 1843. [Bristol: Phoenix Print, 1943.] [24]p. RBrHi.
      Fire co.

1403 KNOWLES, HARRY. "Bristol and the land of Pokanoket." NEM, n.s. 35 (1907), 609-628.

1404 KNOWLTON, JOSEPHINE GIBSON. Longfield: the house on the Neck. (1856) 3d ed. Providence: Oxford Pr., 1956. 366p. RHi. +

1405 Bristol

1405 LANE, JAMES PILLSBURY. Historical sketches
of the First Congregational Church, Bristol,
R.I., 1687-1872. Providence: Providence
Pr., 1872. 126p. RHi. +
This history also appeared in the church
Manual (1873).

1406 LARNED, ALBERT CECIL. Two hundred years of
St. Michael's rectors, 1721-1955....
Bristol: Bristol Phoenix Publishing, 1957.
84p. RHi.
Episcopal.

1407 MacDONALD, W. A. "Bristol's quaintness
charms the visitor." PM, 30 (1918),
299-304.
Includes historical sketch.

1408 MANCHESTER, ANNA B. "Old Bristol."
American Monthly Magazine, 3 (1893),
247-255.

1409 [MIDDLETON, ALICIA HOPTON.] Life in
Carolina and New England during the
nineteenth century: as illustrated by
reminiscences and letters of the Middleton
family of Charleston, South Carolina, and
the DeWolf family of Bristol, Rhode Island.
Bristol: Priv. Print., 1929. xii, 233p.
RHi. +

1410 MILLER, WILLIAM J. "Mr. Miller's historical
narrative." RIHSPr (1876-1877), 56-60.
Death of King Philip (1676).

1411 MINER, LILIAN BURLEIGH. "Old homes of
Bristol, Rhode Island." House Beautiful, 46
(1919), 218-220.

1412 MOONEY, ELIZABETH C. "The house on Hope
Street." Yankee, 39 (Jan. 1975), 64, 66-67,
140-141.
Linden Place, built for General George
DeWolf in 1810.

1413 MUNRO, WILFRED HAROLD. Address at the
laying of the cornerstone of the Guiteras
Memorial School, Bristol, R.I., Dec. 20,
1925. n.p., n.d. [9]p. RHi.
Brief history of Bristol schools.

1414 _____. The history of Bristol, R.I: The
story of the Mount Hope lands, from the
visit of the Northmen to the present time;
containing accounts of the Indian wars, the
character and lives of the early settlers in
Bristol, the events of the Revolution, the
privateers of the War of 1812, details of
the commerce of the port, and sketches of
its distinguished men. Providence:
J. A. & R. A. Reid, 1880. 396p. RHi. +

1415 _____. The most successful American
privateer: an episode of the War of 1812.
Worcester, Mass.: American Antiquarian
Society, 1913. 53p. RHi. +
The Yankee, of Bristol.

1416 _____. Some legends of "Mount Hope." n.p.:
George D. Flynn, R. F. Haffenreffer, Jr.,
1915. 61p. RHi. +

1417 _____. Tales of an old sea port: a general
sketch of the history of Bristol, Rhode
Island, including, incidentally, an account
of the voyages of the Norsemen...and
personal narratives of some notable voyages
accomplished by sailors from the Mount Hope
lands. Princeton, N.J.: Princeton Univ.
Pr., 1917. 292p. RHi. +

1418 NELSON, EVERETT B. "Roger Williams College:
history of a 'lively experiment.'" RIY
(1971), 38-42.

1419 PALMER, HENRY ROBINSON. "The Herreshoffs
and their boats." NEM, n.s. 12 (1895),
515-532.
Yacht-builders.

1420 PARDEE, ALICE DeWOLF. Blithewold: Bristol,
Rhode Island. n.p., 1978. 160p. RHi. +
Historic house and grounds.

1421 PRESTON, HOWARD WILLIS. "Point Pleasant:
William Vassall's confiscated estate."
RIHSC, 18 (1925), 1-8.
Loyalist.

1422 RHODE Island tercentenary, town of Bristol,
1636-1936. [Bristol: Phoenix Print, 1936.]
[23]p. RHi.
Includes "An ethnic history of Bristol."

1423 RICHMOND, WILLIAM E. Mount Hope: an
evening excursion. Providence: Miller and
Hutchens, 1818. 69p. RHi.
Early history, partly in verse.

1424 RUSSELL Warren in Bristol: one man's
legacy. Bristol: Roger Williams College,
1980. 24p. RHi.
Architect.

1425 SCOTT, KENNETH. "The privateer Yankee in
the War of 1812." American Neptune, 21
(1961), 16-22.

1426 SHEPARD, THOMAS. Two discourses,
by...pastor of the Catholic Congregational
Church, in Bristol, R.I. Providence:
Sayles, Miller & Simmons, 1857. 55p.
RHi. +
History of the church. Name later changed
to First Congregational Church.

1427 SOCIETY OF COLONIAL WARS. RHODE ISLAND.
A letter from Major William Bradford to the
Reverend John Cotton, written at Mount Hope
on July 21, 1675, and containing an account
of the operations leading up to an
unsuccessful attempt to capture Metacom
alias King Philip the Wampanoag chieftan.
Reproduced in facsimile and published for
the first time from the original document
preserved in the John Carter Brown
Library.... Providence, 1914. 16p. RHi. +
  Includes historical introduction.

1428 THOMAS, RAYMOND A. Two hundred years of the
Bristol Train of Artillery, Rhode Island
Militia (1776-1976). n.p., 1976. 98p.
RHi.

1429 THOMPSON, CHARLES O. F. Sketches of old
Bristol. Providence: Roger Williams Pr.,
1942. xiii, 418p. RHi. +

1430 TOMAS, MARJORIE S. "The Haffenreffer
Museum." RIY (1968), 77-81.
  Haffenreffer Museum of Anthropology.

1431 TROTTER, WILLIAM R. History of the choir of
Trinity Church, Bristol, R.I., 1875-1900.
Bristol: Pr. of the Semi-weekly Phoenix,
1900. 18p. RHi.
  Episcopal.

1432 WESTON, FRANK. "A historic mansion and
modern home." RIY (1964-1965), 76-79.
  "Linden Place," designed by Russell
Warren for General George DeWolf.

  SEE ALSO entries 433, 476, 478, 554, 675,
763, 1153.

## BURRILLVILLE (PROVIDENCE CO.)

1433 BARNES, HARRY LEE. "The Wallum Pond
estates." RIHSC, 15 (1922), 33-55, 77-93,
109-128; 16 (1923),21-31.
  Also published separately.

1434 BLEIWEIS, LOUIS. Austin T. Levy.
Cambridge, Mass.: Riverside Pr., 1953.
89p. RHi.
  Local textile manufacturer, writer on
economic subjects, Republican candidate for
U.S. Senate in 1950.

1435 FITZ, WILLIAM. An historical sketch of the
public schools of Burrillville. Providence:
Providence Pr., 1876. 32p. RHi. +

1436 GREENE, SHIRLEY. "Churches of
Burrillville." WRICHSH, 12 (Oct. 1968),
[2].

1437 KEACH, HORACE A. Burrillville: as it was,
and as it is. Providence: Knowles,
Anthony, 1856. x, 170p. RHi. +

1438 LAPHAM, LEAH INMAN. "Burrillville's town
meeting house." WRICHSP, 2, No. 2 (1955),
[14-17].

1439 MAPLEVILLE, R.I. OUR LADY OF GOOD HELP
CHURCH. Our Lady of Good Help, Mapleville,
Rhode Island: 75th anniversary, 1905-1980.
n.p., [1980]. 64p. RG1.
  Roman Catholic.

1440 _____. Tenth anniversary of Our Lady of
Good Help, Mapleville, R.I., Sunday,
September 5th, 1915. n.p., [1915]. [12]p.
RPD.
  Roman Catholic. Text mostly in French.

1441 NASONVILLE, R.I. SHRINE OF THE LITTLE
FLOWER. Tenth anniversary, 1923-1933,
Shrine of the Little Flower, Nasonville,
Rhode Island, Sunday, September 24, 1933.
n.p., [1933]. [69]p. RWoU. +
  Roman Catholic. Text in English and
French.

1442 O'BRIEN, WILLIAM B. "Counterfeiters of
Wallum Lake." WRICHSP, 2, No. 2 (1955),
[18-20].

1443 PASCOAG HERALD (newspaper). Souvenir
historical number (June 1894). 8, 28p.
DLC. +

1444 RHODE ISLAND. HISTORICAL PRESERVATION
COMMISSION. Historic and architectural
resources of Burrillville, Rhode Island:
a preliminary report. Providence, 1982.
ii, 86p. RHi.
  Author: Walter Nebiker.

1445 RHODE ISLAND. STATE SANATORIUM, WALLUM
LAKE. Rhode Island State Sanatorium: forty
eventful years, 1905-1945. [Providence,
1945.] 84p. RHi. +

1446 RIDER, SIDNEY S. "The history of Wallum
Pond, or Lake, in Burrillville, R.I." BN,
26 (1909), 145-148.

1447 _____. "Pascoag." BN, 13 (1896), 36-39.
  Origin of the place name.

1448 RYAN, THOMAS E. Burrillville, R.I., and the
Catholic Church: a historical sketch.
[Providence: Remington Pr., 1925.] 168p.
RHi. +

1449 WEIS, ROBERT LEWIS. A history of the First
Universalist Church of Burrillville, Rhode
Island. Harrisville, 1944. 56p. RBuH.

## CENTRAL FALLS (PROVIDENCE CO.)

1450 ADDRESSES and poem in commemoration of the Captain Michael Pierce fight, March 26, 1676.... Memorial services at Central Falls, Rhode Island, October 15, 1904. Dedication of monument, September 21, 1907. Thomas Williams Bicknell, ed. n.p., 1908. 41p. RPB. +
   During King Philip's War. The exact site of the fight has been a subject of some debate. See index for other entries concerning Pierce's Fight.

1451 CENTRAL FALLS, R.I. "Friends and neighbors"; "a solid mile of solid citizens": souvenir program, issued upon the occasion of the diamond jubilee celebration, Central Falls, R.I., September 20th to 27th 1970. n.p., [1970?]. [168]p. RHi.
   Includes "History of Central Falls," by Thomas J. Curley.

1452 _____. Reference book of the city of Central Falls, R.I., containing a brief historical sketch of the city, the city charter, government, committees and officials.... Central Falls: E. L. Freeman, 1895. 95p. RHi. +

1453 CENTRAL FALLS, R.I. BAPTIST CHURCH. Faith and covenant of the Central Falls Baptist Church, Central Falls, R.I., with a list of present members. Pawtucket: R. Sherman, 1868. 16p. RHi.
   Includes historical sketch.

1454 CENTRAL FALLS, R.I. BROAD STREET BAPTIST CHURCH. Historical sketch, covenant, articles of faith, and rules of order.... Central Falls, 1894. 12p. RPB. +

1455 CENTRAL FALLS, R.I. CHURCH OF SAINT BASIL THE GREAT. Church of St. Basil the Great, Central Falls, Rhode Island: dedication, October 26, 1975. n.p., 1975. [158]p. RPD.
   Melkite Greek Catholic Church. This parish was established in 1908 for Syrian immigrants in Central Falls. Book includes historical sketch of the parish and of the Melkites in America.

1456 CENTRAL FALLS, R.I. CONGREGATIONAL CHURCH. The articles of faith, covenant, and standing rules of the Congregational Church, Central Falls, with a brief history of the church, and a roll of its membership. (1876) Central Falls, 1888. 35p. RHi.

1457 _____. Confession and covenant...with a brief history of the church and list of members. Central Falls, 1871. 24p. RHi. +

1458 _____. Jubilee celebration of the Congregational Church, Central Falls, R.I., June sixteenth and eighteenth, 1895. Central Falls: E. L. Freeman, [1895]. 115p. RHi.

1459 _____. Manual...containing a brief history...with a list of officers and members. Central Falls, 1896. 60p. RPB. +

1460 CENTRAL FALLS, R.I. HOLY TRINITY CHURCH. Souvenir of the Parish of the Holy Trinity, Central Falls, R.I., published on the occasion of the dedication of the convent and school...October 29, 1905. n.p., n.d. 27p. RP.
   Roman Catholic.

1461 CENTRAL FALLS, R.I. [NOTRE DAME CHURCH.] Dédicace de la nouvelle église de Notre-Dame du Sacré-Coeur, Central Falls, R.I., Dimanche, le 15 octobre à 10.30 heures. Central Falls: U. S. Sabourin, 1933. [69]p. RWoU.
   Roman Catholic. French parish. Includes historical sketch. Text in French.

1462 _____. Notre Dame Church, Central Falls, Rhode Island. South Hackensack, N.J.: Custombook, 1974. 25, [11]p. RHi.

1463 CENTRAL FALLS, R.I. SAINT JOSEPH'S CHURCH. ...In commemoration of the golden jubilee of St. Joseph's Parish, Central Falls, R.I. n.p., 1957. [208]p. RPa. +
   Roman Catholic. Text in English and Polish.

1464 CENTRAL FALLS, R.I. [SAINT MATTHEW'S CHURCH.] Le cinquintenaire sacerdotal de Mgr. Joseph-Alfred Laliberté, prélat de sa sainteté curé-fondateur de la Paroisse de Saint-Mathieu de Central-Falls Rhode Island, Dimanche, le 27 avril, 1941; trente-cinquième année de fondation. [Central Falls: U.S. Sabourin, 1941.] 63p. RCe.
   Roman Catholic. French parish. Text in French.

1465 _____. Program-souvenir des fêtes du jubilé d'or de la Paroisse Saint-Mathieu, Central Falls, Rhode Island, 1906-1956. n.p., n.d. [85]p. RWoU.
   Includes brief historical sketch. Text in French.

1466 _____. St. Matthew's Church, Central Falls, Rhode Island, 1906-1981; and a history of Catholic America. South Hackensack, N.J.: Custombook, 1981. 20, [68]p. RWoU.

1467    CENTRAL FALLS POLICE RELIEF ASSOCIATION.
        History of Central Falls Police Department.
        (1935) Central Falls, 1954. 128p. RCe.
            Cover title:  50th anniversary Central
        Falls annual policeman's ball.

1468    GRIMES, J. CLEMENT.  "Growing up in Central
        Falls." RIer (Aug. 20, 1972), 6-11.
            1920s.

1469    McGUIRE, JOHN P.  History of Holy Trinity
        Parish, Central Falls, Rhode Island. n.p.,
        1939. 93, [25]p. RHi.
            Roman Catholic.

1470    RHODE ISLAND.  HISTORICAL PRESERVATION
        COMMISSION.  Central Falls, Rhode Island:
        statewide historical preservation report
        P-CF-1. [Providence], 1978. vi, 78p.
        RHi. +
            Author:  Pamela A. Kennedy.

1471    SACRED HEART ACADEMY, CENTRAL FALLS.
        ...Golden jubilee, 1959. n.p., n.d.  [87]p.
        RWoU.
            Text in French and English.

1472    WALDEN, GEORGE F.  "Pierce's Fight."  RIY
        (1974), 18-22.
            During King Philip's War (1676).

        SEE ALSO entries 554, 601, 1240, 1242, 1246,
        1249, 2598.


## CHARLESTOWN (WASHINGTON CO.)

1473    BOISSEVAIN, ETHEL, and RALPH ROBERTS III.
        "The minutes and ledgers of the Narragansett
        tribe of Indians, 1850-1865: an intimate
        glimpse into the economic and social life of
        an acculturated Indian tribe on the
        threshold of detribalization." Man in the
        Northeast, No. 7 (Spring 1974), 3-27.

1474    BRADNER, LEICESTER.  "Ninigret's Fort:  a
        refutation of the Dutch theory."  RIHSC, 14
        (1921), 1-5.
            Attributes early fort in Charlestown to
        Niantic Indians, rather than Dutch traders.
        See also entries 1478-1479.

1475    CAROLINA, R.I.  SAINT MARY'S CHURCH.  Saint
        Mary's, Carolina, Rhode Island.  South
        Hackensack, N.J.: Custombook, 1972. 24p.
        RPD.
            Roman Catholic.

1476    CHARLESTOWN BICENTENNIAL BOOK COMMITTEE.
        Reflections of Charlestown, Rhode Island,
        1876-1976: a memorial to the bicentennial
        celebration of the United States of America.
        Westerly: Utter, 1976. xi, 154p. RHi. +

1477    FISH, JOSEPH.  Old light on separate ways:
        the Narragansett diary of Joseph Fish,
        1765-1776.  William Scranton Simmons and
        Cheryl L. Simmons, eds.  Hanover, N.H.:
        Univ. Pr. of New England, 1982.  188p.
        RHi. +
            Missionary to Narragansett Indians in
        Charlestown.

1478    GOODWIN, WILLIAM B.  "Notes regarding the
        origin of Fort Ninigret in the Niantic
        country at Charlestown." RIHSC, 25 (1932),
        1-16.
            See also entries 1474, 1479.

1479    [HALEY, JOHN WILLIAMS.]  Fort Ninigret.
        Providence: "Old Stone Bank," 1932. 10p.
        RHi.
            Supports the theory that the fort was
        built by Dutch traders.  See also entries
        1474, 1478.  This entry was part of the "Old
        Stone Bank" historical pamphlet series.  See
        note, entry 432.

1480    MANDEVILLE, FRANCES WHARTON.  The historical
        story of Charlestown, Rhode Island.
        [Charlestown:]  Charlestown Historical
        Society, 1979. ix, 84p. RHi.

1481    RHODE ISLAND.  COMMISSION ON THE AFFAIRS OF
        THE NARRAGANSETT INDIANS.  Fourth annual
        report of the Commission on the Affairs of
        the Narragansett Indians, made to the
        General Assembly at its January session,
        1884. Providence: E. L. Freeman, 1884.
        35p. RHi.
            Includes addresses at the dedication of
        the memorial boulder at Fort Ninigret, 1883.

1482    RHODE ISLAND.  HISTORICAL PRESERVATION
        COMMISSION.  Preliminary survey report:
        town of Charlestown.  Providence, 1981. ii,
        57p. RHi. +
            Author:  Walter Nebiker.

1483    SHINN, RIDGWAY F., JR.  "An arithmetic
        workbook of 1827-1828 as a source for Rhode
        Island social history." RIH, 25 (1966),
        43-50.
            Belonged to Reynolds C. Crandall, of
        Charlestown.

1484    TUCKER, WILLIAM FRANKLIN.  Historical sketch
        of the town of Charlestown, in Rhode Island,
        1636 to 1876.  Westerly: G. B. & J. H.
        Utter, 1877. 88p. RHi. +

        SEE ALSO entries 1266, 1268-1271, 1276,
        1286, 1318, 1333, 1336, 1344, 3763.

## COVENTRY (KENT CO.)

1485 ARNOLD, AGNES A. "Said to be built." WRICHSH, 11 (June 1968), [2]; (July 1968), [1-2].
History of the Paine House, home of the Western R.I. Civic Historical Society.

1486 ____. "When Greene was younger." WRICHSH, 15 (Apr. 1972), [2]; (May 1972), [2].
Village of Greene.

1487 ARNOLD, HENRY N. "Arnold Spring Rock Shelter." Narragansett Archaeological Society of R.I., Reports (Jan. 1969), 1-4.
Indian site.

1488 BARBOUR, ARDIS W. "Coventry, our town, 1741-1941." WRICHSP, 1, No. 3 (1950), 11-21.
Includes brief historical sketches of Coventry's villages.

1489 BATES, FRANK G. "Incomplete notes on Washington Village." WRICHSH, 3 (Mar. 1960), [2].

1490 ____. "Recollections of olden times." WRICHSH, 3 (Oct. 1959), [2]; (Mar. 1960) [2].
Elder Stone Meetinghouse Neighborhood.

1491 BRANT, ROSA E. Historical sketch of the Quidnick Baptist Church, Quidnick, R.I., prepared...for the centennial celebration, February 1951. n.p., n.d. [10]p. RHi.

1492 BRIGGS, FRANK J. "Smallpox in Coventry." WRICHSH, No. 1 (June 1957), [2].

1493 CHAMPLIN, RICHARD L. "Cranberries galore." RIY (1971), 70-71.
Coventry Cranberry Company.

1494 COVENTRY, R.I. CHURCH OF OUR LADY OF CZENSTOCHOWA. Our Lady of Czenstochowa, Coventry, Rhode Island. South Hackensack, N.J.: Custombook, 1981. 35, [41]p. RPD-H.
Roman Catholic. Polish parish.

1495 ____. ...Souvenir of the golden jubilee of Our Lady of Czenstochowa Parish, Quidnick, Rhode Island, 1907-1957. n.p., n.d. 124p. RPD-H.
Text in Polish and English.

1496 COVENTRY PUBLIC LIBRARY. Reflections of Coventry's yesterdays (1741-1900). Coventry, 1976. 34p. RCo.

1497 FOWLER, WILLIAM S. "Archaic discoveries at Flat River." Narragansett Archaeological Society of R.I., [Reports] (Jan. 1968), 17-36.
Indian site.

1498 ____. "Discoveries at Wilcox Brook Site." Narragansett Archaeological Society of R.I., Report (Oct. 1974), 1-8.
Indian site.

1499 ____. "Early archaics at the Bluff Site." Narragansett Archaeological Society of R.I., Report (Oct. 1971-Jan. 1972), 1-10.
Indian site.

1500 FREEMASONS. COVENTRY. MANCHESTER LODGE, NO. 12. Manchester Lodge, No. 12, Free and Accepted Masons of Coventry, R.I.: one hundredth anniversary, November 29 and 30, 5908. Central Falls: E. L. Freeman, 1910. 55p. RHi.

1501 [HALEY, JOHN WILLIAMS.] The legend of Carbuncle Pond. Providence: "Old Stone Bank," 1931. 10p. RHi.
This entry was part of the "Old Stone Bank" historical pamphlet series. See note, entry 432.

1502 HARPIN, MATHIAS P. Prophets in the wilderness: a history of Coventry, Rhode Island. Volume 1 of two volumes. Oneco, Conn.: Harpin's Connecticut Almanac, 1974. 182p. RHi. +

1503 "HOPKINS Hollow and Roaring Brook." WRICHSH, 9 (June 1966), [1-2]; (July 1966), [2].

1504 PLACE, JOHN W. "The McGregor District (land of the carbuncle)." WRICHSP, 2, No. 1 (1953), [20-26].

1505 ____. "Speech of John W. Place, rededication of Rice City Christian Church." R.I. Roots, 6 (1980), 35-39.

1506 RHODE ISLAND. HISTORICAL PRESERVATION COMMISSION. Preliminary survey report: town of Coventry. Providence, 1978. iv, 57p. RHi.
Author: Vivienne F. Laskey.

1507 "RHODE Island's historic Mount Vernon." PM, 32 (1920), 123-124, 126.
Nathanael Greene Homestead, where the future Revolutionary War general moved from Warwick in 1770.

1508 SALISBURY, VIRGINIA GREENE. Christ Church, Coventry, Rhode Island, 1917-1957. n.p., [1957]. 23p. RHi.
Episcopal.

1509 "THE STORY of the counterfeiters." WRICHSP, 2, No. 1 (1953), [17-19].
19th century.

1510 225th anniversary celebration, 1741-1966: souvenir booklet, Coventry, R.I. np., n.d. [18]p. RHi.

1511 WASHINGTON, R.I. CHRISTIAN UNION CHURCH. A sketch of the organization, together with the articles of faith, covenant, address, general principles and rules, adopted by the Christian Union Church at Washington Village, Coventry, R.I. Providence: J. Flagg Carr, 1858. 16p. RHi.
Nondenominational.

1512 WOOD, SQUIRE GREENE. A history of Greene and vicinity, 1845-1929. Providence: Priv. Print., 1926. 101p. RHi. +

SEE ALSO entries 341, 418, 1157.

## CRANSTON (PROVIDENCE CO.)

1513 ANDREWS, ELLIOTT E., and HENRY H. SMITH. "Drag strip for horseless carriages." RIer (Dec. 2, 1956), 12-14.
Early auto racing at Narragansett Park.

1514 BOWSHER, PRENTICE. "Garden City: it went according to plan." RIer (Oct. 3, 1965), 17-21.
Post-World War II development.

1515 BRAYTON, GLADYS W. "Arlington District Hall." CHSN [Feb. 1980, 3-6].

1516 _____. "Arlington Public Library." CHSN [Nov. 1974].

1517 _____. "Auburn's Church of the Ascension." CHSN [Dec. 1976].
Episcopal.

1518 _____. "The Cranston story." RIY (1963), 55-67.

1519 _____. "Cranston's cycledrome." CHSN [Dec. 1977].
Bicycle racing, ca. 1920s.

1520 _____. "Cranston's theatres." CHSN (June 1970).

1521 _____. "Early welfare and Cranston's town poor farm." CHSN (Feb. 1973).

1522 _____. "The fate of a village's schools." CHSN (Sept. 1971).
Oaklawn.

1523 _____. "Following the trail." CHSN [Mar. 1980, 3-6].
Local history in street names.

1524 _____. "Friends' Meeting House, Cranston's first church." CHSN [Nov. 1976].

1525 _____. "If only a house could talk." CHSN [May 1977].
Benjamin Brayton house.

1526 _____. "A mile of memories." CHSN [June 1977].
Places and events associated with "a winding country road in the western part of Cranston."

1527 _____. "Milestones of progress and change." CHSN [Jan. 1978].
"Firsts" in the town's history.

1528 _____. "'The mill by the side of the road.'" CHSN [Oct. 1976].

1529 _____. Other ways and other days. East Providence: Globe Printing, [1975]. 176p. RHi. +
Collection of brief articles on many phases of life in Cranston and R.I., previously published in Cranston Historical Society Newsletter. Articles by this author that were not included in Other ways and other days are cited individually in this bibliography.

1530 _____. "Pawtuxet Baptist Church." CHSN (Apr. 1970).

1531 _____. "Rhode Island State Fair days at Narragansett Park." CHSN [Oct. 1977].

1532 _____. "St. Bartholomew's Church." CHSN (Dec. 1970).
Episcopal.

1533 _____. "Signs of the times in Arlington." CHSN [Apr. 1980, 4-7].
History of street names in a part of Cranston.

1534 _____. "What's in a name?" CHSN [Mar. 1977].
Place names in Cranston.

1535 _____. "Wrestling with change in the gay nineties." CHSN [Nov. 1977].
Social change.

1536 BURNHAM, CHRISTIE W. Historical sketch of the Pawtuxet Baptist Church, from its organization, Nov. 17, 1806, to Sept. 1, 1890. n.p., n.d. 8p. RHi. +

1537 CLAUSON, JAMES EARL. Cranston: a historical sketch. Providence: T. S. Hammond, 1904. 52p. RHi. +

1538 CRANSTON, R.I. CHURCH OF THE ANNUNCIATION. Church of the Annunciation: 75th anniversary celebration. [Providence,] 1981. 279, [4]p. RHi.
   Greek Orthodox church, originally located in Providence.

1539 CRANSTON, R.I. FRANKLIN CONGREGATIONAL CHURCH. Manual of the Franklin Congregational Church, Pettaconset, Cranston, R.I., organized September 26, 1873. Providence: Providence Pr., 1875. 15p. RHi.
   Includes historical sketch.

1540 CRANSTON, R.I. KNIGHTSVILLE CONGREGATIONAL CHURCH. Knightsville Congregational Church, 1928-1938. n.p., n.d. 6p. RHi.

1541 _____. The Knightsville Meetinghouse, with a story of the Sunday school that was founded in 1864. Cranston, 1927. 22p. RPB. +

1542 CRANSTON, R.I. SAINT PAUL'S CHURCH. 50th anniversary, St. Paul's Church, Cranston, Rhode Island, 1929-1979. n.p., 1979. 52p. RHi.
   Roman Catholic.

1543 CRANSTON BICENTENNIAL COMMITTEE. Cranston bicentennial, 1754-1954...celebrating 200 years of progress. Official souvenir book. [Cranston, 1954.] 76p. RHi. +

1544 GOLDEN, JANET, and ERIC C. SCHNEIDER. "Custody and control: the Rhode Island State Hospital for Mental Diseases, 1870-1970." RIH, 41 (1982), 113-125.

1545 [HALEY, JOHN WILLIAMS.] Early Cranston. Providence: "Old Stone Bank," 1933. 10p. RHi.
   This and the next entry were part of the "Old Stone Bank" historical pamphlet series. See note, entry 432.

1546 [_____.] Who killed Amasa Sprague? Providence: "Old Stone Bank," 1932. 10p. RHi.
   1843 murder of the Cranston businessman and manufacturer, for which John Gordon, an Irish immigrant, was convicted on circumstantial evidence and executed--the last execution in the state.

1547 JONES, HENRY AARON. The dark days of social welfare at the state institutions at Howard, Rhode Island. [Providence:] Dept. of Social Welfare, [1943?]. 87p. RHi. +

1548 JOYCE, WILLIAM L. "The first race, and other automobilia." RIer (Oct 8, 1972), 23-24, 26.
   Reputedly the first automobile race in America (1896).

1549 McCARTHY, LAWRENCE T. "'Poosha' Madonna is now a pizza pusher." RIer (Oct. 30, 1955), 8-10, 12.
   Bicycle racing in the Cranston Open Air Cycledrome (1920s).

1550 OAK LAWN, R.I. BAPTIST CHURCH. LADIES' UNION SOCIETY. Mashanticut: a souvenir issued by the Ladies' Union Society of Oak Lawn, R.I., on the anniversary of their twenty-fifth May breakfast, May 2, 1892. Providence: Snow & Farnham, 1892. 68p. RHi. +
   Includes history of Friends' Meeting House and the Oak Lawn Baptist Church.

1551 PHENIX NATIONAL BANK. ..."The attraction of opposites." [Providence,] 1945. 10p. RHi.
   Universal Winding Co., manufacturer of Universal Winding Machine. This entry was part of the Romance of R.I. Industry pamphlet series. See note, entry 768.

1552 RHODE ISLAND. HISTORICAL PRESERVATION COMMISSION. Cranston, Rhode Island: statewide historical preservation report P-C-1. Providence, 1980. vi, 81p. RHi.
   Author: Robert Eliot Freeman.

1553 THORNTON, R.I. SAINT ROCCO'S CHURCH. 50th anniversary, 1903-1953: Saint Rocco's Church, Thornton, R.I. n.p., [1953]. 17p. RPD.
   Roman Catholic. Italian parish.

1554 WADDICOR, ARTHUR. "Church Brook Rock Shelter No. 1." Narragansett Archaeological Society of R.I., Report (Jan. 1969), 10-15.
   Indian site.

1555 _____, and MORRIS MITCHELL. "Furnace Brook Site: a salvage dig." Narragansett Archaeological Society of R.I., Report (Jan. 1969), 4-10.
   Indian site.

1556 WYSS, BOB. "'They did not know what they were doing.'" RIer (July 19, 1981), 24-26.
   1845 execution of John Gordon for the murder of Amasa Sprague--the last execution in the state.

SEE ALSO entries 68, 70, 95, 355, 576, 637, 764, 785, 839, 1231-1232.

## CUMBERLAND (PROVIDENCE CO.)

1557 BLACKSTONE MONUMENT ASSOCIATION. An address delivered at the formation of the Blackstone Monument Association, together with the preliminaries and proceedings at Study Hill, July 4, 1855. Pawtucket: James L. Estey, 1855. 39p. RP. +
Rev. William Blackstone, first white settler in the area.

1558 [CUMBERLAND, R.I. OUR LADY OF FATIMA CHURCH.] [Commemorative book.] n.p., [1978?]. 99p. RHi.
Roman Catholic. Portuguese parish. Text in English and Portuguese.

1559 CUMBERLAND, R.I. SAINT JOAN'S CHURCH. St. Joan's Church, Cumberland Hill, Rhode Island, and a history of Catholic America. South Hackensack, N.J.: Custombook, 1980. 48, [68]p. RP.
Roman Catholic.

1560 CUMBERLAND, R.I. SAINT JOHN BAPTIST MARY VIANNEY CHURCH. Solemn dedication, Saint John Vianney Church, Cumberland, Rhode Island, Sunday, November 23, 1958.... n.p., n.d. 99p. RPD.
Roman Catholic. Includes historical sketch.

1561 HAYDEN, EDWARD J. Cumberland, Rhode Island: historical story. (1968) 3d ed. [Cumberland,] 1976. 26p. RHi.

1562 McLOUGHLIN, WILLIAM G. "Free love, immortalism, and perfectionism in Cumberland, Rhode Island, 1748-1768." RIH, 33 (1974), 67-85.

1563 PROVIDENCE EVENING REPORTER (newspaper). [Series of articles concerning Cumberland in the American Revolution] (June 19, July 12, 14, 1897).
Includes debate between Mrs. James H. Rickard and Sidney S. Rider over the existence of a beacon used for signaling.

1564 RHODE ISLAND. HISTORICAL PRESERVATION COMMISSION. Preliminary survey report: town of Cumberland. Providence, 1977. iii, 35p. RHi.
Authors: Walter Nebiker, Russell Wright.

1565 RIDER, SIDNEY S. "A chapter of Rhode Island lore: the beautiful prophetess of Cumberland." BN, 33 (1916), 97-101, 105-106.
Jemima Wilkinson, the "Universal Friend."

1566 SIMPSON, ROBERT V. North Cumberland: a history. [Chelsea, Vt.: Acorn Pr. & Design,] 1975. 63p. RHi.

1567 SOCIETY OF COLONIAL WARS. RHODE ISLAND. The first record book of the Society of Colonial Wars in the State of Rhode Island and Providence Plantations, 1897-1902: constitution and by-laws, officers and members, historical papers. Providence: Snow & Farnham, 1902. 134p. RHi. +
Includes "The Rehoboth fight, 1676," by Joseph Ballard Murdock, contending that the military engagement with Indians, also known as "Pierce's Fight," took place at what is now Valley Falls, in Cumberland. See index for other references to "Pierce's Fight."

1568 WHEELER, ROBERT L. "Conductor's watch slow, 14 die." RIer (Oct. 25, 1953), 12-13.
1853 train wreck at Valley Falls.

SEE ALSO entries 458, 1242, 1252.

## EAST GREENWICH (KENT CO.)

1569 AMERICAN LEGION. RHODE ISLAND. Sixth annual state convention of the American Legion, East Greenwich, Rhode Island, August 15 and 16, 1924. n.p., n.d. [48]p. RHi.
Includes "Historic East Greenwich," by Emily Gertrude Arnold.

1570 BIRD, ASA GARDINER. "General James M. Varnum of the Continental Army." Magazine of American History, 18 (1887), 185-193.
Includes his years in East Greenwich.

1571 BOESCH, MARGIE. "Quilting in East Greenwich." East Greenwich Packet, 3 (Winter 1973-1974), 1, 3-4.

1572 CARPENTER, ESTHER BERNON. Huguenot influence in Rhode Island...a paper read before the Rhode Island Historical Society, November 17, 1885. Providence: Kellogg Printing, [1885]. 33p. RHi. +

1573 EAST GREENWICH, R.I. EXECUTIVE COMMITTEE. That there may be a permanent and enduring record of the two hundred and fiftieth anniversary celebration of the founding of the town of East Greenwich, Rhode Island, September 4th to 8th, inclusive, 1927. The souvenir program, 1627-1927. Providence: Akerman Standard, [1927?]. 96p. RHi.
Includes historical sketch by Emily Gertrude Arnold.

1574 EAST GREENWICH, R.I. OUR LADY OF MERCY CHURCH. Our Lady of Mercy Parish celebrates one hundred and five years of growth in Christ's love and truth, 1867-1972. n.p., [1972]. 32p. RPD-H.
Roman Catholic.

1575 EAST GREENWICH SEMINARY. Sketch of East Greenwich Seminary; its relation to public schools, and advantages for giving normal instruction. Providence: A. Crawford Greene, 1865. 20p. RHi. +
Became Greenwich Academy.

1576 [EAST GREENWICH TERCENTENARY COMMISSION.] The tercentenary book, East Greenwich, R.I., 1677-1977. East Greenwich: R.I. Pendulum, 1977. 96p. RHi.

1577 EAST GREENWICH VOLUNTEER FIRE DEPARTMENT. 150th anniversary celebration, East Greenwich Volunteer Fire Dept., June 29th - July 5th, 1947: 150 years of community service. n.p., [1947]. [80]p. REaG.
Includes brief historical sketch.

1578 "FOUNDING of the Academy in 1802." East Greenwich Academy Alumnus, 23 (May 1936), 7-9.

1579 FREEMASONS. EAST GREENWICH. KING SOLOMON'S LODGE, NO. 11. King Solomon's Lodge, No. 11, F. & A.M., East Greenwich, Rhode Island: program, 150th anniversary, June 3-5-9, 1956. n.p., n.d. 24p. RHi.
Includes historical sketch.

1580 GOODWIN, DANIEL. An historical address delivered...in St. Luke's Church, East Greenwich, R.I., before the Kentish Guards, on the occasion of its one hundred and twenty-fifth anniversary, on October the fifteenth, eighteen hundred and ninety-nine. East Greenwich: W. J. McClure, n.d. 24p. RHi.

1581 GREENE, DANIEL H. History of the town of East Greenwich and adjacent territory, from 1677 to 1877. Providence: J. A. & R. A. Reid, 1877. 263p. RHi. +

1582 HESS, JEFFREY A. "Black settlement house, East Greenwich, 1902-1914." RIH, 29 (1970), 113-127.
"...a mission for the town's Negro population."

1583 "THE HUGUENOT settlement in Rhode Island." PM, 33 (1921), 132-136.
In East Greenwich.

1584 KENTISH GUARDS, EAST GREENWICH. One hundred and ninety-second anniversary ball, Kentish Guards, Rhode Island Militia.... n.p., [1966?]. [16]p. RHi.
Includes a history of the unit by Warren F. Dietzel.

1585 _____. Two hundredth anniversary, Kentish Guards, Rhode Island Militia, member Centennial Legion of Historic Military Commands, East Greenwich...October 1974. Robert Allen Greene, ed. n.p., [1974]. [104]p. RHi.
Includes historical sketches.

1586 KENTISH Guards: a history. n.p., n.d. 96p. REaG.

1587 KING, HENRY IRVING. An account of the 250th anniversary celebration of the founding of the town of East Greenwich. East Greenwich: Greenwich Pr., 1930. 52p. RP.

1588 LADD, PAUL R. "Windmill Cottage and Longfellow." RIH, 26 (1907), 1-11.
Henry Wadsworth Longfellow in East Greenwich.

1589 LARSON, PAMELA H. "Men who created a craftsmen's heritage for East Greenwich: they left their mark." East Greenwich Packet, 3 (Spring 1973), 1-3.

1590 McPARTLAND, MARTHA R. The history of East Greenwich, Rhode Island, 1677-1960; with related genealogy. East Greenwich: East Greenwich Free Library Association, 1960. 300p. RHi. +

1591 [MEADER, CHARLES A.] The Casey family of East Greenwich: an account of "some men who lived on Main Street in a small town"....East Greenwich: East Greenwich News, 1927. 43p. RHi. +

1592 MILLER, WILLIAM DAVIS. Notes and queries concerning the early bounds and divisions of the township of East Greenwich, as set forth in William Hall's plat, 1716. Providence: Society of Colonial Wars, R.I., 1937. 19p. RHi. +

1593 MURRAY, THOMAS HAMILTON. Charles MacCarthy: a Rhode Island pioneer, 1677. Somerset, Ohio, n.d. 15p. RHi. +
Early Irish settler.

1594 OLDHAM, NEILD B. "They've made their last sausage." RIer (Mar. 29, 1959), 10-11.
Munson Bros. Grocery Store, in business nearly 60 years.

1595 "ORIGIN of name East Greenwich." NHR, 4 (1886), 249-250.

1596 PALFY, ELEANOR. "The glorious Fourth in Rhode Island." Town and Country, 101 (July 1947), 54-55, 102.
Fourth of July celebrations in East Greenwich.

1597 POTTER, ELISHA R. Memoir concerning the French settlements and French settlers in the Colony of Rhode Island. (1879) Baltimore: Genealogical Publishing, 1968. 138p. RHi. +

1598 PRESTON, HOWARD WILLIS. "General Varnum House." RIHSC, 20 (1927), 115-120.
James Mitchell Varnum.

1599 REILLY, HENRY F. "The might-have-been story of Gallaudet." RIer (Nov. 29, 1959), 6-8, 10.
Gallaudet Aircraft Corp.

1600 RHODE ISLAND. HISTORICAL PRESERVATION COMMISSION. East Greenwich, Rhode Island: statewide preservation report K-EG-1. [Providence,] 1974. vi, 43p. RHi. +
Author: James H. Gibbs.

1601 RIDER, SIDNEY S. The meaning of the phrase "the manor of East Greenwich in our County of Kent," in the charter of Rhode Island in 1663. n.p., n.d. 22p. RHi. +

1602 TURNER, HENRY E. Historical address delivered before the alumni of Greenwich Academy, at East Greenwich, R.I., June 22, 1882. Newport: John P. Sanborn, 1882. 25p. RHi. +

1603 _____. Reminiscences of East Greenwich: address delivered before the East Greenwich Businessmen's Association, December 1891. (1892) East Greenwich: East Greenwich Free Library, 1934. [29]p. RHi. +
According to 1892 ed., date of address was Apr. 11, 1892.

1604 THE VARNUM House, built 1773, East Greenwich, Rhode Island: home of Major General James Mitchell Varnum. n.p., n.d. 8p. RNoK.

1605 WHEELER, ROBERT L. "A 'ghost village' without ghosts." RIer (Apr. 19, 1953), 20-21.
Frenchtown Village, an early textile-mill village.

1606 _____. "James Mitchell Varnum's house." RIer (May 31, 1953), 3-4, 6.
Historic house.

1607 WORTHINGTON, WILLIAM. Historical address delivered...on the morning of St. Luke's Day, Sunday, October 18, 1908, in commemoration of the seventy-fifth anniversary of the organization of the Parish of St. Luke's, East Greenwich, R.I. [East Greenwich, 1908.] [7]p. REaG.
Episcopal.

SEE ALSO entries 149, 455, 458, 466.

## EAST PROVIDENCE (PROVIDENCE CO.)

1608 ANDERSON, ROBERT E. The history of Squantum on the occasion of the 100th anniversary of the incorporation of the association. [East Providence: Squantum Association, 1972.] 58p. RHi.
Squantum Association (club).

1609 BLISS, GEORGE N. An historical sketch of the town of East Providence, delivered before the town authorities and citizens of East Providence, July 4th, 1876. Providence: John F. Greene, 1876. 52p. RHi. +

1610 BROWN, JOHN C. The Jones Pond shell heap: an excavation by the Narragansett Archaeological Society of Rhode Island. n.p., 1939. 25p. RHi. +

1611 [CONFORTI, JOSEPH.] Our heritage: a history of East Providence. White Plains, N.Y.: Monarch Publishing, 1976. vii, 196p. RHi. +

1612 EAST PROVIDENCE, R.I. CHURCH OF THE SACRED HEART. "In the hands of the Lord": Sacred Heart Parish centennial, 1876-1976, East Providence, Rhode Island. n.p. [1976]. [132]p. RPD.
Roman Catholic.

1613 EAST PROVIDENCE, R.I. FIRST BAPTIST CHURCH. Historical address, including Baptist history in ancient Rehoboth, and poems, delivered in the First Baptist Church in East Providence, Nov. 14, 1894, in commemoration of the founding of the First Baptist Church, East Providence, R.I. [Providence: Narragansett Publishing,] n.d. 50p. RPB. +

1614 _____. Historical sketch of the First Baptist Church of East Providence. n.p., n.d. 9p. RHi.

1615 EAST PROVIDENCE, R.I. HAVEN UNITED METHODIST CHURCH. 1875-1975: souvenir program of one hundredth anniversary. n.p., [1975]. 12p. RHi.

1616 HART, GEORGE THOMAS. "Squantum: its origin and significance." PBTJ, 16 (1904), 268-272.
Squantum Association.

1617 HINCKLEY, ANITA W. "'Let's put the clams in our middy blouses.'" RIer (June 8, 1969), 28.
Summer visits to Crescent Park in Riverside.

1618 HORTON, ELMER S. The story of Squantum: presented on the occasion of the 80th anniversary of the association...September 17, 1951. [Providence: Bank Lithograph, 1952.] 34, [2]p. RHi. +
Squantum Association (club).

1619 "HOW Squantum derived its name." PBTJ, 27 (1915), 429-432.
Squantum Association.

1620 HOYT, HAROLD W. The story of Hunt's Mills, East Providence, R.I. (1895) 2d ed. Providence: Snow & Farnham, 1897. 31p. RHi. +
Gristmill and sawmill site.

1621 PHENIX NATIONAL BANK. ..."A latter-day pioneer." [Providence,] 1945. 10p. RHi.
Abrasive Machine Tool Co. This and the next entry were part of the Romance of R.I. Industry pamphlet series. See note, entry 768.

1622 _____. ..."The plant with 100 histories." [Providence,] 1945. 10p. RHi.
Rumford Chemical Works.

1623 RHODE ISLAND. HISTORICAL PRESERVATION COMMISSION. East Providence, Rhode Island: statewide preservation report P-EP-1. [Providence,] 1976. vi, 79p. RHi. +
Author: Richard W. Longstreth.

1624 RIDER, SIDNEY S. A retrospect from the round tower of the Pomham Club. Providence: Priv. Print., 1889. 19p. RHi. +
Reflections on the early history of what is now East Providence.

1625 ROTARY CLUB, EAST PROVIDENCE. Rep art exhibition. n.p., n.d. 40p. RHi.
Catalog includes "History of East Providence," by Otho Smith.

1626 RUMFORD, R.I. NEWMAN CONGREGATIONAL CHURCH. Articles of faith of the Newman Congregational Church of Seekonk and East Providence. Providence: Snow & Farnham, 1902. 26p. RHi.
Includes "Historical notice."

1627 _____. Historical address and poem delivered in the Newman Congregational Church, in East Providence, June 7th, 1893, in commemoration of the 250th anniversary of the founding of the Newman Congregational Church and the ancient town of Rehoboth. [Pawtucket: Charles A. Lee, 1893.] 55p. RPB. +

1628 _____. Newman Congregational Church, Rumford, Rhode Island. n.p., 1968. 15p. RHi.
Includes historical sketch by Robert H. Simonton.

1629 RUMFORD CHEMICAL WORKS. Eighty years of baking powder history. Rumford, 1939. 23p. RHi. +

1630 TRIM, ROBERT S. "Newman Cemetery." R.I. Roots, 3, No. 1 (Spring 1977), 1, 3-7.

1631 WANNAMOISETT COUNTRY CLUB, EAST PROVIDENCE. 1898-1948: fiftieth anniversary year, Wannamoisett Country Club. Helen B. Perkins and Roy F. Perkins, eds. n.p., 1948. 47p. RP.

1632 _____. Fourteenth National Professional Golf Championship, 1931. n.p., [1931]. [40]p. RHi.
Includes "The story of Wannamoisett," [31-32].

1633 WOOD, W. LeROY. "First settlers in East Providence." RIHSC, 24 (1931), 92-96.

SEE ALSO entry 1239.

## EXETER (WASHINGTON CO.)

1634 ARNOLD, WILLET H. Historical sketch of the Baptist Church in Exeter, R.I. Central Falls: E. L. Freeman, 1883. 23p. RHi. +

1635 HARVEY, W. WARD. Miskiania Camp: an abstract of title, with a short introductory history. Newport: Harvey Publishing, 1970. iii, 126p. RNHi.
Owned by a club. See also next entry.

1636 _____. The Yawcoak Farm: the story of the origins of Miskiana Camp in Exeter, R.I. Newport, 1974. vi, 186p. RNHi.
See also preceding entry.

1637 HULING, MARY KENYON. Historical sketch of the Baptist Church in Exeter, Rhode Island (Chestnut Hill). Cranston: Pendleton Pr., [1939]. 27p. RHi. +

1638 NARRAGANSETT GUN CLUB, EXETER. Golden anniversary of the Narragansett Gun Club, Inc., Austin Farm Road, Exeter, R.I.... n.p., 1957. [56]p. RHi.
Includes historical sketch.

1639 RHODE ISLAND. HISTORICAL PRESERVATION COMMISSION. Preliminary survey report: town of Exeter. Providence, 1976. iii, 18p. RHi.
Authors: Walter Nebiker, Russell Wright.

1640 SCHNEIDER, ERIC C. "Mental retardation, state policy, and the Ladd School, 1908-1970." RIH, 40 (1981), 133-143.
R.I. School for the Feeble-minded.

1641 SIMISTER, FLORENCE PARKER. A short history of Exeter, Rhode Island. [Exeter: Exeter Bicentennial Commission,] 1978. 105p. RHi. +

## FOSTER (PROVIDENCE CO.)

1642 BEAMAN, CHARLES C. "Sketches of Foster." Providence Journal (1857-1858).
At least 14 articles in the series. Rider Collection, Brown Univ., has installments 5 (Jan. 6, 1858), 6 (Jan. 21, 1858), 14 (Aug. 26, 1858).

1643 BONGARTZ, ROY. "Endsville." RIer (July 21, 1974), 28-29.
The Snagwood, once a nightclub in Foster.

1644 _____. "'I'll stay here until my end or Foster's.'" RIer (Aug. 16, 1981), 6-9, 11.
Reflections on Foster's 200th anniversary.

1645 CASEY, B. T. "Reminiscences of Foster." Pawtuxet Valley Gleaner (Aug. 27, 1892-Mar. 4, 1893).
Series of articles, reprinted from early numbers of the newspaper.

1646 CLEMENCE, CLARA E. "Dolly Cole's Hill." WRICHSP, 1, No. 4 (1950), 19-21.

1647 _____. "The Drowne Homestead." WRICHSP, 2, No. 2 (1955), [7-9.]
Once owned by Dr. Solomon Drowne.

1648 FOSTER, R.I. MOOSUP VALLEY CHURCH. Reflections, Moosup Valley Church, 1868-1968. n.p., [1968]. 9p. RHi.
Congregational.

1649 FOSTER: a bicentennial celebration, 1781-1981. Foster, 1981. 86p. RHi.
Primarily a photographic history.

1650 "THE FOSTER gold mine." WRICHSH, 1 (Apr. 1958), [2]; (May 1958), [2].

1651 HOWARD, DANIEL. "Some facts about Foster, Rhode Island." WRICHSP, 1, No. 2 (1949), 14-17.

1652 MATTHEWS, MARGERY I., VIRGINIA I. BENSON, and ARTHUR E. WILSON. Churches of Foster: a history of religious life in rural Rhode Island. Foster: North Foster Baptist Church, 1978. 165p. RHi. +

1653 MURRAY, THOMAS HAMILTON. "Sketch of an early Irish settlement in Rhode Island." American-Irish Historical Society, Journal, 2 (1899), 152-157.
Dorrance Purchase.

1654 YE OLDE historical town map of Foster; also fair to middlin street map by Bill Turner; history by your people. Pascoag: W. R. P. Turner, 1974. RNoP.
Folded map with text.

1655 OLSON, SANDRA, MARCIA M. BOWDEN, MARGERY I. MATTHEWS, and ELIZABETH OLAUSEN. Foster and the patriots' dream: a bicentennial reflection. [Foster:] Foster Preservation Society, 1976. 22p. RHi.

1656 POTTER, HENRY B. "Tent life for consumptives in Rhode Island: a brief history of Pine Ridge Camp; its inception, achievements and plans." PMJ, 4 (1903), 185-191.

1657 RHODE ISLAND. HISTORICAL PRESERVATION COMMISSION. Foster, Rhode Island: statewide historical preservation report P-F-1. [Providence,] 1982. 74p. RHi.
Author: Ancelin V. Lynch.

1658 SAUNDERS, MRS. WINTHROP H. "Hopkins Mills Union Chapel." WRICHSP, 1, No. 4 (1950), 9-18.

1659 TAYLOR, PEARL E., and ELSIE M. FASTESON. Bits and pieces from the general store ledgers, Foster, Rhode Island. Foster: Ladies Auxiliary of the Foster Center Volunteer Fire Company, 1965. [18]p. RFo.

1660 _____. Foster, R.I. n.p., 1963. 15p. RFo.

1661 _____. The one room schoolhouse, Foster, Rhode Island. Foster: Ladies Auxiliary of the Foster Center Volunteer Fire Company, 1964. [30]p. RFo.

SEE ALSO entries 341, 1235, 1238, 1257-1258.

## GLOCESTER (PROVIDENCE CO.)

1662 CHAPIN, HOWARD M. "Glocester, R.I." RIHSC, 26 (1953), 64-65.
Spelling of the name.

1663 CHEPACHET, R.I. SAINT EUGENE'S CHURCH. St. Eugene's Church, Chepachet, Rhode Island, 1956-1981. n.p., 1981. Unp. RGl.
Roman Catholic.

1664    FALLON, WILLIAM P.  "America's oldest
        (continuously operated) grocery store!"
        Yankee, 32 (Apr. 1968), 112-115, 117.
            In Chepachet.

1665    FITCH, MARTHA R.  "History of Glocester."
        WRICHSP, 1, No. 2 (1949), 2-5.

1666    GLOCESTER BICENTENNIAL COMMISSION.
        Glocester:  the way up country; a history,
        guide and directory.  Edna Kent, comp.
        [Glocester,] 1976.  iv, 192p.  RHi.

1667    [HALEY, JOHN WILLIAMS.]  The Chepachet
        elephant.  Providence:  "Old Stone
        Bank," 1932.  10p.  RHi.
            Exhibited there in 1822, and shot and
        killed by some local residents as a prank.
        This entry was part of the "Old Stone
        Bank" historical pamphlet series.  See note,
        entry 432.

1668    MANTON FREE PUBLIC LIBRARY, CHEPACHET.
        Early history of Glocester.  [Chepachet,]
        n.d.  19p.  RG1.
            Reprinted from entry 1244.

1669    MOWRY, J. B.  Historical sketch of the
        Chepachet churches.  [Chepachet:]  Old Home
        Day Committee, 1911.  19p.  RG1.

1670    MOWRY, JESSE B.  Glocester, R.I.:  the
        town's pioneers and Indians; an address on
        Old Home Day, August 19, 1933.  n.p., n.d.
        12p.  RHi. +

1671    OBSERVER PUBLICATIONS.  Glocester 250:
        published by Observer Publications, Inc., in
        commemoration of the 250th anniversary of
        Glocester.  [Greenville,] 1980.  28p.  RG1.

1672    PERRY, ELIZABETH A.  A brief history of the
        town of Glocester, Rhode Island, preceded by
        a sketch of the territory while a part of
        Providence.  Providence:  Providence Pr.,
        1886.  136p.  RHi. +

1673    RHODE ISLAND.  HISTORICAL PRESERVATION
        COMMISSION.  Preliminary survey report:
        town of Glocester.  Providence, 1980.  iv,
        62p.  RHi.
            Author:  Walter Nebiker.

1674    SARKESIAN, BARBARA.  "Found:  a ledger and
        a family."  Family Heritage, 2 (1979),
        68-69.
            Welcome Allen Shippee's mid-19th-century
        account book.

1675    WORTHINGTON, W. CHESLEY.  "A love letter to
        Chepachet."  RIer (July 5, 1953), 3-7.

        SEE ALSO entries 1061, 1235, 1258.

## HOPKINTON (WASHINGTON CO.)

1676    ANDREWS, HOPE G.  "The Nichols family."
        Hopkinton Historical Association, Hopkinton
        Notes, 1, No. 6 (Nov. 1978), 1-3.

1677    ASHAWAY, R.I.  CHURCH OF OUR LADY OF
        VICTORY.  Twenty-fifth anniversary jubilee,
        Our Lady of Victory Parish, Ashaway, Rhode
        Island, September 19, 1946 - October 24,
        1971.  n.p., [1971].  [4]p.  RPD-H.
            Roman Catholic.

1678    "CARRIAGE shops."  Hopkinton Historical
        Association, Hopkinton Notes, 2, No. 5
        (Sept. 1979), 1-3.

1679    CRANDALL, D. ALVA.  "Schools of other days:
        northern Hopkinton."  Hopkinton Historical
        Association , Hopkinton Notes, 5, No. 2
        (Mar. 1982), 2-4.

1680    CRANDALL, JULIAN T.  "A love letter to
        Ashaway."  RIer (Dec. 7, 1958), 33-34,
        36-37.

1681    FIRST HOPKINTON CEMETERY ASSOCIATION.
        Historical addresses, delivered at the
        dedication of the Ministers' Monument in the
        First Hopkinton Cemetery, near Ashaway,
        R.I., August 28, 1899.  Plainfield, N.J.:
        American Sabbath Tract Society, 1899.  26p.
        RHi. +
            "Memorial to the early pastors of the
        second Seventh-day Baptist Church in
        America."

1682    GRISWOLD, S. S.  An historical sketch of the
        town of Hopkinton, from 1757 to 1876,
        comprising a period of one hundred and
        nineteen years...delivered July 4th, 1876.
        Hope Valley:  Wood River Advertiser Pr.,
        1877.  94p.  RHi. +

1683    [HILL, FRANK M.]  The biography of the
        Honorable Frank Hill and history of the
        Ashaway National Bank.  n.p., [1976?].  39p.
        RHi.

1684    "HISTORY and legends of Meeting House
        Bridge."  Hopkinton Historical Association,
        Hopkinton Notes, 5, No. 5 (Sept. 1982), 1-4.

1685    HOPE Valley revived.  The recorded past:
        photographs and oral history.  Betty Salomon
        and Tess Hoffman, comps.  n.p., 1977.
        [48]p.  RHi.

1686    HOPKINTON, R.I.  FIRST SEVENTH-DAY BAPTIST
        CHURCH.  Bi-centennial celebration of the
        First Seventh-day Baptist Church of
        Hopkinton, located in Ashaway, R.I.,
        September 25 and 26, 1908.  [Alfred, N.Y.:
        Alfred Pr., 1908.]  111p.  RHi.

1687 HOPKINTON BICENTENNIAL COMMITTEE. History of the town of Hopkinton, Rhode Island, 1757-1976. 181p. RHi. +

1688 HOPKINTON TERCENTENARY COMMITTEE. Tercentenary map and description of early Hope Valley (Carpenter's; or Middle Iron Works) and Wyoming (Brand's Iron Works). [Westerly: Utter, 1936.] 14p. RHi. +

1689 MacLURE, JOHN. "'Please don't turn your back on me.'" Yankee, 43 (Mar. 1979), 88-89, 167.
1976 rescue of badly injured truck driver.

1690 "MOVIES." Hopkinton Historical Association, Hopkinton Notes, 3, No. 3 (May 1980), 3-4.
Early motion picture shows in Hopkinton.

1691 "THE NINIGRET Cycling Club." Hopkinton Historical Association, Hopkinton Notes, 2, No. 6 (Nov. 1979), 3-5.
Organized 1894.

1692 "THE OLD Locustville Store." Hopkinton Historical Association, Hopkinton Notes, 1, No. 3 (May 1978), 3-6.

1693 RANDOLPH, CORLISS F. "The old Westerly, or the First Hopkinton Church." Sabbath Recorder, 63 (1907), 1414-1422.
First Seventh-Day Baptist Church.

1694 RHODE ISLAND. HISTORICAL PRESERVATION COMMISSION. Preliminary survey report: town of Hopkinton. Providence, 1976. iii, 23 p. RHi.
Authors: Walter Nebiker, Russell Wright.

1695 "THE SECOND Seventh Day Baptist Church of Hopkinton, R.I." Hopkinton Historical Association, Hopkinton Notes, 4, No. 1 (Jan. 1981), 1-6; No. 2 (Mar. 1981), 1-3.

1696 STILLMAN, ELISHA C. "Old homes, old men and old letters." WHSR (1927), 7-15.
Ashaway and vicinity.

1697 _____. "Old houses and their occupants on the old Hopkinton Road three-quarters of a century ago." WHSR (1913-1915), 27-32.

1698 "THE TAN yard at Hopkinton City." Hopkinton Historical Association, Hopkinton Notes, 2, No. 6 (Nov. 1979), 1-3.

1699 "THE THURSTON Store." Hopkinton Historical Association, Hopkinton Notes, 3, No. 4 (July 1980), 1-3.

1700 "TOMAQUAG Brook." Hopkinton Historical Association, Hopkinton Notes, 2, No. 4 (July 1979), 3-5.
Historical sketch, written ca. 1900.

1701 WILLIAMS, J. HAROLD. Yawgoog story: a half century of Scout camping in Rhode Island. Providence: Narragansett Council, Boy Scouts of America, 1965. 58p. RHi.
Boy Scout camp on Yawgoog Pond.

SEE ALSO entries 1286, 1344-1345.

## JAMESTOWN (NEWPORT CO.)

1702 AMACKER, MILTON W. "Conanicut, gem of Narragansett Bay." RIY (1973), 104-108.
Conanicut Island.

1703 BRINLEY, FRANCIS. "Conanicut Island." NHM, 2 (1882), 193-197.

1704 CARR, MARIA A. "Old Jamestown." JHSB, No. 6 (1932), 1-7.

1705 CHAMPLIN, RICHARD L. "Rhode Island's first lighthouse." NH, 43 (1970), 49-64.
Beavertail Lighthouse.

1706 CHAPIN, HOWARD M. "Quetenis Island or Dutch Island." RIHSC, 19 (1926), 88-91.

1707 CLARKE, LENA. "Some old houses in Jamestown." JHSB, No. 1 (1920), 1-10.

1708 DEMBER, IRA. "Rhode Island's movable Chapel of the Transfiguration." Yankee, 34 (July 1970), 80, 134-135, 137-138, 141.
Episcopal. See also entry 1717.

1709 FRANKLIN, SUSAN BRALEY. "The Beavertail Lighthouse." RIH, 10 (1951), 97-101.

1710 _____. "A short history of the west ferries of Jamestown." JHSB, No. 8 (1941), 3-16.

1711 GARLICK, REUBEN W. "My ferrying days at Jamestown." RIer (Dec. 28, 1958), 8-11.

1712 HAUN, EUGENE. "Jamestown, R.I., 1657-1961." Yankee, 25 (May 1961), 60-67.

1713 A HISTORY of Jamestown and early days around Narragansett Bay. Compiled by Elizabeth Helmick for Jamestown Public Library. n.p., n.d. [65]p. RJa.
Series of newspaper articles on Jamestown history that appeared originally in Newport Daily News.

1714    HISTORY of the Portuguese of Conanicut
        Island, 1895-1980. Collected by Shirley
        Tiexiera Quattromani. Catharine Morris
        Wright, ed. Jamestown: Jamestown
        Philomenian Library, 1980. 233p. RHi.
            For accounts of Portuguese Americans in
        other Newport County towns, see entry 1770
        and Donald Reed Taft, Two Portuguese
        communities in New England (1923). The
        latter work relates in part to Portsmouth.

1715    JAMESTOWN, R.I. Souvenir program,
        celebration of the 300th anniversary of the
        purchase of Jamestown, Conanicut Island,
        from the Narragansett Indians, August 10th
        thru August 17th, 1957, Jamestown, Rhode
        Island. n.p., n.d. [20]p. RNHi.
            Includes historical sketch by Walter Leon
        Carr.

1716    _____. That there may be a permanent record
        of the two hundred and fiftieth anniversary
        of the incorporation of the town of
        Jamestown, Rhode Island, August 4th, 1928.
        n.p., [1928]. 55p. RHi. +
            Includes historical sketch by Lena Clarke
        and Walter Leon Watson.

1717    JAMESTOWN, R.I. CHAPEL OF THE
        TRANSFIGURATION. The first movable church:
        the Chapel of the Transfiguration, Conanicut
        Island, Diocese of Rhode Island; the only
        complete church on wheels in the world....
        Newport: F. W. Marshall, 1899. 135p.
        RHi. +
            Episcopal. See also entry 1708.

1718    LEAVENS, JOHN M. "Catboats and Conanicut,
        1880-1920." NH, 48 (1976), 77-94.

1719    LIPPINCOTT, BERTRAM. Jamestown sampler.
        Ambler, Pa.: John J. Gaghan, 1980. x,
        128p. RHi. +
            Social life and customs.

1720    _____. "King James's other island." NH, 54
        (1981), 101-112.
            Conanicut.

1721    LOW, WILLIAM GILMAN. "A short history of
        the Beaver Tail Light, Conanicut, Rhode
        Island." JHSB, No. 7 (1936), 3-15.

1722    POTTER, MARGARETTA WOOD. "How we saved the
        Jamestown Windmill." NH, 48 (1975),
        233-246.
            Jamestown Historical Society.

1723    RIDER, SIDNEY S. "Conanicut." BN, 9 (1892),
        157-159.

1724    SIMMONS, WILLIAM SCRANTON. "The ancient
        graves of Conanicut Island." NH, 40 (1967),
        153-175.
            Archaeological excavation of Narragansett
        Indian burial ground.

1725    _____. Cautantowwit's house: an Indian
        burial ground on the island of Conanicut in
        Narragansett Bay. Providence: Brown Univ.
        Pr., 1970. xix, 178p. RHi. +

1726    STEVENS, MAUD LYMAN. The Jamestown
        windmill. Newport: Remington Ward, 1926.
        32p. RHi. +

1727    TAYLOR, A. O'D. "Jamestown." NHSB, No. 52
        (1925), 1-15.

1728    WATSON, WALTER LEON. "The early Quakers and
        the old Quaker Meeting House." JHSB, No.
        5 (1930), [2-15].

1729    _____. History of Jamestown on Conanicut
        Island in the State of Rhode Island.
        Providence: John F. Greene, 1949. 104p.
        RHi. +

1730    _____. The house of Carr: an historical
        sketch of the Carr family from 1450 to
        1926...written for the 150th anniversary of
        the Carr Homestead, built by Nicholas Carr
        in 1776. n.p., 1926. 57p. RHi. +

1731    _____. Random thoughts regarding Jamestown:
        a paper read before the Jamestown Historical
        Society. n.p., n.d. [15]p. RHi. +

1732    _____. "A short history of Jamestown on the
        island of Conanicut, Rhode Island." RIHSC,
        26 (1933), 40-59, 79-90.

1733    WHEELER, ROBERT L. "Beavertail Light."
        RIer (Oct. 23, 1949), 20-21.

1734    WILLIAMS, ROGER. An answer to a scandalous
        paper which came to my hand from the
        Massachusetts clamouring against the
        purchasers of Qunnunnagut Iland, and
        subscribed by John Easton.... Providence:
        Society of Colonial Wars, R.I., 1945.
        [15]p. RHi. +
            Includes historical introduction
        concerning 17th-century dispute over
        ownership of Conanicut Island.

        SEE ALSO entries 351, 1021, 1104, 1171,
        1184, 1189.

## JOHNSTON (PROVIDENCE CO.)

1735 ALLENDALE MUTUAL INSURANCE COMPANY. The triumph of an idea. n.p., [197_]. 51p. RHi.
Includes historical sketch of the company.

1736 CADY, JOHN HUTCHINS. "The Thomas Clemence House (c. 1680), 38 George Waterman Road, Johnston, R.I." RIHSC, 34 (1941), 65-77.
See also this author's article under same title in Old-time New England, 39 (1948), 17-24.

1737 [HALEY, JOHN WILLIAMS.] Fenner Castle. Providence: "Old Stone Bank," 1931. 10p. RHi.
Built in late 17th century by Capt. Arthur Fenner; destroyed in 1880s. This entry was part of the "Old Stone Bank" historical pamphlet series. See note, entry 432.

1738 JOHNSTON, R.I. Town of Johnston, R.I., incorporated March 6, 1759: 200th anniversary celebration, November 11th, 1959. n.p., 1959. [17]p. RPa.
Historical sketch by Ralph S. Mohr.

1739 RHODE ISLAND. HISTORICAL PRESERVATION COMMISSION. Preliminary survey report: town of Johnston. Providence, 1976. iii, 22p. RHi.
Authors: Walter Nebiker, Russell Wright.

1740 SAVILLE, FOSTER H. "Steatite quarry at Johnston, R.I." RIHSC, 12 (1919), 103-105.
Narragansett Indian site.

1741 SWEET, RALPH N. Old times in Graniteville: a boy's life in the 90's. n.p., n.d. 24p. RNoP.

SEE ALSO entries 1226, 1259.

## LINCOLN (PROVIDENCE CO.)

1742 "THE BUTTERFLY Factory, Lincoln, R.I." Old Slater Mill, The Flyer, 4 (Apr. 1973), 3-4.
Cotton mill.

1743 CHURCH, LOUISA RANDALL. "My New England grandmother and grandfather." Old-time New England, 32 (1941), 67-72.
Louisa Elizabeth Clark and Samuel Clark.

1744 CUMMINGS, ABBOTT LOWELL. "The restoration of the Eleazer Arnold House in Lincoln, Rhode Island." Antiques, 77 (1960), 490-493.

1745 DORIS, VIRGINIA L. "Rhode Island's Great Road." Yankee, 27 (Apr. 1963), 68-71, 134.
In Lincoln.

1746 DUNNIGAN, KATE, and RICHARD QUINNEY. "Work and community in Saylesville." Radical History Review, No. 17 (1978), 173-180.

1747 FALES, EMMA C. Lime Rock "before the turn of the century." n.p., n.d. 34p. RHi.
Written 1950.

1748 FOWLER, WILLIAM S. "Twin Rivers: four culture sequence at a Rhode Island site." Narragansett Archaeological Society of R.I. [Report, 1952], 1-16.
Site of archaeological dig.

1749 GREENE, WELCOME ARNOLD. "An historic bell in the Moshassuck Valley." RIHM, 5 (1885), 328-341.
In Butterfly Mill.

1750 _____. Historical sketch of the town of Lincoln, in the State of Rhode Island. Central Falls: E. L. Freeman, 1876. 26p. RHi. +

1751 ISHAM, NORMAN MORRISON. "An old house at Saylesville, R.I." Genealogical Magazine, 1 (1905), 171-174.

1752 LEAGUE OF WOMEN VOTERS, LINCOLN. The Lincoln latch-string: know your town. n.p., [196_]. 39p. RHi.
Includes brief historical sketch of Lincoln.

1753 LINCOLN, R.I. Once in a hundred years: a pictorial history.... Lincoln, 1971. 168p. RHi. +

1754 LONSDALE, R.I. CHRIST CHURCH. "Reminiscences of Christ Church, Lonsdale." Christ Church, Parish Guide, 1 (June 1872), 12-14; (July 1872), 13-15; (Sept. 1872), 14-16; (Oct. 1872), 5-7; (Nov. 1872), 9-11; (Dec. 1872), 6-8; (Jan. 1873), 5-6; (Feb. 1873), 5-8; (Mar. 1873), 9-12.
Episcopal. Articles signed M.E.K.

1755 LONSDALE, R.I. FIRST BAPTIST CHURCH. Articles of faith and covenant, of the Baptist Church in Lonsdale, R.I. Providence: A. Crawford Greene, 1875. 22p. RHi.
Includes historical sketch.

1756 MANVILLE, R.I. [SAINT JAMES CHURCH.]
Programme-souvenir commémorant la
bénédiction des cloches de la nouvelle
église, a l'occasion des noces de diamant
de la Paroisse St. Jacques de Manville.
n.p., 1934. 76p. RHi.
Roman Catholic. French Parish. Includes
historical sketch of the village and the
parish. Text in French.

1757 _____. St. James Church, Manville,
R.I. South Hackensack, N.J.: Custombook,
1974. 17, [7]p. RHi.
Roman Catholic.

1758 MOSHASSUCK Bleachery, W. F. & F. C. Sayles,
proprietors. n.p., [1904]. 10p. RHi.
Includes historical information.

1759 PHENIX NATIONAL BANK. ..."Old king cotton."
[Providence,] 1945. 10p. RHi.
Lonsdale Co. (textile manufacturer). This
and the next entry were part of the Romance
of R.I. Industry pamphlet series. See note,
entry 768.

1760 _____. ...Sayles Finishing Plants, Inc.
[Providence,] 1946. 10p. RHi.
Bleachers, dyers, and finishers.

1761 RHODE ISLAND. HISTORICAL PRESERVATION
COMMISSION. Lincoln, Rhode Island:
statewide historical preservation report
P-L-1. Providence, 1982. vi, 70p. RHi.
Author: Pamela Kennedy.

1762 RIDER, SIDNEY S. "Louisquisset." BN, 12
(1895), 85-87.
Origin of the place name. See also BN, 33
(1916), 177-178.

1763 SAYLESVILLE, R.I. MEMORIAL CONGREGATIONAL
CHURCH. Manual of the Memorial
Congregational Church in Saylesville, R.I.
Providence: Providence Pr., 1882. 27p.
RHi.
Includes historical sketch.

1764 WHITNEY, JAMES O. A paper read before the
Rhode Island Historical Society, Tuesday,
October 1, 1889...the location of "Pierce's
Fight." n.p., n.d. Broadside. RHi.
King Philip's War (1676).

SEE ALSO entries 1242, 1252, 3803.

## LITTLE COMPTON (NEWPORT CO.)

1765 BROWNELL, CARLTON C. A history of Little
Compton Commons. Little Compton: Brownell
Library, n.d. 15p. RHi.

1766 _____. Little Compton architecture. n.p.,
n.d. [16]p. RP-Harrington.
Includes accounts of several historic
houses.

1767 BURCHARD, ROSWELL B. The town of Little
Compton: an historical address....
[Providence: Snow & Farnham,] 1906. 50,
12p. RHi. +

1768 DARLING, FAYREEN B. "Just for spite!"
Yankee, 31 (Aug. 1967), 81, 102-103.
"Spite Tower," a building in Adamsville.

1769 EDDY, ROBERT LEIGH. The United
Congregational Church of Little Compton,
1704-1954: an historical essay. n.p.,
1954. 40, v p. RHi. +

1770 GRACIA, FRANCES SYLVIA. Early Portuguese
settlers in Little Compton, Rhode Island.
Portsmouth: Bob's Pr., 1974. 14p. RHi. +
For accounts of Portuguese Americans in
other Newport County towns, see entry 1714
and Donald Reed Taft, Two Portuguese
communities in New England (1923). The
latter work relates in part to Portsmouth.

1771 [HALEY, JOHN WILLIAMS.] Awashonks and
Church. Providence: "Old Stone
Bank," 1933. 10p. RHi.
Alliance between English settlers and
Sakonnet Indians, arranged by Benjamin
Church and Awashonks, the Sakonnet tribe's
female sachem. This entry was part of the
"Old Stone Bank" historical pamphlet series.
See note, entry 432.

1772 HISTORY of the Ladies' Aid Society. n.p.,
n.d. [15]p. RLit.

1773 HOWLAND, FRANK HOWARD. "Historical sketch
of Seaconet, Little Compton, R.I." New
Bedford, Mass., Evening Standard (Apr.
1875-Jan. 1876).
Series of 15 articles. Scrapbook, RHi.
Identifiable dates are Apr. 27, May 12, June
5, 16, July 30, Aug. 12, 26, Sept. 14, Oct.
7, Nov. 4, 19, 1875.

1774 LITTLE COMPTON, R.I. Three centuries:
Little Compton tercentennial, 1675-1975.
George E. Stretch, ed. n.p., [1975]. 96p.
RHi.

1775 LITTLE COMPTON, R.I. UNITED CONGREGATIONAL
CHURCH. Manual of the United Congregational
Church, Little Compton, R.I., revised 1903;
church organized November 20, 1704. n.p.,
[1903]. 43p. MBNEH. +
Includes historical sketch.

1776 LITTLE COMPTON, R.I. UNITED CONGREGATIONAL CHURCH. The one hundred and seventy-fifth anniversary of the organization of the United Congregational Church, Little Compton, R.I., celebrated June 2d, 1880. Providence: Providence Pr., 1880. 76p. RHi. +

1777 _____. The two-hundredth anniversary of the organization of the United Congregational Church, Little Compton, Rhode Island, September 7, 1904. Little Compton: United Congregational Society, 1906. 120p. RHi. +

1778 LITTLE Compton families. Benjamin Franklin Wilbour, comp. Little Compton: Little Compton Historical Society, 1967. xvii, 817p. RHi. +

1779 LITTLE COMPTON HISTORICAL SOCIETY. Friends' Meeting House, Little Compton, R.I. n.p., n.d. [4]p. RHi.

1780 _____. Wilbour House. n.p., n.d. [16]p. RHi.
Includes information about Friends' Meeting House.

1781 PATTEN, DAVID. Adventures in a remembered world. n.p., [1977?]. 255p. RHi.
A collection of his Providence Journal-Bulletin articles about life in Little Compton.

1782 _____. "A love letter to S'cunnet." RIer (Feb. 3, 1952), 12-15.
Sakonnet.

1783 _____. "The mystery of the house within a house." RIer (Jan. 8, 1967), 9-10.
Architectural curiosity.

1784 _____. "The new Vikings: a S'cunnet story." RIY (1970), 93-97.
Pogy-fishing industry.

1785 _____. "The story of S'cunnet's restless old windmill." RIer (Feb. 14, 1965), 14-15.

1786 _____. Three sides to the sea: memories of a S'cunnet childhood. N.Y.: Rinehart, 1956. 243p. RHi. +
Sakonnet.

1787 RIDER, SIDNEY S. "Saconet corruptions." BN, 14 (1897), 121-122.
History of the place name.

1788 SHURTLEFF, BERTRAND L. "A love letter to Adamsville." RIer (Sept. 27, 1953), 3-6, 8.

1789 SIMPSON, ALAN. What's in a name? The case of Little Compton, Rhode Island. [Little Compton:] Little Compton Historical Society, 1982. 20p. RLit.

1790 SOCIETY OF COLONIAL WARS. RHODE ISLAND. Purchase of the lands in Little Compton, 1672/1673, from the Saconet Indians. Philip B. Simonds, ed. Providence, 1977. [10]p. RHi. +

1791 THREE centuries: Little Compton tercentennial, 1675-1975. George E. Stretch, ed. n.p., [1975?]. 96p. RHi.

1792 WAINWRIGHT, NICHOLAS B. "The West Island Club." NH, 50 (1977), 21-37.
Fishing.

1793 WILBOUR, BENJAMIN FRANKLIN. Notes on Little Compton. Carlton C. Brownell, ed. Little Compton: Little Compton Historical Society, 1970. 290p. RHi. +

1794 WILBOUR, ISAAC C. An address relative to the early history of the town of Little Compton, R.I., delivered upon the occasion of the removal from the old to the new town hall, April 5, 1882.... Providence: Angell, 1882. 14p. RHi. +

SEE ALSO entries 433, 1181, 1187.

## MIDDLETOWN (NEWPORT CO.)

1795 ARNOLD, SAMUEL GREENE. An historical sketch of Middletown, R.I., from its organization, in 1743, to the centennial year, 1876. Newport: John P. Sanborn, 1876. 48, xiv p. RHi. +
Reprinted by Middletown Historical Society (1976).

1796 BIGELOW, BRUCE M. "A love letter to Middletown." RIer (Nov. 28, 1954), 3-5, 8-10.
Highlights of the town's past.

1797 BUELL, WILLIAM A. "'Yea, team': review of athletics, 1896-1946." Saint George's School, Alumni Bulletin, 29 (Spring 1946), 40-43.
St. George's School.

1798 BUELL, WILLIAM ACKERMAN. My life and St. George's School. Newport: St. George's School Alumni Association, 1967. 37p. RNHi. +
Headmaster, 1951-1961.

1799 CHAMPLIN, RICHARD L. "Lazy Lawn." NH, 55 (1982), 26-29.
Historic house and its grounds.

1800 Middletown

1800 CHASE, NANCY C. History of the Church of the Holy Cross, Middletown, Rhode Island, 1844-1977. n.p.: [Ward's Printers,] n.d. 18p. RHi.
Episcopal.

1801 DIMAN, J. LEWIS. The capture of General Richard Prescott by Lt.-Col. William Barton: an address delivered at the centennial celebration of the exploit at Portsmouth, R.I., July 10, 1877. Providence: Sidney S. Rider, 1877. 65p. RHi. +
Revolutionary War incident. The house in which Prescott was captured is in Middletown.

1802 DIMAN, JOHN HUGH. "Recollections of ten years." Saint George's School, The Dragon, 8 (June 1906), 138-141.
The first 10 years of the school.

1803 FALKNER, LEONARD. "Captor of the barefoot general." American Heritage, 11 (Aug. 1960), 29-31, 98-100.
Col. William Barton's capture of the Newport-area British commander, Gen. Richard Prescott, in a Middletown farmhouse (1777).

1804 GREGG, JAMES E. "Rev. James E. Gregg's address." Saint George's School, Alumni Bulletin, 7 (Dec. 1921), 12-16.
Early years of the school.

1805 "THE GROWTH of St. George's School." Saint George's School, The Dragon, 24 (Oct. 1921), 7-8.
Signed E.S.

1806 "I remember: the history of St. George's by its sons." Saint George's School, Alumni Bulletin, 29 (Spring 1946), 11-37.

1807 LATTU, ARLENE MURRAY RINGER. Taylor-Chase-Smythe House: John Taylor, a founder of Middletown, 1702-1741. 1st ed. Newport: Naval Supply Depot, 1954. [25]p. RNR. +

1808 MIDDLETOWN, R.I. SAINT COLUMBA'S CHURCH. Memorial services at fiftieth anniversary of the laying of the corner stone of St. Columba's, the Berkeley Memorial Chapel. n.p., [1934?]. 12p. RNR.
Episcopal church. Includes "Middletown as it was fifty years ago," by Helena Sturtevant.

1809 NATIONAL SOCIETY OF THE COLONIAL DAMES OF AMERICA. RHODE ISLAND. Whitehall, near Newport, Rhode Island: built in 1729 by George Berkeley, British philosopher and divine, Dean of Londonderry in Ireland. n.p., [1950]. 12p. RHi.
Includes "Bishop Berkeley," by Bertha Borden Davis.

1810 PAUL, EDWARD J. The part borne by Sergeant John White Paul, of Col. John Topham's regiment of the Rhode Island Brigade, in the capture of Brigadier General Richard Prescott, commander of the British forces, near Newport, R.I., in 1777. Milwaukee: Swain & Tarte, 1887. 22p. RHi. +

1811 RHODE ISLAND. HISTORICAL PRESERVATION COMMISSION. Preliminary survey report: town of Middletown. Providence, 1979. ii, 43p. RHi.
Author: Walter Nebiker.

1812 RIDER, SIDNEY S. "Sachusest." BN, 14 (1897), 261-262.
Indian village.

1813 SAINT GEORGE'S SCHOOL, MIDDLETOWN. Saint George's School in the War. [Newport:] Alumni Association of Saint George's School, 1920. xii, 168p. RHi.
World War I.

1814 SAVOIE, RONALD P. "The Chapel: an architectural history." Saint George's School, Bulletin, 54 (Spring-Summer 1978), 4-9.
50th anniversary of the consecration of the school's Episcopal chapel.

1815 STURTEVANT, MARY CLARK. "The east shore of Middletown since 1872." NHSB, No. 54 (1925), 13-18.

1816 _____. Records and memories of St. Columba's, the Berkeley Memorial Chapel, 1874-1928. [Newport: Remington Ward, 1928.] 52p. RP. +
Episcopal.

1817 TERRY, RODERICK. "The story of Green End Fort at the Siege of Newport." NHSB, No. 51 (1924), 7-14.
Revolutionary War.

1818 WALSH, KENNETH M., and DAVID S. WALSH. "Memo on location of 'Green End Fort.'" NH, 49 (1976), 1-13.
Built by British during Revolution.

SEE ALSO entries 452, 1167, 1169.

## NARRAGANSETT (WASHINGTON CO.)

1819 CARROLL, CHARLES. "Narragansett Pier." Harper's, 59 (July 1879), 161-177.

1820 CHAMPLIN, RICHARD L. "Point Judith Light: the early years." NH, 45 (1972), 83-89.

1821 DRAGO, CHARLES ROBERT. "Casa Nostra." RIer
(Nov. 6, 1977), 24-25, 27, 29, 31-32.
    Estate of Mrs. Theresa Lownes Noble, sold
in 1972 and torn down.

1822 GERSUNY, CARL, and JOHN J. POGGIE, JR.
"Harbor improvements and fishing at Point
Judith." RIH, 32 (1973), 23-32.

1823 HOYT, ERNEST M. Historical sketch of St.
Peter's-by-the-Sea, of Narragansett, Rhode
Island, 1852-1956. n.p., [1956]. 36p.
RHi.
    Episcopal church.

1824 KISSOUTH, WINIFRED J. W. "Wrecks off the
shores of Narragansett." PR, 2 (1964),
56-58.

1825 KLEIN, MAURY. "Summering at the Pier."
American History Illustrated, 13 (May 1978),
32-43.
    "A look at turn-of-the-century
Narragansett."

1826 MILLER, WILLIAM DAVIS. The capture of His
Majesty's Ship Syren. [Providence:] R.I.
Historical Society, 1923. 7p. RHi.
    1777. See also this author's article of
same title in RIHSC, 17 (1924), 24-28.

1827 NARRAGANSETT TIMES (newspaper).
Narragansett Pier special edition.
Wakefield (Apr. 1887). [4]p. RPB. +
    Includes historical sketch.

1828 RHODE ISLAND. HISTORICAL PRESERVATION
COMMISSION. Narragansett Pier,
Narragansett, Rhode Island: statewide
historical preservation report W-N-1.
[Providence,] 1978. iv, 40p. RHi.
    Author: Robert O. Jones.

1829 A SKETCH of Narragansett Pier: its past,
present and future. Wakefield:
Narragansett Times, 1888. 16p. RHi.

1830 TAFT, LEWIS A., and ANNIE TOTTEN. "Lost at
sea on Christmas Day." Yankee, 33 (Dec.
1969), 134-139.
    1885 shipwreck off Point Judith.

1831 TARASEVICH, CHRISTINE DUERR. "South Ferry:
Rhode Island's forgotten seaport." Univ. of
R.I. Alumni Quarterly, 60 (Fall 1981), 2-5.
    Now the site of the Univ. of R.I.
Narragansett Bay campus.

1832 TAYLOR, WILLIAM HENRY. "An eyewitness
recalls the birth of Narragansett Pier."
RIer (Aug. 29, 1971), 14-16, 18, 20.
    Written ca. 1920.

    SEE ALSO entries 181, 459, 554, 1309,
1322-1323.

## NEW SHOREHAM (WASHINGTON CO.)

1833 BECKWITH, HENRY TRUMAN. The history of
Block Island. (1858) n.p., [1873?]. 20p.
RHi. +

1834 BENSON, FREDERICK J. Research, reflection
and recollections of Block Island.
Westerly: Utter, 1977. x, 147p. RPB. +

1835 BLOCK Island scrapbook, by Maizie. N.Y.:
Pageant Pr., 1957. 345p. RHi. +
    [Maizie Rose.]

1836 BROWN, ARTHUR W. "New England cities and
towns: XIX, Block Island." NEM, 6 (1888),
107-125.

1837 BURGESS, GEORGE R. "The earliest known
white settlement on Block Island." RIHSC,
19 (1926), 81-88.

1838 "THE DISCOVERY of the real Palatine ship."
RIHSC, 16 (1923), 33-38.
    Signed H.M.C. (Howard M. Chapin).
18th-century shipwreck.

1839 FIELDERS, THOMAS B. Block Island fact and
fancy. n.p., n.d. 45p. RHi.

1840 GEMMING, ELIZABETH. "Block Island: 'a
little sandy place.'" RIer (July 9, 1972),
14-16, 18-19.
    Historical sketch.

1841 [HALEY, JOHN WILLIAMS.] "The Island of
Manisses." Providence: "Old Stone
Bank," 1932. 10p. RHi.
    Block Island's early history. This and
the next entry were part of the "Old Stone
Bank" historical pamphlet series. See note,
entry 432.

1842 [_____.] The Palatine Light.
Providence: "Old Stone Bank," 1931. 10p.
RHi.
    Legend relating to 18th-century shipwreck
off Block Island.

1843 HANKS, CARLOS C. "Toll of the stumbling
block: Block Island and its thousand
shipwrecks." Yankee, 8 (Apr. 1942), 48-51.

1844 HAYMAN, ROBERT W. The history of the
Catholic Church on Block Island. n.p., n.d.
[5]p. RPD-H.
    "Memento of the dedication of St. Andrew
Parish Center, Oct. 14, 1979."

1845 "HISTORICAL sketch." Block Island
Historical Society, Occasional Papers, No.
1 (1946), [7-8].
    History of Block Island Historical Society
(inc. 1942).

1846 KINOY, ARTHUR. The real mystery of Block Island: the origins of the island colony. [New Shoreham:] Block Island Historical Society, 1961. 32p. RHi. +

1847 LANMAN, CHARLES. "Block Island." Harper's, 53 (1876), 168-178.

1848 LIVERMORE, SAMUEL TRUESDALE. Block Island: an illustrated history, map and guide; revised and brought down to date, 1901. Providence: C. C. Ball, 1901. 156, [12]p. RHi. +
  Various earlier eds.

1849 _____. History of Block Island, Rhode Island. Reproduced and enhanced by the Block Island Committee of Republication for the Block Island Tercentenary Anniversary. (1877) Forge Village, Mass.: Murray Printing, 1961. 371, [17]p. RHi. +

1850 McHUGH, VINCENT. "A love letter to Block Island." RIer (Aug. 31, 1952), 3-6.

1851 MENDUM, SAMUEL W. "Block Island." NEM, n.s. 16 (1897), 738-751.

1852 MORIARTY, G. ANDREWS. "The Scottish prisoners at Block Island." RIHSC, 13 (1920), 28-35.
  Early settlers.

1853 _____. "Some notes on Block Islanders of the seventeenth century." New England Historical and Genealogical Register, 105 (1951), 162-182.

1854 _____. "Some notes on eighteenth century Block Island." New England Historical and Genealogical Register, 105 (1951), 249-272.

1855 NEW Shoreham, Rhode Island: three centuries of progress, 1661-1961. n.p., 1961. 31, [12]p. RNeS.

1856 NICHOLSON, PAUL C. Atlantic Tuna Club: then and now, 1914-1954. [Providence: Akerman-Standard,] 1954. 47p. RHi.
  Fishing club.

1857 _____. "The Block Island 'Double Ender.'" RIHSC, 16 (1923), 97-103.
  Fishing boat.

1858 PERRY, CHARLES E. "Block Island's story." NEM, n.s. 30 (1904), 515-524.

1859 PETTEE, EDWARD E. Block Island, R.I., illustrated; with a descriptive sketch and outline of history. Boston: Pr. of Deland & Barta, 1884. 122, vi p. RHi. +

1860 POWELL, NOEL. "Block Island's fiery ghost." Yankee, 20 (July 1956), 58-60.
  Legend of the Palatine (18th-century shipwreck).

1861 RITCHIE, ETHEL COLT. Block Island lore and legends. Block Island: F. Norman, 1956. 98p. RHi. +

1862 ROSE, MAIZIE. "'The sky looks awful queer...'" RIer (Sept. 19, 1976), 4-9, 11-12, 21.
  1938 hurricane.

1863 SHEFFIELD, WILLIAM P. A historical sketch of Block Island. Newport: John P. Sanborn, 1876. 62p. RHi. +

1864 TUCKER, KATHERINE PATRICIA. "Block Island." RIY (1973), 94-103.

1865 WILLIAMSON, CHILTON, JR. Saltbound: a Block Island winter. N.Y.: Methuen, 1980. 263p. RSc. +
  Diary of a winter on Block Island, with historical information.

SEE ALSO entries 181, 437, 715, 1082.

## NEWPORT (NEWPORT CO.)

1866 ADELMAN, DAVID C. "They broke in--to pray." RIJHN, 2 (1958), 226-237.
  Touro Synagogue (1902).

1867 ALLEN, FRANK JAMES. The ruined mill, or round church of the Norsemen, at Newport, Rhode Island, U.S.A., compared with the round church at Cambridge and others in Europe. From the Cambridge Antiquarian Society's Proceedings, Vol. XXII. [Cambridge, England,] 1921. [17]p. RHi. +

1868 ALLEN, HELEN FARRELL. "Newport: birthplace of championship tennis." RIY (1969), 27-32.

1869 _____. "Newport: capital and shrine of championship tennis." RIY (1970), 22-26.

1870 [ALMY, BENJAMIN.] A history of the grading of Channing Street and the way things are done by the city government of Newport, R.I. [Newport, 1890.] 34p. RNHi. +

1871 ALMY, MARY GOULD. "Mrs. Almy's journal: Siege of Newport, R.I., August, 1778." NHM, 1 (1880), 17-36.

1872 AMACKER, MILTON W. "The Brenton remembered." NH, 50 (1977), 1-5.
  Lightship.

1873   AMACKER, MILTON W.  "A century at Castle
       Hill."  RIY (1974), 56-59.
          Castle Hill Hotel.

1874   AMES, WINSLOW.  "The transformation of
       Chateau-sur-Mer."  Society of Architectural
       Historians, Journal, 29 (1970), 291-306.
          Historic house.

1875   AMORY, CLEVELAND.  "Newport:  there she
       sits."  Harper's, 196 (Feb. 1948), 118-127.
          Newport society.

1876   AMORY, THOMAS C.  The Siege of Newport,
       August, 1778.  n.p., n.d.  30p.  RHi. +

1877   ATWELL, CHARLES C.  "From Newport to
       anywhere...."  Yankee, 35 (Feb. 1971),
       94-95, 100-103.
          Newport Aero, an air taxi and charter
       service.

1878   AUCHINCLOSS, LOUIS S.  "Oaklawn."  NH, 44
       (1971), 19-24.
          Cottage of Charles Handy Russell.

1879   BAIN, JUNE.  "A tale of two husbands."
       Yankee, 24 (Sept. 1960), 64, 69, 106.
          Samuel Cranston returned in 1763 from
       years of captivity on a pirate ship to find
       his wife about to re-marry.  See also entry
       2342.

1880   BAKER, DARIUS.  "The Coddington portrait."
       NHSB, No. 25 (1918), 1-23.
          William Coddington.

1881   _____.  "The Newport Bannisters."  NHSB, No.
       43 (1923), 1-20.
          Bannister family.

1882   BALLARD, MARGARET.  "Early silver in Trinity
       Church, Newport, Rhode Island."  Antiques,
       120 (1981), 922-925.
          Episcopal.

1883   BANNING, EVELYN I.  "A boarder in Sleepy
       Hollow."  NH, 48 (1975), 247-254.
          Helen Hunt and Newport's literary
       community.

1884   BARBER, JAMES A., JR.  "The school of naval
       warfare."  Naval War College Review, 21
       (Apr. 1969), 89-96.
          U.S. Naval War College.

1885   BARE, BRENTON.  History of the United
       Congregational Church, Newport, Rhode
       Island, 1895-1945:  sermons preached at the
       250th anniversary celebration, October,
       1945....  n.p., n.d.  [9]p.  RNHi.

1886   BARROWS, COMFORT EDWIN.  Historical sketch
       of the First Baptist Church, Newport, R.I.:
       a discourse delivered on Thanksgiving Day,
       November 30, 1876.  Newport:  John P.
       Sanborn, 1876.  64p.  RHi. +

1887   BARTLETT, JOHN RUSSELL.  History of the
       Wanton family of Newport, Rhode Island.
       Providence:  Sidney S. Rider, 1878.  152p.
       RHi. +

1888   BARTON, GEORGE.  "The Naval War College at
       Newport."  Society's Season (Sept. 1935),
       28-29, 40, 45.

1889   BAVIER, ROBERT NEWTON.  America's Cup fever:
       an inside view of fifty years of America's
       Cup competition.  (1980) Rev. ed.  N.Y.:
       Ziff-Davis Publishing, 1981.  xv, 239p.
       RNR. +
          International yacht races, held in Newport
       since 1930.

1890   BENSON, ESTHER FISHER.  "The history of the
       John Stevens Shop."  NHSB, No. 112 (1963),
       7-33.
          Stonecutting shop.

1891   BENSON, JOHN HOWARD.  Flags of the Old State
       House, Newport, R.I.  Newport:  Old State
       House, Inc., [1943?].  [18]p.  RHi. +

1892   BERGNER, JONAS.  "The old house on Franklin
       Street."  NHSB, No. 40 (1922), 1-7.

1893   BICKNELL, THOMAS WILLIAMS.  "The Quakers in
       ancient Newport."  NHSB, No. 13 (1914), 1-2.

1894   BIELLO, JOSEPH A.  "U.S. Naval Hospital,
       Newport, R.I.:  historical sketch."  RIMJ,
       24 (1941), 98-99.

1895   BIGELOW, BRUCE M.  "Aaron Lopez:  colonial
       merchant of Newport."  NEQ, 4 (1931),
       757-776.

1896   _____.  "The Walter Newbury shipping book."
       RIHSC, 24 (1931), 73-91.
          17th-century merchant.

1897   BLISS, RICHARD.  "The hailstorm of July 14,
       1894."  Newport Natural History Society,
       Proceedings, No. 9 (1900), 29-33.

1898   BLISS, ZENAS R.  "Racing for the Cup:  then
       and now."  RIer (Sept. 14, 1958), 4-7.
          America's Cup yacht races.

1899   BOGART, DAVID, RICHARD GROSVENOR, and JOHN
       PEPPER.  "Prohibition and rum running in
       Newport."  Saint George's School, The
       Dragon, 58 (Spring 1966), 13-17.

1900 Newport

1900 BOGGS, WILLIAM E. "The rebirth of an abandoned school." NH, 55 (1982), 143-150.
Callender School, closed in 1974 and later transformed into townhouses by architect George Ranalli.

1901 BOLHOUSE, GLADYS E. "Abraham Redwood: reluctant Quaker, philanthropist, botanist." NH, 45 (1972) , 17-35.

1902 _____. "18th century building agreements." NH, 43 (1970), 9-16.

1903 _____. "The Moravian Church in Newport." NH, 52 (1979), 10-17.

1904 _____. "The Muenchinger-King Hotel." NH, 41 (1968), 57-66.

1905 BOOTH, GLADYS BACHELLER. "Requiem for the old abandoned neighborhood schools." NH, 55 (1982), 151-154.

1906 BOSS, JUDITH A. Newport: a pictorial history. Norfolk, Va.: Donning, 1981. 217p. RNHi.

1907 BOWEN, DONALD F. "A clock case by John Goddard." Antiquarian, 15, No. 2 (Aug. 1930), 37, 74.
18th-century Newport cabinetmaker.

1908 BOWEN, RICHARD LeBARON. "Godfrey Malbone's armorial silver." RIH, 9 (1950), 37-51, 84-94.

1909 _____. "The Scott family needle work." RIH, 2 (1943), 11-21, 49-57.

1910 BOWER, ANTHONY. "Newport observed." Art in America, 53 (June 1965), 120-123.
Interiors of Newport historic houses and historic buildings.

1911 [BRAYTON, ALICE.] The burying place of Governor Arnold: an account of the establishment, destruction, and restoration of the burying place of Benedict Arnold, first governor of Rhode Island and Providence Plantations.... Newport: Priv. Print., 1960. 135p. RHi. +

1912 _____. George Berkeley in Newport. Newport, 1954. xvii, 129p. RHi. +
The noted Irish philosopher and clergyman lived in Newport, 1729-1731.

1913 BRENTON, ELIZABETH C. A history of Brenton's Neck, from 1638, with incidents relative to the settlement of Newport, and the Revolutionary War. Newport: John P. Sanborn, 1877. 50p. RHi.

1914 "THE BRICK Market." NG, No. 6 (1959), [3-5].
See also NG, No. 70 (1977), [10-11].

1915 BRIDENBAUGH, CARL. "Charlestownians at Newport, 1767-1775." South Carolina Historical and Genealogical Magazine, 41 (1940), 43-47.
"Among the colonial gentry who made Newport our first social capital were the planters of South Carolina" who summered there.

1916 _____. "Colonial Newport as a summer resort." RIHSC, 26 (1933), 1-23.

1917 _____. Peter Harrison: first American architect. Chapel Hill, N.C.: Univ. of North Carolina Pr., 1949. xvi, 195p. RHi. +
Includes his years in colonial Newport. See also this author's accounts of colonial and Revolutionary-era Newport in his Cities in the wilderness (1938) and Cities in revolt (2d ed., 1971).

1918 BRIGHAM, CLARENCE SAUNDERS. "James Franklin and the beginnings of printing in Rhode Island." Massachusetts Historical Society, Proceedings, 65 (1936), 536-544.
Colony's first printer, located in Newport.

1919 BRIGHAM, HERBERT OLIN. The old Stone Mill. (1948) 2d ed. Newport: Franklin Printing, 1955. 32p. RHi. +
Famous landmark, the origins of which have been much debated.

1920 [BROOKS, CHARLES T.] The controversy touching the old Stone Mill, in the town of Newport, Rhode-Island.... Newport: Charles E. Hammett, Jr., 1851. 91p. RHi. +

1921 _____. A history of the Unitarian Church in Newport, Rhode Island; read in the church Sunday, January 10, 1875. Newport: Davis & Pitman, 1875. 48p. RHi. +
Channing Memorial Church.

1922 BROOKS, HOWARD E. The Negro in Newport, R.I.: a short history. n.p., 1946. Unp. RNHi.

1923 BROOKS, JEROME E. The $30,000,000 cup: the stormy history of the defense of the America's Cup. N.Y.: Simon and Schuster, 1958. xii, 275p. RNR. +

1924 BROWN, MADELAINE R. "Three examples of the work of Lawrance Langworthy, Newport pewterer." RIHSC, 32 (1939), 56-60.

1925 BROWN, RALPH ADAMS. "The Newport Gazette: Tory newssheet." RIH, 13 (1954), 97-108; 14 (1955), 11-20.

1926 BROWN UNIVERSITY. DEPARTMENT OF ANTHROPOLOGY. Archaeological investigations in Queen Anne Square, Newport, Rhode Island, June 1979. n.p., n.d. vi, 206p. RNR.
Stephen Mrozowski, principal researcher.

1927 BROWNE, HOWARD S. The Newport Hospital: a history, 1873-1973. Newport, 1976. xiv, 175p. RHi. +

1928 _____. "Newport's Revolutionary physicians." NH, 54 (1981), 5-34.

1929 BROWNELL, W. C. "Newport." Scribner's, 16 (1896), 135-156.

1930 BUELL, WILLIAM A. "The golden age of the Newport Casino Theatre." NH, 46 (1973), 29-33.

1931 BUFFUM, MRS. WILLIAM P. "The story of the old Friends' Meeting House." NHSB, No. 40 (1922), 8-11.

1932 BULL, HENRY IV. "The Bull family of Newport." NHSB, No. 81 (1931), 1-31.

1933 BULLOCK, ORIN M., JR. "The Friends Meeting House, 1699-1922: an architectural research report." NH, 42 (1969), 25-[57].

1934 BURKE, JOHN C. "The break in." RIJHN, 6 (1974), 532-541.
Controversy over ownership of Touro Synagogue (1902).

1935 BURNELL, R. D. Races for the America's Cup. London: Macdonald, 1965. 222p. RNR. +

1936 BYRNES, GARRETT D. "Another Newport 'cottage' goes public." RIer (Apr. 9, 1972), 8-9, 11-12, 14.
Rosecliff and its past.

1937 _____. "A love letter to Newport." RIer (July 2, 1967), 6-8, 10.
Historical.

1938 CABLE, MARY. "The marble cottages." Horizon, 7, No. 4 (Autumn 1965), 19-26.

1939 [CAHOONE, SARAH S.] Sketches of Newport and its vicinity; with notices respecting the history, settlement and geography of Rhode Island. N.Y.: John S. Taylor, 1842. 213p. RHi. +
First published in 1840 as Visit to Grand-papa; or, a week in Newport.

1940 "THE CAP of the Newport Light Infantry Co." RIHSC, 20 (1927), 7-11.

1941 CARPENTER, RALPH E., JR. The arts and crafts of Newport, Rhode Island, 1640-1820. Newport: Preservation Society of Newport County, 1954. xiii, 216p. RHi. +

1942 _____. "Discoveries in Newport furniture and silver." Antiques, 68 (1955), 44-49.

1943 _____. "The Newport exhibition." Antiques, 64 (1953), 38-45.
Exhibition by the Preservation Society of Newport County of locally-made furniture, silver, paintings, and prints.

1944 [_____.] Washington-Rochambeau celebration in historic Newport, Rhode Island, 1780-1955. n.p., [1955]. [8]p. RHi.
Commemorating French presence in Newport during American Revolution.

1945 CARRICK, ROBERT W. The pictorial history of the America's Cup races. N.Y.: Viking Pr., 1964. 194p. RNR. +

1946 CARTER, SAMUEL III. "The great nautical jam." Yankee, 31 (Aug. 1967), 86, 88, 93, 148-155.
Crowds at the America's Cup races.

1947 CHADWICK, MRS. FRENCH E. "The visit of General Washington to Newport in 1781." NHSB, No. 6 (1913), 1-19.

1948 CHAMPLIN, RICHARD L. "The art, trade, or mystery of the ropemaker." NH, 46 (1973), 81-93.

1949 _____. "Beacon Rock." NH, 56 (1983), 6-9.
Historic house, built 1891.

1950 _____. "High time: William Claggett and his clockmaking family." NH, 47 (1974), 157-190.

1951 _____. "James Wady: 'the life so short, the craft so long to learn.'" NH, 48 (1975), 348-355.
Clockmaker.

1952 _____. "Newport estates and their flora." NH, 53 (1980), 49-66, 89-100; 54 (1981), 45-50.

1953 _____. "Quaker clockmakers of Newport." NH, 50 (1977), 77-89.

1954 _____. "Rose Island centennial." NH, 43 (1970), 65-70.
Rose Island Lighthouse.

1955 _____. "Spouting Rock: thar she blew." NH, 45 (1972), 1-6.

1956 CHAMPLIN, RICHARD L. "Thomas Claggett: silversmith, swordsman, clockmaker." NH, 49 (1976), 57-68.

1957 CHANNING, GEORGE G. Early recollections of Newport, R.I., from the year 1793 to 1811. Newport: A. J. Ward, 1868. 284p. RHi. +

1958 CHAPIN, HOWARD M. Calendrier Francais pour l'année 1781 and the printing press of the French fleet in American waters during the Revolutionary War. Providence: Preston & Rounds, 1914. [9]p. RHi. +
French-language almanac.

1959 _____. "Was Claggett, the clock-maker, an engraver?" RIHSC, 22 (1929), 41-45.

1960 CHASE, DAVID. "Notes on the Colonial Revival in Newport." NH, 55 (1982), 38-62.
"...The story of six pre-Revolutionary landmarks...and what befell them in the nineteenth century."

1961 "CHATEAU-sur-Mer." NG, No. 40 (Nov. 1969), [1-5].
Historic house.

1962 CHEROL, JOHN A. "Chateau-sur-Mer in Newport, Rhode Island." Antiques, 118 (1980), 1220-1225.
Historic house.

1963 _____. "Designed for another age: decorative arts in Newport mansions." Antiques 118 (1980), 498-501.

1964 _____. "Kingscote in Newport, Rhode Island." Antiques, 118 (1980), 476-485.
Historic house.

1965 _____. "Restoration of the butternut rooms, Chateau-sur-Mer, Newport, R.I." Nineteenth Century, 7, No. 1 (Spring 1981), 34-36.
Historic house.

1966 CHOULES, J. O. A sermon, preached November 26, 1829, being the day of thanksgiving, containing a history of the Second Baptist Church, Newport, R.I. Providence, 1830. 27p. RPB. +

1967 CHYET, STANLEY F. "Aaron Lopez: a study in buenafama." American Jewish Historical Quarterly, 52 (1963), 295-309.
See also next entry.

1968 _____. Lopez of Newport: colonial American merchant prince. Detroit: Wayne State Univ. Pr., 1970. 246p. RHi. +
Aaron Lopez: his involvements in Newport's commerce, Jewish community, etc.

1969 _____. "A synagogue in Newport." American Jewish Archives, 16 (1964), 41-50.
Touro Synagogue.

1970 CLARK, KENNETH. "Newport: an early American seaport." White Pine Series of Architectural Monographs, 8 (June 1922), 3-16.

1971 CLARKE, CHARLES H. The Old Stone Mill, Touro Park, Newport, Rhode Island. [Newport, 1910.] 23p. RHi. +

1972 COGGESHALL, W. J., and J. E. McCARTHY. The Naval Torpedo Station, Newport, Rhode Island, 1658 through 1925. (1920) Newport: Remington Ward, 1944. 37p. RNW-Hi.

1973 COMER, JOHN. ...The diary of John Comer. Edited with notes by C. Edwin Barrows...with an introduction and a few additional notes by James W. Willmarth. [Providence: R.I. Historical Society], 1893. 132p. RHi. +
Baptist minister. Published as RIHSC, 8.

1974 CONANT, KENNETH J. "Newport Tower or Mill." RIH, 7 (1948), 2-7.

1975 CONFORTI, JOSEPH. "Samuel Hopkins and the Revolutionary antislavery movement." RIH, 38 (1979), 39-49.
Pastor of First Congregational Church.

1976 COOPER, JOSEPH. "The Methodist Church in Newport." NHSB, No. 101 (1940), 45-48.

1977 CORNELL, JOHN. "The Cornell Farm of Newport." Americana, 6 (Feb. 1911), 109-111.

1978 CORR, EDWARD J. "'I remember I was in a phone booth, and it was lifting off the floor.'" RIer (Sept. 17, 1978), 24, 26.
1938 hurricane.

1979 COST, HARRY FULTON. "Presbyterian Church in Newport." NHSB, No. 101 (1940), 51-53.

1980 COVELL, ELIZABETH GREENE. "The visits of Benjamin Franklin to Newport, Rhode Island." NHSB, No. 103 (1945), 1-16.

1981 COVELL, WILLIAM KING. "Newport, Rhode Island, houses: before and after." Old-time New England, 25 (1935), 128-135; 28 (1937), 1-2.
Houses no longer standing and the buildings that replaced them.

1982 _____. The organs of Trinity Church, Newport, R.I. London: Musical Opinion, 1935. 14p. RNR. +
Episcopal. Pamphlet reprinted from The Organ, 14 (1955).

1983 COVELL, MRS. WILLIAM W. "Historic types of Newport houses." NHSB, No. 48 (1924), 1-10.

1984 CRANE, ELAINE F. "Uneasy coexistence: religious tensions in eighteenth century Newport." NH, 53 (1980), 101-111.

1985 CURTIS, EDITH ROELKER. "Girlhood in Newport in the golden age." RIer (Aug. 28, 1960), 10-13.

1986 DALLETT, FRANCIS JAMES. "The Newport Marine Society certificate: discoveries in American engraving." NH, 37 (1964), 125-132.

1987 DANIELS, BRUCE C. "Governing Rhode Island's metropolitan: the town meeting and its officers in colonial Newport, 1770-1776." NH, 52 (1979), 101-117.

1988 DARLING, FAYREEN B. "The most elegant house in Newport." Yankee, 31 (Apr. 1967), 79-80, 128-130.
    Villa Marina, built in 1870 by Milton H. Sanford.

1989 DARLING, PAUL A. "Rhode Island's Cliff Walk: its wild origins and bright future." Yankee, 36 (Nov. 1972), 62-66, 68, 70.

1990 DAUGHTERS OF THE AMERICAN REVOLUTION. RHODE ISLAND. WILLIAM ELLERY CHAPTER, NEWPORT. 300th aniversary of Newport, Rhode Island, 1639-1939. [Newport: Beans Pr., 1939.] [29]p. RNR.

1991 DAVIS, LUCIUS D. History of the Methodist Episcopal Church, in Newport, R.I. Newport: Davis & Pitman, 1882. 136p. RHi. +

1992 DAWLEY, JESSIE ROSE. The story of Emanuel Church, Newport, R.I. n.p., n.d. 153p. RNHi.
    Episcopal.

1993 DEAR, IAN. The America's Cup: an informal history. N.Y.: Dodd, Mead, 1980. 192p. RP. +

1994 DEARDEN, PAUL F. "The Siege of Newport: inauspicious dawn of alliance." RIH, 29 (1970), 17-35.
    1778. See also entry 1178.

1995 DEFENDING the America's Cup. Robert W. Carrick and Stanley Z. Rosenfeld, eds. N.Y.: Knopf, 1969. xv, 189p. RNR. +

1996 DEMBER, IRA. "The grandest dames of Newport's gilded age." RIer (Nov. 21, 1971), 19-20, 23-24.
    Mamie Fish, Alva Belmont, and Tessie Oelrichs.

1997 DEUTSCH, SARAH. "The elusive Guineamen: Newport slavers, 1735-1774." NEQ, 55 (1982), 229-253.

1998 DEXTER, LORRAINE LeH. "Steps from Trinity Church to the Point: the Zabriskie Memorial Church of St. John." NH, 48 (1975), 329-346.
    Episcopal.

1999 "DID Jews settle in Rhode Island in 1658?" RIJHN, 2 (1958), 216-218.
    Signed D.C.A. (David C. Adelman).

2000 [DIX, JOHN ROSS.] A hand-book of Newport, and Rhode Island. Newport: C. E. Hammett, Jr., 1852. xii, 170p. RHi. +
    Includes historical information.

2001 DODGE, DONALD. "The Corné House, ca. 1799-1822(?)." NH, 42 (1969), 14-21.
    Home of painter Michele Felice Corné.

2002 DOW, CHARLES H. Newport, the city by the sea; four epochs in her history: an age of shadowy tradition, an era of commercial success and social splendor, a generation of decadence, a half century of unparalleled development. Newport: John P. Sanborn, 1880. 120p. RHi. +

2003 DOW, RICHARD ALAN, and E. ANDREW MOWBRAY. Newport. Providence: Mowbray, 1976. [62]p. RHi. +
    Pictorial, descriptive, historical.

2004 DOWNING, ANTOINETTE FORRESTER. "History of the Friends Meeting House in Newport, Rhode Island." NH, 41 (1968), 137-167.

2005 _____. "The story of Pitt's Head Tavern, Ebenezer Flagg's Newport home." NG, No. 1 (1947), [3-12].

2006 _____, and VINCENT J. SCULLY, JR. The architectural heritage of Newport, Rhode Island, 1640-1915. (1952) 2d ed. N.Y.: C. N. Potter, 1967. xvi, 526p. RHi. +

2007 DUNLAP, G. D. America's Cup defenders. N.Y.: American Heritage Pr., 1970. 91p. RHi. +

2008 DUNTON, GARDNER. "Building The Breakers." RIer (July 3, 1960), 8-10.
    Historic house.

2009 _____. "Covering the end of a glittering era of Newport." RIer (Aug. 24, 1958), 4-5, 7-8, 10.
    Changing scene along Bellevue Ave.

2010 Newport

2010 DUNTON, GARDNER. "The day George Washington disappeared." Yankee, 33 (Nov. 1969), 100, 132-134.
Gilbert Stuart portrait of Washington in the Old State House.

2011 _____. "'Men...safe from female intrusion.'" RIer (Oct. 11, 1953), 12-14.
Newport Reading Room (club).

2012 _____. "The Newport story." RIY (1965-1966), 49-55.

2013 _____. "This was the Newport that was." RIer (Aug. 2, 1964), 8-12.
Newport society.

2014 EDEL, LEON. Henry James, Edith Wharton, and Newport: an address delivered...at the opening of the exhibition held at the Redwood Library and Athenaeum, Newport, Rhode Island, July and August, 1966. Newport, 1966. 28p. RHi. +

2015 EDWARD, JAMES G. The Newport story. Newport: Remington Ward, 1952. 71p. RHi. +

2016 ELLICOTT, J. M. "Three Navy cranks and what they turned." U.S. Naval Institute Proceedings, 50 (1924), 1615-1628.
U.S. Naval War College.

2017 ELLIOTT, MAUD HOWE. "The Navy at Newport." U.S. Naval Institute Proceedings, 59 (1933), 842-843.

2018 _____. "Newport, the cradle of American sports." NHSB, No. 89 (1933), 2-28.

2019 _____. "Some recollections of Newport artists." NHSB, No. 35 (1921), 1-32.

2020 _____. This was my Newport. Cambridge, Mass.: Mythology Company, 1944. xxiv, 279p. RHi. +

2021 ELLIOTT, MRS. R. SHERMAN. "The Seventh Day Baptist Meeting House, Newport, Rhode Island: excerpts from a paper read before the Newport Historical Society, November 18, 1929." NH, 48 (1975), 265-278.
Includes information about building's removal and restoration by Newport Historical Society. See also NHSB, No. 73 (1930), 1-15.

2022 ELLIS, F. R. "The U.S. Naval War College story." NH, 37 (1964), 57-73.
See also this author's article of same title in Navy: the Magazine of Sea Power, 6 (June 1963), 16-21, 32-33.

2023 "THE ELMS." NG, No. 18 (1963), [6-9].
Historic house.

2024 "FACT and fancy about the old Stone Mill." Newport Herald (Mar. 29, Aug. 25, 1899).

2025 FANTA, J. JULIUS. Winning the America's Cup: twenty challenges, 1870-1970. N.Y.: Sea Lore Publishing, 1969. 200p. RP. +

2026 FARRELL, JOHN E. "'The air of Rhode Island is good.'" RIMJ, 59 (1976), 317-327, 339-342.
Colonial and Revolutionary-era medicine in Newport.

2027 FAUVEL GOURAUD, J. B. G. L'Hercule et la Favorite; ou la capture de l'Alexandre de Bordeaux, et des Pirates Bordelais, effectuée à New-port, Rhode Island, états-Unis de l'Amérique du Nord, le 21 mai 1838. Paris: Chez l'Auteur, 1840. 2v. RHi. +
Arrested and held for a time in Newport, the pirates eventually were returned to France and hanged. The author was French vice consul in Newport at the time of the incident.

2028 FERBER, LINDA S. "William Trost Richards at Newport." NH, 51 (1978), 1-15.
Landscape painter.

2029 FERGUSON, J. WALTON. "Kingscote grounds." NG, No. 67 (1976), 11-14.
Historic house and grounds.

2030 _____. Kingscote: Newport cottage orné. Newport: Preservation Society of Newport County, 1977. 42p. RNR. +

2031 _____. Rosecliff. Newport: Preservation Society of Newport County, 1977. 25p. RHi. +
Historic house.

2032 FERREE, BARR. "'Castlewood,' the villa of Louis Bruguiere, Esq., Newport, Rhode Island." American Homes and Gardens, 5 (1908), 299-303.

2033 FLATHER, RANDOLPH. "Ida Lewis was quite a woman." RIer (Oct. 16, 1977), 28-30, 32, 34.
Noted for her rescues of shipwreck victims.

2034 FLIFLET, THORLEIF. A layman looks at Newport Tower. n.p., n.d. [4]p. RHi.
Stone Mill.

2035 FOOTE, HENRY WILDER. "John Smibert and Robert Feke in Newport." RIH, 9 (1950), 33-36.
Painters.

2036 FOOTE, HENRY WILDER. "Robert Feke, portrait painter." RIH, 6 (1947), 35-43.
See also preceding entry.

2037 "FORT Adams." NG, No. 24 (1965), [13-15].
Former U.S. Army post.

2038 FRANKLIN, ROBERT S. "Newport cemeteries." NHSB, No. 10 (1913), 3-45.

2039 FRANKLIN, RUTH B. A short history of the Civic League of Newport, Inc., 1905-1940. Newport: Franklin Printing, n.d. 12p. RHi.

2040 _____. "Some early schools and schoolmasters of Newport." NHSB, No. 96 (1936), 13-31.

2041 FRANKLIN, SUSAN BRALEY. "Division Street: a memory and a warning." NHSB, No. 104 (1948), 1-40.

2042 _____. Historical sketch of Second Baptist Church, Newport, Rhode Island, 1656-1936. [Newport, 1936?] 21p. RNHi. +

2043 FRANKLIN PRINTING HOUSE. Two centuries in Newport, Rhode Island, 1727-1928. Newport, [1928]. [12]p. RHi.
History of the business.

2044 FREEMASONS. NEWPORT. VAN RENSSELAER LODGE OF PERFECTION. Van Rensselaer Lodge of Perfection, Ancient Accepted Scottish Rite, Valley of Newport, Rhode Island; Seventy-fifth anniversary, December the sixteenth, nineteen hundred and twenty-four. Newport: Mercury Publishing, n.d., 20, [3]p. RNHi.

2045 "THE FRENCH fleet at Newport, 1778." RIY (1965-1966), 64-65.
From a French officer's diary.

2046 "THE FRENCH in Newport, 1781, 1881." NHM, 2 (1882), 176-178.
Signed J.E.M.

2047 FRIEDMAN, LEE M. "The Newport synagogue." Old-time New England, 36 (1946), 49-57.
Touro Synagogue.

2048 GALE, MARIE J. "Some old Newport houses." NHSB, No. 36 (1921), 1-20.

2049 GALVIN, JOHN. "Tennis lessons." RIer (June 27, 1976), 20-24.
Tournament tennis in Newport (1950s).

2050 GARDNER, WILLIAM F. "Robert Gardner and the founding of Trinity Church, Newport, R.I." NHM, 7 (1887), 197-200.
Episcopal.

2051 GARRETT, WENDELL D. "The furnishings of Newport houses, 1780-1800." RIH, 18 (1959), 1-19.

2052 _____. "The Goddard and Townsend joiners of Newport: random biographical and bibliographical notes." Antiques, 121 (1982), 1153-1155.
Cabinetmakers.

2053 GIFFORD, BARBARA L. "James Franklin and his press: being an account of the introduction of printing into the Colony of Rhode island and Providence Plantations, wherein appears something of the history of the first printer and his press." RIY (1973), 76-87.

2054 GIROUARD, MARK. "Newport, Rhode Island: an eccentric among American towns." Country Life, 134 (1963), 478-481, 545-549.

2055 GLEESON, PAUL FRANCIS. "The Newport Light Infantry." RIHSC, 33 (1940), 1-13.

2056 GODFREY, WILLIAM S., JR. "The archaeology of the old Stone Mill in Newport, Rhode Island." American Antiquity, 17 (1951), 120-129.

2057 _____. "The Newport puzzle." Archaeology, 2 (1949), 146-149.
Stone mill.

2058 _____. "Newport Tower, II." Archaeology, 3 (1950), 82-86.
See also preceding entry.

2059 GOLDBLATT, BURT. Newport Jazz Festival: the illustrated history. N.Y.: Dial Pr., 1977. xxix, 287p. RHi. +

2060 GOLDOWSKY, SEEBERT J. "More on Aaron Lopez." RIJHN, 6 (1973), 313-326.
Jewish merchant.

2061 _____. "Newport as Ararat." RIJHN, 6 (1974), 604-609.
Proposed migration of European Jews to Newport in 1820s.

2062 _____. "Where they lived and worked in old Newport." RIJHN, 5 (1970), 382-385.
Early Jewish residents.

2063 GOOD, L. DOUGLAS. "Colonials at play: leisure in Newport, 1723." RIH, 33 (1974), 9-17.

2064 GOODMAN, ABRAM VOSSEN. "A distinct people." RIJHN, 5 (1970), 327-331.
Touro Synagogue as a symbol for American Jews.

2065 Newport

2065 GOODWIN, DANIEL. "'The making of Trinity Church, Newport'": a sermon before the Rhode Island Episcopal Convention held June 14 and 15, A.D. 1898, in Trinity Church, Newport, on the occasion of the two hundredth anniversary of the parish. Providence: Snow & Farnham, 1898. 22p. RHi. +

2066 _____. "Newport under British occupation." Magazine of History, 13 (1911), 14-19, 81-86.
American Revolution.

2067 GRAY, CHANNING. "Those ill-fated Newport fests." RIer (July 5, 1981), 10-11.
Music festivals.

2068 GREENE, JOHN H., JR. "A brief history of the Catholic Church in Newport." NHSB, No. 101 (1940), 19-30.

2069 _____. The building of the Old Colony House at Newport, Rhode Island. 2d ed. Newport: Old State House in Newport, Rhode Island, Inc., 1952. [9]p. RHi. +

2070 GUINNESS, DESMOND, and JULIUS TRUESDALE SADLER, JR. Newport preserv'd: architecture of the 18th century. N.Y.: Viking Pr., 1982. 152p. RHi. +

2071 GUTSTEIN, MORRIS A. Aaron Lopez and Judah Touro: a refugee and a son of a refugee. N.Y.: Behrman's Jewish Book House, 1939. xii, 118p. RHi. +

2072 _____. "A Newport ledger, 1760-1770." American Jewish Historical Society, Publications, 37 (1947), 163-169.
Attributed to Naphtaly Hart and Company, merchants.

2073 _____. The story of the Jews of Newport: two and a half centuries of Judaism, 1658-1908. N.Y.: Bloch Publishing, 1936. 393p. RHi. +

2074 _____. To bigotry no sanction: a Jewish shrine in America, 1658-1958. N.Y.: Bloch Publishing, 1958. 191p. RP. +
Touro Synagogue.

2075 _____. The Touro family in Newport. Newport: Newport Historical Society, 1935. 39p. RHi. +
Reprinted from NHSB, No. 94 (1935), 3-39.

2076 GUTTMAN, ALEXANDER. "Ezra Stiles, Newport Jewry, and a question of Jewish law." American Jewish Archives, 34 (1982), 98-102.

2077 HACKETT, WALTER. "The remarkable Count Axel de Fersen." RIer (Mar. 24, 1968), 12-13.
Swedish nobleman and French officer, who served in Newport during the American Revolution.

2078 HALE, STUART O. "How Fort Adams will come to life again." RIer (Jan. 17, 1965), 10-12.
Includes sketch of the former U.S. Army post's past.

2079 [HALEY, JOHN WILLIAMS.] "Aaron Lopez." Providence: "Old Stone Bank," 1932. 10p. RHi.
Early Jewish merchant. This and the following entries by the same author were part of the "Old Stone Bank" historical pamphlet series. See note, entry 432.

2080 [_____.] Admiral de Ternay. Providence: "Old Stone Bank," 1932. 10p. RHi.
Commander of French fleet at Newport during American Revolution.

2081 [_____.] Belles of colonial Newport. Providence: "Old Stone Bank," 1930. 10p. RHi.
Newport and the French troops stationed there during the American Revolution.

2082 [_____.] A gentleman's journal. Providence: "Old Stone Bank," 1931. 10p. RHi.
William Jefferay, who settled in Newport in 1650.

2083 [_____.] Ida Lewis. Providence: "Old Stone Bank," 1931. 10p. RHi.
Known for her rescues of shipwreck survivors, "She was more famous, particularly during the latter half of her life, than any American woman of the past or present."

2084 [_____.] Newport and our Navy. Providence: "Old Stone Bank," 1933. 10p. RHi.

2085 [_____.] The Newport assemblies. Providence: "Old Stone Bank," 1931. 10p. RHi.
Dances for Newport's upper classes (18th century).

2086 [_____.] A Newport landmark. Providence: "Old Stone Bank," 1930. 10p. RHi.
The Vernon House.

2087 [_____.] "The old synagogue in Newport." Providence: "Old Stone Bank," 1932. 10p. RHi.
Touro Synagogue.

2088 HALEY, JOHN WILLIAMS. "Peter Harrison, a great colonial architect." Old-time New England, 36 (1946), 58-61.
His work in Newport.

2089 [_____.] An unknown destination. Providence: "Old Stone Bank," 1932. 10p. RHi.
The French troops sent to Newport in 1780.

2090 [_____.] William Brenton of Hammersmith. Providence: "Old Stone Bank," 1933. 10p. RHi.
One of the first settlers of Newport.

2091 HAMMOND, GEOFFREY F. Showdown at Newport: the race for the America's Cup. N.Y.: Walden Publishing, 1974. vii, 216p. RNR. +

2092 HANLON, JOHN. "The cradle of tennis was meant to be rocky." Sports Illustrated, 28 (Nov. 11, 1968), E3-E4.
Newport Casino.

2093 _____. "Newport's sporting life was never dull." RIer (Aug. 11, 1968), 4-7.

2094 _____. "The prickly pioneer of golf." Sports Illustrated, 29 (Feb. 26, 1968), S3-S4.
First official national amateur golf championship, held in Newport, 1895.

2095 _____. "Tennis in Newport: how it all began." RIer (Aug. 1, 1971), 15-17.

2096 HARRIS, FRANK G. History of the re-union of the Sons and Daughters of Newport, R.I., July 4th, 1884. Newport: Davis & Pitman, 1885. 171p. RHi. +

2097 HARRISON, SANDRA LYNNE. "The Cotton House." NG, No. 11 (1960), [3-5].
Historic house.

2098 HATFIELD, R. G. "The 'old mill' at Newport: a new study of an old puzzle." Scribner's, 17 (1879), 632-641.
Stone Mill.

2099 HAYES, JOHN D. "Stephen B. Luce and the beginnings of the U.S. Naval War College." Naval War College Review, 23 (Jan. 1971), 51-59.

2100 HAYWARD, JOHN T. "I had a dream: the story of the Naval War College." Shipmate, 37 (Oct. 1974), 16-19.

2101 HECKSCHER, MORRISON H. "John Townsend's block-and-shell furniture." Antiques, 121 (1982), 1144-1152.
Newport cabinetmaker.

2102 HELFNER, FRANCINE GAIL. "Where credit is due: Jewish contributions to life in Newport." RIJHN, 6 (1972), 226-235.

2103 HENIN, BENJAMIN LOUIS ANTOINE. American historical oration, delivered at the inauguration of the monument erected in Newport, R.I., to commemorate the landing in 1780 on the cliffs of Newport, of the French troops which came to help the American colonists obtain their independence; Newport, R.I., July 14th, 1928. n.p., 1929. 13p. RHi. +

2104 HERBST, JURGEN. "The charter for a proposed college in Newport, Rhode Island: a chapter in the history of eighteenth century higher education in America." NH, 49 (1976), 25-49.

2105 HEWETH, LIDA. "The old mill at Newport." American Monthly Magazine, 5 (1894), 1-5.
Stone Mill.

2106 HIGGINSON, THOMAS WENTWORTH. "Old Newport days." Outlook, 91 (1909), 876-880.

2107 "HISTORY of yachting in Newport: from the Providence Sunday Journal of August 2, 1885; reprint from the Newport Mercury, Whole Number 6,344, for the week ending November 1, 1885." NH, 47 (1974), 121-126.
Signed H.G.W. (Horatio G. Wood).

2108 "HMS Rose: the ship that started a navy." All Hands (July 1976), 28-29.

2109 NO ENTRY

2110 HOFER, PHILIP. John Howard Benson & his work, 1901-1956. N.Y.: The Typophiles, 1957. x, 56p. RHi. +
"Artist, calligrapher, sculptor, scholar, and humanist, he was unquestionably America's leading designer of incised letters."

2111 HOLAND, HJALMAR R. "The Newport Tower mystery." RIH, 12 (1953), 55-62, 83-89.

2112 _____. "The origin of the Newport Tower." RIH, 7 (1948), 65-73.

2113 HOLMES, OBADIAH. Baptist piety: the last will and testimony of Obadiah Holmes. Edwin S. Gaustad, ed. Grand Rapids, Mich.: Christian Univ. Pr., 1978. xii, 171p. RNHi. +
Early Baptist clergyman; settled in Newport ca. 1650.

2114 HORNE, CHARLES E. III. "United States Naval War College." RIY (1972), 10-15.

2115 HOWE, BRUCE. "Early days of the Art Association." NHSB, No. 110 (1963), 5-29.
Art Association of Newport.

2116 HOWLAND, BENJAMIN B. "The streets of Newport, R.I." Magazine of New England History, 2 (1892), 77-93.

2117 HOYT, EDWIN P. The defenders. South Brunswick, N.J.: A. S. Barnes, 1969. 107p. RHi. +
America's Cup.

2118 HOYT, NORRIS D. The twelve meter challenges for the America's Cup. N.Y.: Dutton, 1977. 252p. RNR. +

2119 HUGHES, STANLEY C. "Early days of Trinity Church." NHSB, No. 101 (1940), 31-41.
Episcopal.

2120 HUHNER, LEON. The Jews of Newport... address delivered on the occasion of unveiling the memorial tablet in the old Jewish synagogue at Newport, R.I., Sept. 7, 1908. n.p., 1908. 11p. DLC. +

2121 HUNTER, ANNA F. "A decade of Newport, as seen by two wandering sons." NHSB, No. 53 (1925), 1-23.
Charles Hunter and Thomas R. Hunter (1840s).

2122 ____. "Kay Street during my life." NHSB, No. 83 (1932), 1-12.

2123 ____. "A Newport romance of 1804." NHSB, No. 61 (1927), 1-21.
Courtship.

2124 HUNTER, WILLIAM. Address...before the Redwood Library and Athenaeum, Newport, R.I., August 24, 1847. Newport: John P. Sanborn, 1882. [40]p. RHi. +
History of the library.

2125 HYDE, J. A. LLOYD. "Pagoda House, in Newport, Rhode Island." Antiques, 84 (1963), 158-161.
Historic house.

2126 ILLINGWORTH, JOHN H. Twenty challenges for the America's Cup. N.Y.: St. Martin's Pr., 1968. 158p. RNR. +

2127 THE INTERNATIONAL Tennis Hall of Fame, Newport, Rhode Island. n.p., [1979?]. 32p. RNHi.
Includes articles on tennis in Newport and the history of the Newport Casino.

2128 "THE IROQUOIS visit Rochambeau at Newport in 1780: excerpts from the unpublished journal of the Comte de Charlus." RIH, 11 (1952), 73-81.
During the American Revolution. Durand Echeverria, ed.

2129 ISHAM, NORMAN MORRISON. "A Goddard tea-table." Antiquarian, 14, No. 1 (Jan. 1930), 51.
John Goddard, 18th-century Newport cabinetmaker.

2130 ____. "Report on the old Brick Market or old City Hall, Newport, Rhode Island." Society for the Preservation of New England Antiquities, Bulletin, 2 (1916), 3-11.

2131 ____. Trinity Church in Newport, Rhode Island: a history of the fabric. Boston: [D. B. Updike,] 1936. xi, 111p. RHi. +
Episcopal.

2132 ISLAND CEMETERY COMPANY, NEWPORT. An historical sketch of the Island Cemetery Company, in Newport, Rhode Island.... Boston: Pr. of John Wilcox and Son, 1872. 45, [2]p. RNHi.

2133 "ITEMS relating to the Gould family and the Jews of Newport." American Jewish Historical Society, Publications, 27 (1920), 423-442.
Edited documents.

2134 "ITEMS relating to the Jews of Newport." American Jewish Historical Society, Publications, 27 (1920), 175-216.
Edited documents.

2135 "ITEMS relating to the Newport cemetery." American Jewish Historical Society, Publications, 27 (1920), 413-415.
Jewish Cemetery.

2136 "ITEMS relating to the Newport Synagogue." American Jewish Historical Society, Publications, 27 (1920), 404-412.
Edited documents.

2137 "ITEMS relating to the Touro family, Newport." American Jewish Historical Society, Publications, 27 (1920), 417-422.
Edited documents.

2138 JACKSON, HENRY. An historical discourse, delivered in the Central Baptist Meeting House, Newport, R.I., January 8th, 1854;...also, the articles of faith, and the covenant, adopted in church meeting, Jan. 7th, 1847, together with a catalogue of its members and its first letter to the Warren Association. Newport: Cranston & Norman, 1854. 72p. RHi. +
Historical discourse also published separately.

2139 JACOBSON, JACOB MARK. "Jewish merchants of Newport in pre-Revolutionary days." RIJHN, 5 (1970), 332-381.

2140 JAFFE, RALPH S. "The Rhode Island Tercentenary Half Dollar." NH, 44 (1971), 8-18.

2141 JASTROW, MORRIS, JR. "References to Jews in the diary of Ezra Stiles." American Jewish Historical Society, Publications, 10 (1902), 5-36.
During his residence in Newport (1755-1778).

2142 JEFFREYS, C. P. BEAUCHAMP. "The case of the crewless brig Sea Bird, 1750: a nautical Newport mystery." NH, 46 (1973), 1-20.

2143 _____. "An eighteenth century summer visitor to Newport." NH, 42 (1969), 1-14.
Dr. Alexander Hamilton.

2144 _____. "The identification of a previously unrecorded Malbone miniature in Newport." NH, 41 (1968), 19-33.
Edward G. Malbone, miniature painter.

2145 _____. Newport, 1639-1976: an historical sketch. Newport: Newport Historical Society, 1976. 64p. RHi.

2146 JETER, HENRY N. Historical sketch of the Shiloh Baptist Church at Newport, R.I., and the pastors who have served. Newport: B. W. Pearce, 1891. 30, xxxi p. RHi. +
Black church.

2147 JONES, THEODORE A. Challenge '77: Newport and the America's Cup. N.Y.: Norton, 1978. 266p. RNHi. +

2148 JONES, WILIAM SAFFORD. Unitarian beginnings in Newport: a sermon preached...in the Channing Memorial Church, Newport, Rhode Island, October 23, 1910, the day before the seventy-fifth anniversary of the Unitarian Congregational Church. n.p., n.d. [12]p. RNHi.
Channing Memorial Church.

2149 KAPLAN, MARILYN. "The Jewish merchants of Newport, 1740-1790." RIJHN, 7 (1975), 12-32.

2150 KAULL, JAMES T. "What now for Stanford White's little gem?" RIer (Sept. 11, 1966), 26-28.
Casino Theater.

2151 KAVANAGH, EDGE. "The palace cottages of Newport." Munsey's, 17 (Sept. 1897), 833-840.

2152 KENNY, ROBERT W. "The Rhode Island Gazette of 1732." RIHSC, 25 (1932), 97-107.
Newspaper.

2153 KERR, ROBERT J. II. "'Let justice prevail though the heavens may fall': a short history of the Newport Artillery Company." NHSB, No. 109 (1963), 3-20.

2154 KING, DAVID. An historical sketch of the Redwood Library and Athenaeum, in Newport, Rhode Island. Boston: John Wilson, 1860. liii p. RHi. +
A later imprint under the same title (1876, 12p.), includes historical information after 1860.

2155 KNIGHTS OF COLUMBUS. NEWPORT COUNCIL, NO. 256. Diamond jubilee ball, Newport Council No. 256, 75th anniversary year, 1897-1972.... n.p., n.d. [16]p. RNHi.
Includes historical sketches.

2156 KNOWLTON, JOSEPHINE GIBSON. "The gay nineties." RIY (1967), H97-H100.

2157 KOHLER, MAX J. "The Jews in Newport." American Jewish Historical Society, Publications, 6 (1897), 61-80.

2158 _____. "The Lopez and Rivera families of Newport." American Jewish Historical Society, Publications, 2 (1894), 101-106.

2159 KRUMBHAAR, EDWARD BELL. Doctor William Hunter of Newport. Reprinted from Annals of Surgery, January 1935. n.p., n.d. [23]p. RNHi. +
18th-century physician.

2160 KUSINITZ, BERNARD. "The 1902 sit-in at Touro Synagogue." RIJHN, 7 (1975), 42-72.

2161 _____, and SAMUEL KOSCH. "A half century of Judah Touro Lodge No. 998, Independent Order of B'nai B'rith." RIJHN, 7 (1975), 73-78.

2162 LaFARGE, MARGARET. "Old Newport." Scribner's, 62 (1917), 542-553.

2163 "LANDMARK revisited." NH, 40 (1967), 69-83.
Stone Mill.

2164  LeBOURGEOIS, JULIEN J.  The United States
Naval War College.  N.Y.:  Newcomen Society
in North America, 1975.  21p.  RNoP. +

2165  LEWIS, THEODORE.  "Touro Synagogue:
National Historic Site."  NH, 48 (1975),
281-320.
    See also next entry.

2166  _____.  "Touro Synagogue, Newport, R.I.,
1763-1963."  NHSB, No. 111 (1963), 3-20.
    See also preceding entry.

2167  LIPSCOMB, FRANK WOODGATE.  A hundred years
of the America's Cup.  Greenwich, Conn.:
New York Graphic Society, 1971.  52p.
RNR. +

2168  LOBSEN, ANDREA FINKELSTEIN.  "Newport's Jews
and the American Revolution."  RIJHN, 7
(1976), 258-276.

2169  "THE LONG Wharf."  NHSB, No. 57 (1926), 5-7.
Signed M.E.P. (Mary E. Powel).

2170  LUCE, STEPHEN B.  "The U.S. Naval War
College."  U.S. Naval Institute Proceedings,
36 (1910), 559-586, 683-696.

2171  LYMAN, ELIZA B.  A reminiscence of Newport
before and during the Revolutionary War.
(1869) Newport:  Milne Printery, 1906.
40p.  RHi. +

2172  McCABE, CAROL.  "A jewel of a church gets
a proper setting."  RIer (July 29, 1979),
14-16, 18.
    The story of Queen Anne Square.

2173  McCRILLIS, JOHN O. C.  "The apothecary
shop."  New-England Galaxy, 10 (Fall 1968),
31-39.
    Recollections of Downing Brothers Pharmacy
as it was in 1929.

2174  McDONALD, WILLIAM.  "The Old State House at
Newport."  NHSB, No. 11, (1914), 1-9.

2175  McHUGH, FRANCIS J.  "Eighty years of war
gaming."  Naval War College Review, 21 (Mar.
1969), 88-89.
    U.S. Naval War College.

2176  McKILLOP, LUCILLE.  "The Touro influence:
Washington's spirit prevails."  RIJHN, 6
(1974), 614- 621.
    George Washington's reply to the Jews of
Newport.

2177  McLEAN, JOHN P., FRANK P. KING, and HENRY Y.
BABCOCK.  A history of Saint George's
Church, 1833-1933:  prepared for the
centennial celebration, February 19-26,
1933.  n.p.:  Beans Pr., n.d.  22p.  RNHi.
    Episcopal.

2178  MacNUTT, J. SCOTT.  "Happy school by the
sea."  NH, 56 (1983), 10-20.
    Cloyne School, a boys' preparatory school
in Newport, 1895-1917.

2179  MACONI, CAROLE J.  Belcourt Castle, Newport,
Rhode Island.  Southborough, Mass.:  Yankee
Colour Corp., 1978.  35p.  RNHi.
    Historic house.

2180  "MALBONE."  NG, No. 77 (1979), [11-14].
    Historic house and grounds.

2181  MALLERY, ARLINGTON H., GARDNER C. EASTON,
and JOHN HOWIESON.  The Newport Tower:  it
was not a colonial windmill or the summer
house of Benedict Arnold.  It may have been
a Viking tower or Christian church, but
undoubtedly is the oldest European building
standing on the mainland of America.  A
special interim report made to the Council
of the city of Newport, R.I., October 20,
1955.  n.p., [1955].  4, [17]p.  RNR. +

2182  MANUEL, ELTON MERRITT.  Description of
colonial uniforms, 1744-1859, of the Newport
Artillery Company, Newport, Rhode Island,
compiled from the records of the Newport
Artillery Company.  [Newport, 1965.]  11p.
RPB-ASKB.

2183  _____.  Merchants and mansions of bygone
days:  an authentic account of the early
settlers of Newport, Rhode Island.  Newport:
Remington Ward, 1939.  32, vi p.  RHi. +

2184  MASON, GEORGE CHAMPLIN.  Newport and its
cottages.  Newport:  George C. Mason & Son,
1875.  viii, 109p.  RHi. +

2185  _____.  Newport illustrated, in a series of
pen & pencil sketches.  Newport:  C. E.
Hammett, Jr., 1854.  115p.  RHi. +
    Contains historical information.  Various
later eds.

2186  _____.  "Nicholas Easton vs. the city of
Newport."  RIHSC, 7 (1885), 329-344.
    His claim to Easton's Pond, Marsh and
Beach (1780s).

2187  _____.  Reminiscences of Newport.  Newport:
Charles E. Hammett, Jr., 1884.  407p.
RHi. +

2188  MASON, GEORGE CHAMPLIN, JR.  "The old Stone
Mill at Newport:  construction versus
theory."  Magazine of American History, 2
(1879), 541-549.

2189  "THE MAUDSLEY-Gardner-Watson-Pitman House,
Newport, R.I."  Old-time New England, 28
(1938), 79-84.

2190 MAYER, LLOYD M. "New lights from old history." NHSB, No. 87 (1933), 2-12.
French role at Newport in the American Revolution.

2191 MEANS, PHILIP AINSWORTH. Newport Tower. N.Y.: Holt, 1942. xxi, 344p. RHi. +
Stone Mill.

2192 "MEDICAL history in Newport." RIMJ, 24 (1941), 91-92.

2193 MENDES, A. P. "The Jewish Cemetery at Newport, R.I." RIHM, 6 (1885), 81-105.

2194 METCALF, PAULINE C. "The interiors of Ogden Codman Jr. in Newport, Rhode Island." Antiques, 118 (1980), 486-497.

2195 MILLAR, JOHN FITZHUGH. "Flora." RIY (1974), 28-31, 45.
British frigate, captured from the French; sunk by the Americans at Newport in 1778, it was later raised and operated under both American and French flags.

2196 _____. "HMS Rose was a constant thorn in the side." RIer (June 9, 1974), 14, 16-19.
British frigate, operating out of Newport, 1774-1776.

2197 _____. "It all really began here." RIer (July 4, 1976), 7, 9-10.
"...the first shots of the American Revolution were fired in Newport at the British schooner St. John, in 1764."

2198 _____. "Newport's early composers." NH, 53 (1980), 67-76.

2199 _____. "Operation Clapboard." RIY (1973), 9-19.
Historic preservation.

2200 _____. "Pachelbel and Gardner: two early Newport composers." NH, 55 (1982), 63-65.
Charles Theodore Pachelbel and Newport Gardner.

2201 MILLER, G. WAYNE. "The long years of waiting are over: Touro Synagogue finally gets its stamp." RIer (Aug. 22, 1982), 5-6.
Commemorative postage stamp.

2202 "MISCELLANEOUS items relating to Jews of Newport." American Jewish Historical Society, Publications, 27 (1920), 443-459.
Edited documents.

2203 MONTROSE, J. GRAHAM. "H.M.S. Rose: the only ship of the Revolutionary War in existence." RIY (1973), 26-37.

2204 _____. "Newport mansions." RIY (1974), 60-95.

2205 MOOZ, R. PETER. "The origins of the Newport block-front furniture design." Antiques, 99 (1971), 882-886.

2206 MORIARTY, G. ANDREWS. "Herodias (Long) Hicks-Gardiner-Porter: a tale of old Newport." RIH, 11 (1952), 84-92.
17th-century Newport woman, whose marriages, divorces, and conduct caused a stir locally.

2207 _____. "Newport's old Stone Mill." NEQ, 19 (1946), 111-114.

2208 MORRIS, ANNA WHARTON. "The romance of the two Hannahs." NHSB, No. 46 (1923), 1-33.
Redwood and Rodman.

2209 MORRIS, EVERETT B. Sailing for America's Cup. N.Y.: Harper & Row, 1964. 216p. RNR. +

2210 MORSE, JARVIS M. "The Wanton family and Rhode Island Loyalism." RIHSC, 31 (1938), 33-44.

2211 MOSES, LIZA, and MICHAEL MOSES. "Authenticating John Townsend's and John Goddard's Queen Anne and Chippendale chairs." Antiques, 121 (1982), 1130-1143.

2212 MOWBRAY, E. ANDREW. "The French 'conquest' of Newport." RIer (May 30, 1976), B44-B51, B53.
French troops in Newport during the American Revolution.

2213 MOWREY, DWIGHT F. "Founding of Unitarianism." NHSB, No. 101 (1940), 48-50.
In Newport.

2214 MURDOCH, RICHARD K. "British 'naval intelligence' reports on the fortifications of Newport in 1814." NH, 38 (1965), 1-8.

2215 NARRAGANSETT BAY MARINE REPAIR SHOPS. 112TH AREA SERVICE UNIT, FORT ADAMS. History of Fort Adams, Rhode Island. n.p., n.d. 13p. RP-Harrington.
Former U.S. Army installation.

2216 "THE NAVY at Newport: a British view, 1864." RIH, 25 (1966), 110-116.
Frank J. Merli, ed.

2217 NELSON, WILBUR. "Dr. John Clarke and the Baptist beginnings in Newport." NHSB, No. 101 (1940), 41-45.

2218 NEWPORT, R.I. CENTRAL BAPTIST CHURCH. Manual of the Central Baptist Church, in Newport, R.I., 1879. Providence: J. A. & R. A. Reid, 1879. 28p. RNHi.
Includes historical sketch.

2219   NEWPORT, R.I.  CONGREGATION JESHUAT ISRAEL.
Dedication Services, Congregation Jeshuat
Israel; community building, Newport, Rhode
Island, August 29th, 1926.  Newport, 1926.
[8]p.  RHi. +

2220   _____.  Fiftieth anniversary of the
reconstruction of the Synagogue of
Congregation Jeshuat Israel, Newport, Rhode
Island, 5643-5693, 1883-1933.  n.p., [1933].
17p.  RHi.
         Touro Synagogue.

2221   _____.  Touro Synagogue of Congregation
Jeshuat Israel, Newport, Rhode Island;
founded 1658, dedicated 1763, designated as
a National Historic Site, 1946.  Newport:
Society of Friends of Touro Synagogue
National Historic Shrine, 1948.  55p.
RHi. +

2222   NEWPORT, R.I.  FIRST BAPTIST CHURCH.
Covenant of the First Baptist Church, in
Newport, R.I., adopted May 4, 1727; with an
appendix.  Newport: James Atkinson, 1847.
24p.  RHi. +
         Includes historical sketch.

2223   _____.  Directory of the First Baptist
Church, Newport, R.I., organized 1638....
n.p., 1900.  46p.  MBNEH.
         Includes brief historical sketch.

2224   _____.  Historical sketch of the First
Baptist Church, in Newport.  n.p., n.d.
[8]p.  RPB.

2225   NEWPORT, R.I.  FIRST METHODIST EPISCOPAL
CHURCH.  Historical sketch and directory of
the First Methodist Episcopal Church,
Marlboro Street, Newport, Rhode Island....
Newport: Milne Printery, 1903.  52p.  RNHi.

2226   NEWPORT, R.I.  FIRST PRESBYTERIAN CHURCH.
Fifty years of service and blessing.
Newport: Remington Ward, 1938.  65p.  RHi.

2227   NEWPORT, R.I.  MOUNT ZION AFRICAN METHODIST
EPISCOPAL CHURCH.  Official souvenir
program, 100th anniversary, mortgage burning
and New England Annual Conference, Mt. Zion
A.M.E. Church:  70 years at present site,
1875-1945; 8 Bellevue Avenue, Newport, Rhode
Island, May 24-25-26-27, 1945.  n.p.,
[1945].  44p.  RNHi.
         Includes historical sketch.

2228   NEWPORT, R.I.  ROGERS HIGH SCHOOL.  Rogers
High School:  one hundred years, 1873-1973.
n.p., n.d.  [49]p.  RNR.

2229   NEWPORT, R.I.  SAINT AUGUSTIN'S CHURCH.
Silver jubilee, St. Augustin's Church,
Newport, R.I....  [Newport,] 1936.  68p.
RNHi.
         Roman Catholic.

2230   NEWPORT, R.I.  SAINT JOSEPH'S CHURCH.  Saint
Joseph's Church reference book, Newport,
Rhode Island, 1935.  n.p., [1935].  72p.
RNR.
         Includes historical sketch.  Roman
Catholic church.

2231   _____.  A souvenir book commemorating the
consecration of Saint Joseph's Church,
Newport, Rhode Island, by the Right Reverend
William A. Hickey, D.D., October the
twelfth, one thousand nine hundred and
twenty-two.  [Newport:]  Saint Joseph's High
School Alumni Association, n.d.  64p.  RNHi.
         Includes historical sketches of the parish
and of the Catholic Church in Newport.

2232   NEWPORT, R.I.  SAINT MARY'S CHURCH.  Golden
jubilee of the Church of the Holy Name of
Mary, Our Lady of the Isle, Newport, R.I.,
Sunday, August the seventeenth, 1902.
[Providence: Livermore & Knight,] n.d.
[17]p.  RNR.
         First Roman Catholic church in R.I.

2233   _____.  A history, St. Mary's Parish,
Newport.  n.p., [1978?].  [34]p.  RHi.

2234   _____.  One hundred years:  the Church of
the Holy Name of Mary; Our Lady of the Isle.
n.p., n.d.  93p.  RHi.

2235   _____.  St. Mary's Parish, 1828-1978.  n.p.,
n.d.  83p.  RHi.
         Roman Catholic.  Includes historical
sketch.

2236   NEWPORT, R.I.  SAINT PAUL'S METHODIST
CHURCH.  Dedication of the sanctuary, March
24, 1946:  St. Paul's Methodist Church,
Newport, Rhode Island.  n.p., n.d.  [24]p.
RNHi.
         Includes "Vignettes of our changing
sanctuary," by Mae Stenhouse.

2237   NEWPORT, R.I.  SAINT SPYRIDON'S GREEK
ORTHODOX CHURCH.  Saint Spyridon's Greek
Orthodox Church, Newport, Rhode Island:
fiftieth anniversary, 1915-1965.  n.p., n.d.
[56]p.  RNHi.

2238   NEWPORT, R.I.  SHILOH BAPTIST CHURCH.
Pastor Henry N. Jeter's twenty-five years
experience with the Shiloh Baptist Church
and her history; corner School and Mary
Streets, Newport, R.I.  Providence:
Remington Printing, 1901.  98p.  RHi.
         Black church.

2239 NEWPORT, R.I. TRINITY CHURCH. Annals of Trinity Church, Newport, Rhode Island, 1698-1821. George Champlin Mason, ed. Newport: George C. Mason, 1890. 358p. RHi. +
Episcopal.

2240 _____. Annals of Trinity Church, Newport, Rhode Island, 1821-1892. George Champlin Mason, ed. 2d series. Newport: V. Francis Mott, 1894. 463p. RHi. +

2241 _____. Trinity Church in Newport: parish organized 1698, first church built 1701, present church built 1726. [Newport, 1955?] [31]p. RNHi. +

2242 NEWPORT, R.I. UNITED BAPTIST CHURCH. 310 years of Christian service, 1638-1948: the United Baptist Church, John Clarke Memorial, Newport, Rhode Island. Newport, 1948. 56p. RHi. +

2243 NEWPORT, R.I. UNITED CONGREGATIONAL CHURCH. The articles of faith, and church covenant, of the United Congregational Church, of Newport, R.I., with a brief notice of the origin and history of the church, prepared...by the pastor, Rev. A. Henry Dumont.... Newport: James Atkinson, 1834. 46p. MWA. +
"First free black church in America."

2244 _____. Manual of the United Congregational Church, Newport, R.I. Newport: John P. Sanborn, 1891. 38p. RHi. +
Includes historical sketch.

2245 NEWPORT, R.I. ZABRISKIE MEMORIAL CHURCH OF SAINT JOHN THE EVANGELIST. A century on the Point: notes from the history of the Zabriskie Memorial Church of St. John the Evangelist, founded 1875. [Newport: Centennial Committee, 1975.] 113p. RNR.
Episcopal.

2246 _____. History of the Free Chapel of Saint John the Evangelist, Newport, R.I., 1875-83. n.p.: Marshall & Flynn, n.d. 31p. RHi.

2247 "NEWPORT a hundred years ago." Lippincott's Magazine, 26 (1880), 351-362.

2248 NEWPORT ASSOCIATION OF MECHANICS AND MANUFACTURERS. Historical sketch of the Newport Association of Mechanics and Manufacturers, 1792-1887. Newport: T. T. Pitman, 1887. 32p. RNHi. +

2249 "THE NEWPORT Casino." NG, No. 19 (1963), [3-5].

2250 NEWPORT CHAMBER OF COMMERCE. Historic Newport. Newport, 1933. 61p. RHi. +
Later eds., 1937, 1941.

2251 "THE NEWPORT church." Sabbath Recorder, 63 (1907), 962-963, 966.
Seventh-Day Baptist.

2252 NEWPORT Daily News: its history, its building, its personnel, 1846-1892. [Newport:] Daily News Job Print, [1892]. 48p. RHi. +
Newspaper.

2253 "NEWPORT Harbor sixty years ago." NHSB, No. 57 (1926), 8-12.
Signed L.M.M. (Lloyd M. Mayer).

2254 NEWPORT historical and social; first published 1854 in Harper's Monthly. Newport: Arnold Art Store, 1969. [29]p. RMi.
Reprinted from Harper's, 9 (1854), 289-317.

2255 NEWPORT HISTORICAL SOCIETY. Early religious leaders of Newport: eight addresses delivered before the Newport Historical Society, 1917. Newport, 1918. 184p. RHi. +

2256 _____. Items of interest concerning Oliver Hazard Perry in Newport and Newport in the War of 1812. Newport: Mercury Publishing, 1913. 32p. RHi. +

2257 _____. Newport Historical Society, Newport, R.I. n.p., n.d. 10p. RPB. +
Includes historical sketch.

2258 "NEWPORT in 1842." NHR, 7 (1889), 201-208.
Newport Artillery Company's role in suppressing the Dorr Rebellion.

2259 NEWPORT mansions: the gilded age. Photography by Richard Cheek; text by Thomas Gannon; introduction by David Chase. Little Compton: Foremost Publishers, 1982. 88p. RHi.

2260 "NEWPORT society in the last century." Harper's, 59 (1879), 497-505.

2261 NICHOLS, ARTHUR HOWARD. "Bells of Trinity Church, Newport, R.I." New England Historical and Genealogical Register, 70 (1916), 147-150.
Episcopal.

2262 OAKLEY, CHESTER A., JR. America's Cup. Newport: Franklin Printing, 1974. 17p. RNR. +
Includes history of the races.

2263 "OCHRE Point: the home of an American jurist." NHM, 3 (1882), 33-55.
William Beach Lawrence. Article signed "H.G.W."

2264   O'CONNOR, RICHARD.  The golden summers:  an antic history of Newport.  N.Y.:  Putnam, 1974.  344p.  RHi. +

2265   O'HANLEY, DONALD M.  Newport--by trolley! Cambridge, Mass.:  Boston Street Railway Association, 1976.  96p.  RHi. +

2266   "THE 'OLD MILL' at Newport:  a new study of an old puzzle."  Scribner's, 17 (1879), 632-641.

2267   OLDPORT ASSOCIATION, NEWPORT.  The Wanton-Lyman-Hazard House, built before 1700; owned and maintained by the Newport Historical Society.  [Newport,] 1974.  [20]p.  RHi.

2268   OLIVER, E. WESLEY, JR.  The America's Cup, 1851-1967.  Woodside, N.Y.:  Palmer & Oliver, 1967.  32p.  RHi. +

2269   _____.  The America's Cup, 1977.  n.p., 1977.  63p.  RJa. +
       Includes history of the races.  See also 1970, 1974 eds. (RHi).

2270   O'LOUGHLIN, KATHLEEN MERRICK.  Newport Tower.  St. Catharines, Ontario, 1948.  20p. RHi. +
       Stone Mill.

2271   OPPENHEIM, SAMUEL.  "The first settlement of the Jews in Newport:  some new matter on the subject."  American Jewish Historical Society, Publications, 34 (1937), 1-10.

2272   _____.  "Jews of Newport in history:  some false statements regarding a Jewish senator of Rhode Island, and also regarding the early Israelites of Newport, exposed.  How history is distorted by a professional Rhode Island historian."  Menorah, 39 (Aug. 1905), 81-90.

2273   OSBORNE, ROBERT SCOTT.  "The Naval War College."  Munsey, 12 (1895), 638-640.

2274   OTT, JOSEPH K.  "Abraham Redwood's chairs?"  Antiques, 119 (1981), 669-673.

2275   PACKARD, J. K.  "Longfellow and the Jewish cemetery at Newport."  RIJHN, 5 (1968), 168-174.

2276   PANAGGIO, LEONARD J.  Portrait of Newport. [Newport:]  Savings Bank of Newport, 1969. xiii, 136p.  RHi. +

2277   _____.  "Side-wheelers and sight-seers." NG, No. 12 (1960), [3-6].
       Steamboat trips to Newport.

2278   _____.  "Thomas Galvin:  an early professional gardener."  NH, 41 (1968), 85-89.
       19th-century horticulture.

2279   PEARCE, B. W.  Matters and men in Newport, as I have known them, 1858-1892.... Newport:  Enterprise Pr., 1892.  52p.  RHi.

2280   PELL, HERBERT.  "An answer to the Norse theory."  RIH, 12 (1953), 120-122.
       Stone Mill.

2281   _____.  "The old Stone Mill, Newport."  RIH, 7 (1948), 105-119.

2282   PERRY, J. TAVENOR.  "The Scandinavian tower of Newport, Rhode Island, U.S.A." Antiquary, n.s. 9 (1913), 463-465.
       Stone Mill.

2283   "PERRY to the rescue!"  Yankee, 37 (Jan. 1973), 100-102.
       1816 rescue of shipwreck survivors off Newport by U.S. Navy personnel commanded by Commodore Oliver Hazard Perry.

2284   PHELPS, HARRIET JACKSON.  Newport in flower: a history of Newport's horticultural heritage.  Newport:  Preservation Society of Newport County, 1979.  153p.  RHi. +

2285   PHILLIPS, N. TAYLOR.  "The Levy and Seixas families of Newport and New York."  American Jewish Historical Society, Publications, 4 (1896), 189-214.

2286   PITMAN, T. T.  "Some recollections of the founders."  NHSB, No. 70 (1929), 4-14.
       Newport Historical Society.  Article followed by "Notes on founders and contemporaries," 15-28.

2287   PLATT, VIRGINIA BEVER.  "'And don't forget the Guinea voyage':  the slave trade of Aaron Lopez of Newport."  William and Mary Quarterly, 3 ser. 32 (1975), 601-618.

2288   _____.  "Tar, staves, and New England rum: the trade of Aaron Lopez of Newport, Rhode Island, with colonial North Carolina." North Carolina Historical Review, 48 (1971), 1-22.

2289   _____.  "Triangles and tramping:  Captain Zebediah Story of Newport, 1769-1776." American Neptune, 33 (1973), 294-303.
       Patterns of commerce.

2290   POHL, FREDERICK J.  "A key to the problem of Newport Tower."  RIH, 7 (1948), 75-83.
       Stone Mill.

2291   _____.  "Was the Newport Tower standing in 1632?"  NEQ, 18 (1945), 501-506.

2292  POINT ASSOCIATION OF NEWPORT. Here and
there on the Point; reprinted from the Green
Light, bulletin of the Point Association of
Newport, Rhode Island, Inc.  Newport, 1962.
[35]p.  RHi.
        The Point, place in Newport.

2293  _____. Now and then on the Point; reprinted
from the Green Light, Bulletin of the Point
Association of Newport.  Newport, 1980.
44p.  RNHi.

2294  POLAND, WILLIAM CAREY. Robert Feke, the
early Newport portrait painter, and the
beginnings of colonial painting:  a paper
read before the Rhode Island Historical
Society, April 5, 1904.  Providence, 1907.
26p.  RHi. +

2295  POOL, D. DE SOLA. "The Touro Synagogue:
aspects of the missing half-century of its
history (1850-1900)."  American Jewish
Historical Society, Publications, 38 (1948),
57-76.

2296  PORTER, DANIEL R. The Hunter House:
"'mansion of hospitality.'"  Newport:
Preservation Society of Newport County,
1976. 20p.  RHi. +

2297  POWEL, H. W. H.  "Early defenses of Newport
during Siege of 1778."  NHSB, No. 47 (1923),
23-24.

2298  POWEL, MARY E.  "Election day in Newport."
NHSB, No. 8 (1913), 1-12; No. 15 (1915),
1-16.
        Election-day customs.

2299  _____. "A few French officers to whom we
owe much."  NHSB, No. 38 (1921), 1-19.
        American Revolution.

2300  _____. "A few words about some old
buildings in Newport."  NHSB, No. 55 (1925),
1-28.

2301  _____. "Miss Jane Stuart, 1812-1888; her
grandparents and parents."  NHSB, No. 31
(1920), 1-16.
        Artist and daughter of Gilbert Stuart.

2302  _____. "The old Easton Farm."  NHSB, No. 64
(1928), 1-15.

2303  _____. "Presidential visits to Newport."
NHSB, No. 45 (1923), 16-31.

2304  _____. "Some of our founders, sixty years
ago."  NHSB, No. 16 (1915), 1-31.
        Newport Historical Society.

2305  POWERS, W. A.  "The gentlemen and their
cup."  Town and Country, 112 (Sept. 1958),
74-78, 132-134, 136, 139.
        America's Cup.

2306  PRATT, W. V.  "The Naval War College:  an
outline of the past and description of the
present."  U.S. Naval Institute Proceedings,
53 (1927), 937-947.

2307  [PRESERVATION SOCIETY OF NEWPORT COUNTY.]
Marble House, the William K. Vanderbilt
mansion, Bellevue Avenue, Newport, Rhode
Island. [Newport, 1965.] 17p.
RP-Harrington.

2308  _____. Washington-Rochambeau celebration,
1780-1955, Newport, Rhode Island.  Newport,
[1955]. 40p.  RHi. +
        Cover title:  Official souvenir program,
Washington-Rochambeau celebration,
1780-1955.

2309  PRICE, EDITH BALLINGER.  "A child's memories
of Wiliam Trost Richards."  NH, 52 (1979),
1-9.
        Landscape painter.

2310  _____. "The court end of town."  NHSB, No.
108 (1962), 4-22.

2311  _____. "The three Johns."  NG, No. 7
(1959), [3-6].
        Stevens family, stone carvers, and the
John Stevens Shop.

2312  PRINGLE, MURRAY T.  "Rhode Island's first
reckless road rascal."  Yankee, 40 (Feb.
1976), 92-93.
        Michael Woods, "first motorist in history"
to be arrested for speeding (1904).

2313  THE PROCEEDINGS of the Free African Union
Society and the African Benevolent Society,
Newport, Rhode Island, 1780-1824.  William
H. Robinson, ed.  Providence:  Urban League
of R.I., 1976.  xiv, 196p.  RHi. +

2314  PROVIDENCE, R.I.  FIRST BAPTIST CHURCH.  A
review of a report, presented to the Warren
Baptist Association, at its meeting in 1849,
on the subject of the true date of the First
Baptist Church in Newport, R.I., prepared by
a committee of the First Baptist Church in
Providence, and read to the Warren Baptist
Association, September 12, 1850.
Providence:  H. H. Brown, 1850.  26p.
RHi. +
        See also entry 7.

2315 Newport

2315 PROVIDENCE PARTNERSHIP (architects). The
urban design plan: Historic Hill, Newport,
Rhode Island, project No. R.I. R-23,
September, 1971. Prepared for the
Redevelopment Agency of the city of Newport,
Rhode Island, by the Providence Partnership,
Providence, Rhode Island, and Russell
Wright.... n.p., 1971. 44p. RHi. +
   Includes historical sketch.

2316 PUTNEY, MARTHA S. "Black merchant seamen of
Newport, 1803-1865: a case study in foreign
commerce." Journal of Negro History, 57
(1972), 156-168.

2317 "THE QUEEN of Aquidneck." Harper's, 49
(1874), 305-320.
   I.e., Newport.

2318 RAND, BENJAMIN. Berkeley's American
sojourn. Cambridge: Harvard Univ. Pr.,
1932. xi, 79p. RHi. +
   Bishop George Berkeley.

2319 RAY, JOHN MICHAEL. "Newport's golden age:
a study of the Newport slave trade." Negro
History Bulletin, 25 (1961), 51-57.

2320 REDWOOD LIBRARY AND ATHENAEUM, NEWPORT.
Annals of the Redwood Library and Athenaeum,
Newport, R.I. George Champlin Mason,
ed. Newport: Redwood Library, 1891. 528p.
RHi. +

2321 _____. A catalogue of the Redwood Library
and Athenaeum, in Newport, R.I.... Boston:
John Wilson and Son, 1860. liii, 383p.
RHi. +
   Includes historical sketch.

2322 _____. One hundred and seventy-fifth
anniversary of the incorporation of the
Redwood Library.... Newport, 1922. 49p.
RHi. +

2323 _____. Redwood Library and Athenaeum:
addresses commemorating its 200th
anniversary, 1747-1947. [Providence:
Akerman-Standard,] n.d. 31p. RHi. +

2324 _____. Redwood papers: a bicentennial
collection. Lorraine Dexter and Alan
Pryce-Jones, eds. Newport, 1976. 139p.
RHi. +
   Collection of articles relating to the
institution, its founder, collections,
furnishings, etc.

2325 _____. A short sketch of the Redwood
Library of Newport, Rhode Island.
[Newport:] Mercury Publishing, 1917. 21p.
RHi. +

2326 REED, HENRY HOPE. The Elms: the Edward J.
Berwind mansion, Bellevue Avenue, Newport,
Rhode Island. n.p., n.d. 24p.
RP-Harrington. +

2327 RE-UNION of the Sons and Daughters of
Newport, R.I., August 23, 1859. George
Champlin Mason, ed. Newport: Fred A.
Pratt, 1859. vi, 297p. RHi. +
   Includes historical sketch of Redwood
Library and Athenaeum.

2328 RHODE ISLAND. HISTORICAL PRESERVATION
COMMISSION. The Kay Street-Catherine
Street-Old Beach Road neighborhood, Newport,
Rhode Island: statewide preservation report
N-N-1. Providence, 1974. vi, 46, [17]p.
RHi. +

2329 _____. The southern Thames Street
neighborhood in Newport, Rhode Island:
statewide historical preservation report
N-N-3. Providence, 1980. vi, 42p. RHi.
   Author: John F. A. Herzan.

2330 _____. The West Broadway neighborhood,
Newport, Rhode Island: statewide historical
preservation report N-N-2. Providence,
1977. vi, 59p. RHi.
   Author: John F. A. Herzan.

2331 RHODE ISLAND HISTORICAL SOCIETY. Gazette
Francoise: an account of the French
newspaper printed on the press of the French
fleet at Newport, Rhode Island, 1780 and
1781. Providence, 1926. 11p. RHi. +

2332 RICHARDS, T. ADDISON. "Newport."
Knickerbocker, 54 (1859), 337-352.

2333 RICHARDSON, EDWARD ADAMS. "The builder of
the Newport (Rhode Island) Tower." Journal
of the Surveying and Mapping Division,
Proceedings of the American Society of Civil
Engineers, 86, No. SU1 (1960), 73-95.
   Stone Mill. Investigation of the
structural design.

2334 RIDER, SIDNEY S. "The real history of 'my
stone built windmill.'" BN, 31 (1914),
137-142.
   Stone Mill.

2335 _____. "The story of the Rhode Island
Almanack of 1728, printed at Newport in 1727
by James Franklin." BN, 28 (1911), 193-198.

2336 ROBERTS, ARTHUR S. Redwood Library and
Athenaeum, Newport, Rhode Island.
Providence: Priv. Print., [1948]. 58p.
RHi. +
   Also published as Two centuries of the
Redwood Library and Athenaeum, 1747-1947
(1948).

2337 ROBINSON, WILLARD B. "Fort Adams: American example of French military architecture." RIH, 34 (1975), 77-94.
See also next entry.

2338 _____. Report on the restoration of Fort Adams. n.p., 1972. 33, [2]p.
RP-Harrington.
Former U.S. Army installation. Includes historical sketch.

2339 ROBSON, LLOYD A. "Newport begins." NH, No. 113 (1964), 7-32; 37 (1964), 74-79, 93-119, 133-153; 38 (1965), 9-38, 71-95, 110-127, 151-179; 39 (1966), 39-75, 89-129, 139-168; 40 (1967), 22-51, 176-190.
Early history.

2340 _____. "Newport, one hundred years ago." NHSB, No. 106 (1961), 3-18.

2341 ROELKER, WILLIAM GREENE. "Governor Samuel Ward, farmer and merchant." RIH, 6 (1947), 54-58.
18th century.

2342 A ROMANCE of Newport in 1755, together with pencilings along the way; also a street and avenue directory, 1874. Newport: A. J. Ward, 1874. 34p. RNR. +
"A husband taken by pirates; his return after seven years' captivity upon the eve of his wife's marriage." See also entry 1879.

2343 ROSEN, BENTON H. "King David's Lodge, A.F. & A.M., No. 1, of Newport, Rhode Island." RIJHN, 6 (1974), 578-585.
Jewish lodge of Freemasons.

2344 _____. "The Touro Jewish Synagogue Fund: a fiscal review." RIJHN, 6 (1972), 236-244.

2345 ROSENGARTEN, J. G. "The German soldiers in Newport, 1776-1779, and the siege of 1778." NHM, 7 (1886), 81-118.

2346 RUDOLPH, RICHARD H. "Eighteenth century Newport and its merchants." NH, 51 (1978), 21-38, 45-60.

2347 RUSSELL, JOHN HENRY. "A fragment of Naval War College history." U.S. Naval Institute Proceedings, 58 (1932), 1164-1165.

2348 RUSSELL, KAY. "Stephen Bleecker Luce and the Naval War College." Naval War College Review, 32 (Mar.-Apr. 1979), 20-41.

2349 SAINT GEORGE'S SCHOOL, MIDDLETOWN. Newport architecture: a collection of papers of the architecture class of St. George's School, 1965-1966. n.p., n.d. 39p. RNR.

2350 SANBORN, MRS. ALVAH H. "The Newport Mercury." NHSB, No. 65 (1928), 1-11.
Newspaper.

2351 SANFORD, PELEG. The letter book of Peleg Sanford of Newport, merchant (later governour of Rhode Island), 1666-1668. Transcribed from the original in the Massachusetts Archives by Howard W. Preston, with an introduction and notes by Howard M. Chapin, and additional notes by G. Andrews Moriarty, Jr. Providence: R.I. Historical Society, 1928. vi, 84p. RHi. +

2352 SAVINGS BANK OF NEWPORT. One hundred years of the Savings Bank of Newport: glimpses of the past of an old town, together with brief accounts of some of the men who have filled a part in the bank's history and in the town affairs. Newport, 1919. 48p. RHi. +

2353 SCHLESS, NANCY HALVERSON. "Peter Harrison, the Touro Synagogue, and the Wren city church." Winterthur Portfolio, 8 (1973), 187-200.
English sources of Harrison's architectural design.

2354 SCHREIER, EUGENE. The old Jewish community of Newport, R.I.; with sketch of the ancient Touro Synagogue and cemetery. Newport: Milne Printery, 1905. 27p. RHi. +

2355 SCHUMACHER, ALAN T. "A gentleman's library." NH, 52 (1979), 29-36.
William Shepard Wetmore.

2356 _____. "George Champlin Mason: architect, artist, author; 1820-1894." NH, 43 (1970), 21-29.

2357 _____. "Hammett's bibliography." NH, 41 (1968), 93-117.
Bibliography of Newport imprints, compiled by Charles E. Hammett, Jr. (1887). This work is listed under Supplementary Bibliographies.

2358 _____. "Newport's first directory." NH, 44 (1971), 93-105.
1856-1857.

2359 _____. "19th century Newport guide books." NH, 51 (1978), 73-93.

2360 SCHWARTZ, ESTHER I. "Restoration of the Touro Synagogue." RIJHN, 3 (1959), 106-131.

2361 _____. "Touro Synagogue restored, 1827-29." Society of Architectural Historians, Journal, 17 (1958), 23-26.

2362 SCOTT, KENNETH. "The counterfeiting venture of Abel and Samuel Chapin." RIH, 11 (1952), 93-95.
1723.

2363 _____. "George Scott, slave trader of Newport." American Neptune, 12 (1952), 222-228.

2364 _____. "A Newport street fight in 1768." RIH, 18 (1959), 119-121.
Between American and British sailors; one man killed.

2365 SEARS, ROBERT S. "The ancient 'tower' of Newport, Rhode Island." Potter's American Monthly, 5 (1875), 753-754.
Stone Mill.

2366 SERVICES at the dedication of the school house erected by the Trustees of the Long Wharf, at Newport, Rhode Island, May 20th, 1863, with an appendix. Newport: Pratt & Messer, 1863. 106p. RHi. +
Includes history of Long Wharf and Newport schools; historical sketches of Newport.

2367 THE 1764 catalogue of the Redwood Library Company at Newport, Rhode Island. Marcus A. McCorison, ed.; preface by Wilmarth S. Lewis. New Haven, Conn.: Yale Univ. Pr., 1965. xxiii, 109p. RHi. +

2368 SHEA, MARGARET M. The story of colonial Newport. n.p.: Priv. Print., 1962. 28p. RN. +

2369 SHEFFIELD, WILLIAM P. An address delivered...before the Rhode Island Historical Society, in Providence, February 7, A.D. 1882; with notes. Newport: J. P. Sanborn, 1883. 67p. RHi. +
"Privateersmen of Newport."

2370 _____. Address...to Newport Artillery on attaining its 150th year of existence, September 10, 1891. Newport: Daily News Job Print, 1891. 16p. RHi. +

2371 _____. Historical address, of the city of Newport, delivered July 4th, 1876; with an appendix. Newport: John P. Sanborn, 1876. 68, xv p. RHi. +

2372 _____. "The scope and purpose of an historical society in Newport." NHSB, No. 20 (1916), 1-22.
History of Newport.

2373 SHELTON, F. H. More light on the old mill at Newport.... Newport, 1917. 23p. RP. +
Stone Mill. Reprinted from NHSB, No. 21 (1917), 1-23.

2374 SHERMAN, ARCHIBALD C. Newport and the Savings Bank. Newport: A. Hartley, G. Ward, 1944. 69p. RHi. +
Savings Bank of Newport.

2375 SHIPTON, CLIFFORD K. "John Callender." RIH, 6 (1947), 45-51.
18th-century Baptist minister in Newport and author of one of the earliest histories of R.I. (entry 143).

2376 SHIPTON, NATHANIEL N. "General Joseph Palmer: scapegoat for the Rhode Island fiasco of October, 1777." NEQ, 39 (1966), 498-512.
Attempted American invasion of British-occupied Newport.

2377 "THE SIEGE of Newport, day by day: from contemporary records and later historians." NHSB, No. 51 (1924), 16-19.
1778.

2378 SIMISTER, FLORENCE PARKER. "'...And one bill of 3 dollars....'" NH, 39 (1966), 29-38.
Rhode Island Union Bank and the issuance of paper money.

2379 _____. "Ida Lewis: keeper of the light." New-England Galaxy, 10 (Fall 1968), 55-65.
See note, entry 2083.

2380 _____. Streets of the city: an anecdotal history of Newport. Providence: Mowbray, 1969. xiii, 164p. RHi. +

2381 SIMS, W. S., JR. "The golden age of Newport." St. George's School, The Dragon (n.d.), 178-294.
Article found in Redwood Library, Newport.

2382 SKEMP, SHEILA. "George Berkeley's Newport experience." RIH, 37 (1978), 53-63.
Berkeley, the Irish philosopher and clergyman, lived in Newport, 1729-1731.

2383 SKINNER, HARRIET DAYTON. "Newport, Rhode Island, during the Revolution." American Monthly Magazine, 4 (1894), 103-117.

2384 SMALES, HOLBERT T. "The Breakers": an illustrated handbook. Newport: Preservation Society of Newport County, 1950. 40p. RHi. +
Historic house.

2385 SMITH, DIANA LANIER. "Robinson House." NH, 50 (1977), 6-14.
Historic house.

2386 SMITH, GEORGE B. Historical sketch of the Second Baptist Church, Newport, Rhode Island, 1656-1903. Newport: Remington Ward, 1903. 17p. RNHi.

2387 SMITH, GEORGE B. "Memories of the long ago, 1839-1925." NHSB, No. 56 (1926), 1-13.

2388 SOUVENIR program of the eighteenth international yacht race for the America's Cup, 1962. n.p., [1962]. 80p. RP.
Includes "History of the America's Cup," by Everett B. Morris.

2389 SPAWN, WILLMAN, and CAROL M. SPAWN. "Francis Skinner, bookbinder of Newport: an eighteenth-century craftsman identified by his tools." Winterthur Portfolio, 2 (1965), 47-61.

2390 SPECTOR, RONALD. Professors of war: the Naval War College and the development of the naval profession. Newport: Naval War College Pr., 1977. viii, 185p. RHi. +

2391 STAPLER, JOHN. "The Naval War College: a brief history." U.S. Naval Institute Proceedings, 58 (1932), 1157-1163.

2392 STERN, MALCOLM H. "Myer Benjamin and his descendants: a study in biographical method." RIJHN, 5 (1968), 133-144.
Colonial Jewish resident.

2393 _____. "Newport Jewry: whence and whither?" RIJHN, 5 (1970), 313-326.

2394 STEVENS, JOHN AUSTIN. The French in Rhode Island. Newport in the Revolutionary period, 1778-1782; the French occupation, 1780-1781. An address delivered in Newport...in 1897. [Newport:] Franklin Printing House, 1928. 40p. RHi. +
For a more detailed account of the same subject, see Edwin Martin Stone, Our French allies... (1884), a lengthy treatment of French contributions to the American Revolutionary cause. Newport and R.I. figure prominently in the discussion. See also Stephen Bonsal, When the French were here...(1945).

2395 STEVENS, MAUD LYMAN. "The antiquities of Newport, Rhode Island." Old-Time New England, 21 (1930), 51-59.
Historic buildings.

2396 _____. "Colonel Higginson and his friends in Newport." NHSB, No. 49 (1924), 1-15.
Thomas Wentworth Higginson and Newport's literary community.

2397 _____. A history of the Vernon House in Newport, R.I. [Newport:] Charity Organization Society of Newport, 1915. 56p. RHi. +

2398 _____. "Mawdsley House." NHSB, No. 97 (1936), 14-22.
Historic house.

2399 _____. "Measures of defence in old Newport." NHSB, No. 26 (1918), 3-11.

2400 _____. "Newport streets." NHSB, No. 67 (1928), 1-13.

2401 _____. "The old Hazard House." NHSB, No. 33 (1920), 25-42.

2402 _____. "The old house at 17 Broadway." NHSB, No. 59 (1926), 3-7.
Wanton-Lyman-Hazard House.

2403 _____. "The romance of Newport." NHSB, No. 24 (1918), 1-30.

2404 _____. "Trinity Church in Newport and some of its members." NHSB, No. 77 (1930), 2-12.
Episcopal.

2405 _____. "Washington and Newport." NHSB, No. 84 (1932), 2-20.
George Washington.

2406 STEVENS, WILLIAM B., JR. "Joseph Blackburn and his Newport sitters, 1754-1756." NH, 40 (1967), 95-107.
Portrait painter.

2407 _____. "Newport's beautiful Irish." Yankee, 41 (Sept. 1977), 76-85, 188, 191-194, 197.
Irish Americans.

2408 STILES, EZRA. The literary diary of Ezra Stiles, D.D., LL.D., president of Yale College. Franklin Bowditch Dexter, ed. N.Y.: Scribner's, 1901. 3v. RHi. +
Diary (1769-1795) includes years in Newport as minister of Second Congregational Church.

2409 STOCK, ELY. "Longfellow's 'The Jewish cemetery at Newport.'" RIH, 20 (1961), 81-87.

2410 STONE, FRANCIS H., JR. "The Newport Citizens Cup race." RIH, 6 (1947), 111-115.
Yacht race (1886).

2411 STONE, HERBERT L., WILLIAM H. TAYLOR, and WILLIAM W. ROBINSON. The America's Cup races. N.Y.: Norton, 1970. viii, 311p. RHi. +
Various earlier eds.

2412 STOW, CHARLES MESSER. "John Goddard, stubborn master craftsman." Antiquarian, 8, No. 1 (Feb. 1927), 19-21.
18th-century Newport cabinetmaker.

2413 THE STUYVESANT staircase, Ayrault House, Newport. Newport: Priv. Print., 1956. 12p. RNR. +

2414 Newport

2414 SWAN, BRADFORD FULLER. "Frontier justice in Newport, 1652." RIH, 33 (1974), 3-7.
Trial, conviction, and execution of Alexander Partridge.

2415 SWAN, FRANK H. The Colony House. Providence: Akerman-Standard, [1930]. 18p. RHi. +
Old State House.

2416 TAYLOR, ERICH. Charles Theodore Pachelbel and the Berkeley organ at Trinity Church, Newport, R.I. Newport, 1939. Unp. RHi. +
Episcopal church.

2417 TERRY, RODERICK. "The coming of the French fleet." NHSB, No. 66 (1928), 8-15.

2418 _____. "The history of the liberty tree of Newport, Rhode Island." NHSB, No. 27 (1918), 1-35.

2419 [_____.] "History of the old Colony House at Newport." NHSB, No. 63 (1927), 1-36.

2420 [_____.] "The influences leading to the first settlement of Newport...." NHSB, No. 49 (1924), 16-22.

2421 _____. "Some old Newport broadsides." NHSB, No. 77 (1930), 13-18.

2422 [_____.] "Some old papers relating to the slave trade." NHSB, No. 62 (1927), 10-34.

2423 THEODORE, CONSTANTINE. The history of St. Spyridon Greek Orthodox Church and community, Newport, Rhode Island, 1915-1956. [Newport: Wilkinson Pr.,] n.d. 28p. RNR.

2424 THOMAS, J. RICHARD. "The birth of the United States Naval War College." U.S. Naval Institute Proceedings, 79 (1953), 273-279.

2425 THURSTON, C. R. "Newport in the Revolution." NEM, n.s. 11 (1894), 3-19.

2426 TIFFANY, OSMOND. "Old Newport." Cosmopolitan, 15 (1893), 664-673.

2427 TILLEY, EDITH MAY. "David Melville and his early experiments with gas in Newport." NHSB, No. 60 (1927), 1-17.
"First practical demonstration of gas lighting in this country."

2428 _____. Historic spots in Newport. Newport: Mercury Publishing, 1914. 16p. RHi. +

2429 _____. "Items of Newport interest in early Boston newspapers." NHSB, No. 69 (1929), 1-15; No. 74 (1930), 2-22.

2430 _____. "The Newport Historical Society in its earlier days." NHSB, No. 12 (1914), 1-16.

2431 _____. "A Newporter's wanderings in genealogical by-paths." NHSB, No. 78 (1931), 2-18; No. 88 (1933), 3-15.

2432 TILLEY, JOHN HENRY. "Newport from 1700 to 1775." Newport Herald (Nov. 10, 11, 1896).

2433 TOMPKINS, HAMILTON B. "Address." NHSB, No. 17 (1915), 1-4.
Early history of Newport Historical Society.

2434 _____. "On the so-called portrait of Governor William Coddington in the City Hall at Newport." NHSB, No. 9 (1913), 1-4.

2435 THE TORPEDO Station. n.p., n.d. 8p. RNHi.
Naval station established on Goat Island in 1869.

2436 "TREATS and holidays in old Newport." NHSB, No. 57 (1926), 1-5.
Signed H.L.S.

2437 [TUCKERMAN, ARTHUR.] The Newport Reading Room, 1853-1953: an informal history. Newport: Newport Reading Room, 1954. x, 37p. RHi. +
Men's club.

2438 _____. When Rochambeau stepped ashore: a reconstruction of life in Newport in 1780. Newport: Preservation Society of Newport County, 1955. xii, 24p. RHi. +

2439 TUCKERMAN, HENRY THEODORE. "The graves at Newport." Harper's, 39 (1869), 372-388.
Cemeteries and epitaphs.

2440 TUNNELL, DANIEL R., and ADELAIDE HECHTLINGER. "Life in Newport." Early American Life, 1 (Feb. 1975), 39-41; (Apr. 1975), 27-31.

2441 TURNER, HENRY E. Newport, 1800-1850: a paper read before the Unity Club, Newport, R.I....March 23, 1897. n.p., n.d. 12p. RHi. +

2442 _____. [Paper on Newport loyalists during the American Revolution.] RIHSPr (1874-1875), 48-51.

2443 _____. "Schools and schoolmasters of Newport: an address...before the alumni of the Rogers High School, Newport, R.I., Dec. 31, 1883." NHM, 4 (1884), 203-225.

2444 TURVILLE, GEORGE L. Newport down under. Wakefield: HELPS Secretarial Service, 1977. 22p. RNoK.
Social life and customs. Reprinted from NH, 52 (1979), 37-52.

2445 "TWO accounts of the Wanton-Lyman-Hazard House." NH, 46 (1973), 43-49.

2446 "TWO branches of the Newport Townsends." Antiques, 31 (1937), 308-310.
Furniture makers.

2447 U.S. COAST GUARD. "History of Castle Hill Light Station, Newport, Rhode Island." RIH, 10 (1951), 103-108.

2448 U.S. NAVAL HOSPITAL, NEWPORT. Rededication, Chapel, Naval Hospital, Newport, Rhode Island, November 23, 1947. n.p., n.d. [24]p. RHi.
Includes historical sketch.

2449 U.S. NAVAL TRAINING STATION, NEWPORT. Souvenir history of the Naval Training Station, Newport, R.I. Newport: Naval Aid Society, 1915. 32p. RHi.

2450 U.S. NAVAL WAR COLLEGE, NEWPORT. History of the United States Naval War College, 1884-1963, and succeeding annual command historical report supplements. Prepared in accordance with OpNavInstruction 5790.9 of 5 May 1959. [Newport, 1964.] 75, [78]p. RNW.

2451 _____. The United States Naval War College: a staff study of its historical background, mission and educational philosophy, principles and concepts, from which the second year of the course in naval warfare was derived. [Newport,] 1954. 117, [176]p. RNW.

2452 U.S. NAVAL YEOMAN SCHOOL, NEWPORT. History of the United States Naval Yeoman School, Newport, Rhode Island, 1907-1921. n.p., n.d. 33p. RNW-Hi.

2453 VAN RENSSELAER, MARY (KING). Newport: our social capital. Philadelphia: Lippincott, 1905. 402p. RHi. +
A history of Newport.

2454 VANDERBILT, HAROLD S. On the wind's highway: Ranger, Rainbow and racing. N.Y.: Scribner's, 1939. xi, 259p. RHi. +
America's Cup racing.

2455 VAUGHAN, ROGER. The grand gesture: Ted Turner, Mariner, and the America's Cup. Boston: Little, Brown, 1975. 298p. RNHi. +
1974.

2456 VEEDER, PAUL L. II. "The outbuildings and grounds of Chateau-sur-Mer." Society of Architectural Historians, Journal, 29 (1970), 307-317.
Historic house.

2457 VERNON, THOMAS. The diary of Thomas Vernon, a loyalist, banished from Newport by the Rhode Island General Assembly in 1776; with notes by Sidney S. Rider.... Providence: Sidney S. Rider, 1881. viii, 150p. RHi. +

2458 VLAHOS, MICHAEL. The blue sword: the Naval War College and the American mission, 1919-1941. Newport: Naval War College Pr., 1980. v, 214p. RHi. +

2459 _____. "The Naval War College and the origins of war-planning against Japan." Naval War College Review, 33 (July-Aug. 1980), 23-41.

2460 VON BULOW, CLAUS. "Clarendon Court, Newport, R.I.: a house and its ghosts." NH, 47 (1974), 218-226.

2461 WADLEIGH, JOHN R. "Fifty years ago, when Newport remembered Rochambeau." NH, 54 (1981), 123-125.
1931 celebration remembering the French general based at Newport during American Revolution.

2462 WALLACE, ROBERT W. Sermons on Congregationalism in Newport.... Newport: Daily News Job Print, 1896. 92p. RHi. +

2463 WARD, A. JUDSON. Fiftieth anniversary celebration: history of Rhode Island Lodge, No. 12, I.O.O.F., Newport, R.I. [Providence:] Snow & Farnham, 1897. 59p. RHi.

2464 WARD, J. STEDMAN. "The trolley car days of Newport, R.I." NH, 47 (1974), 129-152.

2465 WARREN, MRS. GEORGE HENRY. "Newport, and its Preservation Society." Historic Preservation, 18 (Mar.-Apr. 1966), 69-75.
Preservation Society of Newport County.

2466 WATERBURY, THEODORE E. "John P. Newell, 1832?-1898." NH, 41 (1968), 67-73.
Lithographer.

2467 WAX, DAROLD D. "Thomas Rogers and the Rhode Island slave trade." American Neptune, 35 (1975), 289-301.
Newport ship captain, who made seven voyages to Africa between 1756 and 1773.

2468    WEAVER, PAULINE K. The Newport National
        Bank: one hundred and forty-seventh
        anniversary, 1803-1950: a chronicle of
        service to the community, selected from the
        records. Newport: Newport National Bank,
        1950. 28p. RHi.

2469    WEBB, THOMAS HOPKINS. Account of an ancient
        structure in Newport, Rhode Island, the
        Vinland of the Scandinavians, in letters to
        C. C. Rafn, with remarks by him.... n.p.,
        [1839?]. [15]p. RPB. +
            Stone Mill.

2470    WEBER, HILMAR H. "On a German regiment
        stationed at Newport." RIHSC, 27 (1934),
        1-4.
            In 1778, during the British occupation.

2471    WEEDEN, WILLIAM BABCOCK. Ideal Newport in
        the eighteenth century. Worcester, Mass.:
        Davis Press, 1907. 14p. RHi. +

2472    WEINBERG, HELENE BARBARA. "The decoration
        of the United Congregational Church." NH,
        47 (1974), 109-120.

2473    WEINHARDT, CARL J. "Newport preserved."
        Art in America, 53 (June 1965), 114-119.
            Newport architecture.

2474    WELCH, EDWARD B. Hunter House and its
        occupants during the Revolutionary War era.
        Newport: Preservation Society of Newport
        County, n.d. 14p. RNR.

2475    WHARTON, KATHARINE JOHNSTONE. "An old
        Newport Loyalist." NHSB, No. 32 (1920),
        1-14.
            Francis Brinley.

2476    WHEELER, GERALD E. "The War College years
        of Admiral Harris Laning, U.S. Navy." Naval
        War College Review, 21 (Mar. 1969), 69-87.

2477    WHEELER, ROBERT L. "Opinionists to
        opulence." RIer (June 22, 1952), 3-6, 8,
        10.
            Newport architecture.

2478    WHITE, DONALD C. "The Newport Artillery
        Company." Naval War College Review, 22 (May
        1970), 71-74.
            Militia company.

2479    WICK, BARTHINIUS L. Did the Norsemen erect
        the Newport Round Tower? n.p., n.d. 26p.
        RHi. +

2480    WILLIAMS, CATHERINE READ (ARNOLD).
        "Sketches of Newport." Family Circle and
        Parlor Annual, 14 (1852), 57-62, 90-94,
        143-148.

2481    WILLIAMS, THOMAS J. Coasters Harbor Island
        and the Newport Naval Training Center:
        their activities and growth. [Newport:]
        Training Station Pr., [1937?]. 34p. RHi.

2482    WINSHIP, GEORGE PARKER. "Newport newspapers
        in the eighteenth century." NHSB, No. 14
        (1914), 1-19.

2483    WOOD, ANNA WHARTON. "The Robinson family
        and their correspondence with the Vicomte
        and Vicomtesse de Noailles." NHSB, No. 42
        (1922), 1-35.
            Includes information on Quakers in
        colonial R.I.; French in Newport during the
        Revolution.

2484    WOODBRIDGE, GEORGE. "Rochambeau: two
        hundred years later." NH, 53 (1980), 5-21.
            French army in Newport.

2485    WOODS, ARLENE. "A Baldacchino-Puteal
        ensemble and its origins." NH, 55 (1982),
        92-113.
            "...A stone well head and its canopy
        [that] graced the famous rose gardens of
        Vinland, a Newport...summer residence."

2486    "THE WORLD-famous mug." RIY (1967), 88-89.
            America's Cup.

2487    WORMELEY, KATHARINE PRESCOTT.
        "Reminiscences of Newport in the fifties."
        NH, 41 (1968), 1-17.
            Richard L. Champlin, ed. (1850s).

2488    WRIGHT, C. M. "Newport Quakers and their
        Great Meeting House: or how we came to
        restore the Great Meeting House." NH, 47
        (1974), 197-216.

2489    WRIGHT, REDWOOD. "Fort Adams: doomed to
        live again?" RIer (Apr. 20, 1958), 4-8.
            Former U.S. Army installation.

2490    "YANKEE explores the legend of the old
        Newport Tower." Yankee, 18 (Mar. 1954),
        24-35.
            Stone Mill.

2491    YEAGER, HENRY J. "The French fleet at
        Newport, 1780-1781." RIH, 30 (1971), 87-93.

2492    YOUNG, JOHN. Two tall masts: the America's
        Cup challenge from Cambria to Sovereign.
        London: Stanley Paul, 1965. 123p. RNR. +

        SEE ALSO entries 32, 96, 105, 124, 131, 181,
        246, 277, 317, 357, 359, 432, 478, 482, 513,
        554, 601, 663, 715, 725, 758, 782, 906, 934,
        946, 968, 981, 1020, 1032, 1061, 1094, 1098,
        1164, 1168, 1171, 1175, 1178-1180, 1184,
        1186, 1188-1190, 1193, 1195, 1206-1207,
        1211, 1217, 1219-1220, 2656, 3019.

Entries for Cities and Towns

## NORTH KINGSTOWN (WASHINGTON CO.)

2493 BAKER, DAVID SHERMAN, JR. An historical sketch of North Kingstown, delivered at Wickford, July 4th, 1876. Providence: E. A. Johnson, 1876. 26p. RHi. +

2494 A BRIEF history of the Baptist church, in Wickford, R.I., constituted August 9, 1834; comprising the principal facts connected with the late difficulties, which resulted in its dissolution, April 4, 1844. Providence: Knowles & Vose, 1844. 36p. RHi.

2495 CADY, JOHN HUTCHINS. "Cocumscussoc." Old-time New England, 39 (1949), 61-70.
    Historic house, also known as Smith's Castle. See note, entry 2543.

2496 CARPENTER, ESTHER BERNON. "The old Narragansett glebe." NHR, 1 (1883), 287-290.
    Residence and land connected with St. Paul's Church (Episcopal), Wickford.

2497 CHAPIN, HOWARD M. The trading post of Roger Williams, with those of John Wilcox and Richard Smith.... Providence: Society of Colonial Wars, R.I., 1933. 26p. RHi. +

2498 CHIPMAN, WILLIAM P. "Historical sketch of the Quidnessett Baptist Church, North Kingstown, R.I." NHR, 2 (1883), 81-97.

2499 CONLEY, PATRICK T. North Kingstown: an historical sketch. [Providence: R.I. Bicentennial Commission,] n.d. 11p. RHi. +

2500 DAUGHTERS OF THE AMERICAN REVOLUTION. RHODE ISLAND. PETTAQUAMSCUTT CHAPTER, WICKFORD. Facts and fancies concerning North Kingstown, Rhode Island. North Kingstown, 1941. 143p. RHi. +

2501 EARLE, ALICE MORSE. "The oldest Episcopal church in New England." NEM, n.s. 7 (1893), 577-593.
    St. Paul's Church, Wickford.

2502 EARLE, JOHN M. A brief history of Quidnessett Baptist Church: sesquicentennial, 1828-1978.... Newport: Ward's Printing, n.d. iv, 60p. RNoK.

2503 FOWLER, WILLIAM S. "Rhode Island prehistory at the Green Point site." Report of the Narragansett Archaeological Society of Rhode Island (July 1954), 65-80.

2504 FREEMASONS. WICKFORD. WASHINGTON LODGE, NO. 5. One hundredth anniversary, Washington Lodge, No. 5, A.F. & A.M., Wickford, R.I. [Providence:] Snow & Farnham, [1898]. 63p. RHi. +

2505 GARDINER, GEORGE W. Lafayette, Rhode Island: a few phases of its history from the ice age to the atomic. Pawtucket: J. C. Hall, 1949. xvi, 267p. RHi. +

2506 GARDINER, J. WARREN. "Roger Williams: the pioneer of Narragansett." NHR, 2 (1883), 25-34.

2507 "THE GILBERT Stuart house." NHR, 1 (1883), 247-255.

2508 GOODWIN, DANIEL. A golden vial full of odours: a sermon preached at the old Narragansett Church, St. Paul's Parish, Wickford, Rhode Island, September 9th, 1907, on the two hundreth anniversary of its erection. Boston: Merrymount Pr., 1908. 22p. RHi. +
    Episcopal.

2509 GREEN, FRANCES. "Wickford, my village of dreams." New-England Galaxy, 17 (Summer 1975), 14-24.

2510 GRISWOLD, FRANCES IRENE BURGE. Old Wickford: "the Venice of America." Milwaukee: The Young Churchman, 1900. 240p. RHi. +

2511 HAZARD, CAROLINE. The Gilbert Stuart Birthplace: a brief history of the birthplace, its purchase and restoration; the forming of the corporation and future projects. [Providence: Roger Williams Pr., 1935.] 21p. RHi. +

2512 _____. "The Gilbert Stuart House." RIH, 1 (1942), 105-108.

2513 _____. "Gilbert Stuart's birthplace." Daughters of the American Revolution Magazine, 71 (1937), 205-207.

2514 HINCKLEY, ANITA W. "Mother Prentice." RIer (June 27, 1965), 16.
    "Kept the best boarding house in Wickford."

2515 _____. "My friend, the rumrunner." RIer (Oct. 19, 1969), 26-27.
    During Prohibition.

2516 _____. Wickford memories. Boston: Branden Pr., 1972. 118p. RHi. +

2517 _____. "Wickford tales." American Heritage, 16, No. 4 (June 1965), 80-90.

2518    HULING, RAY GREENE. "The Greenes' of Quidnesset." NHR, 2 (1883-1884), 137-144, 161-176, 253-264; 3 (1884), 20-33.

2519    ISHAM, NORMAN MORRISON. Wickford and its neighborhood. n.p., 1922. [4]p. RHi.
        Historic houses.

2520    JACKSON, HENRY G. "The Quonset hut." RIH, 6 (1947), 6-10.
        Famous building-type, developed at U.S. Naval installation at Quonset during World War II.

2521    LAFAYETTE, R.I. ADVENT CHRISTIAN CHURCH. Manual of the Advent Christian Church, Lafayette, Rhode Island.... (1884) Lafayette, 1888. 47p. RHi.
        Includes historical sketch.

2522    LAWRENCE, H. NEWMAN. The old Narragansett church (St. Paul's), built A.D. 1707: a constant witness to Christ and his church.... n.p., 1915. 86p. RHi.
        Episcopal.

2523    "THE LONE Eagle was there before the Blue Eagles." RIer (Feb. 23, 1964), 32-33.
        Historical sketch of site of the U.S. Naval Air Station, Quonset Point.

2524    McHALE, JULIA B. "The old Narragansett church." Daughters of the American Revolution Magazine, 71 (1937), 210-211.
        Saint Paul's Church (Episcopal), Wickford.

2525    MacSPARRAN, JAMES. A letter book and abstract of our services, written during the years 1743-1751 by the Revd. James MacSparran, Doctor in Divinity and sometime rector of Saint Paul's Church, Narragansett, Rhode Island. Daniel Goodwin, ed. Boston: D. B. Updike, 1899. xliv, 197p. RHi. +
        Episcopal.

2526    MARKHAM, ALTON, and ROBERT A. SCHRACK. "Was this the first farm forestry in America?" Journal of Forestry, 45 (1947), 900-902.
        Francis Willett of Saunderstown (18th century).

2527    MORGAN, JOHN HILL. "What was Gilbert Stuart's name?" RIHSC, 34 (1941), 33-44.
        I.e., his full name.

2528    "NOTES on Quidnessett." NHR, 1 (1883), 305-311; 5 (1886), 61-66.

2529    RHODE ISLAND. HISTORICAL PRESERVATION COMMISSION. North Kingstown, Rhode Island: statewide historical preservation report W-NK-1. [Providence,] 1979. vi, 65p. RHi.
        Author: Ellen Weiss.

2530    RHODE ISLAND. UNIVERSITY. COASTAL RESOURCES CENTER. The redevelopment of Quonset/Davisville: an environmental assessment prepared for the Rhode Island Department of Economic Development. [Kingston,] 1977. 200p. RHi.
        Sites of Quonset Naval Air Station and Davisville Advanced Base Depot during World War II. Report includes brief historical sketch.

2531    RIDER, SIDNEY S. "Wickford." BN, 13 (1896), 157-159.

2532    SAUNDERS, LAURA SMITH, and JOHN A. SAUNDERS. "The shipbuilding Saunderses: echoes of the caulking iron on Narragansett Bay." NH, 46 (1973), 53-70.
        John Aldrich Saunders and descendents.

2533    SIMISTER, FLORENCE PARKER. Streets of the city: an anecdotal history of North Kingstown. North Kingstown: Simister's Bookshop, 1974. 108p. RHi. +

2534    "SMITH'S Castle at Cocumscussoc, Rhode Island." RIY (1965-1966), 86.
        Historic house.

2535    STETS, DAN. "'The spirit of Fort Kearney.'" RIer (July 18, 1982), 4-5, 7, 9, 12.
        World War II camp in which German prisoners of war were held and indoctrinated.

2536    UPDIKE, DANIEL BERKELEY. Richard Smith: first English settler of the Narragansett Country, Rhode Island; with a series of letters written by his son, Richard Smith, Jr., to members of the Winthrop family, and notes on Cocumscussuc, Smith's estate in Narragansett. Boston: Merrymount Pr., 1937. xix, 118p. RHi. +

2537    UPDIKE, WILKINS. A history of the Episcopal church in Narragansett, Rhode Island, including a history of other Episcopal churches in the state.... With a transcript of the Narragansett parish register, from 1718 to 1774; an appendix containing a reprint of a work entitled: America dissected, by the Revd. James MacSparran, D.D., and copies of other old papers; together with notes containing genealogical and biographical accounts of distinguished men, families, &c. 2d ed., newly edited, enlarged, and corrected, by the Reverend Daniel Goodwin.... (1847) Boston: D. B. Updike, 1907. 3v. RHi. +
        Saint Paul's Church, Wickford.

2538    WARD, JOHN. "At Saunderstown: no more flags flying." RIer (Mar. 7, 1965), 4-5.
        U.S. Weather Bureau storm-warning station.

2539 WHITE, ELIZABETH NICHOLSON. Anne of Kings Towne. 2d ed. [East Providence: Watchemoket Pr., 1955.] 51p. RHi.
Ann Coddington Willett (1653-1751); history of Willett Farm, Saunderstown.

2540 WHITE, HUNTER C. Old St. Paul's in Narragansett. Wakefield: Wakefield Printing, 1957. 56p. RHi. +
Episcopal church.

2541 _____. Wickford and its old houses; supplemented by a history of North Kingstown and a listing of its historic houses and localities. [Wickford:] Main Street Association, 1960. 95p. RHi. +

2542 WICKFORD, R.I. SAINT BERNARD'S CHURCH. St. Bernard Church, Wickford, R.I. South Hackensack, N.J.: Custombook, 1975. 24, [20]p. RNoK.
Roman Catholic.

2543 WOODWARD, CARL RAYMOND. Plantation in Yankeeland: the story of Cocumscussoc, mirror of colonial Rhode Island. Wickford: Cocumscussoc Association, 1971. ix, 198p. RHi. +
Richard Smith's 17th-century plantation near Wickford. House, still standing, is now popularly known as Smith's Castle.

SEE ALSO entries 131, 458, 1277, 1322.

# NORTH PROVIDENCE (PROVIDENCE CO.)

2544 ANGELL, FRANK C. Annals of Centerdale in the town of North Providence, Rhode Island: its past and present, 1636-1909. Central Falls: E. L. Freeman, 1909. xv, 196p. RHi. +

2545 _____. History of Roger Williams Lodge, No. 32, F. & A.M., Centerdale, Rhode Island, 1875-1923. Centerdale: Centredale Pr., n.d. 148p. RNoP. +

2546 _____. Looking backward four score years, 1845-1925. Centerdale: Centredale Pr., 1925. 178p. RHi. +
Life in Centerdale.

2547 BISSLAND, JAMES H. "When Greystone was a bit of old England." RIer (Sept. 2, 1962), 8-11.
Mill village.

2548 CENTERDALE, R.I. SAINT LAWRENCE CHURCH. St. Lawrence Parish, Centredale, R.I.: golden jubilee, 1907-1957. n.p., n.d. [60]p. RPD-H.
Roman Catholic.

2549 DISABLED AMERICAN VETERANS. GORDON PAUL MILLER CHAPTER NO. 11, NORTH PROVIDENCE. General Marshall's victory report on the winning of World War II in Europe and the Pacific; with an added section featuring the contributions made by our own community toward the winning of the war. Historic handbook for every American. [North Providence,] n.d. 123, [18]p. RNoP.

2550 FREEMASONS. NORTH PROVIDENCE. ROGER WILLIAMS LODGE, NO. 32, CENTERDALE. The first hundred years: a brief history of Roger Williams Lodge No. 32, A.F. & A.M., Centerdale, R.I. n.p., 1976. 60p. RNoP.

2551 GENEVA VOLUNTEER FIRE COMPANY, NORTH PROVIDENCE. Fiftieth anniversary of the Geneva Volunteer Fire Company, Inc., 1902-1952. n.p., n.d. [13]p. RHi.

2552 HARPIN, MATHIAS P. "Lymansville." WRICHSH, 4 (Apr. 1961), [2]; (May 1961), [2]; (June 1961), [2].
Includes its role as a textile-mill village.

2553 HISTORICAL RECORDS SURVEY. RHODE ISLAND. Inventory of the town and city archives of Rhode Island: No. 4, Providence County; Vol. 10, North Providence. Providence, 1942. viii, 159p. RHi. +
Includes historical sketch.

2554 LOVEJOY, DAVID S. "Uncle Brown grabs a town." RIH, 14 (1955), 47-51.
An aspect of the 18th-century Ward-Hopkins controversy in R.I. colonial politics, involving the separation of North Providence from Providence and its incorporation as a town.

2555 NORTH PROVIDENCE, R.I. SAINT ANTHONY'S CHURCH. Saint Anthony Church, North Providence, Rhode Island. South Hackensack, N.J.: Custombook, 1971. 23p. RPD.
Roman Catholic. Italian parish. Includes historical sketch.

2556 NORTH Providence centennial: a report of the celebration at Pawtucket, North Providence, of the one hundredth anniversary of the incorporation of the town, June 24th, 1865; with an address, containing historical matters of local interest. Pawtucket: Robert Sherman, 1865. 91p. RHi. +
Address by Massena Goodrich. Another ed., entitled, Report of the centennial celebration... (Providence, 1865), has 118p.

2557 NORTHERN INTERRELATED LIBRARY SYSTEM. North Providence Union Free Library, 100th anniversary. [Pawtucket, 1970.] 15p. RNoP.

2558 OBSERVER (newspaper). North Providence 200th anniversary issue. (Greenville, Apr. 8, 1965.) 112p. RNoP.

2559 YE OLDE historical town map of North Providence, with indexed street map, by Bill Turner. n.p., 1967. RNoP.
Folding map with text.

2560 RHODE ISLAND. HISTORICAL PRESERVATION COMMISSION. Preliminary survey report: town of North Providence. Providence, 1978. iv, 43p. RHi.
Author: Vivienne F. Laskey.

2561 VENAVA, SULLY W. Fifty years of fire fighting: a history of the Centredale Fire Company. n.p., 1956. [34]p. RNoP.

2562 WEIS, ROBERT LEWIS. Saint James Episcopal Church: history of 100 years. n.p., 1969. 140p. RHi.

2563 WHEELER, ROBERT L. "Dr. Gardner's call book." RIer (Mar. 28, 1954), 14-15.
1832 record book of the medical practice of Dr. Johnson Gardner.

SEE ALSO entry 1251.

## NORTH SMITHFIELD (PROVIDENCE CO.)

2564 "ABNER Bailey tells the story of a North Smithfield landmark." North Smithfield Heritage Association, Newsletter (Sept. 1981), 4-9.
Primrose Grange, No. 9, Patrons of Husbandry.

2565 ARNOLD, FRED A. "The Inman Purchase in North Smithfield." NHR, 6 (1888), 49-92.

2566 BUCK, E. A. An historical discourse, delivered at the semi-centennial anniversary of the Slatersville Congregational Church, Sept. 9, 1866. Woonsocket: S. S. Foss, 1867. 48p. RHi. +

2567 DONNELL, ALBERT. Address delivered...on the seventieth anniversary of the dedication of the Congregational Church building at Slatersville, R.I., November 28, 1908. n.p., n.d. 24p. RHi.

2568 _____. An historical address delivered at the centennial celebration of the Congregational Sunday School at Slatersville, R.I., September 13, 1908. Woonsocket: Charles E. Cook, 1908. 46p. RHi.

2569 _____. Sermon preached at the ninetieth anniversary of the organization of the Congregational Church at Slatersville, Rhode Island, Sept. 9, 1906. Woonsocket: Charles E. Cook, 1906. 40p. RHi. +

2570 FRANKLIN, M. S. "Houses and villages of North Smithfield, Rhode Island." Pencil Points, 16 (1935), 431-446.

2571 NEBIKER, WALTER. The history of North Smithfield. [North Smithfield:] North Smithfield Bicentennial Commission, 1976. xviii, 24p. RHi.

2572 _____. "North Smithfield a century ago." RIY (1972), 73-81.

2573 _____. "The Peleg Arnold Tavern." North Smithfield Heritage Association, Newsletter (Apr. 1977), 4-7.

2574 NORTH Smithfield centennial, 1666-1971. n.p., n.d. 136p. RHi.
Incorporated in 1871, North Smithfield was previously a part of Smithfield.

2575 PAXTON, HELEN THAYER. "North Smithfield's Rock Cliff Farm." North Smithfield Heritage Association, Newsletter (June 1976), 4-6; (Nov. 1976), 6-9.

2576 RHODE ISLAND. HISTORICAL PRESERVATION COMMISSION. Preliminary survey report: town of North Smithfield. Providence, 1980. iii, 69p. RHi.
Author: Walter Nebiker.

2577 "A ROAD by any other name." Smithfield Heritage Association, Newsletter (Dec. 1973), 1-6; (Feb. 1974), 7-15.
The town's "great road system." 2d article by George A. Harvey.

2578 SLATERSVILLE, R.I. SAINT JOHN'S CHURCH. Saint John's centennial. n.p., [1972]. 44p. RPD.
Roman Catholic.

SEE ALSO entry 3803.

## PAWTUCKET (PROVIDENCE CO.)

2579 BARRETT, SHIRLEY. "It all began with apples: the story of America's first Sunday school." Yankee, 33 (Apr. 1969), 168-171.
Young mill workers received both secular and religious teaching in the school established by Samuel Slater in 1795.

2580 BENEDICT, DAVID. Historical and biographical sketches of some of the early and succeeding inhabitants of Pawtucket. n.p., n.d. 14p. RP.

2581 BOUCHER, SUSAN MARIE. The history of Pawtucket, 1635-1976. [Pawtucket:] Pawtucket Public Library, 1976. xv, 215p. RHi. +
    For histories of Pawtucket in addition to those listed in this section, see entry 1240 and Richard LeBaron Bowen, Early Rehoboth [Mass.].... (Rehoboth, 1945-1950; 7v.).

2582 BOURNE, WILLIAM G. Park Place Congregational Church of Pawtucket, R.I.: a record of fifty years of work and achievement, 1882-1932. n.p., 1932. 24p. RPa.

2583 BULLEN, GEORGE. Historical discourse commemorative of the First Baptist Church, Pawtucket, R.I.,...delivered April 10, 1881. Pawtucket: A. D. Nickerson, 1881. 48p. RHi. +

2584 CASSIDY, THOMAS V. Saint Mary Church of Pawtucket, Rhode Island: a sesquicentennial story, 1829-1979. n.p.: E. A. Johnson, 1979. xii, 111p. RPa.
    Roman Catholic.

2585 D'AMBRA, MIKE. "Metropolis by the bridge." RIY (1971), 18-26.

2586 THE DEBORAH Cook Sayles Public Library. [Providence: Standard Printing, 1903.] 102p. RHi. +
    Includes historical sketch.

2587 EDWARDS, WILLIAM H. "Race track 'war.'" RIY (1971), H209-H212.
    Narragansett Racing Association.

2588 FIRE service of Pawtucket, R.I.: presented to the appreciative public of the sister city. [Pawtucket:] Charitable Association of the Pawtucket Fire Dept., 1888. 90p. MWA.
    Includes historical sketch.

2589 GILBANE, BRENDAN F. "Pawtucket Village mechanics: iron, integrity, and the cotton revolution." RIY, 34 (1975), 3-11.

2590 GOODRICH, MASSENA. Historical sketch of the town of Pawtucket. Pawtucket: Nickerson, Sibley, 1876. 189p. RHi. +

2591 _____. "Pawtucket and the Slater centennial." NEM, n.s. 3 (1890), 139-156.
    Samuel Slater and the beginning of the American cotton-textile industry.

2592 GRIEVE, ROBERT, and JOHN P. FERNALD. The cotton centennial, 1790-1890: cotton and its uses, the inception and development of the cotton industries of America, and a full account of the Pawtucket centenary celebration; historical sketches of Samuel Slater and other pioneer manufacturers, with notices of some of the famous cotton men of today.... Providence: J. A. & R. A. Reid, 1891. 176, xxv p. RHi. +

2593 [HALEY, JOHN WILLIAMS.] Builders of Pawtucket. Providence: "Old Stone Bank," n.d. 9p. RHi.
    The Jenks family, early settlers. This entry was part of the "Old Stone Bank" historical pamphlet series. See note, entry 432.

2594 "HISTORICAL sketch of the Pawtucket Business Men's Association." BTJ, 1 (Dec. 1890), 16, 18, 20.

2595 INDUSTRIAL TRUST COMPANY. SLATER BRANCH. In the path of the pioneers. Pawtucket, 1925. 35p. RHi. +
    History of the bank.

2596 JENKS, MARY A. Behind the bars: or, ten years of the life of a police matron. Pawtucket: Priv. Print., 1902. viii, 179p. RPa. +

2597 JOHNSON, MARY-ANNE. "David Wilkinson's lathe." Tools & Technology, 2 (Fall 1978), 9-12.
    Invented 1794.

2598 KELLY, JOSEPH A. "The stop that has almost stopped." RIer (Jan. 17, 1960), 12-13.
    Pawtucket-Central Falls Railroad Depot.

2599 KULIK, GARY. "Pawtucket Village and the strike of 1824: the origins of class conflict in Rhode Island." Radical History Review, No. 17 (1978), 5-37.
    "...Earliest [strike] in the North American textile industry."

2600 _____, and PATRICK M. MALONE. The Wilkinson Mill. n.p.: American Society of Mechanical Engineers, 1977. 6, [3]p., [8]pl. RHi.

2601 LAW, FREDERICK. The history of old St. Paul's of Pawtucket. Pawtucket: Chronicle Printing, n.d. [60]p. RPa. +
    Episcopal church.

2602 LINCOLN, JONATHAN THAYER. "The beginnings of the machine age in New England: David Wilkinson of Pawtucket." NEQ, 6 (1933), 716-732.
    Early builder and inventor of machinery and machine tools.

2603 Pawtucket

2603 McKENNA, JOHN H. The centenary story of old St. Mary's, Pawtucket, R.I., 1829-1929. Providence: Providence Pr., [1929]. 51, [4]p. RHi. +
Roman Catholic church.

2604 "THE MANUFACTURE of nails: Pawtucket developments to 1829." Old Slater Mill, The Flyer, 3 (June 1972), 3-5, 11.

2605 MOTORMEN AND CONDUCTORS SOCIAL CLUB, DIVISION NO. 3, PAWTUCKET. Official souvenir history of the Motormen and Conductors Social Club, Division No. 3, employees of the Rhode Island Company, 1904. n.p., 1904. 28p. RHi.

2606 NORTON, VERNON C. A common man for the common people: the life of Thomas P. McCoy, 1883-1945. 77p. RHi. +
Important and controversial figure as mayor of Pawtucket and in R.I. Democratic politics.

2607 "AN OLD machine shop, where Samuel Slater's first spinning frames were made." BTJ, 1 (Dec. 1889), 14, 16.
James S. Brown's machine shop.

2608 ONE hundredth anniversary of the founding of cotton spinning in America: official programme of the celebration at Pawtucket, Rhode Island...1890. n.p., n.d. 32p. RHi. +

2609 OUR police: a history of the Pawtucket police force, under the town and city. Henry Mann, ed. Pawtucket: J. M. Beers, 1889. vii, 106p. RPa.

2610 PAWTUCKET, R.I. Historical program, city of Pawtucket diamond jubilee, 1886-1961: seventy-five years of history and progress. n.p., 1961. 120p. RHi. +

2611 _____. Souvenir book of the fiftieth anniversary of the incorporation of the city of Pawtucket and the dedication of the new city hall. [Pawtucket, 1936.] 143p. RHi. +
Includes sketches of Pawtucket history.

2612 PAWTUCKET, R.I. CHURCH OF SAINT THERESA OF THE CHILD JESUS. St. Theresa Church, 1929-1979: golden anniversary book. n.p., n.d. 88p. RHi.
Roman Catholic.

2613 PAWTUCKET, R.I. CONGREGATIONAL CHURCH. A century of Christian service, 1829-1929: Pawtucket Congregational Church. n.p.: [E. L. Freeman, 1929]. 57p. RHi. +

2614 _____. Manual of the Congregational Church, Pawtucket, Mass., containing its history, standing rules, confession of faith, and covenant, with a catalogue of its members. Pawtucket: R. Sherman, 1857. 36p. MWA. +
In what is now Pawtucket, R.I.

2615 PAWTUCKET, R.I. FIRST BAPTIST CHURCH. Centennial anniversary exercises of the First Baptist Sunday School of Pawtucket, Rhode Island, October 24, 1897. Pawtucket: John W. Little, n.d. 79p. RHi. +

2616 _____. Exercises in recognition of the centennial of the First Baptist Church, Pawtucket, R.I. n.p., 1905. 27p. RP. +

2617 _____. First Baptist Church, Pawtucket, R.I.: one hundred and fiftieth anniversary, 1805-1955. n.p., n.d. 32p. RP. +

2618 _____. Manual of the First Baptist Church, Pawtucket, R.I., organized August, 1805. Providence: Providence Pr., 1884. 46p. RHi. +
Includes historical sketch.

2619 PAWTUCKET, R.I. OUR LADY OF CONSOLATION PARISH. Our Lady of Consolation Parish, Pawtucket, Rhode Island. Hackensack, N.J.: Custombook, 1975. 28, [8]p. RHi.
Roman Catholic. French parish.

2620 PAWTUCKET, R.I. SAINT JOSEPH'S CHURCH. A history of St. Joseph's Parish, Pawtucket, Rhode Island, 1873-1979. n.p., n.d. 84p. RPD.
Roman Catholic.

2621 PAWTUCKET, R.I. SAINT MARIA GORETTI CHURCH. St. Maria Goretti Church, Pawtucket, Rhode Island. South Hackensack, N.J.: Custombook, 1967. 24p. RPD.
Roman Catholic.

2622 PAWTUCKET, R.I. TRINITY CHURCH. One hundred years, 1843-1943: Trinity Church, Pawtucket, Rhode Island. n.p., [1943]. [20]p. RPB. +
Episcopal.

2623 PAWTUCKET, R.I. WOODLAWN BAPTIST CHURCH. History of the Woodlawn Baptist Church, Lonsdale Avenue at Weeden Street, Pawtucket, Rhode Island, as compiled for the diamond jubilee celebration of the seventy-fifth anniversary, October 27, 1968. n.p., n.d. 11p. RHi.

2624 _____. Woodlawn Baptist Sunday School centennial, 1875-1975. Pawtucket, [1975]. 11p. RHi.

2625 "PAWTUCKET blacksmiths in the eighteenth century." Old Slater Mill, The Flyer, 4 (July 1973), 5, 8-9.

2626 PAWTUCKET BUSINESS MEN'S ASSOCIATION. Fiftieth anniversary of the Pawtucket Business Men's Association, December 7, 1931. [Pawtucket, 1931.] 20p. RPB.

2627 PAWTUCKET INSTITUTION FOR SAVINGS. One hundred years of the Pawtucket Institution for Savings, 1836-1936. Pawtucket, 1936. 44p. RP.

2628 PAWTUCKET sesqui-centennial cotton celebration, 1790-1940: souvenir program. n.p.: [Visitor Printing,] n.d. [34]p. RHi. +
Marking the 150th anniversary of the American cotton-textile industry.

2629 PAWTUCKET TIMES (newspaper). The Pawtucket Times Historical Magazine, 250th anniversary of Pawtucket, R.I., 1671-1921. Pawtucket, 1921. 55p. RHi.

2630 PHENIX NATIONAL BANK. Crown Manufacturing Company, "Crown College." [Providence,] 1946. 10p. RHi.
Textile manufacturer. This entry and those that follow under the heading of Phenix National Bank were part of the Romance of R.I. Industry pamphlet series. See note, entry 768.

2631 _____. ...H & B American Machine Co. [Providence,] 1945. 10p. RHi.

2632 _____. "Horizon unlimited." [Providence,] 1945. 10p. RHi.
Hope Webbing Co.

2633 _____. ...The J. C. Hall Co. [Providence,] 1946. 10p. RHi.
Bank stationers, lithographers, binders, printers.

2634 _____. ...Pawtucket Manufacturing Co. [Providence,] 1946. 10p. RHi.
Manufacturer of nuts and bolts.

2635 _____. ...Pawtucket Spinning Ring Co. [Providence,] 1946. 10p. RHi.
Textile machinery.

2636 _____. ...Raycrest Mills. [Providence,] 1946. 10p. RHi.
Textile manufacturer.

2637 RANDALL, EDWARD H. A discourse, commemorative of the fiftieth anniversary of the consecration of St. Paul's Church, Pawtucket, R.I., delivered on Sunday, October 20th, A.D. 1867.... Pawtucket: R. Sherman, 1868. 28p. RHi. +
Episcopal.

2638 RHODE ISLAND. HISTORICAL PRESERVATION COMMISSION. Pawtucket, Rhode Island: statewide historical preservation report P-PA-1. [Providence,] 1978. vi, 62p. RHi.
Author: Stephen J. Roper.

2639 RIDER, SIDNEY S. "The Sergeant's Trench riot at Pawtucket." BN, 11 (1894), 13-16.
1822 riot and the trial that resulted.

2640 RIVARD, PAUL E. Samuel Slater: a short interpretive essay on Samuel Slater's role in the birth of the American textile industry. [Pawtucket:] Slater Mill Historic Site, 1974. [30]p. RHi. +
Focuses on his career in Pawtucket. Other biographies of Slater that contain significant information about his career in Pawtucket and R.I. include William R. Bagnall, Samuel Slater and the early development of the cotton manufacture in the United States (1890); E. H. Cameron, Samuel Slater: father of American manufactures (1960); George S. White, Memoir of Samuel Slater (2d ed., 1836).

2641 _____. "Slater in Pawtucket: 1790." Old Slater Mill, The Flyer, 2 (Nov. 1971), 3-5, 9.
Samuel Slater's experiments with cotton-textile machinery.

2642 ST.-GODARD, EDWARD G. St. John's Parish, Pawtucket, R.I., 1884-1978. n.p.: [Dennis Printing, 1978]. 88p. RHi.
Roman Catholic. French parish.

2643 "SAMUEL Slater: early history of the cotton industry in Pawtucket." BTJ, 1 (June 1890), 14, 16; (Aug. 1890), 14, 16; (Sept. 1890), 14, 16.

2644 SLATER TRUST COMPANY. Pawtucket past and present: being a brief account of the beginning and progress of its industries and a résumé of the early history of the city. Pawtucket, 1917. vi, 55p. RHi. +

2645 "THE SYLVANUS Brown House." Old Slater Mill, The Flyer, 3 (Apr. 1972), 3-4, 6, 8-9.
Owned by Old Slater Mill; once housed mill workers.

2646 "TEXTILE experiments, 1790: part I, Slater's first 11 weeks." Old Slater Mill, The Flyer, 2 (Sept. 1971), 2-3, 11.

2647    "TIMOTHY Greene & Company:  the leather
        industry."  Old Slater Mill, The Flyer, 3
        (May 1972), 3-4.

2648    "USING the evidence:  the Brown House
        restoration."  Old Slater Mill, The Flyer,
        4 (Jan. 1973), 3-4, 6.
            Sylvanus Brown House.

2649    WELLES, ARNOLD.  "Father of our factory
        system."  American Heritage, 9, No. 3 (Apr.
        1958), 34-39, 90-92.
            Samuel Slater's first experiments in
        Pawtucket (1790).

2650    WHEELER, ROBERT L.  "Martin knows Main
        Street."  RIer (Dec. 12, 1954), 3-6.
            Pawtucket history viewed through the
        career of newspaperman Frank A. Martin, Sr.

2651    "WHEN the bosses ran Pawtucket."  RIer (Oct.
        10, 1971), P10-P13.

        SEE ALSO entries 179, 554, 601, 1009, 1240,
        1242, 1249, 1255, 2556, 3019.


## PORTSMOUTH (NEWPORT CO.)

2652    BOLHOUSE, GLADYS E.  "Incidents through the
        years at the Portsmouth coal mines."  NH, 40
        (1967), 1-21, 61-68.

2653    BOWEN, JOANNE.  "Probate inventories:  an
        evaluation from the perspective of
        zooarchaeology and agricultural history at
        Mott Farm."  Historical Archaeology, 9
        (1975), 11-25.

2654    BOYNTON, RACHAEL CHASE.  "Prudence Island
        shipping in the old days."  RIY (1973),
        119-121.

2655    CADY, STEVE.  "The chimney is a sailing
        mark."  RIer (July 29, 1956), 10-11.
            Site of the R.I. Yacht Club's summer annex
        on Prudence Island.

2656    THE CENTENNIAL celebration of the Battle of
        Rhode Island, at Portsmouth, R.I., August
        29, 1878:  comprising the oration by
        ex-United States Senator Samuel G. Arnold;
        a letter by Sir Henry Pigot, the English
        commander; a German account of the battle;
        the views of General Lafayette.  Providence:
        Sidney S. Rider, 1878.  118p.  RHi. +

2657    CHASE, HALSEY.  History of Prudence
        Island....  n.p.:  Cogen's, 1957.  7p.  RHi.

2658    CHILDS, LUKE.  "A brief history of
        Portsmouth:  the first twenty-five years."
        Portsmouth Abbey School, [Bulletin] (Feb.
        1977), 59-91.
            I.e., the early history of the school.

2659    THE EARLY records of the town of Portsmouth.
        [Clarence Saunders Brigham, ed.]
        Providence:  E. L. Freeman, 1901.  xi, 462p.
        RHi. +

2660    FARNHAM, RALPH WELCOME.  "The life and times
        of Ralph W. Farnham."  RIer (Oct. 14, 1962),
        12-13.
            Life on Prudence Island.

2661    FLOYD, GREGORY.  "Reflections of a
        headmaster."  Portsmouth Abbey School,
        [Bulletin] (Feb. 1977), 7-12.
            50 years of education at Portsmouth Abbey.

2662    FREEMASONS.  PORTSMOUTH.  EUREKA LODGE, NO.
        22.  100th anniversary, Eureka Lodge No. 22,
        Ancient Free and Accepted Masons of the
        State of R.I. and Providence Plantations,
        June 24, 25, 26, 1960, Portsmouth, Rhode
        Island.  [Somerset, Mass.:  Spectator Pr.,]
        n.d.  [18]p.  RNHi.

2663    GARMAN, JAMES E.  Historic houses of
        Portsmouth, Rhode Island.  Newport:
        Franklin Printing, 1976.  64p.  RNR.

2664    _____.  A history of Portsmouth, Rhode
        Island, 1638-1978.  Newport:  Franklin
        Printing, 1978.  54p.  RNR.

2665    GOLDOWSKY, SEEBERT J.  "The hospital at
        Portsmouth Grove."  RIMJ, 42 (1959),
        733-743, 746.
            Lovell General Hospital, a Civil War
        installation.

2666    [HALEY, JOHN WILLIAMS.]  An unsolved murder.
        Providence:  "Old Stone Bank," 1930.  10p.
        RHi.
            That of Rebecca Cornell in Portsmouth
        (1673).  This entry was part of the "Old
        Stone Bank" historical pamphlet series.  See
        note, entry 432.

2667    MAYER, LLOYD M.  "The dedication of Butts
        Hill Fort."  NHSB, No. 47 (1923), 5-18.
            Battle of Rhode Island (1778).

2668    MAYTUM, CHARLES G.  Paragraphs on early
        Prudence Island.  (1964?) n.p., 1976.  212,
        [5]p.  RBr.

2669    NEUSTADTL, SARA.  "Keeping the animals in
        shape."  Yankee, 46 (Oct. 1982), 106-111.
            Green Animals, a topiary garden.

2670 O'TOOLE, DENNIS A. "Democratic balance: ideals of community in early Portsmouth." RIH, 32 (1973), 3-17.

2671 "RECOLLECTIONS of Jacob Chase." NHSB, No. 28 (1919), 1-12.
Lloyd M. Mayer, ed. Social life and customs.

2672 REID, EUGENE G. "We were small, but not small-time: a report on the early years of Portsmouth Priory School, 1929-1931." Portsmouth Abbey School, Summer Bulletin (1981), 9-11.
Now Portsmouth Abbey School.

2673 REYNOLDS, BILL. "Forever locked in a simpler time." RIer (July 25, 1982), 4, 7.
Portsmouth Abbey School.

2674 RHODE ISLAND. HISTORICAL PRESERVATION COMMISSION. Preliminary survey report, town of Portsmouth. Providence, 1979. iv, 59p. RHi.
Author: Walter Nebiker.

2675 "RHODE Island had smallest feudal estate in America." PM, 34 (1922), 39, 41.
On Prudence Island.

2676 UPTON, DELL. "Architectural change in colonial Rhode Island: the Mott House as a case study." Old-time New England, 69 (Winter/Spring 1979), 18-33.
Portsmouth structure, disassembled and moved in 1973.

2677 WALKER, JOHN. "Art and architecture at Portsmouth Abbey." Portsmouth Abbey School, [Bulletin] (Feb. 1977), 14-24.

2678 WEST, EDWARD H. "The lands of Portsmouth, R.I., and a glimpse of its people." RIHSC, 25 (1932), 65-85.

2679 _____. Portsmouth, Rhode Island, before 1800. n.p., n.d. [65]p. RHi. +
Cover title: History of Portsmouth, 1638-1936.

2680 _____. "Portsmouth under the Hutchinsons." New England Historical and Genealogical Register, 105 (1951), 90-94.
William and Anne Hutchinson as leaders of the early settlement.

SEE ALSO entries 45, 277, 1098, 1162, 1164, 1166-1169, 1175, 1178-1180, 1186, 1188, 1190, 1195, 1206-1207, 1211, 1213, 1217, 1219-1220, 1714, 1801.

## PROVIDENCE (PROVIDENCE CO.)

2681 ADELMAN, DAVID C. "Congregation of the Sons of Israel and David (Temple Beth El): the early years." RIJHN, 3 (1962), 195-261.
Jewish synagogue.

2682 _____. "Montefiore Lodge, Ladies Hebrew Benevolent Association." RIJHN, 4 (1963), 47-78.

2683 _____. "Providence Jewish communities unite." RIJHN, 3 (1960), 160-191.
Charitable organizations.

2684 AIKEN, G. FRED. "The case of the missing fire engine." Yankee, 29 (Apr. 1965), 38-40, 49.
Gaspee No. 9, built in 1849, and once owned by the Providence Veteran Fire Association.

2685 THE ALBEE alumni: a history of the eleven years of the Edward F. Albee Stock Company; dedicated to the theatre-goers of Providence whose loyal support has made the continuation of this organization possible. Providence, 1912. 197p. RHi. +

2686 ALBERT, JUDITH STRONG. "Margaret Fuller's row at the Green Street School: early female education in Providence, 1837-1839." RIH, 42 (1983), 43-56.
The famous Transcendentalist and feminist and her students in an experimental Providence school.

2687 ALEXANDER, ROBERT. "The Arcade in Providence." Society of Architectural Historians, Journal, 12, No. 3 (Oct. 1953), 13-16.

2688 ALLAN, DELORA WHITTEN. "Grandma meets the motor age." RIer (May 23, 1954), 16-18, 20.
An early experience with the automobile.

2689 ALLEN, HELEN FARRELL. "The United States Custom House, Providence." RIY (1971), 80-81.

2690 ALLEN, ZACHARIAH. An address delivered before the Rhode Island Historical Society, at its fiftieth anniversary, July 19, 1872...together with other proceedings. Providence: Providence Pr., 1873. 48p. RHi. +
Includes biographical sketches of original members. Reprinted from RIHSPr (1872-1873), 97-144.

2691 Providence

2691 ALMAGNO, R. STEPHEN. The days of our years: Saint Bartholomew's Parish, Providence, Rhode Island, 1907-1969. n.p., n.d. [1969]. vii, 61p. RPD-H.
Roman Catholic. Italian parish.

2692 ANCIENT ARABIC ORDER OF THE NOBLES OF THE MYSTIC SHRINE FOR NORTH AMERICA. PROVIDENCE. PALESTINE TEMPLE. History of Palestine-Temple, Ancient Arabic Order, Nobles of the Mystic Shrine; preceded by a history of the Imperial Council, A.A.O., N.M.S., for North America. (1895) Boston: Hall Publishing, 1913. 519p. RHi. +

2693 "ANCIENT North End landmarks of the town of Providence." NHR, 4 (1886), 269-274.

2694 "ANCIENT signs." WRICHSH, 16 (May 1973), [1-2].
Shop signs.

2695 ANDERSON, GODFREY T. "Respectful student rebels." RIH, 34 (1975), 43-45.
Brown Univ. (1835).

2696 ANTHONY, ALBERT L. Fifty years' record of Calvary Commandery, Number 13, Knights Templars, stationed at Providence, Rhode Island, 1859-1909. Providence: E. L. Freeman, [1909?]. xiv, 650p. RHi.

2697 ANTHONY, MARY B., and GRACE P. CHAPIN. A history of the Young Ladies' School, 1860-1898, and Miss Abbott's School Alumnae Association, 1912-1930. Providence: Akerman-Standard, 1932. 57p. RHi. +

2698 AQUINO, ANTHONY S. "My South Providence, revisited." RIer (Sept. 22, 1968), 16-18, 21.
Changes in an inner-city neighborhood.

2699 ARNOLD, EARLE B. "Reminiscences of the old Court House." Rhode Island Bar Journal, 5, No. 3 (Dec. 1956), 1, 3, 7, 10; No. 4 (Jan. 1957), 10, 12; No. 5 (Feb. 1957), 1, 4.

2700 ARNOLD, FRED A. "The town bridge at Weybossett: an inquiry as to the date of building the first bridge across Providence River." RIHSPubs, n.s. 3 (1895), 112-122.

2701 ARNOLD, SAMUEL GREENE. Address delivered before the Charitable Baptist Society on the one hundredth anniversary of the opening of the First Baptist Church, Providence, R.I., for public worship, May 28, 1875. Providence: J. A. & R. A. Reid, 1875. 39p. RHi. +

2702 _____. An address delivered before the Rhode Island Historical Society, on the evening of June 1st, 1869. Providence: Hammond, Angell, 1869. 22p. RHi. +
The services to the society of three recently deceased members: Albert Gorton Greene, William Reed Staples, Usher Parsons.

2703 _____. The progress of Providence: a centennial address to the citizens of Providence, R.I.,...with a poem, by George William Pettes, delivered July 4th, 1876. Providence: Providence Pr., 1876. 55p. RHi. +

2704 AUSTIN, WALTER. A forgotten duel, fought in Rhode Island between William Austin, of Charlestown, and James Henderson Elliot, of Boston, March 31, 1806. n.p.: Priv. Print., 1914. 68p. RHi. +

2705 AUTOMOBILE MUTUAL INSURANCE COMPANY OF AMERICA. Pathway of progress, 1907-1957: the record of a half-century of achievement. Automobile Mutual Insurance Company of America, Factory Mutual Liability Insurance Company of America. [Providence,] 1957. 81p. RHi. +

2706 BACKUS, ISAAC. "A brief account of the life of James Manning, D.D., president of Rhode Island College." Books at Brown, 22 (1968), 155-160.
Forerunner of Brown Univ. Ed. by William G. McLoughlin.

2707 BAGHDADI, MANIA KLEINBURD. "'Community' and the Providence Jew in the early 20th century." RIJHN, 6 (1971), 56-75.

2708 BAILEY, ARNOLD C. "Betsey's bountiful bequest." RIY (1967), 46-50.
Roger Williams Park.

2709 BAILEY, WILLIAM M. "Turk's Head and the Whitman estate." RIHSPubs, n.s. 5 (1897), 216-222.
Turk's Head Corner (corner of Weybosset and Westminster streets). Named for carved shop sign that once stood near the corner.

2710 BAILEY, WILLIAM WHITMAN. "Brown in the early sixties." BrAlumMo, 7 (1906), 1-6.
Brown Univ.

2711 [BAKER, WALTER M.] Historical sketch of the First Light Infantry Regiment, Providence, R.I.; September sixteenth and seventeenth, nineteen hundred twelve. n.p.: F. H. Townsend, n.d. 88p. RHi. +

2712 BAPTIST YOUNG PEOPLE'S UNION OF AMERICA.
Souvenir programme, 12th annual convention
...July 10, 11, 12, 13, 1902; Providence,
R.I. Providence: W. H. Leland, n.d. 240,
[4]p. RHi. +
    Includes "Baptist churches of Providence,"
by Thomas E. Bartlett.

2713 BARDAGLIO, PETER W. "Italian immigrants and
the Catholic Church in Providence,
1890-1930." RIH, 34 (1975), 47-57.

2714 BARNARD CLUB, PROVIDENCE. The Barnard Club:
history, constitution, by-laws, list of
members, past presidents. n.p., 1975. 20p.
RHi.
    Various earlier eds.

2715 BARRY, JAY. "First Bears to beat the
Bulldog." BrAlumMo, 61 (Jan. 1961), 13-14.
    Brown Univ. football.

2716 _____. Gentlemen under the elms.
[Providence:] Brown Alumni Monthly, 1982.
176p. RHi.
    Biographical sketches of a number of Brown
Univ. faculty members.

2717 _____. "100 years of Brown football."
BrAlumMo, 79 (Oct. 1978), 26-32.

2718 BARTLETT, IRVING H. "The free Negro in
Providence, Rhode Island." Negro History
Bulletin, 14 (Dec. 1950), 51-54, 66, 67.

2719 BATES, LOUISE PROSSER. Y's work for 10
years. [Providence, 1892?] 16p. RPB.
    Young Women's Christian Temperance Union.

2720 "THE BEGINNINGS of the Holy Ghost Church."
The Echo (Sept. 20, 1979), 5, 18-19.
    Roman Catholic. Italian parish.

2721 BELCHER, HORACE G. "The old Hoyle Tavern."
RIHSC, 28 (1935), 33-48, 83-96.

2722 BENSON, SUSAN PORTER. "Business heads and
sympathizing hearts: the women of the
Providence Employment Society, 1837-1858."
Journal of Social History, 12 (1978),
302-312.
    "...The PES devoted itself to aiding
self-supporting seamstresses, providing
employment, relief, and vocational
education."

2723 BEWITCH, JOSIAH B. "Greater Providence:
what annexation has done for the development
of the city." PBTJ, 21 (1909), 458-462,
464-469.

2724 BICKNELL, THOMAS WILLIAMS. A history of the
Rhode Island Normal School, 1852-1865,
1871-1911. n.p., [1911?]. 235p. RHi. +
    Became R.I. College.

2725 BIGELOW, BRUCE M. State of mind.
Providence: Roger Williams Pr., 1954. 21p.
RHi. +
    Providence Athenaeum (library).

2726 _____. "What's in a name? 9 answers."
BrAlumMo, 52 (Jan. 1952), 3-6.
    Brown Univ. men for whom recently built
dormitories were named.

2727 BINNEY, MARCUS. "All in easy circumstances:
Providence, Rhode Island, II." Country
Life, 169 (Apr. 2, 1981), 900-903.
    Architecture and decorative arts. See
also next entry.

2728 _____. "Thriving entrepot of dissent:
Providence, Rhode Island, I." Country Life,
169 (Mar. 26, 1981), 782-784.
    Architecture. See also preceding entry.

2729 "BIRTHDAY of a sport." BrAlumMo, 52 (July
1953), 10-11, 20.
    Beginning of football at Brown.

2730 BLAKE, CHARLES. An historical account of
the Providence stage; being a paper read
before the Rhode Island Historical Society,
October 25th, 1860 (with additions).
Providence: George H. Whitney, 1868. 297p.
RHi. +
    Theater.

2731 BLAKE, MARION, EVELYN WADE, and MARGARET
HORST. Historical sketch of the South
Baptist Church, Providence, R.I.,
prepared...for the 75th anniversary
celebration, October 6-13, 1935. n.p.,
[1935]. 6p. RHi.

2732 BLANDE, WILLIAM H., SR. "The last downtown
blacksmith shop." RIer (Sept. 10, 1961),
13-14, 16.

2733 BLOCH, LOUIS M. "'Calling all houses and
dormitories.'" BrAlumMo, 82 (Oct. 1981),
31-35.
    College radio is claimed to have had its
beginnings at Brown.

2734 BLOOM, BESSIE EDITH. "Jewish life in
Providence." RIJHN, 5 (1970), 386-413.

2735 BOWDITCH, JOSIAH B. "Providence Harbor:
its past, present and future." PBTJ, 21
(1909), 242-244.

2736 BOWEN, RICHARD LeBARON. The Providence Oath
of Allegiance and its signers, 1651-2....
Providence: Society of Colonial Wars, R.I.,
1943. x, 92p. RHi. +

2737 BRAUDE, WILLIAM G. "Ezra: a journal of
opinion." RIJHN, 7 (1977), 432-436.
    Yiddish-language publication (1911).

2738 BRAUDE, WILLIAM G. "We look back." RIJHN, 5 (1967), 120-126.
Temple Beth-El.

2739 BRAYTON, GLADYS W. "Rhode Island's first mall." CHSN [Nov. 1979], [4-7].
Arcade.

2740 _____. "Roger Williams Park." CHSN [Sept., Oct. 1978].

2741 _____. "Signs of the times." CHSN [Apr. 1978].
Shop signs.

2742 BRETT, ROGER. Temples of illusion: the golden age of theaters in an American city. East Providence: E. A. Johnson, 1976. 309p. RHi. +

2743 BRICKMAN, WILLIAM W. "Tax-exemption privileges for professors of Brown University." History of Education Quarterly, 6 (Winter 1966), 65-78.
A long-standing privilege.

2744 BRIGHAM, CLARENCE SAUNDERS. "Old University Hall: an attempt to identify its rooms and occupants." BrAlumMo, 8 (1908), 113-119.

2745 _____. "Unprinted history of Rhode Island College." BrAlumMo, 6 (1905), 31-32.
Original name of Brown Univ.

2746 BRIGHAM, HERBERT OLIN. "The Rhode Island State Library." PM, 28 (1916), 224-226.
Includes historical sketch.

2747 BRONSON, WALTER C. The history of Brown University, 1764-1914. Providence: Brown Univ., 1914. ix, 547p. RHi. +

2748 BROOKS, GEORGE E., JR. "The Providence African Society's Sierra Leone emigration scheme, 1794-1854: prologue to the African colonization movement." International Journal of African Historical Studies, 2 (1974), 183-202.

2749 BROWN, MRS. CHARLES C. A hospital is born: the history of the Miriam Hospital Association. Providence: Miriam Hospital Association, 1944. 12p. RHi. +

2750 BROWN, FRANK CHOUTEAU. "Colonial architecture of old Providence." PBTJ, 27 (1915), 11-16.

2751 _____. "A Providence, Rhode Island, Georgian mansion: the house founded by John Brown, Esq., 1786." Pencil Points, 17 (1936), 97-112.

2752 BROWN, JAMES. "James Brown's diary (1787-1789)." RIH, 6 (1947), 99-107; 8 (1948), 9-11, 51-56.
Oldest son of merchant John Brown. Diary edited by Clarkson A. Collins III.

2753 BROWN, JOHN NICHOLAS. "Legacy on College Hill." BrAlumMo, 60 (July 1960), 28-32.
Brown Univ. architecture.

2754 BROWN, MOSES. "Official record of the great gale of 1815." RIHSPr, n.s. 2 (1894), 232-235.
Explanatory note by John Howland.

2755 BROWN, PATRICIA LEIGH. "Providence: this New England community is thriving again, thanks to a citywide preservation movement." American Preservation, 4, No. 2 [1981], 9-24.

2756 BROWN, WELCOME O. The Providence Franklin Society: an historical address on the occasion of opening the new rooms of the society in Arnold Block. Providence: J. A. & R. A. Reid, 1880. 50p. RHi. +
Scientific society.

2757 BROWN, WILLIAM J. The life of William J. Brown, of Providence, R.I.; with personal recollections of incidents in Rhode Island. Providence: Angell, 1883. 230p. RHi. +
Account of life in black community.

2758 BROWN AND SHARPE MANUFACTURING COMPANY. Brown & Sharpe Mfg. Co., Providence, Rhode Island, U.S.A.: a bit of history and a glimpse of our present plant. Providence, 1924. [22]p. RHi. +
Machinery manufacturer.

2759 _____. Memorial to the employees of the Brown & Sharpe Mfg. Co. who served at home and abroad in the Great World War. n.p., n.d. 95p. RHi. +
World War I.

2760 "BROWN celebrates her 150th anniversary." PM, 26 (1914), 669-676.
Includes historical sketch of Brown Univ.

2761 "THE BROWN Medical School, 1811-1827." BrAlumMo, 5 (1905), 162-164.

2762 BROWN UNIVERSITY. Brief history of Brown University, 1764-1901; reprinted from the annual catalogue. Providence: Remington Printing, 1902. 13p. RHi.
Historical sketches of Brown are to be found in many editions of the annual catalog.

2763 BROWN UNIVERSITY. Brown University: a group of pictures, with a few pages of comment on certain phases of life at one of America's oldest universities. [Providence,] n.d. 51p. RPB. +

2764 _____. Brown University: an illustrated historical souvenir, 1897. E. A. Locke, ed. Providence: Preston & Rounds, 1897. 123p. RHi. +

2765 _____. Brown University in the Civil War: a memorial. Henry Sweetser Burrage, comp. Providence, 1868. xii, 380p. RHi. +

2766 _____. Brown University in the War: a report by the War Records Committee, including a statement of the war work of the university, the biographies of Brown men who died in service, and a directory of the military service of alumni, former students and undergraduates. Providence, 1919. 74p. RHi. +
World War I.

2767 _____. Celebration of the one hundredth anniversary of the founding of Brown University, September 6th, 1864. Providence: Sidney S. Rider, 1865. 178p. RHi. +
Includes historical discourse by Barnas Sears.

2768 _____. Civil War record of Brown University. Henry Sweetser Burrage, comp. Providence, 1920. 69p. RHi. +

2769 _____. Exercises commemorating the restoration of University Hall, Brown University, October the twenty-fourth, A.D. MDCCCCV.... Providence: Standard Printing, 1905. 53p. RHi. +
Includes address by William MacDonald on the early history of Brown.

2770 _____. The growth of Brown University in recent years, 1899-1909. Providence, 1909. 14p. RHi. +

2771 _____. Historical catalogue of Brown University, 1764-1904. Providence, 1905. xii, 866p. RHi. +
Includes historical sketch. This and other eds. of the historical catalogue contain biographical data on alumni of Brown.

2772 _____. The sesquicentennial of Brown University, 1764-1914: a commemoration. [Providence,] 1915. x, 306p. RHi. +

2773 _____. 200th anniversary celebration, Brown University. n.p., [1964?]. 32p. RHi. +
Includes "The origins of Brown University," by John Nicholas Brown.

2774 _____. University Hall: built in 1770, reconstructed in 1940. Providence, 1940. 21p. RHi. +

2775 [BROWN UNIVERSITY. CLASS OF 1854.] "The class of 1854, which celebrates this year the fiftieth anniversary of its graduation." BrAlumMo, 5 (1904), 7-11.

2776 BROWN UNIVERSITY. [Class reunion reports.] Various places, ca. 1870s-.
Irregular. Coverage varies with class. Many reports include biographical data on class members. Most extensive coverage is for classes ca. 1880-1915. Largest collection is in Brown Univ. Archives.

2777 BROWN UNIVERSITY. DAILY HERALD (newspaper). Souvenir edition of the Brown Daily Herald, published in connection with the one hundred and fiftieth anniversary of the founding of Brown University, held from October eleventh to fourteenth, nineteen hundred and fourteen. [Providence, 1914.] [65]p. RHi.
Includes historical sketches.

2778 BROWN UNIVERSITY. EXECUTIVE BOARD. A sketch of the history and the present organization of Brown University. Providence: Knowles, Anthony, 1861. 15p. RP.

2779 BROWN UNIVERSITY. JOHN CARTER BROWN LIBRARY. The dedication of the library building, May the seventeenth, A.D. MDCCCCIIII. Addresses by William Vail Kellen and Frederick Jackson Turner. Providence, 1905. 68p. RHi. +
Includes historical background.

2780 BROWN UNIVERSITY. LIBRARY. A catalogue of the library of Brown University, in Providence, Rhode-Island; with an index of subjects. Providence, 1843. xxvi, 560p. RHi. +
Includes historical preface.

2781 BROWN UNIVERSITY. SECRETARY'S OFFICE. A brief history of Brown University, 1764-1961. [Providence, 1961?]. [28]p. RPB. +

2782 BROWN UNIVERSITY. SOCK AND BUSKIN (dramatic society). Souvenir program, Sock and Buskin and Komians: fortieth anniversary celebration, 1901-1941. February 3-8, 1941. n.p., n.d. 60p. RP. +
Includes historical sketch.

2783 Providence

2783 BROWNE, JAMES. James Browne: his writings in prose and verse concerning the first settling of the town of Providence and a memorandum of his efforts to prevent a separation of the Baptist congregation there in October 1731; together with some metrical observations. Boston: D. B. Updike, 1917. 24p. RPB. +

2784 _____. The letter book of James Browne of Providence, merchant, 1735-1738, from the original manuscript in the library of the Rhode Island Historical Society, with an introduction by George Phillip Krapp...and a biographical sketch by John Carter Brown Woods. Providence: R.I. Historical Society, 1929. xiv, 66p. RHi. +

2785 BRUNKOW, ROBERT DeV. "Officeholding in Providence, Rhode Island, 1649 to 1686: a quantitative analysis." William and Mary Quarterly, 3 ser. 37 (1980), 242-260.

2786 BUCKINGHAM, JAMES S. "Textile processing in Providence, Rhode Island, in 1838." Textile History Review, 4 (1963), 52-55.

2787 BURGES, TRISTRAM. A memoir of Welcome Arnold. n.p., 1850. 45p. RHi. +
  Merchant and Revolutionary-era politician.

2788 BURGESS, A. M., LOUIS J. KRAMER, MIRIAM J. CARPENTER, and HELEN S. MUNRO. "The care of diabetics at the Rhode Island Hospital since 1910." RIMJ, 9 (1926), 90-93.

2789 BURLINGAME, LUTHER D. "The Providence Engineering Society." PM, 30 (1918), 239-245.

2790 "THE BURNING of Providence: our city as it was 200 years ago...." Providence Journal (Apr. 10, 1876).
  Lengthy historical article, signed E.M.S. (Edwin Martin Stone), recounting the burning of Providence in 1676, during King Philip's War.

2791 BUTLER HOSPITAL, PROVIDENCE. The Butler Hospital: its story; an endowed public institution for the treatment of mental illness. Providence: Trustees and Superintendent of Butler Hospital, 1926. [37]p. RHi. +

2792 _____. Butler Hospital: the story of its growth, portrayal of its facilities, and the methods used in restoration of mental health. [Providence: Hobby Print Shop, Butler Hospital,] n.d. 15p. RHi.

2793 _____. A century of Butler Hospital, 1844-1944. Providence, 1944. 49p. RHi. +

2794 BYRNES, GARRETT D. "Downtown was It." RIer (Jan. 28, 1968), 6-7.
  1920s.

2795 _____. "Eating was an art in the twenties (and now look!)." RIer (May 12, 1968), 12-16.
  Restaurants.

2796 _____. "In half a century the Harkins dream came true." RIer (Sept. 28, 1969), 12-14, 16-18.
  Bishop Matthew Harkins and Providence College.

2797 _____. "The night boats." RIer (Mar. 8, 1970), 34-36, 38, 40, 42-43.
  Overnight steamboat service to N.Y. in the 1920s.

2798 _____. "Providence...passenger port." RIer (Sept. 24, 1961), 14-17.
  Providence as an entry point for southern European immigrants.

2799 _____. "The roaring twenties: it was decidedly uncool." RIer (Dec. 17, 1967), 12-13.
  Major events of the decade.

2800 _____. "That wonderful Hanley hitch." RIer (May 25, 1969), 14.
  Hanley's Brewing Company's "world-famous nine-horse team."

2801 _____. "Trinity's new home is a splendidly haunted house." RIer (Oct. 18, 1970), 16-17, 19-20, 22, 24.
  Trinity Square Repertory Company and the Majestic Theater building.

2802 _____. "Vittles aren't what they used to be in Granny's day." RIer (May 1, 1969), 12-19, 15, 18-19.
  Downtown food stores in the 1920s.

2803 _____. "When Field's Point was young." RIer (Sept. 12, 1971), 38-39, 43, 45; (Sept. 19, 1971), 20-21, 23, 25.
  Once a locally popular summer resort, noted for its clambakes. Sept. 19 article entitled, "The cottages of Field's Point." See also entry 1232.

2804 _____. "World Series roars in Eddy Street." RIer (Sept. 29, 1968), 18-19, 21.
  In the 1920s, play-by-play accounts of the World Series were announced to street crowds by Journal-Bulletin staff members using megaphones.

2805 BYRNES, GARRETT D., and CHARLES H. SPILMAN. The Providence Journal: 150 years. Providence: Providence Journal, 1980. 494p. RHi. +
   Newspaper.

2806 _____. "Who was John R. Rathom?" RIer (Apr. 20, 1980), 16-18, 20-21; (Apr. 27, 1980), 12-13, 15, 18, 22, 22-23; (May 4, 1980), 32-35, 37-41, 43.
   Editor of the Providence Journal in early 20th century and an important figure in the newspaper's history.

2807 CADY, JOHN HUTCHINS. The civic and architectural development of Providence, 1636-1950. Providence: The Book Shop, 1957. 320p. RHi. +

2808 _____. "The development of the Neck: a chronicle of the East Side of Providence." RIH, 2 (1943), 22-36, 83-96, 113-127; 3 (1944), 37-51, 119-132; 4 (1945), 37-54.

2809 _____. "The divisions of the home lots of Providence." RIHSC, 31 (1938), 101-107.

2810 _____. Highroads and byroads of Providence. Providence: Akerman-Standard Pr., 1948. 69p. RHi. +

2811 _____. "The Providence Market House and its neighborhood." RIH, 10 (1952), 97-116.

2812 _____. Swan Point Cemetery: a centennial history. Providence: [Akerman-Standard,] 1947. 55p. RHi.

2813 _____. "The Thomas Poynton Ives House." RIH, 14 (1955), 1-10.

2814 _____. "Weybosset Bridge." RIH, 8 (1949), 13-20.

2815 _____. "The William Goddard House." RIH, 17 (1958), 48-55.

2816 CALDWELL, SAMUEL L. Discourse delivered in the First Baptist Meeting House, Providence, Sunday morning, May 28, 1865, ninety years after its first dedication. Boston: Gould and Lincoln, 1865. 22p. RHi. +

2817 [_____, and WILLIAM GAMMELL.] History of the First Baptist Church in Providence, 1639-1877. Providence: J. A. & R. A. Reid, 1877. 23p. RHi. +

2818 CALOGERO, JAMES. "The Pembrokers." RIY (1969), 35-39.
   Pembroke College, Brown Univ.

2819 CAMPBELL, PAUL R., and PATRICK T. CONLEY. The Aurora Club of Rhode Island: a fifty year history. Providence: Aurora Civic Association, 1982. 112p. RHi.
   Italian-American association.

2820 "THE CANAL Market of Providence: corporation period, 1826-1872." NHR, 8 (1890), 1-6.

2821 CANDON, SUE. "Remember red sweater day?" RIer (June 29, 1975), 12-13.
   Student life at Classical High School.

2822 CANONICUS memorial: services of dedication, under the auspices of the Rhode Island Historical Society, September 21, 1883. Providence: Providence Pr., 1883. 31p. RHi.
   Narragansett Indian sachem.

2823 CARPENTER, CHARLES H., JR. Gorham silver, 1831-1981. N.Y.: Dodd, Mead, 1982. xii, 332p. RHi. +
   Silver produced by the Gorham Co. Includes information about the history of the company.

2824 CARPENTER, E. J. "Roger Williams and the plantations at Providence." NEM, n.s. 26 (1902), 353-364.

2825 CARRERE AND HASTINGS (architects). The Central Congregational Church, Providence, Rhode Island: i. history, ii. the present situation, iii. plans. N.Y., 1891. [23]p. RHi.

2826 CARROLL, LEO E. "Irish and Italians in Providence, Rhode Island, 1880-1960." RIH, 28 (1969), 67-74.

2827 CASSEDY, JAMES H. Charles V. Chapin and the public health movement. Cambridge, Mass.: Harvard Univ. Pr., 1962. x, 310p. RHi. +
   Providence Superintendent of Health from 1884 to 1931, who has been called the "city's most famous public servant."

2828 _____. "Charles V. Chapin re-visited: an appreciation." RIMJ, 66 (Jan. 1983), 41-44.
   See also preceding entry.

2829 _____. "Edwin Miller Snow: an important American public health pioneer." Bulletin of the History of Medicine, 35 (1961), 156-162.
   City's first Superintendent of Health, and "to all intents and purposes America's first professional medical health officer."

2830 Providence

2830 CATIR, NORMAN JOSEPH. Saint Stephen's Church in Providence: the history of a New England Tractarian parish, 1839-1964. Providence: St. Stephen's Church, 1964. xvi, 222p. RHi. +
Episcopal.

2831 CHACE, GEORGE I. A discourse commemorative of Francis Wayland, delivered before the alumni of Brown University, September 4, 1866. Providence: Sidney S. Rider & Brother, 1866. 51p. RHi. +
President of Brown.

2832 CHAPIN, HOWARD M. "The Chinese junk Ke Ying at Providence." RIHSC, 27 (1934), 5-12.
Visited port of Providence in 1847.

2833 _____. "George Annable, sculptor." RIHSC, 22 (1929), 119-128.

2834 _____. "The lands and houses of the first settlers of Providence." RIHSC, 12 (1919), 1-8.

2835 _____. Report upon the burial place of Roger Williams. Providence: R.I. Historical Society, 1918. 30p. RHi. +

2836 CHAPIN, WILLIAM W. "First Congregational Society pew holders, 1816." RIH, 10 (1951), 110-118; 11 (1952), 10-13, 46-47, 70-72.
Brief biographical sketches.

2837 CHASE, EVELYN. The library, Rhode Island School of Design. Providence, 1942. 30p. RNHi. +
Historical sketch.

2838 CHIAPPINELLI, S. ROBERT. "Happy birthday, LaSalle boys!" RIer (Sept. 12, 1971), 14, 16-18.
LaSalle Academy's 100th anniversary.

2839 CHUDACOFF, HOWARD P., and TAMARA K. HAREVEN. "From the empty nest to family dissolution: life course transitions into old age." Journal of Family History, 4 (1979), 69-83.
Providence as a case study.

2840 CHUDACOFF, HOWARD P., and THEODORE C. HIRT. "Social turmoil and governmental reform in Providence, 1820-1832." RIH, 31 (1972), 21-31.

2841 CHUDACOFF, NANCY FISHER. "The Revolution and the town: Providence, 1775-1783." RIH, 35 (1976), 71-89.

2842 _____. "Woman in the news, 1762-1770: Sarah Updike Goddard." RIH, 32 (1973), 99-105.
Printer, exemplifying women's contributions to the urban economy of the colonial period.

2843 "CHURCHES of colonial days." PM, 26 (1914), 561-567.
In Providence.

2844 CHURCHILL, DONALD. "Appendicitis at the Rhode Island Hospital, 1891-1900." PMJ, 2 (1901), 86-93.

2845 CITIZENS SAVINGS BANK. The first hundred years, 1871-1971, Citizens Savings Bank; history and development of the Citizens Banks. Providence, 1971. vi, 25p. RHi.

2846 CLAFLIN, ALBERT W. "The Providence Cable Tramway." RIH, 5 (1946), 41-53; 6 (1947), 11-28.

2847 CLAPP, ROGER TILLINGHAST. The Hope Club: a centennial history, 1875-1975. n.p.: [E. A. Johnson,] n.d. 121p. RHi.

2848 _____. "The peach picker's plight." RIer (Jan. 17, 1960), 20.
Jonathan Gray was "unfortunately shot" in 1825 while raiding an orchard; his slayer was charged with murder.

2849 CLARK, HENRY C. Report of the exercises at the dedication of the statue of Ebenezer Knight Dexter, presented to the city of Providence...June 29, 1894. Providence: Snow & Farnham, 1894. 44p. RHi.
Story behind statue to the "city's noblest benefactor and friend of the poor and homeless."

2850 CLARK, THOMAS MARCH. An historical discourse, delivered in St. John's Church, Providence, R.I., on St. Barnabas's Day, June 11, 1872, in commemoration of the one hundred and fiftieth anniversary of the parish. Hartford, Conn.: M. H. Mallory, 1872. 52p. RHi. +
Episcopal.

2851 CLARKE, LOUIS W. "The inception of the Providence Board of Trade." PBTJ, 20 (1908), 497-498.

2852 CLOUGH, ELSIE. "It was fun while it lasted: the story of a book shop." Yankee, 28 (Nov. 1964), 83, 178, 181, 185, 187-189.
The Booke Shop, 75 Westminster Street.

2853 COHEN, ABBY. "Public health and preventive medicine in Providence, 1913." RIH, 36 (1977), 55-63.

2854 COLE, MARION SHIRLEY. The women's college in Brown University: its progress and expansion. Providence, 1917. 47p. RPB. +
Pembroke College.

2855 "THE COLLEGE scene in Providence, 1786-1787." RIH, 27 (1968), 65-70.
Contemporary document. Noel P. Conlon and Clarkson A. Collins III, eds.

2856 COLLIER, THEODORE. "Providence in Civil War days." RIHSC, 27 (1934), 66-84, 98-113.

2857 COLLINS, CLARKSON A. III. "The Providence proprietors." RIY (1964-1965), H22-H27.

2858 COLLINS, JOHN J. "A history of the Providence Water Works and its treatment methods." New England Water Works Association, Journal, 74 (Mar. 1960), 12-21.

2859 "COLONIAL architecture in Providence." PM, 26 (1914), 783-792.

2860 COMMERCE, manufactures and resources of the city of Providence and environs: a descriptive review; industry, development, enterprise. n.p.: National Publishing, 1882. 148p. RHi.
Includes historical sketch.

2861 "COMMONS at Brown." Brunonian, 5 (1872), 163-168.
Commons Hall, Brown Univ.

2862 CONGDON AND CARPENTER COMPANY. One hundred and fifty years, the Congdon & Carpenter Co. Providence, 1940. 20p. RHi. +
Later primarily a supplier of steel, the firm originally was involved in the iron trade, industrial supply, hardware, etc.

2863 CONLEY, PATRICK T., and PAUL R. CAMPBELL. Providence: a pictorial history. Norfolk, Va.: Donning, 1982. 232p. RHi. +
Bibliographical essay, 226-232.

2864 CONROY, VIRGINIA. "Providence was a great show town." RIY (1970), H193-H196.
Theater.

2865 CONTINENTAL Sloop Providence commissioning, October 24, 1976, Providence, Rhode Island. [Newport: Seaport '76,] 1976. [17]p. RNW-Hi.
Includes historical sketch of the original, Revolutionary-era ship, by Hope S. Rider.

2866 COOKE, ABIGAIL WHIPPLE. "Providence Art Club." NEM, 43 (1911), 492-496.

2867 COOLIDGE, ARLAN R. "How Rhode Island nearly lost Reeves and the American Band." RIH, 22 (1963), 33-37.
David Wallis Reeves, director and composer.

2868 _____. "The Providence Opera House, 1871-1931." RIY (1970), H182-H192.

2869 COOPER, WENDY A. "The purchase of furniture and furnishings by John Brown, Providence merchant...." Antiques, 103 (1973), 328-339, 734-743.
Two articles, pertaining to the years 1760-1803.

2870 CORNING, HOWARD. "Sullivan Dorr, China trader." RIH, 3 (1944), 75-90.
19th-century Providence merchant.

2871 CORNWELL, ELMER E., JR. "A note on Providence politics in the age of Bryan." RIH, 19 (1960), 33-40.
I.e., William Jennings Bryan.

2872 _____. "Party absorption of ethnic groups: the case of Providence, Rhode Island." Social Forces, 38 (1960), 205-210.

2873 _____. "Some occupational patterns in party committee membership." RIH, 20 (1961), 87-96.
Political parties, Providence, 1864-1957.

2874 COTTROL, ROBERT J. The Afro-Yankees: Providence's black community in the antebellum era. Westport, Conn.: Greenwood Pr., 1982. xviii, 200p. RHi. +
Bibliography, 183-193.

2875 [CRANE, SILAS A.] Brown University under the presidency of Asa Messer, S.T.D., LL.D. By an alumnus. Boston: Crosby & Ainsworth, 1867. 23p. RHi. +

2876 CRANE, THEODORE R. "Francis Wayland and the residential college." RIH, 19 (1960), 65-78, 118-129.
Wayland's student-housing reforms at Brown Univ.

2877 _____. Francis Wayland: political economist as educator. Providence: Brown Univ. Pr., 1962. 46p. RHi. +
Includes history of Brown Univ. during Wayland's years as president in 2d quarter of 19th century. Reprinted from RIH, 21 (1962), 65-90, 105-124.

2878 CROWE, CHARLES R. "Transcendentalism and 'the newness' in Rhode Island." RIH, 14 (1955), 33-46.
How Transcendentalism related to spiritualism and reform movements in Providence.

2879 _____. "Transcendentalism and the Providence literati." RIH, 14 (1955), 65-78.

2880 CRUMP, STUART F., JR. "Joseph Brown, astronomer." RIH, 27 (1968), 1-12.
Early member of Brown Univ. faculty.

2881 Providence

2881 CULWICK, M. R. "Brown University, Providence, Rhode Island." Alexandra College Magazine, No. 7 (Dec. 1895), 20-24.

2882 CUMMING, RICHARD. "'Places, please...places for the top of the show!'" RIer (Sept. 26, 1976), 20-22, 24.
Professional theater in Providence.

2883 CUSHMAN, FRANKLIN RICHMOND. King's Church--St. John's Church, 1722-1929. Providence, 1949. 18p. RHi. +
Episcopal.

2884 DAMON, S. FOSTER. "Providence theatricals in 1773." RIH, 4 (1945), 55-58.

2885 DANFORTH, WALTER R. "Pictures of Providence in the past, 1790-1820: the reminiscences of Walter R. Danforth." RIH, 10 (1951), 1-13, 45-60, 85-96, 119-129; 11 (1952), 17-29, 50-63.
Clarkson A. Collins III, ed.

2886 DAVIS, HADASSAH F. Providence: the town the Browns built, 1760-1820. Providence: Pafnuty Publishers, [1977?]. 13p. RHi.

2887 DAY, FRANK L. "The Providence Medical Association: its past, present and future." PMJ, 7 (1906), 71-82.

2888 DEALEY, JAMES QUAYLE. "The early history of Providence." PBTJ, 27 (1915), 689-691.

2889 DeCAMP, L. SPRAGUE. Lovecraft: a biography. Garden City, N.Y.: Doubleday, 1975. xvi, 510p. RHi. +
Author H. P. Lovecraft. Includes information about his life in Providence.

2890 DEDICATION concert at the Benedict Monument to Music in Roger Williams Park, Providence, Rhode Island, Sunday afternoon, September twenty-first nineteen hundred twenty-four, at two o'clock. n.p., [1924]. [8]p. RHi. +
Includes historical background.

2891 DEDICATION of the equestrian statue of Major-General Ambrose E. Burnside, in the city of Providence, July 4, 1887, with the oration of General Horatio Rogers; together with some account of General Burnside's funeral, and of the movement resulting in the erection of the statue. Providence: E. L. Freeman, 1887. 60p. RHi. +
Civil War general.

2892 DEL DEO, FRANCIS S. "Impressions of the golden era of the Italian Federal Hill." RIY (1972), 21-31.

2893 DEMBER, IRA. "America's very first shopping center." Yankee, 34 (Nov. 1970), 114-117, 236, 239-240.
Arcade.

2894 DENISON, FREDERIC. "Fields Point Indian relics." NHR, 6 (1888), 25-29.

2895 DeWOLF, HALSEY. "A brief account of the work of the Providence Lying-in Hospital during the fifteen years of its existence." PMJ, 1 (1900), 146-150.

2896 _____. "Memories of the old Rhode Island Hospital, personal and impersonal." RIMJ, 40 (1957), 98-101.

2897 DIDSBURY, A. RUSSELL. "Time cancels out Mr. Freeman's restrictions." RIer (Jan. 3, 1960), 8-10.
Residential restrictions in the John R. Freeman Plat, East Side, Providence.

2898 DINNEEN, WILLIAM. "Early music in Rhode Island churches: II. Music in the First Baptist Church, Providence, 1775-1834." RIH, 17 (1958), 33-44.
See also next entry and entries 146 and 3205-3206.

2899 _____. "Early music in Rhode Island churches: IV. Music in Beneficent Congregational Church and the Richmond Street Congregational Church, 1744-1836." RIH, 17 (1958), 108-118.
See also preceding entry and entries 146 and 3205-3206.

2900 _____. Music at the Meeting House, 1775-1958. Providence: Roger Williams Pr., 1958. 64p. RHi.
First Baptist Church.

2901 DONLEY, JOHN E. "Charles Value Chapin: the man and his work...." RIMJ, 37 (1954), 311-316.
Providence Superintendent of Health.

2902 DONNAN, ELIZABETH. "A nineteenth-century academic cause celebre." NEQ, 25 (1952), 23-46.
Departure of President Elisha Benjamin Andrews from Brown at trustees' request because of his advocacy of free coinage of silver (1896).

2903 DORR, HENRY C. "The early town meetings of Providence." RIHSPr (1874-1875), 27-30.

2904 _____. [Paper on the early town councils of Providence.] RIHSPr (1875-1876), 36-38.

2905 DORR, HENRY C. The planting and growth of Providence, illustrated in the gradual accumulation of the materials for domestic comfort, the means of internal communication and the development of local industries. Providence: Sidney S. Rider, 1882. 267p. RHi. +

2906 _____. The proprietors of Providence, and their controversies with the freeholders. Providence: [R.I. Historical Society,] 1897. 141p. RHi. +

2907 DORWART, JEFFREY M. "Providence conspiracy of 1894." RIH, 32 (1973), 91-96.
"...A conspiracy hatched in Providence ...to destroy the Japanese navy for China during the Sino-Japanese War of 1894-5."

2908 DOW, CHARLES H. History of steam navigation between New York and Providence. N.Y.: Wm. Turner, 1877. 29p. RHi. +

2909 DOWNING, ANTOINETTE FORRESTER. "Benefit Street, 1963." RIY (1964-1965), 57-62.
Historic preservation.

2910 _____. "The fate of the Carrington House." RIH, 21 (1962), 1-7.
Home of Edward Carrington.

2911 _____. "John Brown House." Antiques, 87 (1965), 556-563.
Headquarters of Rhode Island Historical Society.

2912 _____. "New light on the Sullivan Dorr House." RIH, 16 (1957), 33-40.

2913 _____. "Why save Downing Square?" RIer (July 4, 1971), 12-13.
Once the site of several screw factories.

2914 DOWNS, JACQUES M. "The merchant as gambler: Major William Fairchild Megee (1765-1820)." RIH, 28 (1969), 99-110.

2915 DUFFY, DAVID A. "The marble palace: the story of the Rhode Island State House." RIY (1967), 41-45.

2916 _____. "Providence College: a biography." RIY (1965-1966), 61-64.

2917 DURFEE, SARAH C. Twenty-five years: a historical sketch of the Woman's Foreign Missionary Association of the First Baptist Church, Providence, R.I., read at the annual meeting, June 13, 1891. Providence: F. H. Townsend, 1892. 31p. RHi. +

2918 DURFEE, THOMAS. A historical discourse delivered on the two hundred and fiftieth anniversary of the planting of Providence. Providence: Sidney S. Rider, 1887. 69p. RHi. +

2919 DYER, ELISHA. "The old schools of Providence." NHR, 5 (1887), 220-240.

2920 _____. "The old taverns of Providence." NHR, 5 (1886), 129-150.

2921 _____. Sketch and reminiscences of the Providence Fire Department, from 1815 to 1854: read before the Providence Veteran Firemen Association, Tuesday evening, October 27, 1885.... Providence: E. A. Johnson, 1886. 17p. RHi.

2922 "EARLY commercial signs and firms of providence." RIHSPubs, n.s. 6 (1898), 144-166.

2923 "EARLY days of export business of Providence." PM, 34 (1922), 337-338.

2924 "EARLY days of local drama." PM, 28 (1916), 645-648.
Theater.

2925 "EARLY days of the Providence Jewish community." RIJHN, 3 (1960), 148-159.

2926 "EARLY Providence architects leave prominent landmarks." PM, 26 (1914), 799-801.

2927 "EARLY Providence book plates." RIHSC, 30 (1937), 97-101.

2928 "EARLY settlers of Providence Plantations." R.I. Roots, 5, No. 1 (Spring 1979), 1, 3-6.

2929 EASTON, FRANK T. "The Providence Classical High School and its relationship to Brown University." BrAlumMo, 3 (1903), 162-165.

2930 EATON, AMASA M. Roger Williams: the founder of Providence; the pioneer of religious liberty.... [Providence:] Dept. of Education, State of R.I., 1908. 19p. RHi. +

2931 EDDY, MURIEL E. The gentleman from Angell Street. Providence, 1961. 25p. RHi. +
Author H. P. Lovecraft.

2932 _____. "H. P. Lovecraft among the demons." RIer (Mar. 8, 1970), 23, 25-26.
Lovecraft was a native of Providence.

2933 EMLEN, ROBERT P. "From the collections: an ordinary chair." RIH, 31 (1983), 67-68.
Article documents the work of Thomas M. Parker, Providence chairmaker during the second quarter of the 19th century. Chair referred to is in collections of the R.I. Historical Society.

2934 "ENGINEERING at Brown." BrAlumMo, 1 (1900), 72-74.

2935 ESCHENBACHER, HERMAN F. "When Brown was less than a university, but Hope was more than a college." BrAlumMo, 80 (Feb. 1980), 26-33.
Education and student life at Brown and Hope College, its residential hall, in the 19th century.

2936 ESTEY, CHARLOTTE, and ROBERT L. WHEELER. "The story of the Towne Street." RIer (Jan. 13, 1952), 12-14; (Jan. 20, 1952), 12-16; (Jan. 27, 1952), 12-15, 17.
South Main Street.

2937 "THE EVOLUTION of architecture: a contrast afforded by many buildings that have been erected in Providence from 1828 to 1895." PJC, 3 (Apr. 1895), 17-22.

2938 EXERCISES at the dedication of the Doyle Avenue Grammar School, Providence, R.I., Tuesday afternoon, September 5th, 1876. n.p., n.d. 52p. RHi.
Includes historical address on Providence schools, by Edwin M. Stone.

2939 "'A FAITHFUL reporter of the passing news.'" RIer (July 16, 1979), 26-27, 29-35.
150th anniversary of Providence Journal.

2940 FARNHAM, JOSEPH E. C. A brief history of Franklin Lodge, No. 23, I.O.O.F., Providence, R.I., instituted July 13, 1872; also, an obituary of deceased members, and list of members, December 31, 1876. Providence: Providence Pr., 1877. 59p. RHi. +

2941 FEDERAL PRODUCTS CORPORATION. A half century of service to the art of precision. Providence, 1968. 75p. RHi.
Manufacturer of gauges and other precision instruments.

2942 FERGUSON, SUSAN G. "Eighteenth-century wall decoration in the John Brown House in Providence, Rhode Island." Antiques, 107 (1975), 122-129.

2943 FIELD, EDWARD. "The fortifications in and around Providence." NHR, 5 (1887), 209-219.
During the American Revolution.

2944 FIELD, EDWARD II. A history of Company A, of the Young Republican Regiment, of Providence, R.I., in connection with the presidential campaign of 1880. Providence: Providence Pr., 1883. 19p. RHi. +

2945 FIRE service of Providence: a souvenir presented to the appreciative public of Rhode Island. Charles E. White, ed. [Providence:] Providence Permanent Firemen's Relief Association, 1887. 132p. RHi. +
See also entry 3725.

2946 FIRST LIGHT INFANTRY REGIMENT, PROVIDENCE. Centennial, First Light Infantry Regiment, May 11, 1818 - May 11, 1918: honor roll and roster of the command; historical address. Providence, n.d. 36p. RHi.

2947 FIRST LIGHT INFANTRY VETERAN ASSOCIATION, PROVIDENCE. History of the organization of the First Light Infantry Veteran Association, of Providence, R.I., with a roster of the association; to which is added the address of Lt.-Col. Henry Staples, and the poem by Private George W. Pettes, delivered before the association at the first anniversary, May 1870. Vol. 1. [Providence,] 1870. 68p. RHi. +
Militia organization.

2948 _____. Proceedings of the First Light Infantry Veteran Association of Providence, R.I., from 1872 to 1878; with a roster of the association, to which is added the oration of Professor J. Lewis Diman, at the centennial celebration of the capture of General Prescott by Colonel Barton; with a biographical sketch of deceased members. Vol. 3. [Providence,] n.d. 108p. RHi. +

2949 "FIRST mills in the world lighted by electricity." BTJ, 1 (Aug. 1890), 26, 28, 30.
In Olneyville.

2950 "FIRST Universalist Church: closing exercises in the old house; Rev. Mr. Capen's occasional discourse." Providence Daily Journal (Feb. 27, 1872).
E. H. Capen. Lengthy article includes historical sketch of the church.

2951 FLEMING, DONALD. Science and technology in Providence, 1760-1914: an essay in the history of Brown University in the metropolitan community. Providence: Brown Univ., 1952. 54p. RHi. +

2952 "THE FORWARD pass: Irish green or Brown?" BrAlumMo, 69 (Oct. 1968), 30-32.
Brown Univ. football.

2953 FOSTER, WILLIAM E. The first fifty years of the Providence Public Library, 1878-1928. Providence: Providence Public Library, 1928. 46p. RHi. +

2954 "THE FOUNDING of the Providence Bank (October 3, 1791)." RIHSC, 34 (1941), 113-128.
Hope F. Kane and William Greene Roelker, comps.

2955 FRAZIER, JOHN R. History of the Rhode Island School of Design. [Providence: R.I. School of Design, 1961.] 15p. RHi. +

2956 FREE KINDERGARTEN ASSOCIATION, PROVIDENCE. A brief account of the free kindergarten in Providence, charter, by-laws and officers of the Free Kindergarten Association; annual report, April, 1890. Providence: J. A. & R. A. Reid, 1890. 16p. RPB.

2957 FREEMAN, MARTHA K. "My movie career in Providence." RIer (Nov. 26, 1972), 12-15.
Film making in the World War I era.

2958 FREEMASONS. PROVIDENCE. CALVARY COMMANDERY, NO. 13, KNIGHTS TEMPLARS. Calvary Commandery No. 13, Knights·Templars, Providence, R.I., 1859-1909: celebration of the fiftieth anniversary, November 14-16, 1909. Providence: E. L. Freeman, n.d. 59p. RHi. +

2959 _____. Fifty years' record of Calvary Commandery, Number Thirteen, Knights Templars, stationed at Providence, Rhode Island. Albert L. Anthony, comp.... Providence: E. L. Freeman, [1909?]. xiv, 650p. RHi. +

2960 _____. Sixth decade of Calvary Commandery No. 13, Knights Templars, 1909-1919; ending with sixtieth annual and one thousandth conclave; with list of members. Providence: Snow & Farnham, 1920. 131p. RHi.

2961 FREEMASONS. PROVIDENCE. MOUNT VERNON LODGE, NO. 4. Celebration of the one hundredth anniversary of Mount Vernon Lodge, No. 4, Ancient Free and Accepted Masons, February 22, 1899. Providence: [Pr. of Perry Printing,] n.d. 100p. RHi. +

2962 _____. The story of the Mount Vernon Lodge, No. 4, Free and Accepted Masons, Providence, Rhode Island, 1799-1924; to which is appended the by-laws and the list of members. William Evans Handy, historian. Providence, 1924. 230p. RHi. +

2963 FREEMASONS. PROVIDENCE. NESTELL LODGE, NO. 37. Nestell Lodge, No. 37, A.F. & A.M., Providence, R.I.: fiftieth anniversary celebration, 1880-1930. [Providence: Akerman-Standard,] n.d. [28]p. RHi.

2964 FREEMASONS. PROVIDENCE. PROVIDENCE COUNCIL, NO. 1, ROYAL AND SELECT MASTERS. Proceedings of the centennial assembly of Providence Council, Number One, of Royal and Select Masters, Thursday, March 28, A.Dep. 2918, A.D. 1918. Providence: Alpine Printing, 1919. 111p. RP.

2965 FREEMASONS. PROVIDENCE. PROVIDENCE ROYAL ARCH CHAPTER, NO. 1. One hundredth anniversary of the constitution of Providence Royal Arch Chapter, No. 1, Providence, R.I., September 3 and 4, 1893. Providence: E. L. Freeman, 1894. 182p. RHi. +

2966 FREEMASONS. PROVIDENCE. SAINT JOHN'S COMMANDERY, NO. 1, KNIGHTS TEMPLARS. Brief history, charter, and by-laws, and list of members of Saint John's Commandery, from its organization to the present time; with alphabetical list of present members. (1893, 1897) Providence, 1900. 72p. RPB. +

2967 _____. Historical sketch of St. John's Commandery, No. 1, of Knights Templars and the appendant orders, Providence, R.I., together with the charter, by-laws, complete lists of officers and members.... Providence: R.I. Printing, 1875. 215p. RHi. +

2968 _____. History of Saint John's Commandery, Number One, Knights Templars, Providence, Rhode Island, from 1802 to 1902...historical address by Henry W. Rugg.... Providence: E. L. Freeman, 1902. xii, 282p. RHi.

2969 _____. History of Saint John's Commandery, Number One, Knights Templars, Providence, Rhode Island, from 1802 to 1952. Providence: Printers' Service and Supply, 1951. 213p. RHi. +

2970 FREEMASONS. PROVIDENCE. WHAT CHEER LODGE, NO. 21. Charter, act of incorporation and by-laws of Free and Accepted Masons in the city of Providence; also a list of the officers of the lodge and a historical address delivered by Past Master Joshua M. Addeman, on the occasion of the celebration of the fiftieth anniversary of the lodge, November 29, A.C. 5907.... Providence: Standard Printing, 1921. 108p. RHi.
The historical address also appeared in various editions of the lodge manual.

2971 FREEMASONS. PROVIDENCE. WHAT CHEER LODGE, NO. 21. History, charter and by-laws of What Cheer Lodge, No. 21, Providence, R.I. Providence: Pr. of the Freemason's Repository, 1874. 75p. RHi. +

2972 ____. What Cheer Lodge, No. 21, F. & A.M., Providence, Rhode Island: 75th anniversary...nineteen hundred thirty-two. n.p., n.d. [32]p. RHi.
Includes historical sketch.

2973 FREIBERG, MALCOLM. "Brown University's first 'college edifice.'" Old-Time New England, 50 (1960), 85-93.
University Hall.

2974 "THE FRIENDS' New England Yearly Meeting Boarding School: its rise and history, with some notice of its founders and instructors." Providence Daily Journal (June 11, 1859).
Lengthy article concerning the history of what is now Moses Brown School.

2975 FULLER, EDWARD. "The Rhode Island Historical Society." NEM, n.s. 23 (1901), 483-499.

2976 FULLER, MARGARET A. 100 years of music at Central Congregational Church, Providence, Rhode Island. [Providence: Bear Pr., 1952.] [20]p. RHi.

2977 FULTON, FRANK T. The story of the heart station at the Rhode Island Hospital. Providence: Priv. Print., 1955. 44p. RHi. +

2978 GABRIEL, RICHARD A. Ethnic voting in primary elections: the Irish and Italians of Providence, Rhode Island. Kingston: Bureau of Government Research, Univ. of R.I., 1969. 21p. RHi.
See also entry 365.

2979 GALE, WILLIAM K. "'Sure, I remember St. Joe's.'" RIer (Sept. 24, 1972), 4-5, 7-10.
Saint Joseph Hospital.

2980 GAMAGE, DOUGLAS C. "Benefit Street: a path through history." RIY (1972), 93-100.

2981 GAMMELL, WILLIAM. "Sketch of the educational and other benefactions of the late Hon. Nicholas Brown." American Journal of Education, 9 (1857), 291-312.
Including Brown Univ., Providence Athenaeum, Butler Hospital.

2982 [GARDNER, PERCY H.] A century and a half of service, 1800-1950: being a brief account of the founding and growth of the Providence Mutual Fire Insurance Company. [Providence: Akerman-Standard Pr., 1951.] 45p. RHi.

2983 GARLAND, JOSEPH E. To meet these wants: the story of the Rhode Island Hospital, 1863-1963. [Providence:] R.I. Hospital, 1963. 77p. RHi. +

2984 GARRETT, WENDELL D. "Providence cabinetmakers, chairmakers, upholsterers, and allied craftsmen, 1756-1838." Antiques, 90 (1966), 514-519.

2985 GAUSTAD, EDWIN SCOTT. "New light on the six principle controversy in the First Baptist Church, Providence, R.I." The Chronicle, 12 (1949), 181-186.

2986 GEORGE, ROBERT H. Brown University on the eve of the Civil War; Brunonians in Confederate ranks, 1861-1865. Providence: Brown Univ., 1965. 34p. RHi. +
Reprinted from Books at Brown, 20 (1965), 1-34.

2987 ____. "When the University Cadets went to war." BrAlumMo, 62 (Mar. 1962), 5-7.
Brown Univ. and the Civil War.

2988 GEORGI, H. W. "The beginnings of insurance in Providence." RIHSPubs, n.s. 3 (1895), 180-182.

2989 "THE GERMANS in Providence." PBTJ, 22 (1910), 432-435.
German Americans.

2990 GERSUNY, CARL. "Eleanor Marx in Providence." RIH, 37 (1978), 85-87.
Karl Marx's daughter, who lectured in Providence in 1886, sponsored by R.I. Central Labor Union.

2991 ____. "John Francis Smith, heterodox Yankee printer." RIH, 38 (1979), 87-95.
Editor of The People, weekly labor newspaper.

2992 "A GIANT named Chapin." RIer (Aug. 26, 1962), 8-9.
Charles V. Chapin, Providence Superintendent of Health.

2993 "GLORIOUS history of the Benefit Street Arsenal." PM, 31 (1919), 9-12.

2994 GODDARD, M. B. I. "An account of the voyages and wreck of the first ship, 'Ann & Hope,' belonging to Messrs. Brown & Ives, of Providence, R.I." NHM, 5 (1884), 92-105.

2995 GODDARD, WILLIAM GILES. Memoir of the Rev. James Manning, D.D., first president of Brown University, with biographical notices of some of his pupils. Boston: Perkins & Marvin, 1839. 24p. RHi. +

2996 GOLDMAN, ISRAEL M. "The early history of Temple Emanu-El." RIJHN, 4 (1963), 3-46.

2997 _____. "The first twenty years of Temple Emanu-El." RIJHN, 4 (1964), 3-88.

2998 GOLDOWSKY, BERNARD M. "Get that crook!: reminiscences of a private detective." RIJHN, 6 (1971), 102-129.

2999 GOLDOWSKY, SEEBERT J. "Charles V. Chapin: his influence on concepts of public health." RIMJ, 62 (1979), 313-323.
    Providence Superintendent of Health, 1883-1932.

3000 _____. "The Jewish Home for the Aged of Rhode Island: the early years." RIJHN, 2 (1958), 241-253.

3001 _____. "The Jewish Orphanage of Rhode Island." RIJHN, 3 (1959), 88-105.

3002 GOLDSCHEIDER, CALVIN, and SIDNEY GOLDSTEIN. "Generational changes in Jewish family structure." Journal of Marriage and the Family, 29 (1967), 267-276.
    Providence as a case study.

3003 GOLDSTEIN, SIDNEY. "The Providence Jewish community after 125 years of development." RIH, 25 (1966), 51-58.

3004 _____, and CALVIN GOLDSCHEIDER. Jewish Americans: three generations in a Jewish community. Englewood Cliffs, N.J.: Prentice-Hall, 1968. xvii, 274p. RHi. +
    Sociological study of Providence Jewish community.

3005 GOLDSTEIN, SIDNEY, and KURT B. MAYER. "Population decline and the social and demographic structure of an American city." American Sociological Review, 29 (1964), 48-54.
    Providence.

3006 GOODMAN, ABRAM VOSSEN. "Jewish elements in Brown's early history." American Jewish Historical Society, Publications, 37 (1947), 135-145.
    Brown Univ.

3007 GOODRICH, JOSEPH L. "Textron: shooting for a billion in sales this year." RIer (May 1, 1966), 4-6, 8-9, 11-12.
    Includes historical sketch of the corporation.

3008 GOODYEAR, FRANK H., JR. "The painting collection of the Rhode Island Historical Society." Antiques, 100 (1971), 749-757.
    Mainly R.I. artists and/or subjects.

3009 _____. "Paintings at John Brown House." RIH, 31 (1972), 35-51.
    R.I. Historical Society's collection and how it was acquired.

3010 GORHAM, FREDERIC P. "The old medical school in Brown University." PMJ, 16 (1915), 218-227.

3011 GOURLEY, HUGH III. "Carrington House, Providence, Rhode Island." Antiques, 79 (1961), 183-186.

3012 GRAND ARMY OF THE REPUBLIC. RHODE ISLAND. SLOCUM POST, NO. 10, PROVIDENCE. Historical sketch, Slocum Post, No. 10, Department of Rhode Island, G.A.R., chartered February 27th, 1868. n.p., [1894]. 52, [4]p. RHi. +

3013 GRANGER, A. H. Historical discourse, delivered in the Fourth Baptist Meeting House, Providence, R.I., July 9th, 1873; it being the fiftieth anniversary of the organization of the church. Providence: Hammond, Angell, 1874. 36p. RHi. +

3014 THE GREAT gale of 1869, in Providence and vicinity. Providence: Tillinghast & Mason, 1869. 24p. RU.
    Also includes information on the great gale of 1815.

3015 GREEN, THEODORE FRANCIS. One hundred years: an address...delivered at the centennial celebration of Providence the city at Roger Williams Park, June 4, 1932. [Providence:] Centennial Celebration Committee of Providence the City, [1932]. 15p. RHi. +

3016 GREENE, HENRY L. "The Greene-St. School, of Providence, and its teachers; among whom was Sarah Margaret Fuller, afterwards Marchioness d'Ossoli." RIHSPubs, n.s. 6 (1898), 199-219.

3017 _____. "The old Providence Theatre." RIHSPubs, n.s. 6 (1898), 189-191.

3018 GREENE, RICHARD H. "Alumni of Brown University who have held official positions." New-England Historical and Genealogical Register, 43 (1889), 375-377.

3019 GREENE, WELCOME ARNOLD. The Providence Plantations for two hundred and fifty years: an historical review of the foundation, rise, and progress of the city of Providence, with a graphic description of the city at the present time, and of its industries, commerce, manufactures, business interests, educational, religious and charitable institutions, civic, scientific, and military organizations; also, sketches of the cities of Newport and Pawtucket, and the other towns of the state, for which Providence is the commercial center; together with an account of the celebration of the two hundred and fiftieth anniversary of the settlement of Providence.... Providence: J. A. & R. A. Reid, 1886. 468p. RHi. +

3020 ____. "Who saved the Providence records?" NHR, 6 (1888), 391-396.
Claims Roger Williams did so during King Philip's War.

3021 GRIEVE, ROBERT. "The commerce of Providence: a survey of the history of the port, deepening of the channel, contemplated improvements, present commerce." PJC, 5 (Mar. 1897), 17-24.

3022 ____. "Modern Providence." NEM, n.s. 13 (1896), 769-792.

3023 GRINNELL CORPORATION. One hundred years of piping progress: Grinnell, 1850 to 1950. n.p., n.d. [28]p. RHi.
Pipe manufacturer.

3024 "GROWTH of art appreciation in Providence." PM, 26 (1914), 197-203.

3025 "GROWTH of public education in Providence." PBTJ, 27 (1915), 213-223.

3026 GUILD, FREDERICK TAFT. "The old college edifice of Rhode Island College." Daughters of the American Revolution Magazine, 71 (1937), 202-203.
University Hall, Brown Univ.

3027 GUILD, REUBEN ALDRIDGE. "Brown University." NEM, n.s. 1 (1886), 1-12.

3028 ____. Early history of Brown University, including the life, times, and correspondence of President Manning, 1756-1791. Providence: Snow & Farnham, 1897. 631p. RHi. +

3029 ____. "The first commencement of Rhode Island College, and especially the discussion of American independence, which constituted the prominent feature of the commencement exercises." RIHSC, 7 (1885), 267-298.
I.e., Brown Univ. Also printed separately.

3030 ____. Historical sketch of the library of Brown University, with regulations. New Haven, Conn.: Tuttle, Morehouse & Taylor, 1861. [20]p. RHi. +

3031 ____. History of Brown University, with illustrative documents. Providence: Providence Pr., 1867. xv, 443p. RHi. +

3032 ____. Life, times and correspondence of James Manning, and the early history of Brown University. Boston: Gould and Lincoln, 1864. xxii, 523p. RHi. +
First president of Brown.

3033 ____. Sketch of the University Grammar School and of Brown University.... [Providence, 1876.] 14p. RHi. +

3034 ____. Thomas A. Doyle: a sketch of his life.... Providence: J. A. & R. A. Reid, [1889?]. [35]p. RHi. +
Served as mayor every year except one from 1864 until his death in 1881.

3035 ____. "Thomas A. Doyle, late mayor of Providence." NEM, n.s. 2 (1887), 528-532.
See also preceding entry.

3036 HACKETT, WALTER. "Quoth Helen Whitman: 'Goodbye, Edgar.'" RIer (May 18, 1969), 28-29.
Edgar Allan Poe's Providence romance.

3037 HAGUE, WILLIAM. An historical discourse delivered at the celebration of the second centennial anniversary of the First Baptist Church, in Providence, November 9, 1839. Providence: B. Cranston, 1839. 192p. RHi. +

3038 HALE, STUART O. "The life and death of Elsie's book shop." RIer (Dec. 1, 1963), 56-58.
The Booke Shop, 75 Westminster St.

3039 ____. "The main stem from horse-and-buggy days to the dawn of the new mall." RIer (Aug. 29, 1965), 24-27.
Westminster St.

3040 [HALEY, JOHN WILLIAMS.] The American Band. Providence: "Old Stone Bank," 1931. 10p. RHi.
Well-known musical organization in Providence. This and the following entries by the same author were part of the "Old Stone Bank" historical pamphlet series. See note, entry 432.

3041 [_____.] Auton House. Providence: "Old Stone Bank," 1931. 10p. RHi.
Life in the Hoppin family of Providence, described by Augustus Hoppin in his book, Recollections of Auton House.

3042 [_____.] Bicycles and wheelmen. Providence: Old Stone Bank, 1931. 10p. RHi.

3043 [_____.] The Blue Pointers. Providence: "Old Stone Bank," 1932. 10p. RHi.
Closely-knit, working-class neighborhood; its residents and gangs.

3044 [_____.] The cable road. Providence: "Old Stone Bank," 1931. 10p. RHi.
Street railroad over College Hill.

3045 [_____.] A colonial coquette. Providence: "Old Stone Bank," n.d. 10p. RHi.
Unsuccessful courtship of Polly Olney of Providence by William Palfrey of Boston.

3046 [_____.] The Cove. Providence: "Old Stone Bank," 1933. 10p. RHi.
Providence Cove, filled in during the late 19th century.

3047 [_____.] The curse of Clauson. Providence: "Old Stone Bank," 1933. 10p. RHi.
Curse of a 17th-century Providence murder victim on his supposed assailant.

3048 [_____.] Dickens and Thackeray in Providence. Providence: "Old Stone Bank," 1931. 10p. RHi.
Authors Charles Dickens and William Makepeace Thackeray visited and lectured in Providence in 1867 and 1852 respectively.

3049 [_____.] Early printing in Providence. Providence: "Old Stone Bank," 1931. 10p. RHi.

3050 [_____.] Fire! Fire! Providence: "Old Stone Bank," 1932. 9p. RHi.
Fire-fighting in Providence.

3051 [_____.] The First Baptist Meeting House. Providence: "Old Stone Bank," n.d. 10p. RHi.

3052 [_____.] First Light Infantry. Providence: "Old Stone Bank," 1933. 10p. RHi.
Militia unit, organized 1818.

3053 [_____.] "The first mayor of Providence." Providence: "Old Stone Bank," 1932. 10p. RHi.
Samuel Willard Bridgham, who became the new city's first mayor in 1832.

3054 [_____.] Forbes' Museum. Providence: "Old Stone Bank," 1931. 10p. RHi.
19th-century theater.

3055 [_____.] The "Gaspee Room." Providence: "Old Stone Bank," 1931. 10p. RHi.
Room in Sabin's Tavern (no longer standing), where the destruction of the British schooner Gaspee was planned in 1772.

3056 [_____.] "The grand caravan." Providence: "Old Stone Bank," 1933. 10p. RHi.
Circuses and related entertainments in Providence.

3057 [_____.] Jenny Lind and Howard Hall. Providence: "Old Stone Bank," 1931. 10p. RHi.
Her 1850 appearance in the Providence theater.

3058 [_____.] A merchant of Providence. Providence: "Old Stone Bank," 1931. 10p. RHi.
James Brown, Jr. (1698-1739).

3059 [_____.] The middle campus. Providence: "Old Stone Bank," 1931. 10p. RHi.
Brown Univ.

3060 [_____.] "Old Grimes." Providence: "Old Stone Bank," 1932. 10p. RHi.
Albert Gorton Greene, of Providence, and his poem, "Old Grimes," first published in the Providence Gazette (1822).

3061 [_____.] The old Market House. Providence: "Old Stone Bank," 1930. 10p. RHi.
Built in 1770s.

3062 [_____.] Old time commencements. Providence: "Old Stone Bank," 1931. 10p. RHi.
Brown Univ.

3063 [_____.] The old time oyster bars. Providence: "Old Stone Bank," 1931. 10p. RHi.
Eating places in Providence.

3064 [_____.] The passing of Lincoln. Providence: "Old Stone Bank," n.d. 10p. RHi.
How Providence reacted to news of Abraham Lincoln's assassination in 1865.

3065 Providence

3065 [HALEY, JOHN WILLIAMS.] Pembroke College. Providence: "Old Stone Bank," 1931. 10p. RHi.
　　Women's college in Brown Univ.

3066 [_____.] Prospect Terrace. Providence: "Old Stone Bank," 1931. 10p. RHi.
　　Small park and terrace on the East Side, built after the Civil War.

3067 [_____.] Providence prepares for war. Providence: "Old Stone Bank," 1933. 10p. RHi.
　　American Revolution.

3068 [_____.] Stephen Hopkins: Providence's most distinguished citizen. Providence: "Old Stone Bank," n.d. 14p. RHi.
　　Revolutionary-era political leader and signer of the Declaration of Independence.

3069 [_____.] Thomas Poynton Ives. Providence: "Old Stone Bank," 1932. 10p. RHi.
　　Partner of John Brown in the mercantile firm of Brown & Ives.

3070 [_____.] Thomas Smith Webb.... Providence: "Old Stone Bank," n.d. 32p. RHi.
　　Webb was an early-19th-century Providence resident who "framed the present system of Royal Arch Masonry."

3071 [_____.] The Turk's Head. Providence: "Old Stone Bank," 1931. 10p. RHi.
　　Shop sign, long a landmark in downtown Providence.

3072 HALL, EDWARD B. Discourses comprising a history of the First Congregational Church in Providence, delivered June 19, 1836, after the close of a century from the formation of the church. Providence: Knowles, Vose, 1836. 62p. RHi. +
　　Became First Unitarian Church.

3073 HAMMOND, ROLAND. "The Ives family and the Rhode Island Hospital." RIH, 14 (1955), 51-53.

3074 _____, JOHN E. DONLEY, and PETER PINEO CHASE. "The Providence Medical Association, 1848-1948." RIMJ, 31 (1948), 15-30, 33.

3075 HAMMOND, WILLIAM F. "A history of the Fountain Street Methodist Church." NHR, 6 (1888), 37-48.

3076 HANDICRAFT CLUB, PROVIDENCE. Handicraft Club, sixtieth anniversary, 1904-1964, 42 College Hill, Providence, Rhode Island. [19]p. RHi.
　　Includes historical sketch.

3077 HANLON, JOHN. "A rough night for Rocky." RIer (Sept. 15, 1968), 20-22.
　　Controversial heavyweight boxing match in Providence between Rocky Marciano and Tiger Ted Lowry (1949).

3078 _____. "The sporting life at PC." RIer (Nov. 30, 1969), 30-31, 33, 35-36, 39-40, 42.
　　Providence College athletics.

3079 _____. "Who won the first 'World Series?'" RIer (Apr. 20, 1969), 16-18.
　　Providence Grays were unofficial world champions of baseball in 1884.

3080 HANSEN, JAMES E. II. "Students and the Andrews legend at Brown." RIH, 30 (1971), 75-85.
　　Elisha Benjamin Andrews, president (1889-1898).

3081 HARE, ROBERT. Notices of tornadoes. n.p, n.d. 14p. RHi. +
　　Includes account of Providence tornado, Aug. 1838.

3082 HARPIN, MATHIAS P. "A bonnet for Betsy." WRICHSH, 5 (Apr. 1962), [2].
　　Betsy Metcalf and the beginnings of straw braiding in America.

3083 HARRISON, JOSEPH LeROY. The Providence Athenaeum, 1753-1911. n.p., n.d. 39p. RHi. +
　　Library.

3084 HARTWELL, EVERETT S. An historical sketch of the Providence Marine Corps of Artillery, 1801-1951; given at the celebration of the 150th anniversary of the corps at the Benefit Street Armory, Providence, R.I., February 12, 1952. n.p., 1952. 14p. RHi.
　　Militia unit.

3085 HASTINGS, WILLIAM T. The meaning of Brown. Providence, [1939?]. 8p. RHi. +
　　Brown Univ.

3086 _____. "Shakespeare in Providence." Shakespeare Quarterly, 8 (1957), 335-352.
　　"...Public and private reading of the plays, telling mainly the story of the last sixty years...."

3087 _____. "Wars of the Greeks at Brown." NEQ, 5 (1932), 533-554.
　　Controversy over the establishment of a Phi Beta Kappa chapter in 1830.

3088 HATHAWAY, GEORGE E. One hundred years of the Westminster Unitarian Society, 1828-1928. Providence, 1928. 10p. RHi.

3089 HAWK, GRACE E. Pembroke College in Brown University: the first seventy-five years, 1891-1966. Providence: Brown Univ. Pr., 1967. x, 324p. RHi. +

3090 HAYES, FREDERIC. "The First Light Infantry at Brown." BrAlumMo, 12 (1911), 29-32.

3091 HAZLETON, ROBERT MORTON. Let freedom ring: a biography of Moses Brown. N.Y.: New Voices Publishing, 1957. xx, 262p. RHi. +

3092 HEDGES, JAMES B. "The Brown Papers: the records of a Rhode Island business family." American Antiquarian Society, Proceedings, n.s. 51 (1941), 21-36.
       Also published separately.

3093 _____. The Browns of Providence Plantations: colonial years. Cambridge, Mass.: Harvard Univ. Pr., 1952. xviii, 379p. RHi. +
       See also next entry.

3094 _____. The Browns of Providence Plantations: the nineteenth century. Providence: Brown Univ. Pr., 1968. xv, 325p. RHi. +
       See also preceding entry.

3095 _____. "The Browns of Rhode Island." RIY (1965-1966), 34-36.
       See also this author's article of same title in RIY (1974), 115-117.

3096 HESS, JEFFREY A. "Hey, let's burn down the convent!" Yankee, 37 (Mar. 1973), 84-87.
       A mob in 1855 threatened to burn St. Xavier's Convent, home of the Sisters of Mercy.

3097 HESSELTINE, WILLIAM B., and HAZEL C. WOLF. "The New England governors vs. Lincoln: the Providence Conference." RIH, 5 (1946), 105-113.
       1862.

3098 HIGGINS, JOHN SEVILLE. "History of St. John's Cathedral and the Cathedral Close." RIY (1972), 42-44.
       Episcopal.

3099 _____. A narrative of King's Church, St. John's Church, the Cathedral of St. John, 1722-1972. n.p., n.d. 22p. RHi.
       Episcopal.

3100 HINCKLEY, ANITA W. "Mrs. Hinckley's Providence: some details generally glossed over in official histories of the place." RIer (June 4, 1967), 12-13, 15-16, 19.

3101 "THE HISTORIC office of steward at Brown." BrAlumMo, 6 (1905), 93-96.

3102 "AN HISTORICAL account of the planting and growth of Providence." Massachusetts Historical Society, Collections, 2 ser. 9 (1822), 167-203.
       Originally published in Providence Gazette (1765); attributed to Stephen Hopkins.

3103 "HISTORY of Brown University." PBTJ, 20 (1908), 401-406.

3104 "HISTORY of Gaspee House." Daughters of the American Revolution Magazine, 99 (1965), 586-587.
       Owned by Gaspee Chapter, D.A.R.

3105 "HISTORY of Providence shipping." PBTJ, 27 (1915), 147-152.

3106 "HISTORY of the Narragansett Boat Club." The Kiakhta Bomb (Apr. 1887), 4-6.
       "Oldest rowing association in America" (founded 1838).

3107 A HISTORY of the revival of holiness in St. Paul's M.E. Church, Providence, R.I., 1880-1887; or a statement of the circumstances which led to the formation of the South Providence Holiness Association and the Peoples Evangelical Church.... Providence: E. L. Freeman, 1887. 87p. RHi.

3108 HOGROGIAN, JOHN G. "Rhode Island's pro football champions: 1928 Providence Steam Roller." RIH, 36 (1977), 119-128.
       National Football League team.

3109 [HOLBROOK, ALBERT.] The privateer Providence: her unfortunate cruise during the War of 1812-15, together with an account of her commander, Capt. Nicholas Hopkins.... Providence, 1893. 61p. RHi. +

3110 HOLDING, ROBERT S. "George H. Corliss of Providence, inventor." RIH, 5 (1946), 1-16.
       Corliss steam engine.

3111 "HOPE College." BrAlumMo, 57 (Feb. 1957), 4-7, 13.
       Brown Univ. residence hall.

3112 HOPKINS, CHARLES WYMAN. The home lots of the early settlers of the Providence Plantations, with notes and plats.... Providence: [Providence Pr.,] 1886. viii, 78p. RHi. +

3113 HORVITZ, ELEANOR F. "The Jewish Community Center of Rhode Island." RIJHN, 6 (1972), 145-190.

3114 _____. "The Jewish woman liberated: a history of the Ladies' Hebrew Free Loan Association." RIJHN, 7 (1978), 501-512.

3115 Providence

3115 HORVITZ, ELEANOR F. "Marion L. Misch: an extraordinary woman." RIJHN, 8 (1980), 7-65.
Misch (1869-1941) was a Providence businesswoman and feminist. A member of the city's school committee, she was also active in Jewish community activities.

3116 _____. "Max Zinn and the Narragansett Hotel: the end of an era." RIJHN, 6 (1972), 360-384.

3117 _____. "Old bottles, rags, junk!: the story of the Jews of South Providence." RIJHN, 7 (1976), 189-257.

3118 _____. "Pushcarts, surreys with the fringe on top: the story of the Jews of the North End." RIJHN, 8 (1979), 10-50.

3119 _____, and BENTON H. ROSEN. "The Jewish fraternity and Brown University." RIJHN, 8, No. 3 (1981), 299-344.

3120 THE HOUSE of Gladding's: a short review of its century and a half; published as a souvenir on the occasion of its 150th anniversary, October 1916. Providence, [1916?]. [11]p. MWA.
B. H. Gladding Co., "oldest dry goods store in America."

3121 "HOUSING and homes." PM, 28 (1916), 137-142.
House types in Providence over the years.

3122 "HOUSING conditions of Providence." PM, 29 (1917), 79-85.

3123 "HOW Betsey Williams inspired park acquisitions." PM, 28 (1916), 510-511.
Donated land for Roger Williams Park.

3124 "HOW North Main Street didn't come back." PM, 30 (1918), 359-364.
Once the center of retail trade.

3125 HOWLAND, HENRY A. "Providence in 1810 and later." NHR, 6 (1888), 111-121.

3126 "THE HOYLE Tavern." NHR, 6 (1888), 313-314.

3127 HUNTINGTON, HENRY BARRETT. A history of Grace Church in Providence, Rhode Island, 1829-1929; together with an inventory of memorials and funds, compiled by John Hutchins Cady. Providence: Priv. Print., 1931. 237p. RHi. +
Episcopal.

3128 ILLUSTRATED hand-book of the city of Providence, R.I. n.p., [1876?]. xxxiv, 136p. RHi. +
Includes historical information.

3129 INGALL, CAROL K. "The day the anarchist came to town." RIJHN, 8 (1979), 94-98.
Socialist Benjamin Feigenbaum (1905).

3130 IRREPRESSIBLE SOCIETY, PROVIDENCE. Annals of the Irrepressible Society for twenty-five years; incorporated 1873. [Providence: Livermore & Knight,] n.d. [26]p. RHi. +
Club had its beginning during Civil War, when a group of young women met weekly to sew for soldiers.

3131 IRVING, RICHARD F. Toward equal opportunity: the story of the Providence Urban League in the 1940's. [Providence:] Urban League of R.I., 1974. 47p. RHi.
Became Urban League of R.I.

3132 ISELIN, DIANE C. Ivied halls: two centuries of housing at Brown University. Providence: [Brown Univ.,] 1981. 38p. RPB.

3133 ISHAM, NORMAN MORRISON. "The design of the John Brown House." RIH, 7 (1948), 126-128.
John Hutchins Cady, ed.

3134 _____. "The first town mill of Providence." RIHSPubs, n.s. 5 (1897), 192-194.

3135 _____. "George Waterman Cady, F.A.I.A." American Architect and Building News, 91 (1907), 67.
Providence architect.

3136 _____. "The house of Roger Williams." RIHSC, 18 (1925), 33-39.
Report of an archaeological excavation.

3137 _____. The meeting house of the First Baptist Church in Providence: a history of the fabric. Providence: Charitable Baptist Society, 1925. 33p. RHi. +

3138 _____. "Providence and its colonial houses." White Pine Series of Architectural Monographs, 4, No. 3 (1918), 3-13.

3139 "THE JABEZ Gorham House." Providence Preservation Society, Newsletter, 2, No. 1 (Aug. 1961), [1, 4-5].
Recently restored.

3140 JACKSON, HENRY. A discourse in commemoration of the forty-sixth anniversary of the Mite Society; and the two hundred and fifteenth anniversary of the first Baptist church in America. Providence: John K. Stickney, 1854. 32p. RHi. +
Missionary society (Baptist).

3141 JACKSON AND CURTIS (investment bankers). Fifty years of finance: Jackson & Curtis, investment bankers. [Providence,] 1929. 59p. +

3142 JACOBS, FRED. "Isaac Ray and the profession of psychiatry." RIH, 38 (1979), 99-111.
First superintendent of Butler Hospital.

3143 JANUSONIS, MICHAEL. "Can this theater be saved?" RIer (Apr. 17, 1977), 7-8, 14-15, 17-18.
Ocean State Theater. Includes historical sketch.

3144 JOHN BROWN HOUSE, PROVIDENCE. Tercentenary exhibition, June 10 to October 10, 1936. n.p., [1936]. [8]p. RHi.
Includes history of house.

3145 JOHN HOLDEN GREENE: carpenter-architect of Providence. Mrs. Charles Neu, ed. Providence: Providence Preservation Society, 1972. 38, [7]p. RHi. +

3146 "JOHN Kingsbury and the Young Ladies High School." American Journal of Education, 5 (1858), 9-34.
Private school.

3147 JOHNSON, ELIAS HENRY. History of the Third and Brown Street Baptist Churches of Providence, R.I. Providence: J. A. & R. A. Reid, 1880. 43p. RHi. +
Became Union Baptist Church.

3148 JOHNSON, LORENZO D. The spirit of Roger Williams, with a portrait of one of his descendants. Boston: Published for the Author, 1839. vi, 94p. RHi. +
"Descendant" was Roger Williams Baptist Church.

3149 JOHNSON, OLIVER. "A history of the drug business in Providence." NHR, 5 (1887), 345-362.
Pharmacists.

3150 JOHNSON, PEARCE B. "I remember the Steam Roller." RIer (Oct. 23, 1960), 6-10.
Professional football team.

3151 JONES, AUGUSTINE. The history of Friends School, Providence, R.I., from 1779 to 1900. n.p., n.d. [34]p. RHi. +
Became Moses Brown School.

3152 _____. "Moses Brown." NEM, 6 (1888), 34-42.

3153 _____. Moses Brown: his life and services; a sketch read before the Rhode Island Historical Society, October 18, 1892. Providence: R.I. Printing, 1892. 47p. RHi. +
His involvement with the Quakers, antislavery, early cotton manufacturing, etc.

3154 JONES, LESLIE ALLEN. "The old original." RIH, 16 (1957), 114-118.
Clock in the belfry of the First Baptist Church.

3155 JOYCE, WILLIAM L. "'The great day' on the Seekonk." RIer (Mar. 21, 1971), 20-21, 23, 25.
1880 world sculling championships.

3156 _____. "India Point's first schoolmarm." RIer (Dec. 26, 1971), 12-13.
Harriet Ware (1830s).

3157 _____. "Never a wild pitch." Yankee, 37 (Oct. 1973), 223-224.
Exploits of Charlie (Old Hoss) Radbourne, pitcher for the Providence Grays, unofficial world champions of baseball in 1884.

3158 KAULL, JAMES T. "Miss Wheeler said: 'I want my school juicy.'" RIer (Nov. 7, 1965), 8-10, 12-15.
Wheeler School.

3159 KEEN, WILLIAM WILLIAMS. The early years of Brown University, 1764-1770. n.p., [1914]. 37p. RPB. +

3160 KELLNER, GEORGE H., and J. STANLEY LEMONS. "Providence: a century of greatness, 1832-1932." RIH, 41 (1982), 3-18.

3161 KELSEY, RAYNER WICKERSHAM. Centennial history of Moses Brown School, 1819-1919.... Providence: Moses Brown School, 1919. xviii, 178p. RHi. +

3162 KENDALL, KATHLEEN EDGERTON, and JONATHAN C. MESSERLI. "Oratory and learning: Horace Mann at Brown." RIH, 30 (1971), 15-19.
Learning at Brown in the 1810s.

3163 KENNY, ROBERT W. "How the college edifice was built on a spot made for the muses on the inaccessible mountain." BrAlumMo, 72 (Oct. 1971), 26-31.
How Brown Univ. came to Providence.

3164 _____. "George H. Corliss: engineer, architect, philanthropist." RIH, 40 (1981), 49-61.
Inventor of Corliss steam engine.

3165 _____. Town and gown in wartime: a brief account of the College of Rhode Island, now Brown University, and the Providence community during the American Revolution. Providence: University Relations Office, Brown University, 1976. 40p. RHi. +

3166 KIMBALL, GERTRUDE SELWYN. The East-India trade of Providence from 1787 to 1807. Providence: Preston and Rounds, 1896. 34p. RHi. +

3167 Providence

3167   KIMBALL, GERTRUDE SELWYN.  Providence in colonial times.  Boston:  Houghton Mifflin, 1912.  xxi, 392p.  RHi. +

3168   KING, HENRY MELVILLE.  "The First Baptist Church, Providence, Rhode Island:  the oldest church of any denomination in Rhode Island and the oldest Baptist Church in America."  Old-time New England, 34 (1944), 39-43.

3169   _____.  Historical discourse in commemoration of the one hundred and twenty-fifth anniversary of the dedication of the First Baptist Meeting-house, Providence, R.I., Sunday, May 27, 1900.  Providence:  Pr. of F. H. Townsend, 1900.  35p.  RHi. +

3170   _____.  The mother church:  a brief account of the origin and early history of the First Baptist Church in Providence.  Philadelphia:  American Baptist Publication Society, 1896.  85p.  RHi. +

3171   _____.  Remarks at the one hundredth anniversary of the dedication of the First Congregational Church in Providence, R.I., October 31, 1916....  [Providence,] n.d. [4]p.  RHi.

3172   KING, MOSES.  King's pocket-book of Providence, R.I.  Providence:  Tibbitts & Shaw, 1881.  124p.  RHi. +
       Includes brief historical sketches of a number of institutions, businesses, industries, and geographical subdivisions of the city.

3173   KOHN, CATHERINE W.  "The Players."  RIY (1972), 8-9.
       "America's oldest amateur dramatic club still in operation."

3174   KOOPMAN, HARRY LYMAN.  "Poe in Providence."  BrAlumMo, 9 (1909), 137-139.
       Edgar Allan Poe.

3175   LANDMAN, HEDY B.  "The Pendleton House at the Museum of Art, Rhode Island School of Design."  Antiques, 107 (1975), 923-938.
       Charles L. Pendleton House, on Waterman Street.

3176   LANE, GLADYS R.  "Rhode Island's earliest engraver."  Antiques, 7 (1925), 133-137.
       William Hamlin.

3177   LARDNER, ESTHER HOPPIN E.  "The great gale of Sept. 23, 1815."  RIHSPr, n.s. 2 (1894), 202-205.

3178   LARNED, ALBERT CECIL.  The story of old St. John's, 1722-1946.  n.p., n.d.  20p.  RHi. +
       Episcopal church.

3179   LEMONS, J. STANLEY, and FRANCIS M. MARCINIAK.  Strike up the band:  a celebration of the revival of the American Band.  [Providence:]  R.I. College, Office of Publications, [1979].  [16]p.  RHi.

3180   LEONARD, GRACE F.  "Our oldest circulating library."  PM, 28 (1916), 216-219.
       Providence Athenaeum.

3181   _____, and W. CHESLEY WORTHINGTON.  The Providence Athenaeum:  a brief history, 1753-1939.  [Providence:  Providence Athenaeum,] 1940.  60p.  RHi. + Library.

3182   LINCOLN, CHARLES E.  "Passing of a noted Providence building."  PM, 29 (1917), 633-636.
       U.S. Court, Custom House, and Post Office.

3183   _____.  "Police even in days of Roger Williams."  PM, 28 (1916), 785-787.

3184   _____.  "Providence Fire Department antedates Revolution."  PM, 28 (1916), 787-789.

3185   _____.  "Providence musical organizations, past and present."  PM, 28 (1916), 719-726, 758.

3186   _____.  "Public Park Association's notable work."  PM, 28 (1916), 515-519, 589-593.

3187   _____.  "Shops and stores of Providence."  PM, 29 (1917), 9-23.

3188   _____.  "Some local amateur dramatic organizations."  PM, 28 (1916), 705-713.

3189   LINCOLN, JOHN L.  Address delivered on the fiftieth anniversary of the formation of the First Baptist Sunday School, Providence, Sunday, May 30, 1869.  Providence:  Providence Pr., 1869.  38p.  RHi. +
       First Baptist Church.

3190   LIVERMORE AND KNIGHT COMPANY (advertisers).  Fifty years of the pioneer spirit:  a retrospect of a half-century of endeavor which has produced a present-day organization equipped to render a very useful and complete service in advertising and printing.  Providence, 1925.  [51]p.  RHi. +

3191   "LOCAL distilleries."  WRICHSH, 16 (Sept. 1972), [2]; (Oct. 1972), [2].

3192 LORD, AUGUSTUS MENDON. An old church in a new world: commemorative of the two hundredth anniversary of the founding of the First Congregational Church in Providence, delivered...Sunday, December 5, 1920. Providence: First Congregational Society, 1920. 35p. RHi. +
Became First Unitarian Church.

3193 _____. An old New England meeting house: a sermon preached on the one hundredth anniversary of the dedication of the meeting house of the First Congregational Church in the city of Providence...Sunday, October 29, 1916. n.p.: Priv. Print., 1916. 35p. RHi. +
Includes report on 1915 interior restoration, by Henry Bacon.

3194 LORING, JOHN. "Historic houses: American Victorian; the Henry Lippitt House in Providence." Architectural Digest, 35 (Mar. 1978), 148-154.

3195 LOVERIDGE, G. Y. "New light on Tefft." RIer (Sept. 9, 1951), 12-15.
Architect Thomas Alexander Tefft.

3196 LOWE, MOWRY. "The golden era of radio." RIY (1971), H213-H223.
Local, as well as national.

3197 LUTHER, FREDERIC N. "The city of Providence." NEM, 5 (1887), 499-527.

3198 LYNCH, CATHERINE M. "In Sarah's footsteps." RIer (Nov. 24, 1957), 24-25.
75 years of the R.I. Hospital School for Nurses.

3199 _____. "Seventy years of tradition on 'Angell's Lane.'" RIer (Dec. 30, 1956), 8-11.
Providence Art Club.

3200 McCABE, CAROL. "The Providence landmark is 50 years old." RIer (Oct. 1, 1978), 15, 17-18.
Industrial National Bank Building.

3201 McCARTHY, PATRICK J. Autobiographic memoirs of Hon. Patrick J. McCarthy. Mary Josephine Bannon, ed. Providence, 1927. 300p. RHi. +
Progressive-era mayor of Providence.

3202 McCORISON, MARCUS A. "The wages of John Carter's journeyman printers, 1771-1779." American Antiquarian Society, Proceedings, n.s. 81 (1971), 273-303.

3203 McDONALD, WILLIAM. History of Methodism in Providence, Rhode Island, from its introduction in 1787 to 1867. Boston: Phipps & Pride, 1868. 136p. RHi. +

3204 McINTIRE, MRS. WALTER R. The first one hundred years. [Providence, 1959.] 11p. RPB.
Trinity Union Methodist Church.

3205 MANGLER, JOYCE ELLEN. "Early music in Rhode Island churches: I. Music in the First Congregational Church, Providence, 1770-1850." RIH, 17 (1958), 1-9.
See also next entry and entries 146 and 2898-2899.

3206 _____. "Early music in Rhode Island churches: III. Music in King's Church (St. John's), Providence, 1722-1850." RIH, 17 (1958), 73-84.
Episcopal. See also preceding entry and entries 146 and 2898-2899.

3207 MANN, HENRY. Our police: a history of the Providence force from the first watchman to the latest appointee. Providence, 1889. xx, 519p. RHi. +

3208 MANUFACTURERS MUTUAL FIRE INSURANCE COMPANY. The factory mutuals, 1835-1935: being primarily a history of the original of the Factory Mutual Companies during its first one hundred years. Providence, 1935. 384p. RHi. +

3209 "MANY changes on the East Side." PM, 37 (1926), 226-228.
Physical changes since the 1860s.

3210 MASON, WILLIAM H. Reminiscent sketch of "Fire-King Threes" of the Providence Fire Department: including a brief history of Hand Engine Company No. 5, Steam Fire Engine Company No. 3 and Hose Company No. 3. [Providence:] Providence Fire-King Association, 1901. 40p. RHi.

3211 _____. Souvenir offering of "Fire-King Threes" of the Providence Fire Department, including brief histories of the company and association, biographical sketches and reminiscences. [Providence:] Providence Fire-King Association, 1902. 40p. RHi.

3212 _____. Survivors of the Volunteer Fire Department of Providence, R.I.: sketch of the association and how it came to be organized. n.p., 1902. 26p. RHi.
Organization of former volunteer firemen.

3213 MAYO, EDMUND C. "Three men in an industrial century: Jabez Gorham, John Gorham, Edward Holbrook." RIH, 11 (1952), 1-9.
Gorham Manufacturing Company, silverware manufacturers.

3214 MAZET, HORACE S. "The Navy's forgotten hero." U.S. Naval Institute Proceedings, 63 (1937), 347-354.
Abraham Whipple, of Providence, Commodore of R.I. Navy and a leader in the Gaspee affair.

3215 MEMOIR of Dana Pond Colburn, first principal of the R.I. State Normal School, with a sketch of the history of the institution. Republished from Barnard's American Journal of Education for March, 1862. n.p., n.d. 29p. RHi. +
Became R.I. College.

3216 "MEMORIAL Square." RIer (Aug. 1, 1954), 8-9.

3217 MEMORIES of Brown: traditions and recollections gathered from many sources. Robert Perkins Brown, Henry Robinson Palmer, Harry Lyman Koopman, and Clarence Saunders Brigham, eds. Providence: Brown Alumni Magazine, 1909. 495p. RHi. +

3218 MERCHANTS NATIONAL BANK. Old Providence: a collection of facts and traditions relating to various buildings and sites of historic interest in Providence. Providence, 1918. xi, 65p. RHi. +

3219 MESSERLI, JONATHAN C. "Horace Mann at Brown." Harvard Educational Review, 33 (1963), 285-311.
Student life at Brown, 1816-1819.

3220 MICHEL, SONYA. "Children, institutions, and community: the Jewish Orphanage of Rhode Island, 1909-1942." RIJHN, 7 (1977), 385-400.

3221 MILAN, KATHARINE AGATHA. The story of the old Market-house, 1771-1927. Providence: Akerman-Standard, 1927. [16]p. RHi. +

3222 MILLER, ALBERT H. "Alpheus C. Morse." RIMJ, 20 (Feb. 1937), 26.
Providence architect and designer of the R.I. Hospital (dedicated 1868).

3223 _____. "Usher Parsons: a founder of the Rhode Island Hospital." RIMJ, 23 (1940), 168-173.
Includes early history of the hospital.

3224 MINER, GEORGE LELAND. Angell's Lane: the history of a little street in Providence. Providence: Akerman-Standard Pr., 1948. 198, xxxvi p. RHi. +
Includes history of Providence Art Club and list of R.I. painters and sculptors to the end of the 19th century.

3225 _____. "John Brown's Katy, afterwards continental armored sloop Providence." RIH, 2 (1943), 73-82.
American Revolution.

3226 _____. "A Providence packet ship of 1812." RIHSC, 26 (1933), 37-40.

3227 MIRIAM HOSPITAL, PROVIDENCE. Miriam Hospital, Providence, Rhode Island; dedicated December 14, 1952. n.p., [1952?]. [64]p. RHi.
Includes historical background.

3228 A MODERN city: Providence, Rhode Island, and its activities. William Kirk, ed. Chicago: Univ. of Chicago Pr., 1909. ix, 363p. RHi. +
Includes historical information.

3229 MONAHON, ELEANORE BRADFORD. "Providence cabinetmakers." RIH, 23 (1964), 1-22.

3230 _____. "Providence cabinetmakers of the eighteenth and early nineteenth centuries." Antiques, 87 (1965), 573-579.

3231 _____. "The Rawson family of cabinetmakers in Providence, Rhode Island." Antiques, 118 (1980), 134-147.

3232 _____. "Thomas Howard, Jr., Providence cabinetmaker." Antiques, 87 (1965), 702-704.

3233 MONTGOMERY, FLORENCE M. "Furnishing textiles at the John Brown House, Providence, Rhode Island." Antiques, 101 (1972), 496-502.

3234 MOONEY, WILLIAM P. "When Babe Ruth played for Providence." RIer (Apr. 22, 1973), 15-17.
Early in his baseball career, Ruth pitched for the Providence Grays and helped them win the 1914 International League championship.

3235 MOORE, HERBERT G. "Our colonial colleges: Brown University." Daughters of the American Revolution Magazine, 83 (1949), 384-388.

3236 "MORE recent dramatic developments." PM, 28 (1916), 649-654.
Theater in Providence.

3237 MORRIS, CURTIS J. The monument in memory of the R.I. soldiers and sailors who fell victim to the Rebellion. [Providence:] Urban League of R.I., 1974. 19p. RWeW.
Civil War monument.

3238   MOSES, FREDERICK T.  Firemen of industry,
       1854-1954:  the hundredth anniversary of
       Firemen's Mutual Insurance Company, 150
       South Main Street, Providence, Rhode Island.
       [Providence:]  Firemen's Mutual Insurance
       Company, 1954.  111p.  RHi. +

3239   MOWRY, WILLIAM A.  Historical sketch of
       Brown University.  n.p., 1858.  8p.  RPB.

3240   MULROY, RICHARD D.  "Tetanus at the Rhode
       Island Hospital, 1930-1950."  RIMJ, 34
       (1951), 254-257.

3241   MUNRO, WALTER LEE.  "The old back campus."
       BrAlumMo, 28 (1927-1928), 67-68, 119-120,
       166-167, 192-194, 245-246; 29 (1928-1929),
       3-5, 167-168, 189-190, 220-221, 245-247; 30
       (1929-1930), 3-5, 32.
          Brown Univ. See also next entry.

3242   _____.  The old back campus at Brown:  a
       chronicle of student life and activities at
       Brown University in the latter half of the
       last century.  Providence:  Haley & Sykes,
       1929.  47p.  RHi. +
          See also preceding entry.

3243   MUNRO, WILFRED HAROLD.  "The Alpha of Rhode
       Island at Brown."  Phi Beta Kappa Key, 2
       (1915), 327-342.

3244   MURPHY, EDWARD J.  "When death stalked Laura
       Regester."  RIer (Oct. 4, 1959), 16-18;
       (Oct. 11, 1959), 18, 20-21.
          1909 murder.  Concluding article entitled,
       "The stocky man in the derby."

3245   MURRAY, JAMES O.  Francis Wayland.  Boston:
       Houghton, Mifflin, 1891.  vii, 293p.  RHi. +
          Includes his years as president of Brown
       Univ.

3246   _____.  William Gammell, LL.D.:  a
       biographical sketch with selections from his
       writings.  Cambridge, Mass.:  Riverside Pr.,
       1890.  392p.  RHi. +
          Historian, Brown Univ. faculty member,
       president of R.I. Historical Society.
       Selected writings include a biographical
       sketch of R.I. Gov. Samuel Ward.

3247   MURRAY, THOMAS HAMILTON.  "The Irish chapter
       in the history of Brown University."
       American Irish Historical Society, Journal,
       2 (1899), 180-192.

3248   "MUTILATION of the original 'town evidence'
       of Providence."  PM, 23 (1921), 481-484.
          Roger Williams's deed from the Indians.

3249   NAMES of the owners or occupants of
       buildings in the town of Providence, from
       1749 to 1771.  Providence: S. S. Rider &
       Brother, 1870.  25p.  RHi. +

3250   NATIONAL EXCHANGE BANK.  One hundredth
       anniversary, 1801-1901:  the National
       Exchange Bank, Providence, Rhode Island,
       April eighteenth, nineteen hundred and one.
       n.p., n.d.  [31]p.  RHi. +

3251   NEUGEBAUER, OTTO.  "Brown University Library
       and the history of mathematics and
       astronomy."  Books at Brown, 18 (1957),
       78-80.

3252   NORTH AMERICAN EATING HOUSE, PROVIDENCE.
       Bill of fare....  [Providence, 1859?].  76p.
       RPB. +
          Includes historical sketch of Providence.

3253   O'BRIEN, FRANCIS J.  "Down memory lane."
       Rhode Island Bar Journal, 20, No. 4 (Jan.
       1972), 14-16.
          Providence lawyers in the 1920s.

3254   _____.  "Reminiscences of the new
       Courthouse."  Rhode Island Bar Journal, 5,
       No. 7 (Apr. 1957), 1, 11; No. 8 (May 1957),
       8; No. 9 (June 1957), 7.
          Providence County Courthouse.

3255   _____.  "Restaurants and beaneries."  Rhode
       Island Bar Journal, 24, No. 5 (Feb. 1976),
       9.
          Reminiscences of Providence downtown
       eating places.

3256   ODD FELLOWS, INDEPENDENT ORDER OF.
       PROVIDENCE.  ROGER WILLIAMS LODGE, NO. 3.
       A brief history of Roger Williams Lodge, No.
       3, I.O.O.F., from its institution, April
       4th, 1844, to July 1st, 1872; together with
       a concise account of the order in Rhode
       Island from its commencement until the
       organization of Roger Williams Lodge.
       Providence:  Providence Pr., 1872.  34p.
       RPB. +

3257   "OLD builders and carpenters:  Capt. James
       M. Baker, sole survivor of the masters of
       half a century ago."  PBTJ, 23 (1911),
       470-471, 473-474.

3258   OLD COLONY CO-OPERATIVE BANK.  1895-1945:
       half-century anniversary, Old Colony
       Co-operative Bank, Providence, R.I.
       [Providence:  Universal Pr., 1945.]  [13]p.
       RHi.

3259   OLNEYVILLE, R.I.  FIRST FREEWILL BAPTIST
       CHURCH.  The faith, covenant, resolutions
       and by-laws of the First Freewill Baptist
       Church, Olneyville, with a list of members,
       and a brief sketch of its history.
       [Olneyville:]  Published by the Church,
       1878.  33p.  RHi. +

3260 OLNEYVILLE, R.I. FIRST FREEWILL BAPTIST CHURCH. A view of the First Freewill Baptist Church, in Olneyville; comprising its covenant and resolutions...and a brief sketch of its history. [Olneyville,] 1857. 24p. RHi. +

3261 ONE hundredth anniversary of the B. H. Gladding Dry Goods Company, established in October, 1805.... [Providence: Livermore & Knight,] 1905. 13p. RHi.
"Oldest dry goods store in America."

3262 ONORATO, RONALD J. "Providence architecture, 1859-1908: Stone, Carpenter and Willson." RIH, 33 (1974), 87-96.
Alfred Stone, Charles E. Carpenter, Edmund R. Willson.

3263 OSGOOD, SAMUEL. Two sermons, preached in Westminster Congregational Church, Providence, Sept. 9, 1849, on closing his ministry there. Providence: Joseph Knowles, 1849. 31p. MWA.
Sermons relate to history of the church, which later became Westminster Unitarian Church.

3264 OTT, JOSEPH K. "The John Brown House loan exhibition of Rhode Island furniture." Antiques, 87 (1965), 564-571.

3265 _____. "John Innes Clark and his family: beautiful people in Providence." RIH, 32 (1973), 123-132.
Clark was a late-18th-century merchant.

3266 OWNERS and occupants of the lots, houses and shops in the town of Providence, Rhode Island, in 1798, located on maps of the highways of that date; also owners or occupants of houses in the compact part of Providence in 1759, showing the location and in whose names they are to be found on the map of 1798. Henry Richmond Chace, comp. Providence: Livermore & Knight, 1914. 28p. RHi. +

3267 PAINE, GEORGE T. A denial of forgery in connection with the Sachems' deed to Roger Williams: a paper read before the Rhode Island Historical Society, November 17, 1896. Providence: Standard Printing, 1896. 71p. RHi. +
See also entry 3543.

3268 PALMER, HENRY ROBINSON. "Brown University." NEM, n.s. 20 (1899), 293-314.

3269 PARSONS, CHARLES W. The medical school formerly existing in Brown University, its professors and graduates. Providence: Sidney S. Rider, 1881. 59p. RHi. +

3270 PARTRIDGE, HERBERT G. History of the Providence Lying-in Hospital, February 28, 1884 to February 28, 1934. Providence: Board of Trustees, 1934. 71p. RHi. +
This author published an earlier history with similar title in 1903.

3271 "THE PASSING of local landmarks a serious misfortune." PM, 26 (1914), 796-798.

3272 PATTERSON, MERRILL R. "President Messer and the Brown of 1819." RIHSC, 34 (1941), 81-89.
Asa Messer.

3273 PATTON, A. B. "The early land titles of Providence." NHR, 8 (1890), 156-175.

3274 PAXTON, WILLIAM. Moses Brown School: a history of its third half-century, 1919-1969. Providence: Moses Brown School, 1974. xii, 205p. RHi. +

3275 PECKHAM, STEPHEN FARNUM. "A painter of old Providence." Journal of American History, 6 (1912), 649-652.
Edward Lewis Peckham.

3276 _____. "Providence before 1850." Journal of American History, 6 (1912), 661-685.

3277 PERRY, AMOS. The library and cabinet of the Rhode Island Historical Society: their origin and leading features, together with a classified summary of their contents. Providence: Snow & Farnham, 1892. 24p. RHi. +

3278 _____. Memorial of Zachariah Allen, 1795-1882. Cambridge, Mass.: John Wilson, 1883. 108p. RHi. +
Scientist, inventor, author, reformer, textile manufacturer.

3279 _____. "Providence Gazette: its publication, publishers, publication offices, and editors." RIHSPubs, n.s. 5 (1897), 196-202.

3280 PFAUTZ, HAROLD W., HARRY C. HUGULEY, and JOHN W. McCLAIN. "Changes in reputed black community leadership, 1962-72: a case study." Social Forces, 53 (1975), 460-467.
Providence.

3281 PHENIX NATIONAL BANK. ...Arnold, Hoffman & Company, Inc. [Providence,] 1945. 10p. RHi.
Manufacturer of chemicals for textile and other industries. This entry and those that follow under the heading of Phenix National Bank were part of the Romance of R.I. Industry pamphlet series. See note, entry 768.

3282  PHENIX NATIONAL BANK.  ...B. A. Ballou &
Company.  [Providence,] 1945.  10p.  RHi.
Jewelry manufacturer.

3283  _____.  ...Blanding & Blanding, Inc.
[Providence,] 1946.  10p.  RHi.
Downtown drug store.

3284  _____.  ..."A break with the past."
[Providence,] 1945.  10p.  RHi.
National Ring Traveler Co. (textile
machinery manufacturer).

3285  _____.  ...Brown & Sharpe Manufacturing
Company.  [Providence,] 1945.  10p.  RHi.
Machine-tool manufacturer.

3286  _____.  ...Brown University.  [Providence,]
1946.  10p.  RHi.

3287  _____.  ...The Congdon & Carpenter Co.
[Providence,] 1945.  10p.  RHi.
See note, entry 2862.

3288  _____.  ...Elmwood Public Library and the
Knight Memorial.  [Providence,] 1946.  10p.
RHi.
On Elmwood Ave.

3289  _____.  ...Federal Products Corporation.
[Providence,] 1946.  10p.  RHi.
Manufacturer of gauges.

3290  _____.  ..."The firemasters."  [Providence,]
1945.  10p.  RHi.
Factory Mutual System of fire-insurance
companies.

3291  _____.  ...The Franklin Process Company.
[Providence,] 1946.  10p.  RHi.
Dyeing-machinery manufacturers.

3292  _____.  ...Grinnell Company.  [Providence,]
1945.  10p.  RHi.
Pipe manufacturer.  Originated in 1850 as
Providence Steam & Gas Pipe Co.

3293  _____.  ..."History day by day."
[Providence,] 1945.  10p.  RHi.
Providence Journal (newspaper).

3294  _____.  ...The Howard Building.
[Providence,] 1946.  10p.  RHi.
Downtown landmark.

3295  _____.  ...International Braid Company.
[Providence,] 1946.  10p.  RHi.
Manufacturer.

3296  _____.  J. M. Burke Pattern Co., Inc.
[Providence,] 1946.  10p.  RHi.
Pattern-maker and manufacturer of
fire-fighting equipment.

3297  _____.  ...Lamson Oil Corporation.
[Providence,] 1946.  10p.  RHi.
"...R.I.'s largest independent distributor
of gasoline and one of New England's largest
retail distributors of fuel oil."

3298  _____.  ...M. N. Cartier & Sons, Inc.
[Providence,] 1945.  10p.  RHi.
"...Largest wholesale distributor of
roofing materials in the U.S."

3299  _____.  ...Nicholson File Company.
[Providence,] 1946.  10p.  RHi.
Manufacturer.

3300  _____.  ...Phenix Bank notes:  I.
[Providence,] 1946.  10p.  RHi.
Early history of the bank.

3301  _____.  ...Phenix Bank notes:  II.
[Providence,] 1946.  10p.  RHi.
The Phenix National Bank in R.I. history.

3302  _____.  ...Phenix Bank notes:  III.
[Providence,] 1946.  10p.  RHi.
History of the site of the Exchange Bldg.,
which had recently been acquired by Phenix
National Bank.

3303  _____.  ...Phenix Bank notes:  IV.
[Providence,] 1946.  10p.  RHi.
History of the bank.

3304  _____.  ...The Providence Athenaeum.
[Providence,] 1946.  10p.  RHi.
Library.

3305  _____.  ...Providence College.
[Providence,] 1946.  10p.  RHi.

3306  _____.  ...Providence Dyeing Bleaching &
Calendering Company.  [Providence,] 1946.
10p.  RHi.

3307  _____.  ...Providence Gas Company.
[Providence,] 1946.  10p.  RHi.
Natural-gas supplier.

3308  _____.  ...The Providence Mutual Fire
Insurance Company.  [Providence,] 1946.
10p.  RHi.

3309  _____.  ...Providence Public Library.
[Providence,] 1946.  10p.  RHi.

3310  _____.  ...Providence Washington Insurance
Company.  [Providence,] 1946.  10p.  RHi.

3311  _____.  ...Rhode Island Historical Society.
[Providence,] 1946.  10p.  RPB.

3312  _____.  ...Rhode Island Hospital.
[Providence,] 1945.  10p.  RHi.

3313 PHENIX NATIONAL BANK. ...Rhode Island School of Design. [Providence,] 1945. 10p. RHi.

3314 _____. ..."Rhode Island Tool Company." [Providence,] 1945. 10p. RHi.
Tool manufacturer.

3315 _____. ..."The sign of the bunch of grapes." [Providence,] 1945. 10p. RHi.
B. H. Gladding Co., "America's oldest dry-goods store."

3316 _____. ..."The smith of the gods." [Providence,] 1945. 10p. RHi.
Gorham Mfg. Co. (silverware).

3317 _____. ..."A source of heirlooms." [Providence,] 1945. 10p. RHi.
Tilden-Thurber Co. (jewelry retailers).

3318 _____. ...Starkweather & Shepley, Inc. [Providence,] 1946. 10p. RHi.
Insurance brokers.

3319 _____. ..."The story of a life-line." [Providence,] 1945. 10p. RHi.
Davol Rubber Co.

3320 _____. ..."Where ideas are cast in iron." [Providence,] 1945. 10p. RHi.
Builders Iron Foundry, Providence.

3321 _____. ..."Where steam met its master." [Providence,] 1945. 10p. RHi.
Franklin Machine and Foundry Co., a descendant of the Corliss Steam Engine Co.

3322 PHI BETA KAPPA. RHODE ISLAND ALPHA, BROWN UNIVERSITY. Catalogue of the Rhode Island Alpha of Phi Beta Kappa, with the history of the founding of the chapter and its present constitution and by-laws.... (1904) Providence: Palmer Pr., 1914. 112p. RPB. +

3323 _____. A century of scholars: Rhode Island Alpha of Phi Beta Kappa, 1830-1930. William T. Hastings, ed. (1932) 2d ed. Providence, 1943. 255p. RHi. +

3324 _____. More than a century of scholars: Rhode Island Alpha of Phi Beta Kappa, 1830-1954. William T. Hastings, ed. Providence, 1955. 249p. RHi. +

3325 PHILLIPS, JANET. "Divine Providence: after decades of stagnation and neglect a once-wealthy city is 'born again.'" BrAlumMo, 80 (Oct. 1979), 16-24.
Revitalization efforts and their results.

3326 PIGGOTT, FRED. Industrial National Bank of Rhode Island: 170 years of service, 1791-1961. n.p., n.d. [14]p. RHi.

3327 PILLSBURY, WILLIAM M. "Earning a living, 1788-1818: Job Danforth, cabinetmaker." RIH, 31 (1972), 81-93.

3328 "THE PIONEER department store." PBTJ, 21 (1909), 143-144.
The Boston Store, Providence.

3329 "PIONEERS in college hockey." BrAlumMo, 57 (Mar. 1957), 6-11.
Brown Univ. team.

3330 PITMAN, JOHN. Address to the Alumni Association of Brown University, delivered in Providence, on their first anniversary, September 5, 1843. Providence: B. Cranston, 1843. 64p. RHi. +
On the early history of Brown Univ. and the alumni of Brown.

3331 _____. A discourse delivered at Providence, August 5, 1836, in commemoration of the first settlement of Rhode-Island and Providence Plantations; being the second centennial anniversary of the settlement of Providence. Providence: B. Cranston, 1836. 72p. RHi. +

3332 PITTERMAN, MARVIN. "The Hebrew Free Loan Association, 1938-1950." RIJHN, 8 (1980), 91-108.
Gemiloth Chesed Hebrew Free Loan Association.

3333 [THE PLAYERS, PROVIDENCE.] The first sixty-five years: being a chronicle of the history, aspirations and accomplishments of the Players from 1909 to 1974. n.p., n.d. [199]p. RHi.
Amateur theatrical group.

3334 POLAND, WILLIAM CAREY. "The Brown family in its relation to Brown University." BrAlumMo, 2 (1901), 74-78.

3335 "THE POLICE force of Providence: its past and present organization...." Providence Press (1874).
Series of articles beginning Jan. 7, 1874. Rider Collection, Brown Univ.

3336 POLISHOOK, IRWIN H. "An Independence Day celebration in Rhode Island, 1788." Huntington Library Quarterly, 30 (1966-1967), 85-93.
Three contemporary accounts of the pro-Federalist (i.e., pro-U.S. Constitution) celebration in Providence, July 4, 1788.

3337 POMFRET, JOHN E. "Student interests at Brown, 1789-1790." NEQ, 5 (1932), 135-147.

3338 POPKIN, GEORGE. "Macaroni in the street and trouble." RIer (June 10, 1962), 12-13.
Rioting on Federal Hill over food prices (1914).

3339 _____. "What PC has given to Rhode Island." RIer (Sept. 28, 1969), 8-9.
Providence College.

3340 POSTAR, JOSEPH. "They were Hope's 'dream five.'" RIer (Mar. 15, 1959), 6-8.
Hope High School's 1939 R.I. and New England basketball champions.

3341 POTTER, ALFRED L. "The Providence Lying-in Hospital, 1926-1951." RIMJ, 35 (1952), 649-655, 668.

3342 "PRESIDENTS' houses at Brown." BrAlumMo, 2 (1901), 92-94.

3343 PRESTON, HOWARD WILLIS. "The defenders of Providence during King Philip's War." RIHSC, 21 (1928), 56-62.

3344 _____. Notes on old Providence: the old County House in Providence. Providence: Preston & Rounds, 1918. 8p. RHi. +
Courthouse. Reprinted from RIHSC, 11 (1918), 37-44.

3345 _____. Rochambeau and the French troops in Providence in 1780-81-82. Providence, 1924. 30p. RHi. +

3346 _____. "Washington's visits to Providence." RIHSC, 19 (1926), 97-115.
George Washington.

3347 "PROPOSED iron works at Providence in 1655." RIHSC, 28 (1935), 67-70.

3348 PROVIDENCE, R.I. Ceremonies at the unveiling of the monument to Roger Williams, erected by the city of Providence, with the address by J. Lewis Diman, October 16, 1877. Providence: Angell, Hammett, 1877. 52p. RHi. +
Historical address.

3349 _____. Dedication of the French Monument by the city of Providence, R.I.: comprising the historical record, oration, addresses, prayers, ode, and order of exercises, July 4, 1882. Providence: Providence Pr., 1882. 43p. RHi. +
Commemorating French troops in the American Revolution.

3350 PROVIDENCE, R.I. ALL SAINTS' MEMORIAL CHURCH. A history of the choir and music of All Saints' Memorial Church, Providence, R.I. (formerly St. Andrew's): 1858-1923 by Howard Hagan, 1924-1940 by Frank Vinton Brown. Providence: Roger Williams Pr., [1942]. 84p. RHi.
Episcopal.

3351 PROVIDENCE, R.I. ASBURY METHODIST EPISCOPAL CHURCH. Exercises at the laying of the corner-stone of the Asbury Methodist Episcopal Church, Providence, R.I., Monday, November 1, 1886. Providence: Providence Pr., 1886. 45p. RHi. +
Includes historical sketch.

3352 PROVIDENCE, R.I. BENEFICENT CONGREGATIONAL CHURCH. The Beneficent Congregational Church...celebrating the 175th anniversary of the organization of the church.... [Providence, 1919.] [8, 4]p. RPB.

3353 _____. The birthday anniversary of historic Beneficent Meeting House, Providence, Sunday, December 30, 1934; Tuesday, January 1, 1935; Thursday, January 3, 1935; being the 125th anniversary of the dedication of its second and present house of worship. n.p., n.d. [11]p. RHi. +

3354 _____. A brief historical sketch, Beneficent Congregational Church. n.p., 1971. [4]p. RP-Harrington.

3355 _____. Historic Beneficent Meeting House, 1810. n.p., n.d. [7]p. RP-Harrington.

3356 PROVIDENCE, R.I. BROAD STREET CHRISTIAN CHURCH. Manual of the Broad-Street Christian Church, Providence, R.I., 1902. Providence: Standard Printing, [1902]. 89p. RHi.
Includes historical sketch.

3357 PROVIDENCE, R.I. BROWN STREET BAPTIST CHURCH. A brief history of the Brown Street Baptist Church, Providence; with the articles of faith, church covenant, rules and regulations, and list of members. Providence: Knowles, Anthony, 1866. 36p. RHi. +
Became Union Baptist Church.

3358 PROVIDENCE, R.I. CALVARY BAPTIST CHURCH. Manual, Calvary Baptist Church, Providence, R.I., 1899. n.p., n.d. 23p. RHi.
Includes historical sketch.

3359 PROVIDENCE, R.I. CENTRAL BAPTIST CHURCH. The centennial services of the Central Baptist Church, Providence, Rhode Island, April thirtieth, May first, second and fourth, nineteen hundred and five. Providence: Remington Printing, 1906. 82p. RHi.

3360 _____. Complete proceedings of the one hundred and twenty-fifth anniversary of the Central Baptist Church, Providence, R.I., May first, second, fourth and eleventh, 1930. Lloyd and Wayland avenues. n.p., [1930]. 79p. RHi. +

3361 _____. The semi-centennial celebration of the Central Baptist Sunday School, Providence, R.I., May 9, 1877. Providence: Printed for the School, 1878. 30p. RHi. +

3362 _____. Sketch...with a list of members. Providence, 1837. 26p. RPB.

3363 PROVIDENCE, R.I. CENTRAL CONGREGATIONAL CHURCH. The first century of Central Congregational Church, 1852-1952. Providence, 1952. ii, 92p. RHi. +

3364 _____. Historical manual of the Central Congregational Church, Providence, R.I., 1852-1902. Providence: Pr. of E. L. Freeman, 1902. 172p. RHi. +
Includes historical addresses.

3365 _____. Manual of the Central Congregational Society of Providence, R.I. Providence, 1908. 27p. RHi.
Includes historical sketch.

3366 _____. A paper presented at the celebration of the seventy-fifth anniversary of the Central Congregational Church, March tenth, 1927. n.p., n.d. 26p. RHi. +

3367 PROVIDENCE, R.I. CHESTNUT STREET METHODIST EPISCOPAL CHURCH. Seventieth anniversary of the Chestnut Street Methodist Episcopal Church and Sunday School, Providence, R.I., December 13 and 14, 1885. Providence: Providence Pr., 1886. 88p. RHi. +

3368 PROVIDENCE, R.I. CHURCH OF THE BLESSED SACRAMENT. Church of the Blessed Sacrament, Providence, R.I. n.p., 1935. 120p. RPD-H.
Roman Catholic.

3369 PROVIDENCE, R.I. CHURCH OF THE EPIPHANY. The Church of the Epiphany, Providence, Rhode Island: centennial celebration, April 6, 1975. n.p., n.d. [20]p. RHi.
Episcopal.

3370 PROVIDENCE, R.I. CHURCH OF THE REDEEMER. Brief history of the Church of the Redeemer, Providence, R.I., 1859-1889, together with the constitution and by-laws of the parish. [Providence:] Providence Pr., 1890. 18p. RHi.
Episcopal.

3371 PROVIDENCE, R.I. CITY COUNCIL. The city hall, Providence, corner-stone laid June 24th, 1875; dedicated November 14, 1878. Providence, 1881. viii, 108p. RHi. +
Includes historical orations.

3372 _____. Memorial of Thomas Arthur Doyle, mayor of the city of Providence.... Providence, 1887. 86p. RHi. +

3373 _____. Two hundred and fiftieth anniversary of the settlement of Providence, June 23 and 24, 1886. Providence: Providence Pr., 1887. viii, 236p. RHi. +

3374 PROVIDENCE, R.I. CITY PLAN COMMISSION. College Hill: a demonstration study of historic area renewal.... Providence, 1967. x, 230p. RHi. +
Includes historical sketch.

3375 _____. Downtown Providence, 1970: a demonstration of citizen participation in comprehensive planning. Providence, 1971. xiv, 250p. RHi.
Includes historical sketch.

3376 _____. Land use comparison, 1946-1953. Providence, 1955. 61p. RHi.
Providence.

3377 PROVIDENCE, R.I. DEPARTMENT OF PLANNING AND URBAN DEVELOPMENT. Elmwood neighborhood analysis, part one. Providence, 1977. 65, [45]p. RHi.
Includes historical sketch.

3378 _____. Federal Hill neighborhood analysis, part one. Providence, 1980. 38, [46]p. RP.
Includes historical sketch.

3379 _____. Olneyville neighborhood analysis, part one. Providence, 1979. 30, [36]p. RHi.
Includes historical sketch.

3380 _____. Smith Hill neighborhood analysis, part one. Providence, 1979. 45, [42]p. RHi.
Includes historical sketch.

3381 _____. Upper South Providence: neighborhood analysis. Providence, 1980. 45, [44]p. RHi.
Includes "Historic development," 5-29.

3382 PROVIDENCE, R.I. DEPARTMENT OF PLANNING AND URBAN DEVELOPMENT. West End neighborhood analysis, part one. Providence, 1979. 32, [56]p. RHi.
Includes historical sketch.

3383 PROVIDENCE, R.I. EIGHTH BAPTIST CHURCH. The declaration of faith, with the church covenant, rules and regulations, and list of members, of the Eighth Baptist Church, Providence, R.I., constituted, May 20th, 1847. Providence: Albert Crawford Greene, 1850. 12p. RHi.
Includes historical sketch.

3384 PROVIDENCE, R.I. EVANGELICAL ADVENT YAHVEH CHURCH. Origin, covenant, declaration of principles, and by-laws of the Evangelical Advent Yahveh Church, Providence, R.I. Providence: Hammond, Angell, 1867. 21p. RPB.

3385 PROVIDENCE, R.I. FIFTH CONGREGATIONAL CHURCH. Historical sketch, covenant, and articles of faith, of the Fifth Congregational Church, North Main Street, Providence, R.I. Providence: Albro & Hall, 1849. 24p. RHi.

3386 PROVIDENCE, R.I. FIRST BAPTIST CHURCH. The first Baptist church in America, No. Main at Waterman St., Providence, R.I. n.p., [1963?]. 28p. RHi.
Architectural. See also next entry.

3387 _____. The first Baptist church in America, North Main at Waterman Street, Providence, Rhode Island. n.p., [1948]. [4]p. RHi.
Includes "Historical statement," by Henry Melville King and Arthur E. Watson. See also preceding entry.

3388 _____. Historical catalogue of the members of the First Baptist Church in Providence, Rhode Island. Henry Melville King, comp.... Providence: F. H. Townsend, 1908. 189p. RHi. +

3389 _____. History of the First Baptist Church in Providence, 1639-1877. Providence: J. A. & R. A. Reid, 1877. 23p. RHi. +

3390 _____. A list of members of the First Baptist Church in Providence, with biographical sketches of the pastors. Providence: H. H. Brown, 1832. 48p. RHi. +

3391 _____. Manual of the First Baptist Church in Providence, R.I., August, 1910. Providence: F. H. Townsend, 1910. 56p. RHi. +
Includes historical sketch. Earlier manuals containing historical sketches of the church include 1861, 1867, 1873, 1880, 1884, 1890, 1900.

3392 _____. Minutes of the proceedings of the seventy-fifth anniversary of the First Baptist Sunday School, Providence, R.I., held in the First Baptist Meeting House, Sunday, June third, 1894. n.p., n.d. 42p. RHi. +
Includes historical address by Henry Melville King.

3393 _____. The two hundred and fiftieth anniversary of the formation of the First Baptist Church in Providence, Rhode Island, Sunday, April 28, 1889. [Providence:] Snow & Farnham, 1889. 121p. RHi. +
Historical discourse by Samuel L. Caldwell.

3394 PROVIDENCE, R.I. FIRST UNIVERSALIST PARISH. An account of a celebration by the Ladies' Humane Society of the First Universalist Parish, Providence, R.I., of their fiftieth anniversary. n.p., [1882?]. 8p. RHi.
Charitable society.

3395 PROVIDENCE, R.I. FIRST UNIVERSALIST SOCIETY. The centennial book of the First Universalist Society in Providence, Rhode Island, April, 10, 1921. [Providence:] Trustees of the Society, n.d. 93p. RHi. +

3396 _____. The First Universalist Church in Providence, Washington & Greene Streets. n.p., [1971?] [12]p. RHi.
Includes 150th-anniversary historical sketch.

3397 _____. A half-century memorial of the First Universalist Society in Providence, Rhode Island, comprising an historical discourse by Rev. E. H. Capen, a poem by Rev. Cyrus H. Fay.... Providence: Gladding Bros., 1871. 90p. RHi. +

3398 PROVIDENCE, R.I. FOURTH BAPTIST CHURCH. The Fourth Baptist Church: its history, doctrines and membership, Providence, R.I., June, 1879. Providence: J. A. & R. A. Reid, 1879. 52p. RPB. +

3399 PROVIDENCE, R.I. FREE EVANGELICAL CONGREGATIONAL CHURCH. Report of the Free Evangelical Congregational Church, of Providence, R.I., read at the twenty-fifth anniversary of the organization of the church. Providence: Providence Pr., 1868. 12p. RP.

3400     PROVIDENCE, R.I. GRACE CHURCH. Grace Church: a celebration of mission and service in downtown Providence. n.p., [1981?]. [48]p. RHi.
     Episcopal.

3401     _____. The half century jubilee of Grace Church, Providence, Rhode Island, 1829-1879. Providence: Sidney S. Rider, 1880. 88p. RHi. +

3402     PROVIDENCE, R.I. GREENWICH STREET FREE BAPTIST CHURCH. Twentieth anniversary of the Greenwich St. Free Baptist Church and Sunday-school, Providence, R.I.... Boston: Morning Star Publishing House, 1890. 25p. RHi.
     Includes historical sketches of the church and Sunday school. Freewill Baptist.

3403     PROVIDENCE, R.I. HIGH SCHOOL. A brief sketch of the establishment of the High School, Providence, together with the dedicatory exercises of the new building. Providence: J. A. & R. A. Reid, 1878. 129p. RHi. +

3404     PROVIDENCE, R.I. HIGH STREET CONGREGATIONAL CHURCH. Hand-book of the High Street Congregational Church, Providence, R.I., containing the constitution, confession of faith, covenant, rules, officers, calendar, list of members, and items of history. No. 3, 1861. Providence: M. B. Young, 1861. 54p. RHi. +

3405     PROVIDENCE, R.I. HOLY GHOST CHURCH. History of the Holy Ghost Parish, Providence, Rhode Island, published on the seventy-fifth anniversary of the founding of the parish, 1966. n.p., 1966. [28]p. RPD-H.
     Roman Catholic. Italian parish.

3406     [PROVIDENCE, R.I. HOLY NAME CHURCH.] A living memorial, 1882-1982. n.p., [1982]. 48p. RPD.
     Roman Catholic.

3407     PROVIDENCE, R.I. HOPE STREET METHODIST EPISCOPAL CHURCH. Hope St. Methodist Episcopal Church: jubilee souvenir, Providence, R.I., 1874-1904. n.p., n.d. 32p. RHi. +

3408     PROVIDENCE, R.I. JEFFERSON STREET BAPTIST CHURCH. Historical sketch, by-laws and rules of order, articles of faith, church covenant, list of officers and members, 1888. Providence: Baker Publishing, 1888. 16p. RHi.

3409     PROVIDENCE, R.I. MATHEWSON STREET METHODIST EPISCOPAL CHURCH. Souvenir of the Mathewson St. Methodist Episcopal Church of Providence, Rhode Island.... Providence: Snow & Farnham, n.d. 50p. RHi. +

3410     PROVIDENCE, R.I. MOUNT PLEASANT BAPTIST CHURCH. Manual of the Mount Pleasant Baptist Church, Providence, R.I., constituted February 1883. Providence: Yankee Notion Printing, 1884. 48p. RHi.
     Includes historical sketch.

3411     PROVIDENCE, R.I. NORTH CONGREGATIONAL CHURCH. Articles of faith, covenant, and by-laws of the North Congregational Church, Providence, Rhode Island; with a list of members. Providence: [Standard Printing,] 1897. 56p. RHi.
     Includes historical sketch.

3412     PROVIDENCE, R.I. OUR LADY OF MOUNT CARMEL CHURCH. Our Lady of Mt. Carmel Church, Providence, Rhode Island: fifty years of devoted service to Almighty God, 1921-1971. n.p.: [Service Plus Pr.,] n.d. [181]p. RPD.
     Roman Catholic. Italian Parish. Includes historical sketch.

3413     PROVIDENCE, R.I. [OUR LADY OF THE ROSARY CHURCH.] Souvenir da dedicaco da Egreja de Nossa Senhora do Rosario, 9 Setembro de 1906, Providence, R.I. Providence: William R. Brown, 1906. 64p. RHi.
     Roman Catholic. Portuguese parish. Text in Portuguese.

3414     PROVIDENCE, R.I. PARK STREET FREE BAPTIST CHURCH. Manual of the Park Street Free Baptist Church, Providence, R.I., 1880. Dover, N.H.: Morning Star Job Printing House, 1880. 16p. RHi. +
     Includes historical sermon. Freewill Baptist church.

3415     PROVIDENCE, R.I. PILGRIM CONGREGATIONAL CHURCH. Handbook of the Pilgrim Congregational Church, Providence, R.I., organized June 2d, 1869. Providence: Providence Pr., 1870. 24p. MWA.
     Includes historical background.

3416     _____. Manual of the Pilgrim Congregational Church, Providence, R.I., 1890; organized, June 2, 1869. [Providence:] Providence Pr., 1890. 53p. RHi.
     Includes historical sketch.

3417     _____. The twentieth anniversary of the Pilgrim Congregational Church, Providence, R.I.... [Providence:] Providence Pr., 1889. 34p. RHi. +

3418 PROVIDENCE, R.I. PINE STREET BAPTIST
CHURCH. A sketch of the Pine-Street (2d)
Baptist Church, in Providence, with a list
of members. Providence: H. H. Brown, 1837.
36p. RHi.

3419 PROVIDENCE, R.I. POLICE DEPARTMENT. A
brief history of the Providence Police
Department, and 1964 annual report of the
department; centennial issue. Providence,
1965. 69p. RP. +

3420 PROVIDENCE, R.I. RECORD COMMISSIONERS.
First report of the Record Commissioners
relative to the early town records.
Providence: Snow & Farnham, 1892. 34p.
RHi. +
Includes history of town-records
preservation in Providence.

3421 PROVIDENCE, R.I. ROGER WILLIAMS BAPTIST
CHURCH. History of the Roger Williams
Church, Providence, R.I.; with the
discipline and faith of the church, and a
list of members. Providence: R. W. Potter,
1845. 18p. RHi.
Baptist.

3422 _____. Manual of the Roger Williams Church,
Providence, R.I., with a sketch of its early
history. Providence: Hammond, Angell,
1873. 24p. RHi. +

3423 PROVIDENCE, R.I. SAINT ADALBERT'S CHURCH.
St. Adalbert's Church, Providence, Rhode
Island: 75th anniversary, 1902-1977. N.Y.:
Park Publishing, [1977]. 48p. RPD.
Roman Catholic. Polish parish.

3424 PROVIDENCE, R.I. SAINT ANN'S CHURCH. St.
Ann's Roman Catholic Church, Providence,
Rhode Island. South Hackensack, N.J.:
Custombook, 1970. 28, [20]p. RPD.
Roman Catholic. Italian parish.

3425 PROVIDENCE, R.I. SAINT ANTHONY'S CHURCH.
History of St. Anthony's Church. n.p.,
[1975]. [4]p. RPD.
Roman Catholic.

3426 PROVIDENCE, R.I. SAINT BARTHOLOMEW'S CHURCH.
Saint Bartholomew's Church, Providence,
Rhode Island. South Hackensack, N.J.:
Custombook, 1970. 24, [20]p. RPD.
Roman Catholic. Italian parish.

3427 PROVIDENCE, R.I. SAINT EDWARD'S CHURCH.
St. Edward's celebrates its people.
Rejoice: past, present, future. n.p.,
[1972]. 35p. RPD-H.
Roman Catholic.

3428 PROVIDENCE, R.I. SAINT JOSEPH'S CHURCH.
Souvenir booklet commemorating the one
hundredth anniversary of the founding of St.
Joseph's Parish, Hope Street, Providence,
Rhode Island. n.p., [1951?]. [112]p. RHi.
Roman Catholic.

3429 PROVIDENCE, R.I. SAINT MARY'S CHURCH.
Centennial commemoration, Saint Mary's
Parish, Broadway, Providence, Rhode Island,
anno domini 1953: historical, pictorial,
documentary.... [Providence: Hopkins Pr.,]
n.d. 197p. RHi. +
Roman Catholic.

3430 PROVIDENCE, R.I. SAINT MICHAEL'S CHURCH.
Golden jubilee: history of parish and
souvenir program, St. Michael's Church,
Providence, Rhode Island. Providence:
Remington Printing, [1909?]. [60]p. RHi.
Roman Catholic.

3431 _____. One hundred years, St. Michael's
Parish, 1859-1959, Providence, Rhode Island.
n.p., n.d. [68]p. RHi.
Roman Catholic.

3432 PROVIDENCE, R.I. SAINT PATRICK'S CHURCH.
A brief history, St. Patrick's Parish,
1841-1973. Providence: Service Plus Pr.,
[1973]. [88]p. RHi.
Roman Catholic.

3433 PROVIDENCE, R.I. SAINT PAUL'S EVANGELICAL
LUTHERAN CHURCH. "Even so send I you."
Providence, 1966. 61p. RHi.
Includes historical sketch.

3434 PROVIDENCE, R.I. SAINT SAHAG-SAINT MESROB
ARMENIAN CHURCH. Fortieth anniversary
commemoration of the St. Sahag-St. Mesrob
Armenian Church of Providence, 1914-1953.
Providence, 1953. [44]p. MH.
Text in Armenian and English.

3435 PROVIDENCE, R.I. SAINT THOMAS CHURCH.
Saint Thomas Church: 90th anniversary,
parish dinner dance, Saturday, April 16th,
1977; Venus de Milo Restaurant, Swansea,
Massachusetts. n.p., n.d. [10]p. RHi.
Roman Catholic. Includes historical
sketch.

3436 [PROVIDENCE, R.I. SAINTS PETER AND PAUL'S
CATHEDRAL.] The consecration of SS. Peter
& Paul's Cathedral, with the entire
ceremonial, Sunday, June 30th, 1889,
together with illustrations and description
of its interior, history of the church from
1820...and a short history of some of the
leading churches of the diocese.
Providence: J. A. & R. A. Reid, [1889].
77, [7]p. RHi. +
Roman Catholic.

3437 Providence

3437 PROVIDENCE, R.I. SAINTS PETER AND PAUL'S CATHEDRAL. Official souvenir of SS. Peter and Paul's Cathedral, containing a full description of its interior, with illustrations; and sketches of the lives of...Right Rev. Thomas F. Hendricken, D.D.; Right Rev. Matthew Harkins, D.D.; and a short history of the St. Vincent's Orphan Asylum. Providence: F. J. Flanagan, n.d. 103p. RHi. +
    Roman Catholic. Hendricken and Harkins were Bishops of Providence.

3438 PROVIDENCE, R.I. SCHOOL COMMITTEE. Report of the School Committee for the year 1899-1900; centennial celebration of the establishment of the public schools; historical addresses and reports. Providence: Providence Pr., 1901. 367p. RHi. +

3439 PROVIDENCE, R.I. SECOND PRESBYTERIAN CHURCH. A history of the Second Presbyterian Church, 500 Hope Street, Providence, R.I.; sixtieth anniversary, 1891-1951. n.p., n.d. [20]p. RHi.

3440 PROVIDENCE, R.I. STEWART STREET BAPTIST CHURCH. Articles of faith, rules, regulations, and a brief history, with a list of members, of the Stewart-Street Baptist Church, Providence, R.I., constituted Feb. 8, 1851. Boston: Rand, Avery & Frye, 1870. 48p. RHi. +

3441 PROVIDENCE, R.I. TEMPLE EMANU-EL. The Temple Emanu-El has published this dedication journal in the interests of Rhode Island Jewry so that there may be a permanent and enduring record of the founding of Temple Emanu-El, Providence, R.I.... [Providence: Thompson & Thompson, 1927?]. 95p. RHi.

3442 _____. Temple Emanu-El: the first fifty years, 5684-5734. n.p., [1975]. 176p. RHi. +
    Jewish.

3443 PROVIDENCE, R.I. TERCENTENARY COMMITTEE. Religion in Rhode Island. [Providence,] 1936. [14]p. RHi.

3444 PROVIDENCE, the southern gateway of New England: commemorating the one hundred fiftieth anniversary of independence of the State of Rhode Island, May 4, 1926. 1910) n.p.: Historical Publishing, n.d. 264p. RHi. +
    Historical sketches.

3445 PROVIDENCE, R.I. THIRD BAPTIST CHURCH. A list of members with the covenant and sketch of history of the Third Baptist Church in Providence, R.I. Providence: H. H. Brown, 1855. 40p. RHi. +
    Became Union Baptist Church.

3446 _____. A sketch of the Third Baptist Church, Providence; with the covenant and a list of officers and members, 1843. (1840) n.p., [1843]. 24p. RHi.

3447 PROVIDENCE, R.I. UNION BAPTIST CHURCH. A brief history...with the articles of faith, covenant, rules and regulations and list of members. Providence, 1866. 36p. RPB. +
    Union of the Brown Street and Third Baptist Churches.

3448 _____. Thirty years of the Union Baptist Church, Providence, R.I., 1878 to 1908. By the church clerk. n.p., n.d. 23p. RHi.

3449 PROVIDENCE, R.I. UNION CONGREGATIONAL CHURCH. Manual of the Union Congregational Church, in Providence, R.I. Providence: R.I. Printing, 1876. 39p. RHi. +
    Includes historical sketch. 1894 ed. also contains historical notes.

3450 _____. Twentieth anniversary, Union Congregational Church, Providence, R.I., March 31st, 1891. Providence, 1891. 101p. RHi.

3451 PROVIDENCE, R.I. WATERMAN STREET BAPTIST CHURCH. A brief history of the Waterman Street Baptist Church, Providence; with the articles of faith, church covenant, rules and regulations, and list of members. Providence: Knowles, Anthony, 1857. 34p. RHi. +

3452 PROVIDENCE, R.I. WESTMINSTER CONGREGATIONAL SOCIETY. The exercises at the semi-centennial anniversary of the Westminster Congregational Society, held January 5th and 6th, 1878. Providence: [J. A. & R. A. Reid,] n.d. 134p. RHi. +
    Includes historical address by Augustus Woodbury. Became Westminster Unitarian Society.

3453 _____. Sunday school of the Westminster Congregational Society, fiftieth anniversary, Monday, May 5, 1879. Providence: Printed by the Sunday School, n.d. 12p. RHi.

3454 PROVIDENCE ART CLUB. A heritage of rich tradition. n.p., n.d. [12]p. RP-Harrington.
    Thomas Street (formerly Angell's Lane).

3455 "PROVIDENCE as remembered by two old citizens." PM, 32 (1920), 115-118.

3456 PROVIDENCE ATHENAEUM (library). Catalogue of the library of the Providence Athenaeum, to which are prefixed the charter, constitution and bylaws, and an historical sketch of the institution. Providence: Knowles, Anthony, 1853. xxxiv, 557p. RHi. +

3457 "THE PROVIDENCE Athenaeum: for over a half-century a customer of this company." Netopian, 5 (Oct. 1924), 6-11.
Publication of R.I. Hospital Trust Co.

3458 PROVIDENCE ATHLETIC ASSOCIATION. Souvenir club book of the Providence Athletic Association, Providence, Rhode Island. [Providence,] 1899. 212p. RHi. +
Includes historical sketch.

3459 "PROVIDENCE birthplace of America's jewelry and silverware manufacture." PM, 35 (1923), 393-397.
See also next entry.

3460 "PROVIDENCE birthplace of America's jewelry manufacture." PM, 34 (1922), 181-184.
See also preceding entry.

3461 "PROVIDENCE Board of Trade." PBTJ, 20 (1908), 502-510.
Historical sketch.

3462 "PROVIDENCE Board of Trade: its history recounted, the influence it has exerted, and some account of the Providence men who have been identified with it." PJC, 5 (Mar. 1897), 25-32, 41-42.

3463 "PROVIDENCE Chamber of Commerce: its history recounted, the influence it has exerted, and some account of the Providence men who have been identified with it." PBTJ, 15 (1903), 187-195.

3464 PROVIDENCE COUNTY COURTHOUSE COMMISSION. The Providence County Court House, completed A.D. 1933.... Providence, 1933. 23p. RHi. +
Includes historical background of the project.

3465 PROVIDENCE DAILY JOURNAL (newspaper). [Series of articles marking the fiftieth anniversary of the Rhode Island Society for the Encouragement of Domestic Industry.] (Jan. 19, 20, 1870).

3466 "PROVIDENCE export founded about 1700." PM, 35 (1924), 326-328.
Commerce.

3467 PROVIDENCE FEMALE CHARITABLE SOCIETY. A centennial, the fourth of April, nineteen hundred: notable meeting of the Providence Female Charitable Society. [Providence: Livermore & Knight, 1901.] 7p. RHi.

3468 PROVIDENCE FEMALE MITE SOCIETY. Historical sketch of the Providence Female Mite Society, 1806-1884. Providence: J. A. & R. A. Reid, 1885. 11p. RHi. +
"First missionary society in R.I."

3469 PROVIDENCE INSTITUTION FOR SAVINGS. Ships and shipmasters of old Providence: a brief account of some of the famous merchants, sea captains and ships of the past.... Providence, 1919. 51p. RHi. +

3470 PROVIDENCE JOURNAL (newspaper). Brown University, 1764-1964: a special section. (Sept. 27, 1964). 87p. RHi. +
Includes historical sketches.

3471 _____. A hundred years of the Providence Journal ( July 23, 1929). 24p. RHi. +
Supplement to the newspaper.

3472 _____. RISD centennial: a special section of the Providence Sunday Journal (Mar. 20, 1977). 56p. RHi. +
R.I. School of Design. Includes historical sketches.

3473 _____. Semi-centennial of the Providence Journal, January 3, 1870. Providence: Knowles, Anthony & Danielson, 1870. 20p. RHi. +
From that day's issue of the newspaper.

3474 PROVIDENCE JOURNAL (newspaper). RHODE ISLANDER (Sunday magazine). The Evening Bulletin: a special Bulletin centennial issue (Jan. 27, 1963). 112p. RHi. +
Marking the Providence Evening Bulletin's centennial anniversary.

3475 PROVIDENCE JOURNAL COMPANY. Half a century with the Providence Journal: being a record of the events and associates connected with the past fifty years of the life of Henry R. Davis, secretary of the company. [Providence:] Preston & Rounds, 1904. xiii, 235p. RHi. +

3476 PROVIDENCE MEDICAL ASSOCIATION. History and centennial observance. Providence, 1948. 40p. RHi.
Includes historical sketches of the association and of the Providence City Health Department.

3477 PROVIDENCE MUTUAL FIRE INSURANCE COMPANY. A century and a half of service, 1800-1950. Providence: Akerman-Standard Pr., 1951. 45p. RHi.

3478    PROVIDENCE NATIONAL BANK. The centennial of the Providence National Bank, October 3, A.D. 1891. Providence, 1891. 43p. RHi. +

3479    _____. The Providence National Bank: one hundred and fiftieth anniversary, 1791-1941. Providence: Priv. Print., 1941. 52, xiii p. RHi. +

3480    PROVIDENCE of today: its commerce, trade and industries; with biographical sketches and portraits. [Providence]: Providence Telegram Publishing, 1893. 99p. RHi. +
   Includes historical sketches.

3481    "PROVIDENCE pioneer of cotton manufacture in America." PM, 35 (1923), 185, 187.

3482    PROVIDENCE POLICE ASSOCIATION. Providence and her protectors: being a history of the Providence Police Department and the Police Association from the date of its organization up to the present time. [Providence,] 1908. Unp. RHi.

3483    PROVIDENCE PRESERVATION SOCIETY. Broadway: a Victorian boulevard. Providence, n.d. [13]p. RHi.
   Historical sketches of a number of houses in the neighborhood.

3484    _____. Brown University: a microcosm of American architecture. Providence, 1981. 12p. RHi.

3485    _____. Downtown Providence: commerce in architecture. Providence, 1982. 12p. RHi.
   Historical sketches of many downtown buildings.

3486    _____. Elmwood: a Victorian neighborhood. Providence, 1979. [9]p. RHi.
   Brief historical sketches of a number of buildings and houses.

3487    _____. First street festival, May 16, 1958. [Providence, 1958.] 19p. RHi. +
   This and later "street festival" guides, published 1960, 1962, 1964, 1966, 1968, 1971, 1981, and 1982, contain historical sketches of many Providence streets and historic houses.

3488    _____. A mile of history in Providence, R.I.: Benefit Street. Providence, n.d. [10]p. RHi.
   Historical map.

3489    _____. Old buildings--new uses: a festival of re-cycled space. Providence, Rhode Island, October 4th and 5th, 1975. [Providence, 1975.] 22p. RP.
   Includes histories of a number of buildings preserved through adaptive use.

3490    PROVIDENCE PUBLIC LIBRARY. The history and present needs of the Providence Public Library. n.p., [1926?]. 27p. RHi. +

3491    _____. The new building of the Providence Public Library: exercises at the opening of the new building, March 15, 1900, with description of the building. Providence: Snow & Farnham, 1901. 60p. RHi. +
   Includes historical sketch.

3492    "THE PROVIDENCE Tippecanoe Club." RIH, 6 (1947), 97-98.
   Whig supporters of presidential candidate William Henry Harrison (1840).

3493    PROVIDENCE TYPOGRAPHICAL UNION, NO. 33. Printers and printing in Providence, 1762-1907.... [Providence,] 1907. 108, xcviii p. RHi. +

3494    PROVIDENCE UNION NATIONAL BANK AND TRUST COMPANY. Providence Union National Bank and Trust Company opens its newest addition, 35 Weybosset Street. n.p., 1951. [28]p. RHi. +
   Historical commentary by William Greene Roelker and Clarkson A. Collins III concerning the bank's murals. Painted by R. H. Ives Gammell and James Munroe Hewlett, the murals depicted scenes in Providence and events in R.I. history.

3495    PROVIDENCE VISITOR (newspaper). Providence College, 50th anniversary, 1919-1969. Special ed. (Sept. 19, 1969). 48p. RPD-H.

3496    "...PUBLIC eating in Providence: that which is now and that which has been...." Providence Journal (Sept. 11, 1876).
   Lengthy article on the history of restaurants in Providence.

3497    RACKLE, OSCAR W., and JAY BARRY. "When basketball was very young at Brown." BrAlumMo, 68 (Mar. 1968), 22-24.

3498    RAE, JOHN BELL. "The great suffrage parade." RIH, 1 (1942), 90-94.
   1841.

3499    RAMMELKAMP, JULIAN. "The Providence Negro community, 1820-1842." RIH, 7 (1948), 20-33.

3500    RANDALL, GEORGE M. Address delivered on the celebration of the centennial anniversary of St. John's Lodge, No. 2, and the Festival of St. John the Baptist, Providence, R.I., June 24, A.D. 1857.... Providence: St. John's Lodge, No. 2, 1857. 116p. RHi. +
   Freemasons.

3501 RANDALL, JOHN. In God's Providence: the birth of a Catholic charismatic parish. Locust Valley, N.Y.: Living Flame Pr., 1973. 63p. RHi. +
Word of God Prayer Community in Saint Patrick's Parish.

3502 READ, FRANCIS. Westminster Street, Providence, as it was about 1824. Providence: R.I. Historical Society, 1917. [15]p. RHi. +
Drawings made about that date.

3503 REDFIELD, W. C. "Reply to Dr. Hare's further objections relating to whirlwind storms; with some evidence of the whirling action of the Providence tornado of August, 1838." American Journal of Science and Arts, 43 (1842), 301-329.
Refers to entry 3081.

3504 REILLY, HENRY F. "From tavern table to automation." RIer (Oct. 16, 1960), 4-6, 8-9.
Providence post offices.

3505 _____. "Lifetime in a lunchroom." RIer (Mar. 11, 1962), 48, 50, 52-53.
Downtown eating places.

3506 _____. "Telephone grew up fast in Providence." RIer (Apr. 5, 1959), 6-9.
Early improvements by Brown Univ. scientists.

3507 _____. "Where LaSalle grew up." RIer (May 8, 1960), 13-15.
LaSalle Academy's old site on Fountain St.

3508 REILLY, JAMES F. "The Providence Abolition Society." RIH, 21 (1962), 33-48.

3509 "RELIGIOUS conditions in Providence." PM, 26 (1914), 553-560.
Church history.

3510 "RESERVOIR Avenue Cemetery." RIJHN, 1 (1955), 244-261.
Jewish cemetery. Includes burial records.

3511 REYNOLDS, BILL. "God must be a Dominican." RIer (Jan. 11, 1976), 4-5, 7.
Providence College basketball.

3512 _____. "The oldest black men's club-- maybe." RIer (June 11, 1978), 19-23.
Irreproachable Beneficial Association.

3513 _____. "The sandlot heroes." RIer (Aug. 8, 1982), 8-9.
Black baseball teams in the 1930s.

3514 _____. "Thank you, ladies of Miriam's Lodge." RIer (Apr. 25, 1976), 18-20, 23-24.
Miriam Hospital and the Miriam Hospital Association.

3515 REYNOLDS, HORACE. A Providence episode in the Irish literary renaissance. Providence: Study Hill Club, 1929. 39p. RHi. +
William Butler Yeats, Katharine Tynan, et al., as contributors to the Providence Journal.

3516 REYNOLDS, MARY HEWES. John Brown House: guiding manual. Providence: R.I. Historical Society, 1976. 52p. RHi.
Includes historical information on the house and its inhabitants.

3517 RHEA, JAMES N. "A young school with old ideas." RIer (June 8, 1980), 16-17, 19, 22.
Saint Dunstan's Day School.

3518 RHODE ISLAND. HISTORICAL PRESERVATION COMMISSION. Downtown Providence: statewide preservation report P-P-5. [Providence,] 1981. v, 74p. RHi.
Author: William McKenzie Woodward.

3519 _____. Elmwood, Providence: statewide preservation report P-P-3. Providence, 1979. vi, 61p. RHi.
Author: Robert O. Christensen.

3520 _____. Providence industrial sites: statewide historical preservation report P-P-6. Providence, 1981. vi, 62p. RHi.
Author: Lisa C. Link.

3521 _____. Smith Hill, Providence: statewide historical preservation report P-P-4. Providence, 1980. vi, 46p. RHi.
Author: William McKenzie Woodward.

3522 _____. South Providence, Providence: statewide preservation report P-P-2. RHi. Providence, 1978. vi, 82p. RHi. +
Author: Leslie J. Vollmert.

3523 _____. The West Side, Providence: statewide preservation report P-P-1. [Providence,] 1976. vi, 61p. RHi. +
Authors: James H. Gibbs, Pamela Kennedy.

3524 RHODE ISLAND BUSINESS MEN'S ASSOCIATION. [Manual,] 1890-1900. [Providence: Journal of Commerce, 1900.] 117p. RHi. +
Includes "The city of Providence: how it began and how it grew," by Robert Grieve. Other eds., 1907, 1912.

3525    RHODE ISLAND HISTORICAL SOCIETY.
Providence, from provincial village to
prosperous port:  lectures presented at the
First Annual Forum on Rhode Island History,
January, 1975, Providence, R.I., sponsored
by the Rhode Island Historical Society and
the Providence Preservation Society.  Linda
Lotridge Levin, ed.  Providence, 1978.  x,
86p.  RHi. +

3526    RHODE Island Historical Society,
incorporated 1822.  n.p., [1910?].  14p.
RHi. +
        Historical sketch.

3527    RHODE Island Historical Society Museum,
illustrating the history of the state.
Providence:  Standard Printing, 1916.  32p.
RHi. +

3528    RHODE Island Historical Society:  sketch of
its history, with list of papers read at its
stated meetings.  Providence:  Snow &
Farnham, 1890.  37p.  RHi. +
        Reprinted from RIHSPr (1889-1890), 51-85.

3529    RHODE ISLAND HOSPITAL, PROVIDENCE.  Account
of an institution which for over half a
century has been consecrated to the care of
the injured, the healing of the sick, the
relief of human suffering, and the saving of
human life.  Providence, 1923.  58p.  RHi.

3530    RHODE ISLAND HOSPITAL, PROVIDENCE.  NURSES
ALUMNAE ASSOCIATION.  Historical sketch of
the Rhode Island Hospital Training School
for Nurses.  Providence, n.d.  62p.  RHi. +
        Includes history of the hospital.

3531    RHODE ISLAND HOSPITAL TRUST COMPANY.  Brown
University:  a brief historical sketch of
one of our oldest customers.  [Providence,
1924.]  7p.  RPB. +
        Reprinted from the banking company's
magazine, Netopian, 5 (June 1924).

3532    _____.  How this bank got its name.
Providence, 1972.  8p.  RHi.

3533    _____.  The Rhode Island Hospital Trust
Company:  its history, resources and
relations with Brown University.
Providence, 1914.  [24]p.  RHi. +

3534    RHODE Island on Lovecraft.  Donald M. Grant
and Thomas P. Hadley, eds.  Providence:
Grant-Hadley, 1945.  26p.  RHi. +
        Impressions of author H. P. Lovecraft, of
Providence.

3535    RHODE ISLAND SCHOOL OF DESIGN.  MUSEUM OF
ART.  Edward Mitchell Bannister, 1828-1901,
Providence artist:  an exhibition organized
by the Museum of Art, Rhode Island School of
Design, for the Museum of African Art,
Frederick Douglass Institute, Washington,
D.C.  Providence, March 23-April 3, 1966.
[Providence? 1966?]  [14]p.  MB.
        Black landscape painter.  Text by Daniel
Robbins.

3536    RHODE ISLAND STATE NORMAL SCHOOL.  The
dedication of the State Normal School
building, Providence, R.I., on Thursday,
January 23, 1879.  Providence:  E. L.
Freeman, 1879.  66p.  RHi. +
        Includes address by Augustus Woodbury on
the early history of the school, which later
became R.I. College.

3537    RICHARDS, CHARLES AUGUSTUS LEWIS.  The
eternal gospel:  a sermon preached in the
Beneficent Congregational Church on the
seventy-fifth anniversary of the founding of
the Rhode Island Bible Society.  Providence:
Tibbitts & Preston, 1888.  20p. +
        Includes history of the society.

3538    _____.  A sermon on the one hundred and
seventy-fifth anniversary of the founding of
Saint John's Church in Providence,
preached...on the following Sunday, June 13,
1897.  [Providence:  Standard Printing,
1897.]  31p.  RHi. +
        Episcopal.

3539    RIDER, SIDNEY S.  "Annihilation of the claim
for Richard Scott to be the author of the
first compact of government for Providence."
BN, 22 (1905), 105-111.
        See also BN, 5 (1905), 193-198.

3540    _____.  "The Board of Trade Building the
first cotton mill in Rhode Island; some
notes on methods in the olden time, used in
that industry."  BTJ, 1 (Jan. 1810), 29-30.

3541    _____.  "Concerning the alleged baptism of
Roger Williams by Holliman."  BN, 13 (1896),
121-125.
        In Providence (1639).

3542    _____.  "The first (1762) and the second
(1764) printing presses established in
Providence and their earliest product."  BN,
31 (1914), 169-174.

3543    _____.  The forgeries connected with the
deed given by the sachems Canonicus and
Miantinomi to Roger Williams on the land on
which the town of Providence was planted.
Providence:  Sidney S. Rider, 1896.  vi,
128p.  RHi. +
        See also entry 3267.

3544 RIDER, SIDNEY S. "A glimpse of the commerce of Providence a hundred years ago." BTJ, 1 (Nov. 1889), 10, 12, (Dec. 1889), 8.

3545 _____. "Historical notes concerning the transmission of the town of Providence to a city." BN, 31 (1914), 121-123.
1832.

3546 _____. "The history of two books, published here in Providence in 1765, now among the rarest specimens in American literature." BN, 28 (1911), 25-30.
Both were by Timothy Allen: The main point, or saving faith distinghished from counterfeits; and Answer to Pilate's question (what is truth?).

3547 _____. "How men have used a natural creation--coal--to rob the Providence people of money for the last 45 years." BN, 22 (1905), 73-74.
Fluctuating prices.

3548 _____. "The Mantons in Providence, 1840-1848, and Bohuszewicz." BN, 7 (1904), 49-53.
Author Felix Paul Wierzbicki, a Polish exile who lived in Providence for a time, modeled characters in his book, The ideal man (1841), after the Manton family of Providence. He learned about them through a mutual friend, music teacher and composer Edward B. Bohuszewicz, another Polish exile living in the city.

3549 _____. "Notes on the grave of Roger Williams." BN, 24 (1907), 57-64.

3550 _____. "An old almanack with a diary." BN, 11 (1894), 133-134.
1797 almanac, containing manuscript diary entries.

3551 _____. "The one hundred and first anniversary of the September gale of 1815." BN, 33 (1916), 153-160.
Historical sketch.

3552 _____. "The origin of the name Westminster as applied to a street in Providence and some local history connected therewith." BN, 22 (1905), 57-61.

3553 _____. "The place commonly called Goatom." BN, 21 (1904), 17-20.
17th-century place name.

3554 _____. "A Rhode Island fugitive slave case in 1819." BN, 11 (1894), 49-50.
In Providence.

3555 _____. "Something about banks and banking in Providence from 1889 to 1898." BN, 15 (1898), 153-156.

3556 _____. "Street symbol signs." BN, 8 (1891), 121-124.

3557 _____. "The terrible case of Ellen Cosgrove in the Rhode Island courts." BN, 15 (1898), 97-101.
She lost her house and land on Gano Street as a result of a lawsuit (ca. 1890).

3558 _____. "The true date of the founding of Providence." BN, 3 (1886), 127-128.

3559 _____. "Waubosset Plain." BN, 33 (1916), 73.
Place name in early Providence history, now preserved in the name Weybosset Street.

3560 _____. "William White: the first bricklayer in Providence." BN, 15 (1898), 73-74.

3561 RIGGS, DOUGLAS R. "Butler Hospital: at age 125, is it too old to go where the action is?" RIer (May 18, 1969), 10-12, 15-16, 19.
Pioneering mental hospital.

3562 _____. "The Gilbane Building Company: a brother act that's tough to top." RIer (Oct. 16, 1966), 8-12, 14, 16-17, 19.

3563 _____. "The Gorham Corporation: born with a silver spoon in its hat." RIer (Jan. 22, 1967), 5-8.
Silverware manufacturer.

3564 _____. "It all started on Cheapside; now it's the oldest store in the country." RIer (May 8, 1966), 13-14, 16, 18, 20-22, 25-27.
B. H. Gladding Co.

3565 RING, BETTY. "The Balch School in Providence, Rhode Island." Antiques, 107 (1975), 660-671.
Samplers and pictorial embroideries made by students of Miss Mary Balch's Academy: "the largest group of American schoolgirl needlework that may be confidently attributed to a specific school."

3566 _____. "Peter Grinnell and Son: merchant-craftsmen of Providence, Rhode Island." Antiques, 117 (1980), 212-220.
Early-19th-century looking-glass merchants and frame makers.

3567 ROBSON, J. MICHAEL. "Rah, rah, Brunonia, rah, rah...(aw, the hell with it)." RIer (Sept. 20, 1970), 34-35, 37.
Brown Univ. football.

3568 ROCK, R. W. "The growth and progress of the city of Providence." BTJ, 1 (Nov. 1889), 6-7, (Dec. 1889), 6-7, (Mar. 1890), 12; 2 (1891), 92, 94.

3569 Providence

3569 ROCK, R. W. "Providence public schools."
BTJ, 1 (Dec. 1889), 12, (Jan. 1890), 10, 12.

3570 ROELKER, WILLIAM GREENE. "The Browns and
Brown University." BrAlumMo, 49 (Dec.
1948), 3-8.
Brown family.

3571 _____. Francis Wayland: a neglected
pioneer of higher education. Worcester,
Mass.: American Antiquarian Society, 1944.
54p. RHi. +
Includes his presidency of Brown Univ.

3572 _____. "Francis Wayland: president of
Brown University and citizen of Providence."
RIHSC, 32 (1939), 33-55.

3573 _____. "The merger of the two oldest banks
in Providence." RIH, 4 (1945), 107-114.
Providence National Bank and Blackstone
Canal National Bank.

3574 _____, and CLARKSON A. COLLINS III. One
hundred fifty years of Providence Washington
Insurance Company, 1799-1949. Providence:
Providence Washington Insurance Company,
1949. xii, 153p. RHi. +

3575 ROGER WILLIAMS MONUMENT ASSOCIATION,
PROVIDENCE. Historical sketch of the
progress of the Roger Williams Monument
Association, with an appeal to the public in
behalf thereof. Providence: A. Crawford
Greene, 1867. 16p. RHi. +

3576 ROGERS, HORATIO. Oration...delivered at the
laying of the corner stone of the new City
Hall, June 24, 1875. Providence: Priv.
Print., 1875. 20p. RHi. +

3577 _____. Private libraries of Providence,
with a preliminary essay on the love of
books. Providence: Sidney S. Rider, 1878.
iv, 255p. RHi. +

3578 ROOT, JAMES PIERCE. "Pages from the early
records of Providence and the family history
of Mercy Williams." NHM, 3 (1882), 112-130.
Mercy Williams Waterman, youngest daughter
of Roger Williams.

3579 ROSEN, BENTON H. "As the Gentiles saw it:
some observations on the Providence Jewish
community, circa 1909." RIJHN, 6 (1971),
76-80.

3580 _____. "The Providence Conservative
synagogue: Temple Beth-Israel." RIJHN, 5
(1967), 81-99.

3581 ROSENFELD, ALVIN H. "Whitman and the
Providence literati." Books at Brown, 24
(1971), 82-106.
Walt Whitman.

3582 RUBINSTEIN, LOUIS BARUCH. A centennial
history of Redwood Lodge, Number 35, A.F.
& A.M., in the Grand Jurisdiction of Rhode
Island. n.p., [1978?]. xiii, 144p. RHi.

3583 RUGG, HENRY W. An historical discourse
delivered October 29, 1899, the fiftieth
anniversary of the instituting of the Second
Universalist Church, now the Church of
Christ the Mediator, Providence, Rhode
Island.... Providence: E. L. Freeman,
1899. 52p. RHi. +

3584 ST. ARMAND, BARTON L. "Facts in the case of
H. P. Lovecraft." RIH, 31 (1972), 3-19.
Influence of his Providence upbringing on
the author's work.

3585 SAINT JOSEPH'S HOSPITAL, PROVIDENCE.
Official souvenir of the St. Joseph's
Hospital, containing a complete history from
its inception, together with the second
annual report of physicians and surgeons,
etc., 1894. Providence: F. J. Flanigan,
1894. 128p. RHi.

3586 _____. St. Joseph's Hospital dedication
days: dedication day dinner, Sheraton
Biltmore Hotel, Providence, Rhode Island,
Saturday evening, June 26th at 7:30 p.m.;
dedication of Bishop William E. Stang
Building, St. Joseph's Hospital, Sunday,
June 27th at 2 p.m. [Providence, 1965.]
[103]p. RP.
Includes historical sketch.

3587 SAINT MARY'S ORPHANAGE, PROVIDENCE. A brief
historical sketch (with illustrations) of
the infants' department in connection with
the Saint Mary's Orphanage, Providence,
R.I., established May 17th, 1901, by the
Right Rev. Thos. March Clark....
Providence: Franklin Pr., 1903. 33p. RHi.

3588 SAMSON, HENRY T. The Providence World War
Memorial. Providence: Akerman-Standard,
[1930]. 16p. RHi. +

3589 SCARBOROUGH, C. S. "The old taverns of
Providence: their relations to the history
and business of the town." NHR, 8 (1890),
53-68.

3590 SCHACHT, ROBERT H., JR. A commemorative
sermon on the ministers of the First
Congregational Church, Unitarian, in the
city of Providence, Rhode Island....
Providence: First Congregational Society,
1949. 23p. RHi. +
Became First Unitarian Church.

3591 SCOTT, JOHN FRANK. An historical sermon...on the occasion of the two hundredth anniversary of the foundation of St. John's Church in Providence, St. Barnabas Day, June 11, 1922. n.p., n.d. [7]p. MWA.
Episcopal.

3592 SEGAL, BERYL. "Congregation Sons of Zion, Providence, Rhode Island: the Orms Street Synagogue." RIJHN, 4 (1965), 239-277.

3593 _____. Jewish education in Greater Providence: 25th annual meeting of the Bureau of Jewish Education of Rhode Island, June 8, 1977.... Providence: Bureau of Jewish Education of R.I., 1977. 19p. RPJ.
Historical.

3594 _____. "Jewish schools and teachers in metropolitan Providence: the first century." RIJHN, 7 (1977), 410-419.

3595 _____. Know your community: the story of the Jewish institutions and agencies of Greater Providence; a manual for school and home. Providence: Bureau of Jewish Education, Jewish Federation of Rhode Island, 1976. 67p. RHi.

3596 _____. "The Third Seder and the Passover Journals." RIJHN, 8 (1979), 55-61.
Zionist forum and publications.

3597 _____, and SEEBERT J. GOLDOWSKY. "James Jacobs, early Jewish merchant of Providence, Rhode Island." RIJHN, 7 (1978), 461-170.

3598 SEYBOLT, ROBERT FRANCIS. "The second commencement at Brown University." RIHSC, 22 (1929), 72-74.

3599 SHADE, WILLIAM G. "The 'working class' and educational reform in early America: the case of Providence, Rhode Island." The Historian, 39 (1976), 1-23.
19th century.

3600 SHARPE, HENRY DEXTER. Joseph R. Brown, mechanic, and the beginnings of Brown & Sharpe. N.Y.: Newcomen Society, 1949. 32p. RHi. +
Machinery manufacturer.

3601 SHAW, JAMES, JR. Historical sketch of the Sunday School of the First Congregational Society: an address...on the last night in the old chapel, Tuesday, April 10, 1877. Providence: E. A. Johnson, 1884. 39p. RHi. +

3602 SHERMAN, CLARENCE E. The Providence Public Library: an experiment in enlightenment. Providence: Priv. Print., [1937]. 57p. RHi. +

3603 SHERMAN, STUART C. The first ninety years of the Providence Public Library, 1878-1968. Providence: Priv. Print., 1968. 35p. RHi. +

3604 _____. The Providence Public Library: a century of service, 1878-1978. Providence: Providence Public Library, 1978. 39p. RHi. +

3605 SHORE, DEBRA. "An astonishing decade." BrAlumMo, 80 (June 1980), 10-23.
The 1970s at Brown Univ.

3606 _____. "From Babylon to Brown: the Department of the History of Mathematics." BrAlumMo, 79 (1979), 14-23.
Includes historical sketch of the department.

3607 A SHORT history of the African Union Meeting and School-house, erected in Providence (R.I.) in the years 1819, '20, '21; with rules for its future government. Providence: Brown & Danforth, 1821. 32p. RHi. +

3608 SILBERT, WILLIAM G., JR. The 100th anniversary historical sketch of the First Presbyterian Church in the city of Providence, Rhode Island. Providence, 1972. 81, [44]p. RHi. +

3609 "SILVER and silver plate." Harper's, 37 (1868), 433-448.
Gorham Co., Providence.

3610 SIMISTER, FLORENCE PARKER. The first hundred years. Providence: Rhode Island Hospital Trust Company, 1967. 152p. RHi. +
History of the R.I. Hospital Trust Co. (bank).

3611 _____. "Lively lore and legends." RIer (Aug. 29, 1965), 38-39.
Westminster Street.

3612 _____. Old Stone Bank, 1819-1969. n.p., n.d. [7]p. RP.
Providence Institution for Savings.

3613 _____. Streets of the city: an anecdotal history of Providence. Providence: Mowbray, 1968. xi, 164p. RHi. +

3614 SISTERHOOD of the Holy Nativity, Providence, R.I. n.p., [1893?] 14p. RPB. +
Reprinted from The Churchman (Apr. 29, 1893).

3615 SISTERS OF MERCY. PROVIDENCE. The golden jubilee, Saint Francis Xavier's Convent of Mercy, Providence, Rhode Island. [Providence, 1901.] [67]p. RP.

3616 Providence

3616 SISTERS OF MERCY. PROVIDENCE. A little sketch of the work of the Sisters of Mercy in Providence, Rhode Island, from 1851 to 1893. Providence: J. A. & R. A. Reid, 1893. 298p. RHi. +

3617 _____. Seventy-five years in the passing with the Sisters of Mercy, Providence, Rhode Island, 1851-1926. Providence: Providence Visitor Pr., [1926]. vi, 203p. RHi.
See also entry 1001.

3618 A SKETCH of the rise and progress of Grace Church, Providence, compiled by a layman, for the Providence Journal, 1857. n.p., n.d. [4]p. RHi. +
Episcopal.

3619 SLADE, WILLIAM ADAMS. "Early statesmen of Brown." BrAlumMo, 7 (1907), 115-118.
Alumni in politics and government.

3620 [SLATER, ALPHEUS B.] The stamps of the Providence, R.I., postmaster, 1846-1847. Providence: Haley & Sykes, 1930. 104p. RHi. +

3621 SMITH, CHARLES MORRIS. Grace Church in Providence, Rhode Island: a brief summary of the first one hundred years. n.p., 1969. 14p. RP-Harrington.
Episcopal.

3622 SMITH, FRANCIS. A discourse delivered in the Fourth Baptist Meeting-house, Providence, on the re-opening of the house, after its enlargement, October 20, 1850. Providence: John F. Moore, 1851. 22p. RHi. +

3623 SMITH, HENRY H. "Elmhurst." RIer (June 7, 1953), 12-14, 16.
Convent of the Sacred Heart, "one of the oldest girls' schools in R.I."

3624 _____. "The old Howard buildings." RIer (Jan. 6, 1957), 8, 10, 12, 15.

3625 _____. "Reynolds and Duggan threw and threw." RIer (June 12, 1949), 12-14.
20-inning baseball game between Brown Univ. and Providence College in 1924.

3626 SMITH, JOSEPH. "The Providence City Health Department." RIMJ, 31 (1948), 34-36.

3627 SMITH-HOLDEN, INC. (dental supply house). A century of service, 1850-1950: being a brief and interesting history of a successful business, of its pioneer days while a new profession was being born, and its service to that profession through the years that have followed. Nora Scott, comp. Providence, n.d. 30p. RHi.

3628 SNOW, EDWIN M. History of the Asiatic cholera in Providence. n.p., 1832. 8p. RHi. +
From the Providence Journal.

3629 _____. "History of yellow fever in Providence, in years 1797, 1800, 1803, 1805, 1820." (1857) Providence Journal, Sept. 23, 1878.
Lengthy historical article.

3630 SPEAR, CARLTON. "He built first R.I. commercial radio station." RIer (Jan. 12, 1969), 4-5.
Station WEAN, Providence.

3631 SPENCER, ANNA GARLIN. The history of the Bell Street Chapel movement, May, 1888, to July, 1902. Providence: Robert Grieve, 1903. 208p. RHi. +
Nondemoninational.

3632 SPENCER, PAUL J. "Rhode Island's oldest hospital: Butler Hospital, 1844-1944." RIMJ, 27 (1944), 401, 431.
Psychiatric hospital.

3633 SPENGLER, J. J. "Fertility in Providence, Rhode Island, 1856-1929." American Journal of Sociology, 38 (1932), 377-397.

3634 SPICER, WILLIAM A. The high school boys of the Tenth R.I. Regiment, with a roll of teachers and students of the Providence High School, who served in the Army or Navy of the United States during the Rebellion. Providence: N. Bangs Williams, 1882. 83p. RHi. +
Civil War. Includes historical background of enlistment. This entry was part of a series of pamphlets entitled Personal narratives of events of the War of the Rebellion: being papers read before the R.I. Soldiers and Sailors Historical Society. Most titles in the series have been excluded here, because their subject matter is outside the editorial guidelines of this bibliography.

3635 STAPLES, CARLTON A. An historical discourse delivered on the one hundred and fiftieth anniversary of the organization of the First Congregational Church in Providence, R.I., and the ordination of Josiah Cotton, the first minister; Sunday evening, November 1st, 1878. Providence: Sidney S. Rider, 1879. 39p. RHi. +

3636 _____. A sermon preached on the sixtieth anniversary of the dedication of the First Congregational Meeting House, in Providence, October 29th, 1876. Providence: J. A. & R. A. Reid, 1876. 24p. RHi.

3637 STAPLES, WILLIAM R. Annals of the town of Providence, from its first settlement, to the organization of the city government in June, 1832. Providence: Knowles & Vose, 1843. vi, 670p. RHi. +

3638 STARKWEATHER AND SHEPLEY, INC. (insurance brokers). 100 years, a century of experience: Starkweather & Shepley, Inc.; 1979 appointment calendar. n.p., [1978]. [25]p. RHi.
Calendar includes historical sketches of the company.

3639 STEARNS, A. WARREN. "Isaac Ray: psychiatrist and pioneer in forensic psychiatry." American Journal of Psychiatry, 101 (1945), 573-585.
First superintendent of Butler Hospital.

3640 "THE STEPHEN Hopkins House." RIHSC, 23 (1930), 54-56.
Signed N.M.I.

3641 STILLWELL, MARGARET BINGHAM. The Annmary Brown Memorial: a book lover's shrine. (1925) Providence: Priv. Print. for Eugene A. Clauss, 1940. 26p. RHi. +
A library at Brown Univ.

3642 _____. The early days of the John Carter Brown Library: an excerpt from the manuscript, Librarians are human; impressions and experiences in the rare-book world, 1907-1970. [Providence, 1970.] 48p. RPB.
Rare-book library at Brown Univ.

3643 _____. "A man who dared to stand alone: a sidelight of the Dorr Rebellion, 1842-1844." RIH, 36 (1977), 35-41.
Abraham Hermon Stillwell, of Providence.

3644 _____. The pageant of Benefit Street down through the years. Providence: Akerman-Standard Pr., 1945. 144p. RHi. +

3645 _____. While Benefit Street was young. Providence: Akerman-Standard Pr., 1943. 38p. RHi. +

3646 STOKES, HOWARD KEMBLE. The finances and administration of Providence. Baltimore: Johns Hopkins Pr., 1903. vii, 464p. RHi. +

3647 STOLLER, LEO. "Christopher A. Greene, Rhode Island transcendentalist." RIH, 22 (1963), 97-111, 114-116.
Providence resident.

3648 STONE, ALFRED. "Alpheus Morse." American Architect and Building News, 42 (1893), 126-127.
Providence architect.

3649 _____. "Edmund R. Willson, 1859-1906." American Architect and Building News, 91 (1907), 67-72.
Providence architect.

3650 _____. The First Congregational Church and its meeting houses; with suggestions as to memorial windows and tablets. Providence: E. A. Johnson, 1897. 16p. RHi. +

3651 STONE, DEBORAH. "The absent-bodied professor." Yankee, 39 (Nov. 1975), 112-113, 156, 159.
Fictitious Professor Josiah S. Carberry, a Brown Univ. tradition.

3652 STONE, EDWIN MARTIN. The architect & monetarian: a brief memoir of Thomas Alexander Tefft.... Providence: S. S. Rider and Brother, 1869. 64p. RHi. +
Well-known Providence architect, who was also an advocate of a universal currency.

3653 _____. A century of education: being a concise history of the rise and progress of the public schools of the city of Providence. Providence: Providence Pr., 1876. 84p. RHi. +

3654 _____. Mechanics festival: an account of the seventy-first anniversary of the Providence Association of Mechanics and Manufacturers, held in Howard Hall, on Monday evening, February 28, 1860, together with a sketch of the early history of the association.... Providence: Knowles, Anthony, 1860. 119p. RHi. +

3655 _____. A quarter-century review: being the twenty-fifth annual report of the Ministry at Large, in the city of Providence, presented and read at a public meeting held in the First Congregational Church, Sunday evening, January 20th, 1867. Providence: Knowles, Anthony, 1867. 51p. RHi. +
Home missions (Unitarian).

3656 "THE STORY of a successful school." PBTJ, 25 (1913), 219-221, 224.
Bryant & Stratton Business College, Providence (now Bryant College, Smithfield).

3657 STREET CAR MUTUAL BENEFIT ASSOCIATION, PROVIDENCE. Official souvenir history of the Street Car Mutual Benefit Association, Providence, Rhode Island.... Providence: Journal of Commerce, n.d. 64p. RHi.

3658 Providence

3658 SULLIVAN, JOHN F., and VINCENT F. KIENBERGER. Historical sketch of St. Ann's Italian Parish, Providence, R.I....on the occasion of the silver jubilee of its pastor, the Right Reverend Anthony Bove, 1900-1925. n.p., n.d. 72p. RHi.
Roman Catholic. Text in English and Italian.

3659 SWAN, BRADFORD FULLER. "Benefit Street's temple of learning." RIer (Apr. 18, 1971), 10-12.
Providence Athenaeum.

3660 _____. "The city seal of the city of Providence." RIH, 1 (1942), 5-17.

3661 _____. "Dateline: Providence, Sept. '38." RIY (1971), H224-H228.
1938 hurricane.

3662 _____. "Eleven years to fame." RIer (Oct. 7, 1973), 28-30, 32.
Trinity Square Repertory Company.

3663 _____. Gregory Dexter of London and New England, 1610-1700. Rochester, N.Y.: Printing House of L. Hart, 1949. xiii, 115p. RPB. +
Civic, religious, and business leader of early Providence.

3664 _____. "Keeping up with the times for 150 years." RIer (Apr. 16, 1972), 7-8, 10, 12-13.
R.I. Historical Society.

3665 _____. "Moses Brown: the paradoxes of his life." RIer (Feb. 4, 1962), 8-11.

3666 _____. "A new document casts new light on Roger Williams and the Indians." RIer (Nov. 23, 1969), 12-15.
Document relating to the time of an Indian attack on Providence during King Philip's War (1676).

3667 _____. "Recognition at last for John Holden Greene." RIer (May 14, 1972), 32-35, 37.
19th-century architect.

3668 _____. The Rev. Thomas James, the Civil Compact and the Town Evidence. Providence: Roger Williams Pr., 1963. [15]p. RHi.
Contends that the Civil Compact (1638) as well as a significant addendum to the Town Evidence (1638) are in the hand of James. Authorship has been disputed. See also entry 3539.

3669 SWAN, MABEL M. "John Holden Greene, architect." Antiques, 52 (1947), 24-27.

3670 SWAN POINT CEMETERY, PROVIDENCE. Swan Point Cemetery, Providence, R.I. n.p., [1834?]. 57p. RHi.

3671 TAFT, HARRISON SOUTHWICK. "John Brown's mansion house on the hill." RIHSC, 34 (1941), 107-112.

3672 TANNER, EARL C. "Caribbean ports in the foreign commerce of Providence, 1790-1830." RIH, 14 (1955), 97-108; 15 (1956), 11-20.

3673 _____. "Early 19th century Providence exports to Brazil." RIH, 19 (1960), 89-94.

3674 _____. "Early 19th century Providence exports to the Caribbean." RIH, 19 (1960), 42-49.

3675 _____. "Early 19th century Providence imports from the Caribbean and Brazil." RIH, 24 (1965), 116-128.

3676 _____. "The Latin-American trade of E. Carrington & Co., 1822. RIH, 13 (1954), 33-44, 78-85.

3677 _____. "South American ports in the foreign commerce of Providence." RIH, 16 (1957), 65-78.

3678 TATGE, ROBERT O. "A quarantine quandary: ship fever and yellow fever in Providence, Rhode Island, 1797." American Neptune, 40 (1980), 192-210.

3679 TAYLOR, ROBERT J. "The Providence Franklin Society." RIH, 9 (1950), 73-83, 119-129.
Scientific society.

3680 "TELEGRAPHY in Providence: an outline history of the business since 1848." Providence Journal (May 14, 1877).
Lengthy article.

3681 "TELEPHONY in Providence forty years ago." PM, 31 (1919), 107-108.

3682 TELLER, BARBARA GORELY. "Ceramics in Providence, 1750-1800." Antiques, 94 (1968), 570-577.
Evidence from probate inventories.

3683 THOMAS, DONNA. "The Providence Visitor and nativist issues, 1916-1924." RIH, 38 (1979), 51-62.
Official organ of Diocese of Providence (Roman Catholic).

3684 THOMPSON, MACK E. Moses Brown: reluctant reformer. Chapel Hill, N.C.: Univ. of North Carolina Pr., 1962. viii, 316p. RHi. +

3685 THURBER, FREDERICK B. "Random ramble through downtown in the '90s." RIer (Jan. 26, 1958), 12-14.

3686 "TOURO Cadets and Touro Guards." RIJHN, 2 (1957), 99-103.
    Jewish military and fraternal organizations.

3687 TRICKETT, HOMER L. "Preservation of an historic church." Your Church, 3, No. 3 (1957), 11-12, 36-39.
    First Baptist Church.

3688 TRIPP, RUTH. "Some music made in Providence." RIer (Apr. 17, 1960), 5-7.
    Music writing and publishing in Providence, 1910-1920.

3689 TUCKER, MARK. The centennial sermon, preached before the Beneficent Congregational Church and Society, in Providence, R.I., March 19, A.D. 1843.... Providence: Knowles & Vose, 1845. 84p. RHi. +

3690 U.S. DEPARTMENT OF THE INTERIOR. NATIONAL PARK SERVICE. CULTURAL RESOURCES MANAGEMENT DIVISION. Archaeological resource study: Roger Williams National Memorial, Rhode Island. Washington, 1979. v, 91p. RHi.
    Authors: Susan G. Gibson, Stephen Cole, Peter Thorbahn, Cynthia Wood, Myron Stachiw.

3691 "THE UNITED Train centennial: Rhode Island's response to the 'shot heard round the world' one hundred years ago." Providence Daily Journal (Apr. 23, 1875).
    United Train of Artillery. Lengthy article includes historical oration by Nicholas Van Slyck.

3692 UROFF, MARGARET DICKIE. Becoming a city: from fishing village to manufacturing center. N.Y.: Harcourt, Brace & World, 1968. 154p. RHi. +

3693 VAN HOESEN, HENRY BARTLETT. Brown University Library: the library of the college or university in the English colony of Rhode Island and Providence Plantations in New England in America, 1767-1782. Providence: Priv. Print., [1938]. 96p. RHi. +

3694 VAN SLYCK, R. E. NICHOLAS. Address delivered before Calvary Commandery, Knights Templar, No. 13, Providence, R.I., May 22, A.D. 1885; twenty-fifth anniversary of its charter. Providence: J. A. & R. A. Reid, 1885. 29p. RHi.
    Freemasons.

3695 VAN WYE, EUGENE. "William Hamlin: Providence engraver." RIH, 20 (1961), 33-44.

3696 VOSE, JAMES GARDINER. Commemorative discourses preached in the Beneficent Congregational Church, Providence, R.I., October 18, 1868.... Providence: Beneficent Congregational Church, 1869. 135p. RHi. +

3697 _____. Sketches of Congregationalism in Rhode Island, with special reference to the history of the Beneficent Church. N.Y.: Silver, Burdett, 1894. 236p. RHi. +
    Mainly a history of Beneficent Church.

3698 WALSH, RICHARD A. The centennial history of Saint Edward Church, Providence, Rhode Island, 1874-1974. n.p., 1974. xiv, 242p. RHi. +
    Roman Catholic.

3699 WALTER, DOROTHY C. Lovecraft and Benefit Street. [North Montpelier, Vt.: Driftwind Pr., 1943?] [11]p. RHi. +
    Author H. P. Lovecraft.

3700 WARD, JOHN. "Browne & Sharpe: a long way from that tiny shop on So. Main Street." RIer (June 5, 1966), 8-10, 12, 14, 16-17.
    Browne and Sharpe Mfg. Co.

3701 "WASHINGTON and the College." BrAlumMo, 2 (1901), 133-136.
    George Washington's visit to Brown (1790).

3702 WATKINS, LURA WOODSIDE. "The Providence Flint Glass Company." Antiques, 55 (1949), 190-191.

3703 WATSON, ARTHUR E. Angell's apple orchard, 1774-1929. Providence: Akerman-Standard, [1929?]. 22p. RHi. +
    Construction of meetinghouse of First Baptist Church.

3704 WAX, DAROLD D. "The Browns of Providence and the slaving voyage of the brig Sally, 1764-1765." American Neptune, 32 (1972), 171-179.

3705 WAYLAND, FRANCIS, JR., and H. L. WAYLAND. A memoir of the life and labors of Francis Wayland, D.D., LL.D., late president of Brown University, including selections from his personal reminiscences and correspondence. N.Y.: Sheldon, 1867. 2v. RHi. +

3706 WEEDEN, ANNE TILLINGHAST. Women's college in Brown University: its origin and development. Providence, 1912. 30p. RHi. +
    Pembroke College.

3707 Providence

3707 WEEDEN, HARRIET WOOD. "The good ship
Haidie." RIH, 17 (1958), 57-61.
"Last clipper built in Providence."

3708 WEEDEN, WILLIAM BABCOCK. Early commercial
Providence. Worcester, Mass.: Davis Pr.,
1909. 12p. RHi. +
Reprinted from American Antiquarian
Society, Proceedings, n.s. 19 (1909),
420-429.

3709 _____. Early Oriental commerce in
Providence. Cambridge, Mass.: John Wilson,
1908. 45p. RHi. +
Reprinted from Massachusetts Historical
Society, Proceedings, 3 ser. 1 (1907),
236-278.

3710 "WESTMINSTER Street in ye olde towne days."
PM, 29 (1917), 217-218.

3711 WESTON, FRANK. Rhode Island's Cathedral
Close: a dream fulfilled. n.p., n.d.
[7]p. RHi.
St. John's Cathedral (Episcopal).

3712 WHEELER, ROBERT A. "Fifth Ward Irish:
immigrant mobility in Providence,
1850-1870." RIH, 32 (1973), 53-61.

3713 WHEELER, ROBERT L. "The end of an era."
RIer (May 16, 1948), 12-15.
"...Now the streetcars disappear from
Providence streets."

3714 _____. "Five sons were generals:
Providence Marine Corps of Artillery was
ancestor of the famous Battery A." RIer
(Feb. 10, 1952), 3-7.

3715 _____. "From the one-man balloon up to the
'glory of the skies.'" RIer (Oct. 21,
1951), 3-6.
Allen family, 19th-century balloonists.

3716 _____. "Mr. Low's 'hall' comes down." RIer
(May 30, 1948), 12-15.
Empire Theater, originally Low's Opera
House.

3717 _____. "The old Market House comes to life
again." RIer (Sept. 24, 1950), 13-15.

3718 _____. "Old shadow palaces." RIer (Dec.
25, 1955), 12-13.
Beginnings of motion picture entertainment
in Providence.

3719 _____. "1000 performances 1000." RIer (May
12, 1957), 27, 29-32.
The Players (theatrical group).

3720 _____. "The public's library." RIer (Feb.
28, 1954), 3-6, 8.
Providence Public Library.

3721 _____. "Sprague's company store." RIer
(Jan. 8, 1956), 14-16.
A. & W. Sprague Co.

3722 _____. "Tockwotton House." RIer (Sept. 10,
1950), 20-21.
Onetime landmark in Fox Point: "At first
a fine mansion, then a hotel, then a reform
school of grim memory."

3723 "WHEN was Providence founded?" NHR, 5
(1886), 27-42.
Essays by W. E. Foster, Fred A. Arnold,
Sidney S. Rider, H. T. Drowne, Welcome
Arnold Greene.

3724 WHITAKER, GEORGE W. "Reminiscences of
Providence artists." PM, 26 (1914),
137-139, 207-211.

3725 WHITE, CHARLES E. The Providence fireman,
illustrated.... Providence: E. L. Freeman,
1886. 313p. RHi. +
Includes historical sketch. See also
entry 2945.

3726 WHITTEN, W. W. "The automobile in
Providence." PBTJ, 20 (1908), 227-232, 262,
264.

3727 WILKINS, ESTELLE. "Historic Providence."
Daughters of the American Revolution
Magazine, 98 (1964), 573-575, 630.

3728 WILLARD, GEORGE O. History of the
Providence stage, 1762-1891. Providence:
R.I. News, 1891. 298p. RHi. +
Theater.

3729 WILLIAMS, ALONZO R. "The cable tramway
system of Providence." RIH, 4 (1945),
33-36.

3730 WILSON, ARTHUR E. "Liberty: the Rhode
Island variant." Bulletin of the
Congregational Library, 25 (Winter 1974),
4-12.
Mainly about the influence of Beneficent
Congregational Church, Providence.

3731 _____. Paddy Wilson's meeting-house: being
an account of a genial Irish parson who
shaped a community's culture and life.
Boston: Pilgrim Pr., 1950. vii, 278p.
RHi. +
James Wilson, pastor of Beneficent
Congregational Church.

3732 _____. Weybosset Bridge in Providence
Plantations, 1700-1790.... Boston: Pilgrim
Pr., 1947. xi, 275p. RHi. +
Study of religious life in Providence.

3733 WILSON, DOUGLAS C. "Sorry about that,
Mayor." RIer (Jan. 15, 1967), 11-12, 15.
Statue of Mayor Thomas A. Doyle,
threatened by urban renewal. Includes
historical sketch.

3734 WILSON, EDWIN B., CONSTANCE BENNETT,
MARGARET ALLEN, and JANICE WORCESTER.
"Measles and scarlet fever in Providence,
R.I., 1929-1934, with respect to age and
size of family." American Philosophical
Society, Proceedings, 80 (1939), 357-476.

3735 WILSON, GEORGE G. Town and city government
in Providence. Providence: Tibbitts &
Preston, 1889. 77p. RHi. +

3736 WILSON, JAMES WALTER. "The Jenks Museum of
Brown University." Books at Brown, 22
(1968), 41-57.
Includes historical sketch.

3737 _____. "Joseph Brown, scientist and
architect." RIH, 4 (1945), 67-79, 121-128.
An early trustee of Brown Univ. and
Professor of Experimental Philosophy prior
to his death in 1785.

3738 _____. "The next move." BrAlumMo, 61 (Dec.
1960), 4-8.
Biology Dept., Brown Univ.

3739 _____. The old medical school at Brown
University, 1811-1827. Providence: Brown
Univ., 1968. 39p. RPB.

3740 _____. "The Philophysian (Philophusian)
Society at Brown University (1818-1827)."
Books at Brown, 20 (1965), 41-55.
Scientific society, related to the medical
school.

3741 _____, and DIANA FANE. Brown University as
the land grant college of Rhode Island,
1863-1894. Providence: Brown Univ., 1966.
89p. RHi.
Reprinted from Books at Brown, 21 (1966),
3-74.

3742 _____. "The Metcalf estate." Books at
Brown, 21 (1966), 75-89.
Whiting Metcalf estate, left to Brown
Univ.

3743 WINSHIP, GEORGE PARKER. The John Carter
Brown Library: a history. Providence,
1914. 96p. RHi. +
At Brown Univ.

3744 _____. "The Providence Art Club." PM, 26
(1914), 117-119.

3745 WINSOR, EDWARD. Edwards & Angell: a firm
history. n.p., 1978. i, 99p. RHi. +
Law firm in Providence and N.Y.

3746 WINTERICH, JOHN T. "A love letter to
Providence, R.I." RIer (Apr. 8, 1951),
12-14.

3747 WISBEY, HERBERT A., JR. "Plagiarism by a
prophetess." RIH, 20 (1961), 65-71.
Jemima Wilkinson, the "Universal Friend,"
began her career in R.I. and published her
book, Some considerations, in Providence
(1779).

3748 WOLFE, JULIA W. "The first American straw
hat." National Historical Magazine, 75 (May
1941), 22.
First straw hat made in America,
attributed to Betsy Metcalf of Providence
(1798).

3749 WOODS, ALVA. The historical position of
Brown University: remarks made at the
centennial celebration of the Warren
Association, September 11, 1867.
Providence, 1868. 7p. RHi. +

3750 WOODS, JOHN CARTER BROWN. "John Carter."
RIHSC, 11 (1918), 101-114.
Early Providence printer; publisher of the
Providence Gazette (newspaper).

3751 WORTHINGTON, W. CHESLEY. There's this about
the Providence Art Club.... n.p., [1977?].
24p. RHi.
Includes historical sketch.

3752 WRISTON, BARBARA. "The architecture of
Thomas Tefft." R.I. School of Design,
Museum of Art, Bulletin, 27 (1940), 37-45.

3753 _____. "Thomas Tefft, progressive Rhode
Islander." RIHSC, 34 (1941), 60-61.
Well-known Providence architect and
proponent of a universal currency.

3754 WROTH, LAWRENCE COUNSELMAN. The first
century of the John Carter Brown Library:
a history with a guide to the collections.
Providence: The Associates of the John
Carter Brown Library, 1946. 88p. RHi. +
Brown Univ.

3755 _____. "The first press in Providence: a
study in social development." American
Antiquarian Society, Proceedings, n.s. 51
(1941), 351-383.

3756 _____. The John Carter Brown Library in
Brown University, Providence, Rhode Island.
Providence: Priv. Print., [1936]. 35p.
RHi. +

3757 "YEAR 1900: birth of a magazine."
BrAlumMo, 50 (June 1950), 4-6.
Brown Alumni Monthly.

3758 "THE YELLOW fever in Providence, 1800." NHR, 3 (1884), 136-138.

3759 YOUNG, CHARLES M. A historical retrospect of the First Congregational Society in Providence, R.I., read before the Rhode Island Historical Society, Tuesday, March 23, 1909.... Providence: Women's Alliance of the First Congregational Church, 1910. 35p. RHi. +
Later became First Unitarian Church.

3760 YOUNG LADIES' HIGH SCHOOL, PROVIDENCE. Exercises at the reunion of the Young Ladies' High School in Providence, R.I., February 5th, 1858, with a brief notice of its founder. Providence: George H. Whitney, 1858. 36p. RHi. +

3761 ZUCCARELLI, JOHN G. "The Holy Ghost Parish." The Echo (Mar. 2, 1978), 7; (Mar. 9, 1978), 7; (Mar. 16, 1978), 18; (June 8, 1978), 7.
Roman Catholic. Italian parish.

SEE ALSO entries 179, 230, 252, 277, 365, 393, 419, 447, 460, 466-467, 476, 494, 499, 554, 601, 712, 719, 725, 799, 803, 839, 848, 857, 906, 942, 976, 1042, 1061, 1231-1232, 1236, 1239, 1251, 1255-1256, 1259, 1538, 2554, 3331, 3700, 3794.

RICHMOND (WASHINGTON CO.)

3762 BRAYTON, SUSAN STANTON. "The Stanton Purchase." RIHSC, 28 (1935), 101-110.
1662.

3763 BYRNES, GARRETT D. "The terrible wreck at Richmond Switch." RIer (Jan. 3, 1971), 14-17.
1875 train wreck at what is now Wood River Junction.

3764 HAWKINS, MARION DEWLEY. "The Second Baptist Church of Richmond, Shannock, Rhode Island." Richmond Historical Society, Richmond History, 2, No. 6 (Nov. 1969), 31-32; No. 7 (Dec. 1969), 37-38; No. 10 (Mar. 1970), 50-52; 3, No. 2 (Sept. 1970), 9-10; No. 3 (Oct. 1970), 18-19.

3765 IRISH, JAMES R. Historical sketch of the town of Richmond, from 1747 to 1876, comprising a period of one hundred and twenty-nine years...and delivered July 4th, 1876, at Wood River Grove. Hope Valley: L. W. A. Cole, 1877. 96p. RHi. +

3766 MILLAR, PATRICIA SMITH. "Richmond schools--then and now." Richmond Historical Society, Richmond History, 2, No. 1 (June 1969), 2-3, 6.

3767 RHODE ISLAND. HISTORICAL PRESERVATION COMMISSION. Preliminary survey report: Richmond. Providence, 1977. iv, 35p. RHi.
Authors: Walter Nebiker and Russell Wright.

3768 RICHMOND HISTORICAL SOCIETY. Driftways into the past: local history of the town of Richmond, Rhode Island, as remembered and visualized by members of the Richmond Historical Society and the Richmond Bicentennial Commission. Westerly: Utter, 1977. x, 299p. RHi. +

3769 RIDER, SIDNEY S. "Shannock." BN, 13 (1896), 169-170.
Origin of the place name.

3770 TOOTELL, LUCY RAWLINGS. "Indians in Richmond." Richmond Historical Society, Richmond History, 1, No. 7 (Sept. 1968), 31-32.

SEE ALSO entries 1286, 1341, 1344, 3763.

SCITUATE (PROVIDENCE CO.)

3771 BEAMAN, CHARLES C. An historical address, delivered in Scituate, Rhode Island, July 4th, 1876, at the request of the town authorities. Phenix: Capron & Campbell, 1877. 59, 8p. RHi. +

3772 _____. "Sketches of Scituate." Providence Journal (1854-1855).
Series of at least 18 articles, beginning Sept 28, 1854. Rider Collection, Brown Univ., has installments 1-3, 12 (May 14, 1855), 17 (Aug. 7, 1855).

3773 BOSS, RUTH. "Indian times in Scituate." WRICHSP, 2, No. 1 (1953), [29-32].

3774 BRAYTON, GLADYS W. "Lapham Institute." WRICHSH, 2 (June 1959), [2]; 3 (July 1959), [2], (Aug. 1959), [1].
19th-century Freewill Baptist school.

3775 _____. "The old Battey Meeting House." WRICHSH, 2 (Nov. 1958), [1-2].
Baptist.

3776 A BRIEF history of the organization of the Arkwright & Fiskville Baptist Church. Providence: H. H. Brown, 1839. 8p. RHi. +
Fiskeville Baptist Church.

3777 HARPIN, MATHIAS P. "Scituate raises questions." WRICHSH, 5 (Mar. 1962), [2].
About the legal basis of R.I. state government after the Declaration of Independence and about inequalities in the colonial charter.

Smithfield 3800

3778 HISTORICAL street map, Scituate. William Turner, comp. n.p., [1965]. RNoP.
Folded map with text.

3779 LEYLAND, HERBERT T. "Early years of the Hope Cotton Manufacturing Company." RIH, 25 (1966), 25-32.

3780 McDONALD, JAMES H. "How Chopmist Hill won World War II." RIer (Dec. 6, 1981), 36-38.
Site of a "top-secret, radio-monitoring system."

3781 RAFTER, CORINNE. "Only a memory." WRICHSH, 3 (Sept. 1959), [2].
Village of Rockland, displaced by Scituate Reservoir.

3782 RHODE ISLAND. HISTORICAL PRESERVATION COMMISSION. Preliminary survey report: town of Scituate. Providence, 1980. iv, 70p. RHi.
Author: Walter Nebiker.

3783 [SARKESIAN, BARBARA.] A history of the North Scituate Public Library, incorporated 1906; presented on the occasion of the library's seventy-fifth anniversary, 1981. n.p., 1981. 12p. RJo.

3784 SCITUATE, R.I. JUNIOR/SENIOR HIGH SCHOOL. A history of Scituate, R.I.: being an account of its early settlement and events to the present. [Scituate:] Project Heritage, 1977. iii, 87p. RHi.

3785 SCITUATE REPUBLICAN TOWN COMMITTEE. Scituate, incorporated 1730; named for Scituate, Massachusetts; name of Indian origin. n.p., n.d. 30p. RSc.
Includes historical sketch.

3786 SPENCER, JOSEPHINE P. "Early Scituate." WRICHSH, 12 (May 1969), [2]; (June 1969), [2].

3787 TRAINOR, MARY. "A brief history of Hope Library." WRICHSP, 2, No. 2 (1955), [13-15].

3788 WALKER, CYRUS. The history of Scituate, R.I., by Cyrus Walker; adapted and continued for the Scituate Bicentennial Committee by Hedley Smith.... [Scituate:] Scituate Bicentennial Committee, 1976. 196p. RHi. +

3789 WEST, G. M. Homestead of Lieut. Governor William West, Scituate, Rhode Island; house erected 1775. Chicago Heights, Ill., 1904. [3]p. RHi.

SEE ALSO entries 1236, 1238, 1257.

## SMITHFIELD (PROVIDENCE CO.)

3790 APPLE Valley U.S.A.: in recognition of 250 years. Jeanne M. Tracey, principal author; Thomas W. Hall, Henry P. Shepard, contributing writers. Smithfield: Smithfield 250th Anniversary Committee, 1980. 72p. RSmG.

3791 ARNOLD, FRED A. John Checkley's proposed Parish of Montalto in Smithfield, with genealogical and historical notes on the family of Capt. Joseph Olney, U.S.N. Providence, 1897. 10p. RHi. +
Episcopal.

3792 ARNOLD, JAMES N. The Arnold family of Smithfield. [Smithfield, 1907.] 11p. RHi. +

3793 BURGESS, GIDEON A. "The history of Smithfield." WRICHSP, 1, No. 2 (1949), 6-13.

3794 BYRNES, GARRETT D. "A long trail to the groves of academe." RIer (Apr. 23, 1972), B4-B6, B8.
Bryant College, originally located in Providence and now in Smithfield.

3795 GEORGIAVILLE, R.I. SAINT MICHAEL'S CHURCH. Saint Michael's Church, Georgiaville, Rhode Island: a century of faith and sacrifice, 1875-1975. n.p., n.d. [40]p. RHi.
Roman Catholic.

3796 GREENVILLE, R.I. GREENVILLE BAPTIST CHURCH. First Freewill Baptist Church of Smithfield, Greenville, Rhode Island, 1820-1973: pictorial, history, directory. n.p., n.d. [68]p. RHi.

3797 [HALEY, JOHN WILLIAMS.] The story of old Smithfield. Providence: "Old Stone Bank," 1931. 10p. RHi.
This entry was part of the "Old Stone Bank" historical pamphlet series. See note, entry 432.

3798 HOLST, MONTEREY L. "Zachariah Allen, pioneer in applied silviculture." Journal of Forestry, 44 (1946), 507-508.
Management of his forest land in Smithfield (1820-1877).

3799 PHENIX NATIONAL BANK. ...Esmond Mills, Inc. [Providence,] 1946. [10]p. RHi.
Blanket-makers. This entry was part of the Romance of R.I. Industry pamphlet series. See note, entry 768.

3800 RIDER, SIDNEY S. "The floating island in Scott's Pond." BN, 30 (1913), 121-127.

3801 ST. PIERRE, J. L. "Ghost town: Hanton City, Rhode Island; where did they go?" Yankee, 37 (Sept. 1973), 108-109.

3802 "SCHOOLS of Smithfield." WRICHSH, 2 (1959), [2].

3803 STEERE, THOMAS. History of the town of Smithfield, from its organization in 1730-1, to its division in 1871; compiled in accordance with the votes of the towns of Smithfield, North Smithfield, Lincoln and Woonsocket, R.I. Providence: E. L. Freeman, 1881. 230p. RHi. +

SEE ALSO entries 1226, 1245.

## SOUTH KINGSTOWN (WASHINGTON CO.)

3804 ARNOLD, JAMES N. "The Second Free Will Baptist Church, South Kingstown." NHR, 2 (1884), 204-206.

3805 ARNOLD, VIRGINIA. "Queen's River Baptist Church history." Richmond Historical Society, Richmond History, 1, No. 8 (Oct. 1968), 38-39, 37.

3806 "AS we were." R.I. Alumni Bulletin, 40 (Jan.-Feb. 1960), 6-7.
College life at what is now the Univ. of R.I. in early 1900s.

3807 AYOTTE, JOHN U. D. "The Great Swamp Fight." Yankee, 29 (Dec. 1965), 65, 67, 69, 166-167.
During King Philip's War (1675).

3808 BARON, WILLIAM R. "Peace Dale, Rhode Island: a cultural history." PR, 7 (1970-1971), 14-15, 21-22.

3809 BEDFORD, DENTON K. "The Great Swamp Fight." Indian Historian, 4, No. 2 (Summer 1971), 27-41, 58.

3810 BODGE, GEORGE M. The Narragansett fort fight, December 19, 1675. Boston: Priv. Print., 1886. 21p. RHi.
Great Swamp Fight.

3811 BROWNING, C. FOSTER. "Early industry on the 'Back Side.'" PR, 6 (1969), 2-4, 10.
Water-powered mills.

3812 CHURCHILL, IRVING L. "'Now, when I was a student.'" R.I. Alumni Bulletin, 26 (Mar.-Apr. 1947), 5-6.
Student life at what is now Univ. of R.I. after World War I.

3813 CLARK, A. HOWARD. "The Great Swamp Fight." American Historical Register, 1 (1894-1895), 530-532.
During King Philip's War (1675).

3814 COMSTOCK, CHARLES. A history of South-Kingstown. Reprinted with a foreword by William Davis Miller. (1806) Kingston, 1934. 41p. RHi. +

3815 DAMON, S. C. The shade trees on the campus of the Rhode Island State College. Kingston, 1934. 8p. RU.
Now Univ. of R.I.

3816 DAUGHTERS OF THE AMERICAN REVOLUTION. RHODE ISLAND. NARRAGANSETT CHAPTER. The dedication of a tablet placed by the Narragansett Chapter of the Daughters of the Revolution on Tower Hill, August 21, 1936. n.p., 1936. [9]p. RHi.
Commemorating the Pettaquamscutt Purchase (1657). Address by Caroline Hazard.

3817 "DEDICATION of the Soldiers and Sailors Monument at Riverside Cemetery, South Kingstown, R.I., June 10, 1886." NHR, 5 (1886), 81-125.
Civil War monument.

3818 ESCHENBACHER, HERMAN F. The University of Rhode Island: a history of land-grant education in Rhode Island. N.Y.: Appleton-Century-Crofts, 1967. x, 548p. RHi. +

3819 FAGER, CHARLES. "A grisly tercentennial approaches." RIer (Dec. 7, 1975), 30-37.
Great Swamp Fight (1675).

3820 "THE FIRST Baptist Church of South Kingstown." NHR, 1 (1882), 42-49.

3821 FISH, MARIE POLAND. "A love letter to Kingston." RIer (Apr. 6, 1952), 8-11.

3822 FOWLER, WILLIAM S., and HERBERT A. LUTHER. "Cultural sequence at the Potter Pond Site." Massachusetts Archaeological Society, Bulletin, 11 (July 1950), 91-102.
Indian site.

3823 "THE FRIENDS' old meeting house." NHR, 2 (1884), 298-300.

3824 GAMMELL, WILLIAM, and E. G. ROBINSON. Life and services of Rowland Gibson Hazard, LL.D.: papers read before the Rhode Island Historical Society and the corporation and faculty of Brown University, October 30, 1888. Providence: J. A. & R. A. Reid, 1888. 33p. RHi. +
Textile manufacturer, legislator, philanthropist, author.

3825 GLEESON, PAUL FRANCIS. "Coojoot: a graphite mine located in South Kingstown." RIHSC, 32 (1939), 3-7.

3826 "THE GREAT Swamp Fight of 1675." PM, 34 (1922), 357, 359, 361, 363, 365.

3827 GREENE, WELCOME ARNOLD. "The great battle of the Narragansetts, Dec. 19, 1675: a critical analysis of the various accounts and facts of the event." NHR, 5 (1887), 331-343.
    Great Swamp Fight.

3828 [HALEY, JOHN WILLIAMS.] Samuel Casey, silversmith. Providence: "Old Stone Bank," 1930. 10p. RHi.
    18th century. This entry was part of the "Old Stone Bank" historical pamphlet series. See note, entry 432.

3829 HANCOCK, SAMUEL F. History of the First Baptist Church of South Kingstown, R.I., from 1781 to 1878. Providence: J. A. & R. A. Reid, 1878. 9p. RHi. +

3830 HAZARD, CAROLINE. "The burying-ground of the old South Kingstown Meeting-house." RIHSPubs, n.s. 3 (1895), 123-127.
    Quaker.

3831 _____. A precious heritage: an account of the life of Rowland Hazard and his wife, Margaret Anne Rood, who established their home, Oakwoods, in Peace Dale, Rhode Island, 1854. Peace Dale: Priv. Print., 1929. xiii, 368p. RHi. +
    Includes Rowland Hazard's involvement in textile manufacture at Peace Dale.

3832 _____. The seventy-fifth anniversary of the Peace Dale Congregational Church, 1857-1932.... n.p., n.d. 36p. RHi. +

3833 _____. Thomas Hazard, son of Robt., call'd College Tom: a study of life in Narragansett in the XVIIIth century.... Boston: Houghton Mifflin, 1893. viii, 324p. RHi. +

3834 HAZARD, JOSEPH PEACE. "Dalecarlia and vicinity." NHR, 2 (1883), 130-136.
    Dalecarlia Farm.

3835 HAZARD, ROWLAND GIBSON. Letters of Rowland Gibson Hazard; with a biographical sketch by Caroline Hazard. n.p.: Priv. Print, 1922. xv, 349p. RHi. +
    Textile manufacturer, legislator, philanthropist, author.

3836 HAZARD, THOMAS B. Nailer Tom's diary: otherwise the journal of Thomas B. Hazard of Kingstown, Rhode Island, 1778 to 1840; which includes observations on the weather, records of births, marriages and deaths; transactions by barter and money of varying value, preaching Friends and neighborhood gossip. Caroline Hazard, ed. Boston: Merrymount Pr., 1930. xxiv, 808p. RHi. +

3837 HAZARD, THOMAS R. Recollections of olden time: Rowland Robinson of Narragansett and his unfortunate daughter; with genealogies of the Robinson, Hazard, and Sweet familes of Rhode Island. Newport: John P. Sanborn, 1879. 288p. RHi. +

3838 [HELME, BERNON E.] The old court house at Kingston, where the legislature used to meet when it held sessions in Washington County; built in the year of independence one. Providence: E. L. Freeman, n.d. 10p. RHi.

3839 HIGBEE, HOLLY. Historic Kingston, Rhode Island. n.p.: Milkweed Art Pr., 1971. 75p. RHi.

3840 [HOPKINS, BARBARA.] South Kingstown, R.I.... South Kingstown: South Kingstown Chamber of Commerce, [1960?]. 19p. RSoKPea.

3841 [HOXIE, EMILY N.] A brief history of South Kingstown. n.p., 1962. 4p. RSoKPea.

3842 HOXIE, LOUISE M. The history of Peace Dale, Rhode Island. n.p.: Wakefield Printing, 1968. 16p. RHi.

3843 _____. "Recollections of the Dove and Distaff." PR, 2 (1965), 64-66.
    Dove & Distaff Village Industries, a handicraft guild.

3844 HULING, MARY KENYON. The story of Pettaquamscutt. Providence: Reynolds Pr., 1936. 25, [2]p. RHi. +
    Pettaquamscutt region.

3845 JOHNSON, ERWIN H. "Digging into the Great Swamp mysteries." R.I. Alumni Bulletin, 40 (Jan.-Feb. 1960), 4-5.
    Univ. of R.I. archaeological investigation at site of 1675 Great Swamp Fight.

3846 KELLEY, LEONA McELROY. "The Fayerweathers of Kingston, R.I.: or sequel of Prudence Crandall's boarding school." PR, 2 (1965), 74-77.
    Black family, one of whose members (Sarah Harris Fayerweather) was Crandall's first black student in the famous school in Canterbury, Conn.

# Rhode Island: A Bibliography of Its History

3847 [KELLEY, LEONA McELROY.] Welcome to Peace Dale and Wakefield, the home of the Hazard family. n.p., n.d. [18]p. RSoKPea.

3848 KINGSTON, R.I. KINGSTON CONGREGATIONAL CHURCH. Kingston Congregational Church: history, by-laws, membership. Kingston, 1932. 20p. RPB. +

3849 KLEIN, MAURY. SK 1890: letters from the past. Wakefield: South Kingstown Planning Department, 1978. [31]p. RSoKPea.
South Kingstown history in the form of "letters" from a fictitious local resident during the 1890s.

3850 LEAGUE OF WOMEN VOTERS, SOUTH KINGSTOWN. Know your town: South Kingstown, Rhode Island, 1953. [Wakefield: Narragansett Times, 1953.] 27p. RHi.

3851 "LOOKING back: the early '30s are revisited." Univ. of R.I. Alumni Bulletin, 59 (Summer 1978), 9-15.
Student life.

3852 McBURNEY, CHRISTIAN M. Kingston: a forgotten history. Kingston: Pettaquamscutt Historical Society, 1975. 106p. RHi.

3853 METZ, WILLIAM D. "The fortunate village." Univ. of R.I. Alumni Bulletin, 52 (July-Aug. 1972), 5-10.
Kingston.

3854 _____. "Pettaquamscutt: a purchase and an historical society." NH, 39 (1966), 1-12.
Pettaquamscutt Purchase (1658) and Pettaquamscutt Historical Society, Kingston.

3855 MILLER, WILLIAM DAVIS. "Biscuit City." RIHSC, 26 (1933), 72-77.
Place in South Kingstown.

3856 _____. "Dr. Joseph Torrey and his record book of marriages." RIHSC, 18 (1925), 102-111, 142-153.
Congregational minister.

3857 _____. Early houses of the King's Province in the Narragansett Country. Wakefield, 1941. 34p. RHi. +
Houses in what is now South Kingstown.

3858 _____. An early Rhode Island collector. n.p., 1935. 9p. RHi. +
Thomas Mawney Potter (1814-1890), furniture collector.

3859 _____. "General Washington at Little Rest." RIHSC, 25 (1932), 47-53.
1781.

3860 _____. "John Waite, silversmith." RIHSC, 21 (1928), 45-56.

3861 _____. "Joseph Perkins, silversmith." RIHSC, 21 (1928), 77-84.

3862 _____. "Nathaniel Helme, silversmith." RIHSC, 21 (1928), 85-89.

3863 _____. The removal of the county seat from Tower Hill to Little Rest, 1752. n.p., n.d. 8p. RHi. +
Reprinted from RIHSC, 19 (1926), 11-15, 46-48. Little Rest became Kingston.

3864 _____. "Samuel and Gideon Casey, silversmiths." RIHSC, 22 (1929), 103-109.

3865 _____. "Samuel Casey, silversmith." RIHSC, 21 (1928), 1-14.
Sentenced to death for counterfeiting (1770).

3866 _____. "The Samuel Sewall School Land and the Kingston Academy." RIHSC, 23 (1930), 4-10, 42-47, 50.

3867 _____. The silversmiths of Little Rest. Kingston, 1928. xii, 50p. RHi. +

3868 _____. "Some ancient roads in the Pettasquamscutt Purchase." RIHSC, 24 (1931), 105-117.

3869 _____. "Thomas Mount." RIHSC, 20 (1927), 53-58.
Executed in South Kingstown for burglary (1791).

3870 _____. "Thomas Mount and the Flash language." RIHSC, 22 (1929), 65-69.
Language used among criminals. See note, previous entry.

3871 MONAHON, ELEANORE BRADFORD. "A new look at the Jireh Bull excavation." RIH, 20 (1961), 13-24.
Late-17th-century house site.

3872 NORTH, S. N. D. Rowland Hazard of Peace Dale. Boston: Rockwell and Churchill Pr., 1899. 31p. RU.
Textile manufacturer, legislator, philanthropist.

3873 NORTHRUP, FLORENCE PERRY. "An old time school." PR, 2 (1964), 34-36.

3874 OPENING of the Hazard Memorial, Peace Dale, Rhode Island, October 9th, 1891, the ninetieth anniversary of the birth of Rowland Gibson Hazard. n.p., [1891?]. 55p. RHi. +
Memorial address by Edward Everett Hale.

3875 PENDLETON, WILLIAM H. Memorial of the
centennial exercises of the First Baptist
Church of South Kingstown, R.I....
Providence: Providence Pr., 1881. 91p.
RHi. +

3876 PETTAQUAMSCUTT HISTORICAL SOCIETY, KINGSTON.
Cemeteries in South Kingstown, Rhode Island.
Kingston, 1979. [64]p. RHi.

3877 PIERCE, NATHALIE. "The Dove & Distaff."
PR, 8 (1972), 18-20.
  Dove & Distaff Village Industries, a
handicraft guild.

3878 POGGIE, JOHN J., JR., and CARL GERSUNY.
"Risk and ritual: an interpretation of
fishermen's folklore in a New England
community." Journal of American Folklore,
85 (1972), 66-72.
  In South Kingstown.

3879 POTTER, GAIL M. "The Fowler Hill murder."
Yankee, 27 (Feb. 1963), 37-40, 72.
  1751 murder of William Jackson by Thomas
Carter.

3880 RAMLETTES: a decade of women's sports,
Rhode Island State College, Kingston, Rhode
Island, 1931-1941. [Kingston, 1941.] 98p.
RU.
  Now Univ. of R.I.

3881 A RECORD of the ceremony and oration on the
occasion of the unveiling of the monument
commemorating the Great Swamp Fight,
December 19, 1675, in the Narragansett
Country, Rhode Island; erected by the
Societies of Colonial Wars of Rhode Island
and Massachusetts, October 20, 1906.
Boston: Merrymount Pr., 1906. 68p. RHi. +

3882 "REPORT upon the objects excavated at the
Jireh Bull House and now in the museum of
the Rhode Island Historical Society."
RIHSC, 18 (1925), 83-90.

3883 RHODE ISLAND. HISTORICAL PRESERVATION
COMMISSION. Preliminary survey report:
town of South Kingstown. Providence, 1975.
ii, [18]p. RHi.
  Authors: Russell Wright and Walter
Nebiker.

3884 RHODE ISLAND HISTORICAL SOCIETY.
Proceedings at the dedication of a tablet to
the memory of Major Samuel Appleton,
November 3, 1916. Providence, 1917. 25p.
RHi.
  Commemorating his services in the Great
Swamp Fight (1675).

3885 RIDER, SIDNEY S. "Dr. MacSparran's sermon
to a man convicted of murder in 1751." BN,
20 (1903), 113-115.
  Thomas Carter, who was hanged for the
murder of William Jackson. See also BN, 20
(1903), 129-134.

3886 [RODEWIG, MARGARET R.] "The Indian School."
PR, 5 (1968), 18-20.

3887 ROSEN, BENTON H. "'Now, when I was a
student.'" R.I. Alumni Bulletin, 26
(Jan.-Feb. 1947), 5-6, 10.
  Student life during the Great Depression.

3888 ROSS, MAE. History of Wakefield Baptist
Church, 1781-1981. n.p., [1981]. 68p.
RNoK.

3889 SAINSBURY, GAIL GREGORY. "'Now, girls,
what's the matter with you girls?'
Clerical workers organize." Radical
America, 14 (1980), 67-75.
  At Univ. of R.I.

3890 "SIX stores in Kingston." PR, 14 (1978),
17-18, 23-24.

3891 SOCIETY OF COLONIAL WARS. RHODE ISLAND.
A farther brief and true narration of the
Great Swamp Fight in the Narragansett
Country, December 19, 1675. Written a few
days later and first printed at London in
February, 1676. Now reproduced for the
honour of those who won and lost and for the
instruction and edification of a later
generation met to commemorate those of their
own blood who fought on that or other days,
in a general convention of the Society of
Colonial Wars held at Providence on May 17
& 18, 1912. n.p.: S.P.C. for the Society
of Colonial Wars, R.I., [1912]. 12p.
RHi. +
  Includes historical introduction. See
also Norman Morrison Isham, "Preliminary
report...on the excavations at the Jireh
Bull House...," RIHSC, 11 (1918), 3-11.

3892 _____. A plat of the land of Capt. Henry
Bull at Pettaquamscut, drawn by James Helme,
surveyor, January 8, 1729.... Providence:
E. L. Freeman, 1927. 17p. RHi. +
  Includes historical narrative about the
site.

3893 _____. A preliminary report on the
excavations at the house of Jireh Bull on
Tower Hill in Rhode Island.... Providence:
E. A. Johnson, 1917. 16p. RHi. +

3894 STEDMAN, OLIVER H. "The winter of 1920."
PR, 2 (1964), 35-37.

3895 TAYLOR, PHILLIP KITTREDGE. "'Little Rest.'"
NEM, n.s. 28 (1903), 129-143.
Now Kingston.

3896 THETA CHI FRATERNITY. ETA CHAPTER.
UNIVERSITY OF RHODE ISLAND. A glance back,
a thought forward: a 25-year history of Eta
Chapter, Theta Chi Fraternity, Rhode Island
State College, Kingston, R.I., May 2, 1936.
Kingston, 1936. 116p. RU.

3897 [THOMAS, DANIEL H.] The Congregational
Church, Kingston, Rhode Island. n.p.,
[1945]. [17]p. R.

3898 TURNBAUGH, WILLIAM A. "Beginnings: the
earliest days of the URI campus." Univ. of
R.I. Alumni Quarterly, 59 (Summer 1979),
6-11.

3899 WAKEFIELD, R.I. CHURCH OF THE ASCENSION.
The Church of the Ascension, Wakefield,
Rhode Island, 1839-1939. n.p., n.d. 32p.
RHi. +
Episcopal.

3900 WAKEFIELD, R.I. SAINT FRANCIS OF ASSISI
CHURCH. Saint Francis of Assisi Church,
100th anniversary, April 22, 1979 - October
4, 1979. n.p., [1979]. 54p. RHi.
Roman Catholic.

3901 WAKEFIELD BRANCH COMPANY. Wakefield Branch
Company: 100th year anniversary, 1874-1974.
n.p., n.d. [12]p. RU.
Hardware, lumber, fuels, etc.

3902 WHALEY, CARDER H. The hills of Matunuck
(1941) and the Old Post Road (1944).
Matunuck: Robert Beverly Hale Library,
1964. 16, 8p. RSoKPet.

3903 WHALEY, MARY. "Main Street, Wakefield,
R.I., in 1887." PR, No. 23 (1963), 201-204.

3904 WHEELER, ROBERT L. "Murther in Matunuck."
RIer (Apr. 11, 1954), 12-15.
18th-century crime of passion.

3905 WOODWARD, CARL RAYMOND. Education's "lively
experiment" in Rhode Island. N.Y.:
Newcomen Society in North America, 1957.
28p. RHi.
Univ. of R.I.

3906 _____. From college to university,
1941-1958: a summary report. Kingston,
1960. 60p. RPB. +
Univ. of R.I.

3907 _____. "Kingston's cultural heritage." RIY
(1970), 57-68.

3908 _____. "A profile in dedication: Sarah
Harris and the Fayerweather family."
New-England Galaxy, 15 (Summer 1973), 3-14.
Sarah Harris Fayerweather of Kingston,
first student in Prudence Crandall's school
for black girls in Canterbury, Conn.

3909 _____. "Ten years in perspective." R.I.
Alumni Bulletin, 31 (Nov.-Dec. 1951), 1,
14-15.
Summary of developments at the Univ. of
R.I. during his first ten years as
president.

SEE ALSO entries 96, 341, 482, 484, 513,
1277, 1341.

## TIVERTON (NEWPORT CO.)

3910 BURROUGHS, PELEG. Peleg Burroughs's
journal, 1778-1798: the Tiverton, R.I.,
years of the humbly bold Baptist minister.
Ruth Wilder Sherman, ed. Warwick: R.I.
Genealogical Society, 1981. xxvi, 404p.
RNR. +

3911 CHAPIN, HELEN. "'At about 5:30 the waves
looked the worst...three or four I thought
to be at least 20 feet high.'" RIer (Sept.
17, 1978), 6-7, 19, 12, 14.
1938 hurricane.

3912 DAVIS, FELIX G., and GRACE STAFFORD DURFEE.
The history of Amicable Congregational
Church, 1746-1946. n.p., n.d. 138, 95p.
RHi. +

3913 HOWE, GEORGE. "The minister and the mill
girl." American Heritage, 12, No. 6 (Oct.
1961), 34-37, 82-88.
1832 death of Maria Cornell. Ephraim K.
Avery was charged with murder, but
acquitted. See also entries 3921, 3923.

3914 LEONARD, LILIAS SHEFFIELD. A history of the
Amicable Congregational Church, Tiverton,
Rhode Island. Volume II, 1946-1971. n.p.,
n.d. 41, [40]p. RTU.

3915 McLOUGHLIN, WILLIAM G. "Tiverton's fight
for religious liberty, 1692-1724." RIH, 38
(1979), 35-37.

3916 NELSON, WILBUR. A history of the Old Stone
Church. n.p., n.d. 18p. RNR.
First Baptist Church.

3917 NORTH TIVERTON, R.I. BAPTIST CHURCH. North
Tiverton Baptist Church: souvenir year
book, fiftieth anniversary; program for the
observance.... North Tiverton, 1935.
[30]p. RNHi.

3918 PARKER, RODERICK H. "Tiverton, Rhode
Island, and some of its early dwellings."
Pencil Points, 17 (1936), 575-590.

3919 A PATCHWORK history of Tiverton, Rhode
Island; 1976 bicentennial edition. n.p.,
[1976?]. 168p. RHi.

3920 RHODE Island tercentenary, 1636-1936:
historical edition of Tiverton, Rhode
Island. n.p., [1936]. 78p. RHi. +
Historical sketches of Tiverton.

3921 "THE SENSATION of half a century ago:
murder of Sarah M. Cornell; a narrative of
events by a witness." Providence Journal
(Jan. 1, 1883).
Lengthy historical article, dealing with
famous 1832 murder of mill girl. The
Rev. Ephraim K. Avery was tried and
acquitted. See also entries 3913, 3923.

3922 SINGER, MARYBELLE. "When the whipping post
came tumbling down." RIer (June 8, 1969),
24-25.
1806.

3923 THE TERRIBLE hay-stack murder. Life and
trial of the Rev. Ephraim K. Avery, for the
murder of the young and beautiful Miss Sarah
M. Cornell, a factory girl of Fall River,
Mass., whose affections he won, and whose
honor he betrayed. Philadelphia: Barclay,
1876. 62p. RHi. +
1832 murder in Tiverton. See also entries
3913, 3921.

3924 TIVERTON, R.I. CENTRAL BAPTIST CHURCH.
Centennial celebration, 1808-1908, Central
Baptist Church, Tiverton, Rhode Island....
Fall River, Mass.: J. H. Franklin, n.d.
29p. RHi.

3925 _____. Historical notes on Central Baptist
Church of Tiverton, Rhode Island; one
hundred and fiftieth anniversary, November
2-9, 1958.... n.p., n.d. [8]p. RNHi.

3926 TIVERTON, R.I. HOLY TRINITY PARISH. A
history and church directory of Holy Trinity
Parish, Tiverton, R.I., 1933. Tiverton,
1933. [24]p. RHi. +
Episcopal.

3927 TIVERTON Heights, Tiverton, R.I.: its
historic surroundings and its beautiful
scenery. Fall River, Mass.: Daily Evening
News Print, [1884]. 19, [2]p. RHi. +
Signed "A.N.O."

SEE ALSO entries 1160, 1181, 1187, 1213.

WARREN (BRISTOL CO.)

3928 ACKLEY, WILLIAM N. Historical discourse
delivered in St. Mark's Church, Warren,
R.I., Sunday evening, March 10, 1878, being
the fiftieth anniversary of the organization
of the parish. Providence: Providence Pr.,
1879. 39p. RHi. +
Episcopal.

3929 BAKER, VIRGINIA. "Glimpses of ancient
Sowams: reminiscences of the aborigines;
their sayings and doings." RIHSPr., n.s.
2 (1894), 196-202.
Wampanoag Indian village. The site of
Sowams has been debated. See index for
other references to this subject.

3930 _____. A history of the Fire Department of
Warren, Rhode Island. Warren: Roundfield
Pr., 1912. 120p. RHi. +

3931 _____. The history of Warren, Rhode Island,
in the War of the Revolution, 1776-1783.
Warren: Priv. Print., 1901. 68p. RHi. +

3932 _____. Massasoit's town: Sowams in
Pakanoket; its history, legends and
traditions. Warren: Priv. Print., 1904.
43p. RHi. +
Massasoit was a Wampanoag Indian sachem.
The location of Sowams has been disputed.
See index for other entries on the subject.

3933 _____. Sowams, the home of Massasoit:
where was it? Boston: David Clapp, 1899.
8p. RHi. +
See note, preceding entry.

3934 BAKER, WILLIAM A. "Garret archaeology."
American Neptune, 38 (1978), 170-174.
"...the oldest known shipbuilder's draught
of an American vessel lay hidden for over
two hundred years until recently discovered
on the underside of a pine board that was
part of the garret flooring of the James
Maxwell house in Warren, Rhode Island."

3935 BLOUNT MARINE CORPORATION. Taskmasters of
the sea: the story of the Blount Marine
Corporation, Warren, Rhode Island. n.p.,
1961. 89p. RHi. +
Shipbuilders.

3936 DEAN, M. M. "Annals of the Baptist Church
in Warren, R.I., Brown University, and the
Warren Association." American Baptist
Memorial, 14 (1855), 113-118.

3937 DELABARRE, EDMUND B. "Chief Big Thunder: a problematic figure in Rhode Island annals." RIHSC, 28 (1935), 116-128.
Francis Loring, who claimed to be "custodian of the national archives" of the Wampanoag Tribe.

3938 _____. "A unique Indian implement from Warren: inscribed, perforated, double-edged." RIHSC, 12 (1919), 96-100.

3939 FESSENDEN, GUY MANNERING. The history of Warren, R.I., from the earliest times; with particular notices of Massasoit and his family. Providence: H. H. Brown, 1845. vi, 125p. RHi. +

3940 FORGET, ULYSSE. La Paroisse Saint-Jean-Baptiste de Warren, Etat du Rhode Island (1877-1952). Montreal: Imprimerie Populaire, 1952. 395p. RHi. +
Roman Catholic parish. Text in French and English.

3941 GREENE, SHIRLEY M. "Washington Lodge, No. 3, A.F. & A.M., of Warren, 25 June 1896: celebrating their centennial." R.I. Roots, 6, No. 4 (Winter 1980), 73-75.
Chartered 1796.

3942 MASSASOIT MONUMENT ASSOCIATION, WARREN. Exercises under the auspices of the Thalia Club, Warren, R.I., February 8th, 1893, for the benefit of the Massasoit Monument fund; with addresses, poems, etc. Providence: E. A. Johnson, [1893]. 40p. RHi. +

3943 MOTT, FRANK L. "Portrait of an American milltown: demographic response in mid-nineteenth century Warren, Rhode Island." Population Studies, 26 (1972), 147-157.

3944 PECK, HENRY J. 200th anniversary of Warren, Rhode Island: historical sketch. Warren: The Town, 1947. 111p. RHi. +

3945 RHODE ISLAND. HISTORICAL PRESERVATION COMMISSION. Warren, Rhode Island: statewide preservation report B-W-1. Providence, 1975. vi, 61p. RHi. +
Author: Elizabeth S. Warren.

3946 RIDER, SIDNEY S. "Kickemuet, the Indian village." BN, 14 (1897), 255-257.

3947 _____. "Sowams, now Warren, the first Indian name of a location known to the Plymouth settlers, 16th of March, 1620-1." BN, 23 (1906), 57-63, 65-70, 73-79, 81-86.
See note, entry 3929.

3948 _____. "Warren, a Rhode Island town." BN, 2 (1885), 93.

3949 RUSSELL, J. FENIMORE. "Some old houses of Warren, Rhode Island." Pencil Points, 16 (1935), 539-554, 635-650.

3950 SPALDING, AMOS FLETCHER. The centennial discourse on the one hundredth anniversary of the First Baptist Church, Warren, R.I., November 15, 1864.... Providence: Knowles, Anthony, 1865. 76p. RHi. +

3951 "THE STRENUOUS days of Warren." PM, 26 (1914), 685-687.

3952 TALBOT, MICAH JONES. The origin and progress of the Methodist Episcopal Church in Warren, R.I., including notices of many clergymen and others who have contributed to its planting and growth. Providence: Providence Pr., 1876. viii, 232p. RHi. +

3953 TUSTIN, JOSIAH P. A discourse delivered at the dedication of the new church edifice of the Baptist Church and Society in Warren, R.I., May 8, 1845. Providence: H. H. Brown, 1845. viii, 125p. RHi. +

3954 WARD, JOHN. "The Warren waterfront: the good old days are right now." RIer (Sept. 5, 1965), 3-5.

3955 WARREN, R.I. CHURCH OF SAINT MARY OF THE BAY. St. Mary of the Bay, Warren, R.I., July 19, 1970: dedication day. n.p., n.d. [56]p. RPD.
Roman Catholic. Includes historical sketch.

3956 WARREN, R.I. FIRST BAPTIST CHURCH. Discourse at the centennial of the reorganization of the Baptist Church in Warren, Rhode Island, October 26, 1886. Warren: W. H. Martin, n.d. 34p. RHi. +

3957 _____. Manual of the Baptist Church in Warren, R.I., November 15, 1764 - March 1, 1886. Phenix: John H. Campbell, 1886. 55p. RHi. +
Includes historical sketch.

3958 _____. 175th anniversary of the Baptist Church in Warren and Brown University: dedication of memorial tablet in commemoration of the early association of Brown University and the Baptist Church in Warren under the leadership of James Manning, first pastor of the church and first president of the college; with historical notes & church membership roll, November 19, 1939. n.p., n.d. 16p. RHi.

3959 WARREN, R.I. SAINT ALEXANDER'S CHURCH. 30th anniversary celebration, St. Alexander's Church, Warren, Rhode Island, 1949-1979. n.p., n.d. [20]p. RPD-H.
Roman Catholic. Italian parish.

3960 WARREN, R.I. SAINT CASIMIR'S CHURCH.
...Souvenir of the golden jubilee of St.
Casimir's Parish, Warren, Rhode Island,
1908-1958. n.p., n.d. [95]p. RPD-H.
Roman Catholic. Polish parish. Text in
Polish and English.

3961 "WARREN in the whale fishery." Providence
Evening Bulletin (Feb. 5, 1881).
Lengthy historical article.

SEE ALSO entries 459, 976, 1153.

## WARWICK (KENT CO.)

3962 APPONAUG, R.I. SAINT CATHERINE'S CHURCH.
Saint Catherine's festival week, June 11-16,
1977; life of Saint Catherine. n.p.,
[1977]. [12]p. RPD-H.
Roman Catholic. Includes historical
sketch of the parish.

3963 BELCHER, HORACE G. "Old Rocky Point." RIH,
7 (1948), 33-50.
Resort and amusement park.

3964 BRAYTON, GEORGE A. A defence of Samuel
Gorton and the settlers of Shawomet.
Providence: Sidney S. Rider, 1883. 120p.
RHi. +

3965 BUTTONWOODS CENTENNIAL COMMITTEE.
Buttonwoods centennial, 1871-1971. n.p.,
n.d. 139p. RHi.
Place in Warwick.

3966 CAVE, HUGH B. "A love letter to Warwick."
RIer (Oct. 5, 1952), 12-15.

3967 CHAPIN, HOWARD M. "Early house lots in the
east part of the town of Warwick." RIHSC,
12 (1919), 129-136.

3968 CONIMICUT, R.I. WOODBURY UNION CHURCH.
Fiftieth anniversary of the Woodbury Union
Church, Presbyterian, 1907-1957.... n.p.,
n.d. [7]p. RHi.

3969 _____. Souvenir program, thirty-fifth
anniversary of the Woodbury Union Church,
Conimicut, Rhode Island, Saturday and
Sunday, November 14th and 15th, 1942. n.p.,
n.d. [48]p. RHi.
Includes historical sketch. Independent
in 1942, church later became Presbyterian.

3970 CURTIS, EDITH ROELKER. "Sundays at Potowom
in 1900." RIer (Jan. 25, 1959), 10-13.
Potowomut.

3971 CURTIS, HAROLD R. "The tenement on
Conimicut." RIHSC, 12 (1919), 65-74.
Early land division.

3972 _____. "Warwick proprietors' divisions."
RIHSC, 20 (1927), 33-51.

3973 THE EARLY records of the town of Warwick.
[Howard M. Chapin, ed.] Providence: E. A.
Johnson, 1926. vi, 362p. RHi. +

3974 ELY, WILLIAM D. Report on the settlement of
Warwick, 1642; and the seal of the Rhode
Island Historical Society. Providence: J.
A. & R. A. Reid, [1887?]. 38p. RHi. +

3975 FOWLER, WILLIAM S. "Locust Spring Site:
its occupational activities." Narragansett
Archaeological Society of R.I., Site Reports
(Oct. 1962), 6-20.
Indian site.

3976 _____. "Sweet-Meadow Brook: a pottery site
in Rhode Island." Narragansett
Archaeological Society of R.I., Report (Oct.
1956), 1-23.
Archaeological site in Warwick, with
pottery dating from ca. 500 A.D.

3977 FULLER, OLIVER PAYSON. Historical sketches
of the churches of Warwick, Rhode
Island,...to which is added a record of
persons joined in marriage in that town by
Elder John Gorton, from 1754 to 1792.
(1875) Providence: Sidney S. Rider, 1880.
106p. RHi. +

3978 _____. The history of Warwick, Rhode
Island, from its settlement in 1642 to the
present time: including accounts of the
early settlement and development of its
several villages; sketches of the origin and
progress of the different churches of the
town, &c., &c. Providence: Angell,
Burlingame, 1875. vi, 380p. RHi. +

3979 GREEN, THEODORE FRANCIS. "The youth of
General Greene." RIH, 1 (1942), 112-117.
Nathanael Greene, born 1742 in Warwick,
where he lived until 1770.

3980 [HALEY, JOHN WILLIAMS.] The founding of
Warwick. Providence: "Old Stone
Bank," 1932. 11p. RHi.
This and the next two entries were part of
the "Old Stone Bank" historical pamphlet
series. See note, entry 432.

3981 [_____.] The Kentish Artillery.
Providence: "Old Stone Bank," 1932. 10p.
RHi.
Militia unit.

3982 [_____.] Mark Rock. Providence: "Old
Stone Bank," 1932. 10p. RHi.
Inscribed rock.

3983 HOLST, ANNE CRAWFORD ALLEN. "Cowsett Road,
1870-1900." RIH, 30 (1971), 61-68.

3984   HULING, RAY GREENE. "An offer of sale by the proprietors of Warwick in 1652." NHR, 2 (1884), 233-238.

3985   KELCH, KRISTEN. "The glitter is gone, but there is life yet in old Oakland Beach." RIer (June 27, 1982), 6-8, 12.
    Includes historical background.

3986   [LAWRENCE, ANNA M. M.] Potowomut: Warwick, Rhode Island. n.p.: Greenwich Pr., [1931]. 26p. RP.

3987   LOCKWOOD, ERNEST L. Episodes in Warwick history. [Warwick:] City of Warwick Historical Committee of the R.I. Tercentenary Celebration, 1937. 40p. RHi. +

3988   OLSEN, ELIZABETH ANNE, and CLYDE STROUD WILSON. The St. Barnabas story, 1880-1980: a history of St. Barnabas Church, Warwick, Rhode Island. n.p.: Southern R.I. Publications, 1980. 81p. RHi.
    Episcopal.

3989   "POMHAM and his fort." RIHSC, 11 (1918), 31-36.
    Shawomet Indian sachem (17th century). Signed H.M.C (Howard M. Chapin).

3990   PONTIAC, R.I. [SWEDISH LUTHERAN CHURCH.] Minnesskrift historik och Redogörelse över Svenska Ev. Luth. Församlingens i Pontiac, Rhode Island, Femtio-ariga Verksamhet.... [Worcester, Mass.: Svea Pr.,] 1924. 115p. MWA.
    Text in Swedish.

3991   RHODE ISLAND. HISTORICAL PRESERVATION COMMISSION. Statewide historical preservation report K-W-1. [Providence,] 1981. vi, 78p. RHi.
    Author: Robert O. Jones.

3992   RIDER, SIDNEY S. "The struggle for liberty on the lands of Nasauket and Shawomet: Oakland Beach-Buttonwoods, in 1642-1653." BN, 6 (1889), 125-129.
    Founding of Warwick.

3993   RIGGS, DOUGLAS R. "Rocky Hill School: with disadvantages like these, who needs advantages?" RIer (May 28, 1972), 6-11.
    Includes historical sketch of the private school.

3994   SHEFFIELD, WILLIAM P. Samuel Gorton. n.p., n.d. 62p. RHi.
    Early history of Warwick.

3995   STACKHOUSE, DAVID LUDLOW. "The Warwick story." RIY (1968), 55-64.

3996   TURNER, HENRY E. Greenes of Warwick in colonial history: read before the Rhode Island Historical Society, February 27, 1877. Newport: Davis & Pitman, 1877. 68, [3]p. RHi. +

3997   WARWICK, R.I. SAINT GREGORY THE GREAT CHURCH. 1976 yearbook issued by Saint Gregory the Great Church, Cowsett, Warwick, Rhode Island, on the occasion of the fifteenth anniversary reunion dinner and dance, October 2, 1976.... n.p., [1976]. [16]p. RPD-H.
    Roman Catholic. Includes historical sketch.

3998   WARWICK, R.I. SAINT TIMOTHY'S CHURCH. Saint Timothy Church, Warwick, Rhode Island. South Hackensack, N.J.: Custombook, 1969. 16, [16]p. RPD.
    Roman Catholic.

3999   WARWICK, R.I. WARWICK CENTRAL FREE WILL BAPTIST CHURCH. Re-dedication of the Warwick Central Free Will Baptist Church, December 10, 1905, at Apponaug, Warwick, R.I. n.p., n.d. 43p. RHi. +

4000   WILLIAMS, ELSIE B. The John Waterman Arnold House, National Historic Landmark. n.p., [1971?]. 9p. RHi.
    On Roger Williams Avenue, Lakewood.

4001   WOODWARD, CARL RAYMOND. "Rural economy 200 years ago: as revealed in the account books of Benoni Waterman of Warwick, 1733-1740." RIH, 4 (1945), 97-106; 5 (1946), 119-128.

    SEE ALSO entries 68, 70, 95, 265, 277, 355, 365, 403-404, 419, 438, 502, 576, 600, 637, 764, 818.

## WEST GREENWICH (KENT CO.)

4002   [BAKER, ROBERTA.] Bits and pieces of West Greenwich memoranda. n.p., 1976. 123p. RHi.

4003   BATES, JOHN A. "Historical sketch of the West Greenwich Baptist Church." WRICHSP, 2, No. 3 (1956), [17-28].
    Written in 1890.

4004   CLAPP, ROGER TILLINGHAST. "How Acid Factory Brook got its name." RIH, 4 (1946), 97-104.
    Author published another article under the same title in WRICHSP, 1, No. 4 (1950), 1-8.

4005   FOWLER, WILLIAM S. "Rattlesnake Rock Shelter." Narragansett Archaeological Society of R.I., Site Reports (Oct. 1962), 1-5.
    Indian site.

4006 HISTORICAL RECORDS SURVEY. RHODE ISLAND. Inventory of the town & city archives of Rhode Island: No. 2, Kent County; vol. 4, West Greenwich. viii, 80p. RP. +
Includes historical sketch.

4007 HULING, RAY GREENE. "Early owners of land in West Greenwich, R.I." NHR, 3 (1884-1885), 1-5.

4008 LAMOREUX, CORA HARRINGTON. "History of the town of West Greenwich, Rhode Island." WRICHSP, 2, No. 3 (1956), [29-31].

4009 "A PETITION for the settlment of lands west of East Greenwich." RIHSC, 30 (1937), 85-88.
G. Andrews Moriarty and William Davis Miller, eds.

4010 RHODE ISLAND. HISTORICAL PRESERVATION COMMISSION. Preliminary survey report: town of West Greenwich. Providence, 1978. iv, 38p. RHi.
Author: Vivienne F. Laskey.

4011 RIDER, SIDNEY S. "The derivation of the word 'Nooseneck.'" BN, 4 (1886), 77.
Place in West Greenwich. See also BN, 6 (1889), 201-204.

SEE ALSO entry 1157.

## WEST WARWICK (KENT CO.)

4012 BATES, FRANK G. "Some early history of Crompton." WRICHSP, 2, No. 3 (1956), [2-3].

4013 CROMPTON, R.I. WARWICK AND COVENTRY BAPTIST CHURCH. Historical sketch, with the confession and covenant of the Warwick and Coventry Baptist Church, Crompton, R.I. Providence: Knowles, Anthony, 1863. 8p. RPB. +

4014 FIRST annual Natick Old Timers Jamboree, 1952: souvenir history journal, August 1st, 2nd & 3rd. [West Warwick: Clyde Pr., 1952.] 74p. RHi.
Includes "History of Natick, R.I.," by Charles W. Littlefield, 35-38.

4015 GREENE, HENRY L. "The Lippitt Manufacturing Company." NHR, 7 (1889), 156-157.
Cotton manufacturer.

4016 HARPIN, MATHIAS P. Trumpets in Jericho. West Warwick: Commercial Printing and Publishing, 1961. 400p. RHi. +
Village of Arctic.

4017 ____. "Western Warwick's spectacular era." WRICHSH, 3 (May 1960), [2]; (June 1960), [2]; (July 1960), [2]; 4 (Aug. 1960), [2]; (Sept. 1960), [2]; (Oct. 1960), [2]; (Nov. 1960), [2]; (Mar. 1961), [2].
History of village of Arctic.

4018 LEONARD, WARREN A. Seventy-five years for Christ: being a historical sketch of the First Congregational Church, Riverpoint, R.I. Providence: Oxford Pr., 1924. 38p. RHi. +

4019 O'BRIEN, JOHN J., JR. "Tales of a blacksmith shop." RIY (1971), 44-46.
His father's shop in Clyde.

4020 PHENIX, R.I. PHENIX BAPTIST CHURCH. Historical sketch of the Phenix Baptist Church, Warwick, R.I., with the articles of faith.... Phenix: Gleaner Print, 1881. 41p. RHi. +

4021 ____. One hundredth anniversary, Phenix Baptist Church, founded January 10, 1842 - January 10, 1942. n.p., n.d. [31]p. RP.

4022 PHENIX, R.I. SAINTS PETER AND PAUL CHURCH. SS. Peter & Paul Church, Phenix, Rhode Island. South Hackensack, N.J.: Custombook, 1978. 17, [7]p. RPD.
Roman Catholic.

4023 RIDER, SIDNEY S. "Natick: the origin and meaning of the name; a lexigraphic curiosity." BN, 20 (1903), 177-182.

4024 SHIPPEE, RUTH BARTON. "Old days in Crompton." WRICHSP, 2, No. 3 (1956), [4-11].

4025 SPENCER, WILLIAM B. "History of Phenix and adjacent villages." Pawtuxet Valley Gleaner (Warwick), 1888.
Series of newspaper articles beginning Jan. 7, 1888. Scrapbook, RHi.

4026 TWERSKY, REBECCA. "The founding of a Jewish community: the early years of Congregation Ahavath Shalom of West Warwick, Rhode Island." RIJHN, 7 (1977), 420-429.

4027 UNION LIBRARY ASOCIATION, PHENIX. Catalogue of books in the library of the Union Library Association, Phenix Village, Warwick, R.I., with a sketch of the rise and progress of the association, and a copy of its constitution and by-laws. Providence: A. Crawford Greene, 1852. 36p. RHi.
Phenix is now in West Warwick.

4028 VETERANS OF FOREIGN WARS. SERGEANT DAVID LANGEVIN POST, NO. 449, WEST WARWICK. 40th anniversary program, July 16, 1920 - July 16, 1960. n.p., n.d. [36]p. RHi.
Includes brief historical sketch.

4029 WEST WARWICK, R.I. Book of West Warwick, Rhode Island: published as an official souvenir of the celebration of the fiftieth anniversary of the incorporation of the town of West Warwick. West Warwick: Commerical Printing & Publishing, 1963. Unp. RP. +

4030 WEST WARWICK, R.I. PAROISSE DU CHRIST-ROI. Benediction solomnelle de l'Eglise du Christ-Roi, West Warwick, Rhode Island, le 22 septembre, 1957.... Celebration du 25e anniversaire de la fondation de la paroisse du Christ-Roi, le 22 septembre, 1957; 1931-1956. n.p., n.d. 82p. RHi.
Roman Catholic. French parish. Text in French and English.

4031 WEST WARWICK, R.I. SACRED HEART CHURCH. Sacred Heart Church, West Warwick, Rhode Island. South Hackensack, N.J.: Custombook, 1979. 29, [39]p. RWeW.
Roman Catholic. Italian parish.

4032 WEST WARWICK, R.I. SAINT JOHN THE BAPTIST CHURCH. St. John the Baptist Church, West Warwick, Rhode Island. South Hackensack, N.J.: Custombook, 1974. 36, [17]p. RHi.
Roman Catholic. French Parish.

4033 WEST WARWICK, R.I. SAINT JOSEPH'S CHURCH. 100th anniversary, St. Joseph's Church, West Warwick, R.I. n.p., [1973]. [44]p. RPD.
Roman Catholic.

## WESTERLY (WASHINGTON CO.)

4034 BABCOCK, HERBERT A. "When the railroad came to Westerly." WHSR (1927), 53-59.

4035 BABCOCK, MRS. JAMES O. "Old time Lotteryville." WHSR (1915-1916), 7-15.

4036 BARBER, THOMAS. "Contributions to the history of Westerly." NHR, 2 (1883), 34-40.

4037 _____. "The settlement of Westerly." NHR, 1 (1882), 125-127.

4038 BEST, MARY AGNES. The town that saved a state: Westerly; written during the Rhode Island tercentenary in 1936 for the Westerly Rhode Island Committee. Westerly: Utter, 1943. 283p. RHi. +

4039 BRAY, MILDRED H. Central Baptist Church of Westerly, Rhode Island, and its heritage, 1835-1976. Westerly: [Utter,] 1976. 48p. RWe.

4040 BUFFUM, MRS. F. C. "Old lyceums and speakers of Westerly." WHSR (1933), 5-15.

4041 BUTMAN, DEAN P. "The Westerly story." RIY (1971), 57-68.

4042 CARTER, MARGARET WOODBURY. Shipwrecks and marine disasters on the shores of the town of Westerly, Rhode Island, and adjacent waters. Westerly: David G. Carter, 1973. v, 69p. RHi. +

4043 COONEY, RALPH BOLTON. Westerly's oldest witness: how Westerly and the Washington Trust Company have progressed together for 150 years. Westerly: Washington Trust Company, 1950. ix, 84p. RHi. +

4044 COY, SALLIE E. Westerly's living memorial. Westerly: Westerly Historical Society, 1976. RWe.
Westerly Public Library.

4045 DENISON, FREDERIC. Historical sketch of the First Baptist Church in Westerly, R.I. Westerly: G. B. & J. H. Utter, 1867. 12p. RHi. +
See also this author's Westerly (Rhode Island) and its witnesses... (entry 1286), an account of the history of Westerly and several of its Washington County neighbors.

4046 DOWDING, GEORGE R. Military history of Westerly, 1710-1932. Westerly: Blackburn & Benson, n.d. 56p. MWA.

4047 DUNN, CLAUDE GAVITTE. Westerly, Rhode Island. N.Y.: C. G. Dunn, [1902?]. [40]p. RHi.

4048 FOSTER, MRS. E. B. "Rise and progress of Friends in Westerly and vicinity." WHSR (1915-1916), 34-40.
I.e., Quakers.

4049 HICKOX, MRS. CHARLES F. "The Lucy Carpenter House." WHSR (1933), 41-50.

4050 HILLARD, WILLIAM A. Historical sketch of the First Baptist Church of Westerly, September 29, 1935. [Westerly: Utter,] n.d. 46p. RWe.

4051 KIMBALL, CAROL W. "Summer's end: the steamer Metis." New-England Galaxy, 20 (Summer 1978), 30-36.
1872 shipwreck off Watch Hill.

4052 MACOMBER, STEPHEN W. The story of Westerly granite. [Westerly:] Westerly Historical Society, 1958. 38p. RHi. +

4053 MERAS, PHYLLIS. "Weekapaug, the reposeful resort." RIer (May 4, 1969), 16-17, 19.

4054 MOCHETTI, LIDO J. Life's little pleasures: the photographs of J. Henry Burk, 1900-1919. Westerly: Friends of the Westerly Public Library, 1979. 76p. RWe.
    Photographs of life in Westerly during those years. Includes historical introduction.

4055 MOORE, HARRIET. "'The next thing I knew we were clinging to each other in the bay.'" RIer (Sept. 17, 1978), 34-35, 37, 39.
    1938 hurricane.

4056 MUNSON, SAMUEL LYMAN. Weekapaug, Rhode Island: its first one hundred years. Westerly: Utter, 1977. 82p. RHi. +

4057 PAWCATUCK, R.I. PAWCATUCK SEVENTH-DAY BAPTIST CHURCH. The first hundred years: Pawcatuck Seventh Day Baptist Church, Westerly, Rhode Island, 1840-1940. Westerly: Utter, 1940. 331p. RHi. +

4058 PECK, REGINALD E. Early land holders of Watch Hill. [Westerly: Utter,] 1936. 27, [4]p. RHi. +

4059 PENDLETON, ALBERT P. Main Street then and now. [Westerly:] Westerly Historical Society, 1922. 18p. MWA. +

4060 _____. "People I have known." WHSR (1927), 89-120.
    Householders, tradesmen, etc., around Dixon Square.

4061 _____. "The Watch Hill Road: past and present, buildings and tenants." WHSR (1915-1916), 27-33.

4062 PERRY, HARVEY C. "Bungtown chronicles." WHSR (1933), 16-33.
    Place in Westerly.

4063 RATHBUN, HERBERT W., JR. A glow in the sky: a chronicle of fires and firemen in Westerly. Westerly: Utter, 1963. 29p. RWe.

4064 RHODE ISLAND. HISTORICAL PRESERVATION COMMISSION. Preliminary survey report: town of Westerly. Providence, 1978. iv, 52p. RHi.
    Author: Walter Nebiker.

4065 RIDER, SIDNEY S. "Kedinker Island." BN, 14 (1897), 49-50.

4066 ROWE, DOROTHY SNOWDEN. At the end of the pond: historical reminiscences of Weekapaug, R.I. (1963) Stonington, Conn.: Pequot Pr., 1964. 64p. RHi. +

4067 SAUNDERS, ELOISE. Early history of Dunn's Corners: a project of the Dunn's Corners L Club, presented March 14, 1968, at the Westerly Historical Society. n.p., n.d. 35p. RWe.

4068 SOLOVEITZIK, ELLA. "A study of the Jewish population of the town of Westerly, Rhode Island." RIJHN, 3 (1960), 139-147.

4069 SPICER, JULIA M. "Old time Weekapaug." WestHstSoc (1957), 5-22.

4070 STILLMAN, KARL G. The Westerly Hospital, 1925-1950. n.p., n.d. 27p. RWe.

4071 TAYLOR, BESSE. "Elder John Taylor." WHSR (1927), 61-70.
    Preached in Westerly's Christian Church.

4072 VARS, N. B. "The Vars Homestead." NHR, 2 (1883), 125-127.

4073 [VISIGLIO, GERALDINE.] The Pawcatuck Valley Women's Club: history. n.p., [1951]. 16p. RWe.

4074 WASHINGTON TRUST COMPANY. One hundred years of banking in Westerly. Westerly, 1908. [40]p. RHi. +

4075 WATCH Hill Yacht Club, 1913-1963. n.p., n.d. 64p. RWe.

4076 "WESTERLY observes its 250th birthday." PM, 31 (1919), 266-268.
    Includes historical sketch.

4077 WESTERLY, Rhode Island, tercentenary, 1669-1969: commemorative book; including the program of festivities, May 31st - June 7th, 1969. n.p., n.d. [92]p. RWe.

4078 WHEELER, GRACE D. "Sketches of old Westerly." WHSR (1927), 43-51.

4079 WILCOX, ETHAN. "Cookey Hill." WHSR (1915), 8-21.

4080 WOLCOTT, ELEANOR C. "Personal recollections of early schools of Westerly." WHSR (1933), 57-65.

SEE ALSO entries 179, 554, 601, 1094, 1286, 1344.

## WOONSOCKET (PROVIDENCE CO.)

4081 BONIER, MARIE LOUISE. Débuts de la colonie
Franco-Américaine de Woonsocket, Rhode
Island. Framingham, Mass.: Lakeview Pr.,
1920. 342, [vi]p. RHi. +
Text in French.

4082 BRETT, ROGER. "Woonsocket's last encore."
RIer (Dec. 17, 1972), 14, 16-17.
Woonsocket Opera House.

4083 CHMURA, JEFFREY A. The revitalization of
Cato Hill: a study in historic and
neighborhood renewal; Woonsocket, Rhode
Island, 1975. n.p., n.d. [40]p. RHi.

4084 CITY of Woonsocket, Rhode Island: past &
present, progress & prosperity; souvenir,
1907. J. H. Burgess, ed. Uxbridge, Mass.:
Transcript Pr., [1907?]. 48p. RHi. +

4085 FREEMASONS. WOONSOCKET. WOONSOCKET
COMMANDERY, NO. 24, KNIGHTS TEMPLARS. Fifty
years of Woonsocket Commandery, No. 24, of
Knights Templars and the appendant orders:
a historical review of the leading events of
the half-century 1867-1916. Harry Hazlewood
Wardle, comp. Providence: Standard
Printing, 1917. 104p. RHi.

4086 FRIENDS BIBLE SCHOOL, WOONSOCKET. Report of
the exercises of the twenty-fifth
anniversary of the organization of Friends'
Bible School, Friends' Meeting House,
Woonsocket, R.I., first day evening, tenth
month, 7 o'clock, 1887. Woonsocket: Pr. of
Carl Wheelock, 1887. 29p. RPB. +
Sunday school.

4087 GERSTLE, GARY. "The mobilization of the
working-class community: the Independent
Textile Union in Woonsocket, 1931-1946."
Radical History Review, No. 17 (1978),
161-172.

4088 JACKSON, FRANK A. One hundred and forty
years of banking in Woonsocket, Rhode
Island, 1805-1945: an historical sketch of
the Smithfield Union Bank and the National
Union Bank, predecessors of the Woonsocket
Trust Company. Woonsocket: Woonsocket
Trust Company, n.d. 15p. RHi.

4089 MOTTERN, NICHOLAS A. "'There's no reason to
go to Woonsocket.'" RIer (Mar. 1, 1970),
6-7, 9-11.
Traces the city's rise and decline as a
textile center.

4090 NEWMAN, S. C. A numbering of the
inhabitants; together with statistical and
other information relative to Woonsocket,
R.I. Woonsocket: S. S. Foss, 1846. 55p.
RHi. +
Includes historical sketch.

4091 PHENIX NATIONAL BANK. ...American Paper
Tube Co. [Providence,] 1946. 10p. RHi.
"...Makes quills and bobbins of paper to
be bound with packages of yarn." This and
the next entry were part of the Romance of
R.I. Industry pamphlet series. See note,
entry 768.

4092 _____. ...Taft-Peirce Manufacturing
Company. [Providence,] 1946. 10p. RHi.
Machinery, tool, and gauge manufacturer.

4093 RHODE ISLAND. HISTORICAL PRESERVATION
COMMISSION. Woonsocket, Rhode Island:
statewide historic preservation report
P-W-1. Providence, 1976. v, 83p. RHi. +
Author: David Chase.

4094 RICHARDSON, ERASTUS. "Folklore of
Woonsocket." Woonsocket Evening Reporter
(Mar. 16, 1881).
Lengthy article. Rider Collection, Brown
Univ.

4095 _____. History of Woonsocket. Woonsocket:
S. S. Foss, 1876. 264p. RHi. +

4096 RIDER, SIDNEY S. "Origin of the name,
Woonsocket." BN, 12 (1895), 229-233.

4097 SMYTH, JAMES W. History of the Catholic
Church in Woonsocket and vicinity, from the
celebration of the first mass in 1828, to
the present time, with a condensed account
of the early history of the Church in the
United States. (1878) Woonsocket: Charles
E. Cook, 1903. vi, 304p. RHi. +

4098 SORRELL, RICHARD S. "Sentinelle Affair
(1924-1929): religion and militant
survivance in Woonsocket, Rhode Island."
RIH, 36 (1977), 67-79.
French-nationalist movement within the
Roman Catholic Church, centered in
Woonsocket and R.I.

4099 _____. "Sports and Franco-Americans in
Woonsocket, 1870-1930." RIH, 31 (1972),
117-126.

4100 THOMAS, ALTON PICKERING. Old Woonsocket:
Erastus & Doc. Providence: Mowbray, 1973.
159p. RHi. +
Local historians Erastus Richardson and
the author, on Woonsocket's history.

4101 THOMAS, ALTON PICKERING. Woonsocket: highlights of history, 1800-1976. East Providence: Globe Printing, 1976. vi, 166p. RHi. +

4102 WESSEL, BESSIE BLOOM. An ethnic survey of Woonsocket, Rhode Island. Chicago: Univ. of Chicago Pr., 1931. xxi, 290p. RHi. +
    Includes historical sketch of Woonsocket, by Henry W. Lawrence.

4103 WOONSOCKET, R.I. [CHURCH OF THE HOLY FAMILY.] Album-souvenir du jubilé d'or de la Paroisse Sainte-Famile, Woonsocket, Rhode Island, des noces d'or sacerdotales de Monseigneur S. Grenier, P.D. et de son investiture à la prélature Romaine, Dimanche, le 25 mai, 1952. [Central Falls: U. S. Sabourin, 1952.] [127]p. RHi.
    Roman Catholic. French Parish. Text in French. Includes historical sketch of the parish.

4104 _____. Holy Family Parish, 1902-1977, Woonsocket, Rhode Island. n.p., 1977. [48]p. RHi.
    Roman Catholic. French parish.

4105 _____. Vingt-cinquième anniversaire de la fondation de la Paroisse Sainte Famille, Woonsocket, Rhode Island.... [Framingham, Mass.: Lakeview Pr., 1927.] 39p. RWoU. +
    Text in French.

4106 WOONSOCKET, R.I. CHURCH OF THE PRECIOUS BLOOD. Album-souvenir de noces d'or sacerdotales de Mgr Charles Dauray, prélat de sa sainteté, curé inamovible de la Paroisse du Precieux-Sang, Woonsocket, Rhode Island. Woonsocket: La Tribune Publishing, 1920. [79]p. RWoU.
    Roman Catholic. French parish. Includes biographical sketch of Dauray. Text in French.

4107 _____. Church of the Precious Blood, Woonsocket, R.I. South Hackensack, N.J.: Custombook, 1975. 24, [8]p. RHi. +
    Roman Catholic. French parish.

4108 _____. 80e anniversaire de naissance du Rev. M. Charles Dauray, curé de la Paroisse du Precieux-Sang de Woonsocket, R.I. n.p., 1918. [43]p. RWoU.
    Includes historical and biographical sketches. Text in French.

4109 _____. Programme-souvenir à l'occasion du 70e anniversaire de la fondation de la Paroisse du Precieux-Sang et du anniversaire d'ordination de son curé l'Abbe Georges W. Bedard. n.p.: [Vekeman's Print Shop,] 1912. [72]p. RPD-H.
    Roman Catholic. French parish. Text in French.

4110 _____. Souvenir de noces de diamant sacerdotales de Mgr Charles Dauray, protonotaire apostolique, curé inamovible de la Paroisse du Precieux-Sang, Woonsocket, Rhode Island. Woonsocket: La Tribune Pub., 1930. [61]p. RWoU.
    Includes historical and biographical sketches. Text in French.

4111 WOONSOCKET, R.I. CONVENT DE JESUS-MARIE. Album-souvenir des noces d'or du Convent de Jésus-Marie, Woonsocket, R.I. n.p., 1934. [153]p. RWoU.
    Includes historical sketch. Text in French.

4112 [WOONSOCKET, R.I. DEPARTMENT OF PLANNING AND DEVELOPMENT.] Companion essays to...Woonsocket, R.I.: the Americanization of a foreign city. [Woonsocket: New England Printing and Graphics, 1981.] 23p. RHi.
    Essays on Franco-American history and culture in Woonsocket and R.I. Booklet was produced to accompany a multi-media production funded by R.I. Committee for the Humanities.

4113 WOONSOCKET, R.I. FETE-SAINT-JEAN-BAPTISTE, 1922. Celebration de 1922: notes historiques des paroisses et nombreuses biographies. Woonsocket, 1922. 128p. RWoU. +
    Text in French.

4114 WOONSOCKET, R.I. PAROISSE NOTRE DAME DES VICTOIRES. Album-souvenir du jubilé d'or de la Paroisse Notre Dame des Victoires, Woonsocket, Rhode Island, Dimanche, 31 mai 1959. n.p., [1959]. 100p. RPD.
    Roman Catholic. French parish. Text in French.

4115 WOONSOCKET, R.I. SAINT ANTHONY'S CHURCH. Fiftieth anniversary of St. Anthony's Church, 128 Greene Street, Woonsocket, R.I., Saturday, April 20th, 1974.... n.p., [1974]. [108]p. RHi.
    Roman Catholic. Italian parish.

4116 _____. Golden jubilee, Saint Anthony's Church, 1924-1974, Woonsocket, R.I. n.p., n.d. [109]p. RHi.
    Roman Catholic. Italian parish.

4117 WOONSOCKET, R.I. SAINT CHARLES' CHURCH. Saint Charles Borromeo Church, Woonsocket, Rhode Island: centennial celebration, 1868-1968. n.p., [1968]. [24]p. RHi.
    Roman Catholic.

4118    WOONSOCKET, R.I.  SAINT CHARLES' CHURCH.
St. Charles', old and new:  being a brief
record of the origin and development of
Catholic life in Woonsocket in so far as
that life was affected by the origin and
development of St. Charles' Parish. n.p.,
[1928].  25p.  RHi.

4119    WOONSOCKET, R.I.  SAINT JOSEPH'S CHURCH.
Saint Joseph's Parish, Woonsocket, R.I.,
1929-1979:  a community of faith alive.
n.p., n.d.  144p.  RWoU.
    Roman Catholic.  French parish.  Includes
"A fifty-year history of Saint Joseph's
Parish, Woonsocket, R.I., 1929-1979," by
Raymond H. Bacon, 17-69.

4120    WOONSOCKET, R.I.  SAINT LOUIS DE GONZAGUE
CHURCH.  75th anniversary, 1902-1977, Saint
Louis de Gonzague, Woonsocket, Rhode Island.
n.p., n.d.  [68]p.  RPD.
    Roman Catholic.  French parish.  Became
Saint Aloysius Church.

4121    _____.  Souvenir des fêtes jubilaires du
cinquantième anniversaire de la fondation
de la Paroisse Saint Louis de Gonzague de
Woonsocket, Rhode Island, 9 novembre 1952.
n.p.:  [R.I. Manifold,] n.d.  [92]p.  RPD.
    Text in French.

4122    _____.  Souvenir des noces de rubis,
Dimanche, 15 fevrier, Salle Joyland,
Woonsocket, R.I.  n.p., [1942].  [35]p.
RHi.
    Historical sketch.  Text in French.

4123    WOONSOCKET, R.I.  SAINT MICHAEL'S
UKRANIAN-CATHOLIC CHURCH.  ...50th
anniversary, St. Michael's Ukranian Catholic
Church, Woonsocket, R.I., 1908-1958.  Unp.
RPD-H.
    Roman Catholic.  Text in Ukranian and
English.

4124    WOONSOCKET, R.I.  WOONSOCKET SENIOR HIGH
SCHOOL.  Woonsocket historical minutes:  a
bicentennial presentation....  Woonsocket,
[1976?].  xii, 139, [7]p.  RHi.
    Vignettes of local history.

4125    WOONSOCKET HOSPITAL.  "'For the cure of the
sick--for the benefit of the poor and
especially the needy.'"  n.p.:  [R.I.
Manifold Printing,] n.d.  40p.  RHi.
    History of the hospital, 1873-1973.

    SEE ALSO entries 179, 554, 601, 1246, 3803.

# Supplementary Bibliographies and Guides

Bibliographies of categories of material covered by our editorial guidelines are included in the main body of this volume. They are listed in the Index under the heading "Bibliographies" and also under the particular subject headings to which they pertain, where they come first, separated by a semicolon from other entries. Selected materials wholly or partially excluded by our guidelines can be found in the bibliographies and guides listed below. The list is divided into two sections, [1] General and New England (the items listed here provide geographical access to particular states) and [2] Rhode Island. Basic to all bibliographical searching is Eugene P. Sheehy's Guide to Reference Books.


General and New England

AMERICA: HISTORY AND LIFE; a guide to periodical literature. Santa Barbara, Calif.: Clio Pr., 1964-.
     Abstracts of articles, book reviews, and dissertations. Includes state and local history, by state. Published in four parts (A-D) each year since 1974. A useful guide, especially to articles published after the date of this volume.

ANCTIL, PIERRE. A Franco-American bibliography: New England. Bedford, N.H.: National Materials Development Center, 1979. ix, 137p.

ARTS & HUMANITIES CITATION INDEX. Philadelphia: Institute for Scientific Information, 1976-.

ATLANTIC INDEXING COMPANY. Index to New England periodicals: a current index to selected regional publications. Brookline, N.H., 1978-.
     Annual compilation; includes a number of historical society journals.

BASSETT, T. D. SEYMOUR. A list of New England bibliographies. [Boston:] Committee for a New England Bibliography, n.d. 23p.
     Reprinted from New England Quarterly, 44 (1971), 178-200.

BRIGHAM, CLARENCE SAUNDERS. History and bibliography of American newspapers, 1690-1820. Worcester, Mass.: American Antiquarian Society, 1947. 2v.

COMPREHENSIVE DISSERTATION INDEX, 1861-1972. Ann Arbor, Mich.: Xerox University Microfilms, 1973. 37v.
     Supplements carry the coverage forward. Searchable by computer.

DARGAN, MARION. Guide to American biography. Albuquerque, N.M.: Univ. of New Mexico Pr., 1949-1952. 2v.

DICKINSON, ARTHUR TAYLOR. American historical fiction. 3d ed. Metuchen, N.J.: Scarecrow Pr., 1971. 380p.

DICTIONARY OF AMERICAN BIOGRAPHY. Allen Johnson and Dumas Malone, eds. N.Y.: Charles Scribner's Sons, 1928-1937. 20v. and index.
     Includes birthplace index and subject access under "Rhode Island." Supplements 1-7 (1944-1981) extend coverage to persons who died before 1965; they are not indexed.

DISSERTATION ABSTRACTS INTERNATIONAL. Ann Arbor, Mich.: University Microfilms, 1938-.
   Covers dissertations accepted since 1935. Volumes 1-11 entitled "Microfilm Abstracts" and thereafter, "Dissertation Abstracts."

DORNBUSCH, CHARLES EMIL. Histories, personal narratives: United States Army; a checklist. (1956) Cornwallville, N.Y.: Hope Farm Pr., 1967. 399p.

_____. Military bibliography of the Civil War. N.Y.: New York Public Library, 1961-1972. 3v.

DRAKE, MILTON. Almanacs of the United States. N.Y.: Scarecrow Pr., 1962. 2v.
   Covers 1639-1850.

FORBES, HARRIETTE MERRIFIELD. New England diaries, 1602-1800: a descriptive catalogue of diaries, orderly books, and sea journals. Topsfield, Mass.: Priv. Print., 1923. viii, 439p.

GREGORY, WINIFRED, ed. American newspapers, 1821-1936: a union list of files available in the United States and Canada. N.Y.: H. W. Wilson, 1937. 791p.

HARVARD UNIVERSITY. LIBRARY. Widener Library shelflist, 9: American history.... Cambridge, Mass., 1967. 5v.

HAYWOOD, CHARLES. A bibliography of North American folklore and folksong. N.Y.: Greenberg, 1951. xxx, 1292p.

KAMINKOW, MARION J. United States local histories in the Library of Congress: a bibliography. Baltimore: Magna Carta Book Co., 1975. 5v.

KAPLAN, LOUIS. A bibliography of American autobiographies. Madison, Wis.: Univ. of Wis. Pr., 1961. xii, 372p.

KARPEL, BERNARD. Arts in America: a bibliography. Washington: Smithsonian Institution Pr., 1979. 4v.
   Index is vol 4.

KUEHL, WARREN F. Dissertations in history: an index to dissertations completed in history departments of United States and Canadian universities. Lexington, Ky.: Univ. of Ky. Pr., 1965-1972. 2v.
   Covers 1873-1970.

LE GEAR, CLARA EGLI. United States atlases: a list of national, state, county, city, and regional atlases in the Library of Congress. Washington: Govt. Print. Office, 1950-1953. 2v.

NEW YORK PUBLIC LIBRARY. Dictionary catalog of the history of the Americas. Boston: G. K. Hall, 1961. 28v. First supplement, 1973. 9v.

_____. United States local history catalog: a modified shelf list arranged alphabetically by state, and alphabetically by locality within each state. Boston: G. K. Hall, 1974. 2v.

RINK, EVALD. Technical Americana: a checklist of technical publications printed before 1831. Millwood, N.Y.: Kraus International Publications, 1981. xxviii, 776p.

SOCIAL SCIENCES CITATION INDEX. Philadelphia: Institute for Scientific Information, 1966-.

SPEAR, DORTHEA N. Bibliography of American directories through 1860. Worcester, Mass.: American Antiquarian Society, 1961. 389p.
   Business, city, and county directories, arranged by place.

TANSELLE, GEORGE THOMAS. Guide to the study of United States imprints. Cambridge, Mass.: Harvard Univ. Pr., 1971. 2v.

UNION LIST OF SERIALS in libraries of the United States and Canada. (1927, 1943) 3d. ed. N.Y.: H. W. Wilson, 1965. 5v.
   A basic tool for finding periodical literature cited in this bibliography.

U.S. LIBRARY OF CONGRESS. The National Union Catalog of Manuscript Collections, based on reports from American repositories. Ann Arbor, Mich.: J. W. Edwards, 1962-.

# Supplementary Bibliographies and Guides

U.S. NATIONAL HISTORICAL PUBLICATIONS COMMISSION. A guide to archives and manuscripts in the United States. Philip May Hamer, ed. New Haven, Conn.: Yale Univ. Pr., 1961. xxiii, 775p.

U.S. NATIONAL HISTORICAL PUBLICATIONS AND RECORDS COMMISSION. Directory of archives and manuscript repositories in the United States. Washington: National Archives and Records Service, General Services Administration, 1978. 905p.

WOMEN'S HISTORY SOURCES: a guide to archives and manuscript collections in the United States. Andrea Hinding, ed. N.Y.: R. R. Bowker in association with the Univ. of Minnesota, 1979. 2v.


Rhode Island

AGOSTINELLI, ANTHONY J. The Newport Jazz Festival, Rhode Island, 1954-1971: a bibliography, discography and filmography. Providence, 1977. iv, 58, 12, [6]p.

ALDEN, JOHN ELIOT. Rhode Island imprints, 1727-1800. N.Y.: R. R. Bowker, 1949. xxiv, 665p.

BACHMANN, GEORGE T. "A check list of Rhode Island imprints from 1854 to 1856, with a historical introduction." Unpublished thesis, Catholic Univ. of America, 1961. 113p.

THE BAY BIB: a Rhode Island marine bibliography. Coordinated by Charlene Quinn Dunn and Lynne Zeitlin Hale; Anthony Bucci, ed. [Kingston:] Univ. of R.I., 1979. 2v.

BELLAS, LEWIS J. A research bookshelf of historical-geographical resources for the Providence area. [Kingston:] Univ. of R.I., 1967. 30p.

BRIGHAM, CLARENCE SAUNDERS. "A bibliography of the Narragansett Country." Bulletin of Bibliography, 4 (1906), 117-118.

BROWN, HARRY GLENN, and MAUDE O. BROWN. A directory of printing, publishing, bookselling & allied trades in Rhode Island to 1865. N.Y.: New York Public Library, 1958. 211p.

CAIRNS, MARGARET THERESE. "A check list of Rhode Island imprints from 1831-1834; with a historical introduction." Unpublished thesis, Catholic Univ. of America, 1959. iii, 100p.

CHAPIN, HOWARD M. Bibliography of Rhode Island bibliography. Providence: Preston & Rounds, 1914. [9]p.

_____. Check list of maps of Rhode Island. Providence: Preston & Rounds, 1918. 48p.

_____. List of Roger Williams's writings. Providence: Preston & Rounds, 1918. 7p.

CONLEY, PATRICK T. "An annotated bibliography of works relating to the history of Rhode Island's cities and towns." Typescript, R.I. Historical Society, [1974]. Unp.

COYLE, WALLACE. Roger Williams: a reference guide. Boston: G. K. Hall, 1977. xiii, 102p.

CUTTING, HELEN F. "A check-list of Providence, Rhode Island, imprints from 1848-1850, with an historical introduction." Unpublished thesis, Catholic Univ. of America, 1961. iii, 93p.

DUPONT, JULIE A. "A check list of Providence, Rhode Island, imprints for the years 1858 and 1859, with a historical introduction." Unpublished thesis, Catholic Univ. of America, 1965. iii, 115p.

FARKAS, CATHRINE ANN. "A check list of Rhode Island imprints from 1860-1861, with a historical introduction." Unpublished thesis, Catholic Univ. of America, 1965. iii, 79p.

HANCOCK, EVA W. "A check-list of Providence, Rhode Island, imprints from 1842-1843, with an historical introduction." Unpublished thesis, Catholic Univ. of America, 1960. 74p.

HAMMETT, CHARLES E., JR. A contribution to the bibliography and literature of Newport, R.I.: comprising a list of books published or printed in Newport, with notes and additions. Newport: Charles E. Hammett, Jr., 1887. 185p.

GUILD, REUBEN ALDRIDGE. An account of the writings of Roger Williams. n.p., [1862]. 11p.

JONES, AGNES, MARCIA BEGUM, and CONSTANCE CAMERON. A selected biographical and bibliographical list of Rhode Island authors. Providence: Providence Public Library, 1967. 34p.
    Charles W. Crosby, ed.

[KOOPMAN, HARRY LYMAN.] Brown University...bibliography, 1756-1898.... Providence: Remington Printing, 1898. 20p.

MENDELOFF, NATHAN N. "A checklist of Rhode Island imprints, 1821-1830, with a historical introduction." Unpublished thesis, Catholic Univ. of America, 1954. iv, 189p.

MOESON, FLORENCE T'AN. "A checklist of Rhode Island imprints from 1839 to 1841." Unpublished thesis, Catholic Univ. of America, 1959. iii, 57p.

NICOLOSI, ANTHONY S., and EVELYN R. CHERPAK. A guide to source materials in the Naval Historical Collection. Newport: Naval War College, 1980. 39p.

RHODE ISLAND. STATE LIBRARY, PROVIDENCE. Check-list of departmental publications of the State of Rhode Island, 1935-1955. [Providence,] n.d. 33p.
    Supplements, 1956-1972.

RHODE ISLAND BOOKS forming part of the library of Nelson W. Aldrich, Warwick, Rhode Island. n.p.: Priv. Print., 1915. [164]p.

ST.DENIS, GASTON PIERRE. "Checklist of Providence, Rhode Island, imprints from 1801 through 1805, with an historical introduction." Unpublished thesis, Catholic Univ. of America, 1952. iii, 81p.

SCHEKORRA, EVA W. "A check list of Rhode Island imprints for 1863 and 1864, with a historical introduction." Unpublished thesis, Catholic Univ. of America, 1964. 80p.

SHERMAN, STUART C. The voice of the whaleman: with an account of the Nicholson Whaling Collection. Providence: Providence Public Library, 1965. 216p.
    Collection of whaling records in Providence Public Library.

SNUGGS, M. ANN. "A check list of Providence, Rhode Island, imprints for 1865, with a historical introduction." Unpublished thesis, Catholic Univ. of America, 1967. 73p.

TANNER, EARL C. "The Providence Federal Customhouse papers as a source of maritime history since 1780." New England Quarterly, 26 (1953), 88-100.

TSAO, MARY ANN. "A check list of Providence, Rhode Island, imprints for the years 1835-1838, with a historical introduction." Unpublished thesis, Catholic Univ. of America, 1958. iv, 107p.

U.S. WORKS PROJECTS ADMINISTRATION. SURVEY OF FEDERAL ARCHIVES. Ship registers and enrollments of Newport, Rhode Island, 1790-1939. Providence: National Archives Project, 1941. 2v.
    Abstracts of registers and enrollments.

_____. Ship registers and enrollments of Providence, Rhode Island, 1773-1939. Providence: National Archives Project, 1941. 2v.
    Vol. 1 is in two parts.

_____. Ship registers and enrollments: ship licenses issued to vessels under twenty tons; ship licenses on enrollments issued out of the port of Bristol-Warren, Rhode Island, 1773-1939. Providence: National Archives Project, 1941. vii, 354, 72, 9p.

VAMBERY, JOSEPH T. "A checklist of Rhode Island State's imprints, from 1845 through 1847, with an historical introduction." Unpublished thesis, Catholic Univ. of America, 1959. iii, 150p.

WINSHIP, GEORGE PARKER. Brown University broadsides.... Providence, 1913. [4]p.

_____. Rhode Island imprints, 1727-1800: a list of books, pamphlets, newspapers and broadsides printed at Newport, Providence, Warren, Rhode Island, between 1727 and 1800. (1914) Providence: R.I. Historical Society, 1915. 88p.

# Index

This index includes all authors, editors, and compilers, as well as subjects and places. The references are to entry numbers, not pages. If there is a bibliography for a particular heading, it is listed first and is separated from the other entry numbers by a semicolon. To find general works of state history, see "Rhode Island--histories." We distinguish persons with identical names by vital dates or other data.

We alphabetize word by word rather than letter by letter (New Shoreham before Newport). Corporate authors divided by a period (such as Rhode Island. Tercenterary Commission) precede names of institutions not so divided (such as Rhode Island Central Trades and Labor Union).

Headings for places include names of towns and former and present names of places within towns. Where a work is about several towns, each town is indexed; but sections on towns in county or state histories or other works of larger scope are not indexed.

Library of Congress subject headings have usually been preferred. The user can find material about one subject in one place (e.g., Franco-Americans in Woonsocket) by first finding the range of entry numbers for that place, and then looking for numbers under the subject heading that fall within that range. Headings with many entries, such as "Churches, Roman Catholic," have usually been subdivided by towns.

Abbott Run, place in Cumberland
Abrasive Machine Tool Company, 1621
Academies, see Private schools
Accidents, 1568, 1689, 3763
Achtermier, William O., 1
Acid Factory Brook, 4004
Ackley, William N., 3928
Adams, James P., 2
Adams, James Truslow, 3
Adamsville, place in Little Compton, 1788
Adelman, David C., 4-5, 1866, 1999, 2681-2683
Adirondack Mountains, 995
Adlam, Samuel, 7-8
Admiralty courts, 29, 361, 827, 1122
Advent Christian Church, Lafayette, 2521
Adventure (sloop), 9
Advertising, 3190
African Benevolent Society, Newport, 2313
African Methodist Episcopal churches, see
    Churches, African Methodist Episcopal
African Union Meeting and School-house,
    Providence, 3607
Afro-Americans, see Blacks
Aged, 2839, 3000
Agriculture (see also Farm life; Farms and
    farming; Poultry), 86, 405, 422, 533, 649,
    772, 1141, 1319, 1493, 2653
Ahmat, Sharom, 10
Aiken, G. Fred, 2684

Aircraft industry, 1599
Airships, 134
Albee Stock Company, Providence, 2685
Albert, Judith Strong, 2686
Albion, place in Lincoln
Albro, John, 1203
Alderman, Clifford Lindsey, 12
Aldrich, Nelson, 937
Alexander, Robert, 2687
Algeo, Sara M., 13
All Saints' Memorial Church, Providence, 3350
Allan, Delora Whitten, 2688
Allen, Devere, 15
Allen, Frank James, 1867
Allen, Helen Farrell, 1868-1869, 2689
Allen, Margaret, 3734
Allen, R. W., 16
Allen, Samuel H., 17-18
Allen, Zachariah, 19-20, 1262, 2690, 3278, 3798
Allen family, 3715
Allendale, place in North Providence
Allendale Mutual Insurance Company, 1735
Allenton, place in North Kingstown
Allergy, 354
Almagno, R. Stephen, 2691
Almanacs, 183, 760, 762, 1062, 1958, 2335, 3550
Almy, Benjamin, 1870
Almy, Mary Gould, 1871
Alton, Bradley M., 1177

# Index

# Index

# Index

# Index

# Index

# Index

2712, 2731, 2783, 2816-2817, 2898, 2900, 2917, 2985, 3013, 3037, 3051, 3137, 3140, 3147-3148, 3154, 3168-3170, 3189, 3357-3362, 3383, 3386-3393, 3398, 3408, 3410, 3418, 3421-3422, 3440, 3445-3448, 3451, 3622, 3687, 3703--Richmond, 3764--Scituate, 3775-3776--South Kingstown, 3805, 3820, 3829, 3875, 3888--Tiverton, 3916-3917, 3924-3925--Warren, 976, 3936, 3950, 3953, 3956-3958--West Greenwich, 4003--West Warwick, 4013, 4020-4021--Westerly, 4039, 4045, 4050
Churches, Christian (denomination), 1505, 3356, 4071
Churches, Congregational, 983, 3697--Barrington, 1347, 1354, 1359--Bristol, 1360, 1365-1366, 1377, 1405, 1426--Central Falls, 1456-1459 --Cranston, 1539-1541--East Providence, 1626-1628--Foster, 1648--Lincoln, 1763 --Little Compton, 1769, 1775-1777--Newport, 1885, 1975, 2243-2244, 2408, 2462, 2472 --North Smithfield, 2566-2569--Pawtucket, 2582, 2613-2614--Providence, 2825, 2836, 2899, 2976, 3072, 3171, 3192-3193, 3205, 3263, 3352-3355, 3363-3366, 3385, 3399, 3404, 3411, 3415-3417, 3449-3450, 3452-3453, 3590, 3601, 3635-3636, 3650, 3689, 3696-3697, 3730-3731, 3759--South Kingstown, 3832, 3848, 3856, 3897--Tiverton, 3912, 3914--West Warwick, 4018
Churches, Eastern Orthodox, see Churches, Armenian; Churches, Greek Orthodox
Churches, Episcopal, 194, 448, 517-518, 674, 759, 1086, 2537--Bristol, 1406, 1431--Coventry, 1508--Cranston, 1517, 1532--East Greenwich, 1607--Jamestown, 1708, 1717--Lincoln, 1754--Middletown, 1167, 1800, 1808, 1814, 1816--Narragansett, 1823--Newport, 1882, 1982, 1992, 1998, 2050, 2065, 2119, 2131, 2177, 2239-2241, 2245-2246, 2261, 2404, 2416--North Kingstown, 2496, 2501, 2508, 2522, 2524-2525, 2537, 2540--North Providence, 2562--Pawtucket, 2601, 2622, 2637--Portsmouth, 1167--Providence, 2830, 2850, 2883, 3098-3099, 3127, 3178, 3206, 3350, 3369-3370, 3400-3401, 3538, 3591, 3618, 3621, 3711--Smithfield, 3791--South Kingstown, 3899--Tiverton, 3926--Warren, 3928--Warwick, 3988
Churches, Freewill Baptist, 846, 1127, 3259-3260, 3402, 3414, 3796, 3804, 3999
Churches, Greek Orthodox, 1538, 2237, 2423
Churches, Lutheran, 3433, 3990
Churches, Methodist, 1615, 1976, 1991, 2225, 2227, 2236, 3075, 3107, 3203-3204, 3351, 3367, 3407, 3409, 3952
Churches, Moravian, 1903
Churches, Presbyterian, 1979, 2226, 3439, 3608, 3968-3969
Churches, Protestant (see also specific denominations and churches), 1131
Churches, Roman Catholic (see also Monasticism and religious orders), 228, 512; 228, 230, 257, 259, 339, 445, 512, 802-804, 814, 911, 956, 3436--Barrington, 1346, 1348--Bristol, 1367-1369--Burrillville, 1439-1441, 1448--Central Falls, 1246, 1455, 1460-1466, 1469--Charlestown, 1475--Coventry, 1494-1495--Cranston, 1542, 1553--Cumberland, 1558-1560--East Greenwich, 1574--East Providence, 1612--Glocester, 1663--Hopkinton, 1677--Lincoln, 1756-1757--New Shoreham,

1844--Newport, 2068, 2229-2235--North Kingstown, 2542--North Providence, 2548, 2555--North Smithfield, 2578--Pawtucket, 2584, 2603, 2612, 2619-2621, 2642--Providence, 230, 803, 2691, 2713, 2720, 3368, 3405-3406, 3412-3413, 3423-3432, 3435-3437, 3501, 3658, 3683, 3698, 3761--Smithfield, 3795--South Kingstown, 3900--Warren, 3940, 3955, 3959-3960--Warwick, 3962, 3997-3998--West Warwick, 4022, 4030-4033--Woonsocket, 1246, 4097-4098, 4103-4110, 4112-4123
Churches, Seventh-Day Baptist, 416, 1036, 1094, 1681, 1686, 1693, 1695, 2021, 4057
Churches, Six-Principle Baptist, 1337
Churches, Union, 1511, 1658, 2448, 3631, 3968-3969
Churches, Unitarian, 1921, 2148, 2213, 3072, 3088, 3171, 3192-3193, 3263, 3452-3453, 3590, 3601, 3635-3636, 3650, 3655, 3759
Churches, Universalist, 1449, 2950, 3394-3397, 3583
Churchill, Donald, 187-188, 2844
Churchill, Irving L., 3812
Churchward, Lloyd G., 189
Chyet, Stanley F., 1967-1969
Ciaburri, Robert L., 190
Cinema, see Motion pictures
Circus, 91, 3056
Cirillo, Susan E., 1371
Citizens Savings Bank, 2845
Citizenship, 902
City halls, see Municipal buildings
City planning, 2315, 3374-3382
Civic League of Newport, 2039
Civil liberty, 438
Civil rights, 5, 1038
Civil War (1861-1865), 62, 309, 340, 471, 475, 586, 830, 874, 1044, 1350, 2216, 2665, 2765, 2768, 2856, 2891, 2986-2987, 3064, 3097, 3130, 3237, 3634, 3817
Claflin, Albert W., 2846
Claggett, Thomas, 1956
Claggett, William, 317, 1950, 1959
Clambakes, 473, 1053, 2803
Clapp, Roger Tillinghast, 191, 2847-2848, 4004
Clarendon Court (historic house), Newport, 2460
Clark, A. Howard, 3813
Clark, F. C., 192
Clark, Henry C., 2849
Clark, Jane, 193
Clark, John Innes, 3265
Clark, Kenneth, 1970
Clark, Louisa Elizabeth, 1743
Clark, Samuel, 1743
Clark, Thomas March, 194, 2850, 3587
Clark, William Richard, 195
Clark family, 3265
Clarke, Charles H., 1971
Clarke, John, 409, 968, 981, 1161, 1191, 1196, 2217
Clarke, Lena, 1707, 1716
Clarke, Louis W., 2851
Clarke, Prescott O., 196
Clarke, Richard H., 197
Clarkville, place in Glocester
Classical High School, Providence, 2821, 2929
Clauson, James Earl, 199, 1537
Clayville, place in Foster and Scituate
Clemence, Clara E., 1234-1235, 1646-1647
Clemence, Thomas, 1736

# Index

# Index

# Index

# Index

# Index

# Index

# Index

Nicholas, Herbert Newell, 716
Nichols, Arthur Howard, 2261
Nichols, L. Nelson, 717
Nichols family, 1676
Nicholson, Paul C., 1856-1857
Nicholson File Company, 3299
Nicolosi, Anthony S., 718
Nightclubs (see also Restaurants), 1643
Nine Men's Misery, place in Cumberland, 1252
Ninigret (Niantic Indian sachem), 1474, 1478
Ninigret Cycling Club, Hopkinton, 1691
Noailles, Vicomte and Vicomtesse de, 2483
Nobel, Theresa Lownes, 1821
Nobrega, Edith H., 1247
Nooseneck, place in West Greenwich, 4011
Norris, Isaac II, 750
Norsemen, see Northmen
North, S. N. D., 3872
North American Eating House, Providence, 3252
North Carolina, 2288
North Congregational Church, Providence, 3411
North Cumberland, place in Cumberland, 1566
North End, place in Providence, 2693, 3118
North Ferry, place in North Kingstown
North Foster, place in Foster
North Kingstown, R.I., 131, 458, 1277, 1322,
    2493-2543
North Main Street, Providence, 3124
North Providence, R.I., 1251, 2544-2563
North Providence, R.I.  Saint Anthony's Church,
    2555
North Providence Union Free Library, 2557
North Scituate, place in Scituate
North Scituate Public Library, 3783
North Smithfield, R.I., 2564-2578, 3803
North Tiverton, place in Tiverton
North Tiverton, R.I.  Baptist Church, 3917
Northern Interrelated Library System, 1248, 2557
Northmen, 268, 324, 459-460, 1070, 1414,
    1416-1417, 1867, 2181, 2280, 2282, 2469, 2479
Northrup, Florence Perry, 3873
Norton, Vernon C., 2606
Norumbega (colony), 400, 688
Norwood, place in Warwick
Notre Dame Church, Central Falls, 1461-1462
Nova Scotia, 308, 544, 993
Noyes, Isaac Pitman, 719
Numismatics, 1046, 2140
Nursing schools, 3198, 3530

Oak Lawn, R.I.  Baptist Church.  Ladies' Union
    Society, 1550
Oak Valley, place in Burrillville
Oakland, place in Burrillville
Oakland Beach, place in Warwick, 3985, 3992
Oaklawn, place in Cranston
Oaklawn (historic house), Newport, 1878
Oakley, Chester A., Jr., 2262
O'Brien, Francis J., 720, 3253-3255
O'Brien, John J., 721
O'Brien, John J., Jr., 4019
O'Brien, William B., 1442
Observer (newspaper), 2558
Observer Publications, 1671
Occupations (see also Mobility, occupational),
    2873
Ocean State Theater, Providence, 3143
Ochre Point (historic house), Newport, 2263
O'Connor, Richard, 2264
Odd Fellows, Independent Order of, 2463, 2940

Odd Fellows, Independent Order of.  Providence.
    Roger Williams Lodge, No. 3, 3256
Odd Fellows, Independent Order of.  Rhode Island.
    Right Worthy Grand Encampment, 722
Oelrichs, Tessie, 1996
O'Hanley, Donald M., 2265
Olausen, Elizabeth, 1655
Old age, see Aged
Old age homes, 3000
Old City Hall, Newport, 2130
Old Colony Co-operative Bank, 3258
"Old Grimes" (poem), 3060
Old Harbor, place in New Shoreham
Old Post Road, 3902
Old Slater Mill, Pawtucket, 2640, 2645, 2648
Old State House, Newport, 1891, 2069, 2174, 2415,
    2419
Old Stone Bank, see Providence Institution for
    Savings
Old Warwick, place in Warwick
Oldham, Neild B., 1594
Oldport Association, Newport, 2267
Oliver, E. Wesley, Jr., 2268-2269
Olney, Joseph, 3791
Olney, Polly, 3045
Olney, Stephen, 475
Olneyville, place in Providence, 2949, 3379
Olneyville, R.I.  First Freewill Baptist Church,
    3259-3260
O'Loughlin, Kathleen Merrick, 2270
Olsen, Elizabeth Anne, 3988
Olsen, Stephen, 723
Olson, Sandra, 1655
Omega, place in East Providence
Onorato, Ronald J., 3262
Opera House, Providence, 2868
Opera House, Woonsocket, 4082
Operation Clapboard, Newport, 2199
Oppenheim, Samuel, 2271-2272
Organs, see Reed organs
Oriental trade, 10, 3709
Orms Street Synagogue, Providence, 3592
Orphanages, 3001, 3220, 3437, 3587
Orthodox Eastern Church, see Churches, Armenian;
    Churches, Greek Orthodox
Osborne, Robert Scott, 2273
Osgood, Samuel, 3263
Osterberg, J. S., 724
Osterud, Nancy Grey, 589
O'Toole, Dennis A., 2670
Ott, Joseph K., 725-732, 2274, 3264-3265
Our Lady of Consolation Church, Pawtucket, 2619
Our Lady of Czenstochowa Church, Coventry,
    1494-1495
Our Lady of Fatima Church, Cumberland, 1558
Our Lady of Good Help Church, Mapleville,
    1439-1440
Our Lady of Mercy Church, East Greenwich, 1574
Our Lady of Mount Carmel Church, Bristol, 1367
Our Lady of Mount Carmel Church, Providence, 3412
Our Lady of the Rosary Church, Providence, 3413
Outlet Department Stores, 537, 773
Oysters, 3063

Pabodie, W. H., 738
Pachelbel, Charles Theodore, 2200, 2416
Packard, J. K., 2275
Pagoda House, Newport, 2125
Paine, George T., 3267
Paine, John, 1013

212

# Index

Paine House, Coventry, 1485
Painters and paintings, see Art and Artists; Landscape painters and landscape paintings; Portrait painters and portrait paintings
Palace Garden, place in Warwick
Palatine (ship), 1838, 1842, 1860
Palatine Temple, Ancient Arabic Order of the Nobles of the Mystic Shrine for North America, Providence, 2692
Palfrey, William, 3045
Palfy, Eleanor, 1596
Palmer, Fanny Purdy, 621
Palmer, Henrietta R., 873
Palmer, Henry Robinson, 739-740, 870, 1419, 3217, 3268
Palmer, Joseph, 2376
Panaggio, Leonard J., 830, 2276-2278
Panic of 1873, 163
Papermaking and trade, 1106, 4091
Parades, 3498
Pardee, Alice DeWolf, 1420
Parents Council for Retarded Children, 53
Park Place Congregational Church, Pawtucket, 2582
Park Street Free Baptist Church, Providence, 3414
Parker, Roderick H., 3918
Parker, Thomas M., 2933
Parks, 1617, 2708, 2740, 3066, 3123, 3186
Paroisse du Christ-Roi, West Warwick, 4030
Paroisse Notre Dame des Victoires, Woonsocket, 4114
Paroisse Saint Jacques, Manville, see Saint James Church, Manville
Paroisse Saint-Jean-Baptiste, Warren, 3940
Parrington, Vernon L., 741
Parsonages, 2496
Parsons, Charles W., 742-745, 3269
Parsons, Usher, 746-749, 2702, 3223
Parsons, William T., 750
Partridge, Alexander, 2414
Partridge, Herbert G., 3270
Pascoag, place in Burrillville, 1443, 1447
Pascoag Herald (newspaper), 1443
Passover Journal, Providence, 3596
Patience, place in Portsmouth
Patrons of Husbandry, 533, 2564
Patten, David, 751, 1781-1786
Patten, Martha F., 1349
Pattern making, 3296
Patterson, James T., 612
Patterson, Merrill R., 3272
Patton, A. B., 3273
Patykewich, Victoria H. C., 1192
Paul, Edward J., 1810
Paul, John White, 1810
Paulhus, David L., 752
Pawcatuck, R.I. Pawcatuck Seventh-Day Baptist Church, 4057
Pawcatuck River Valley, 1310, 1345
Pawcatuck Valley Women's Club, Westerly, 4073
Pawtucket, R.I., 179, 554, 601, 1009, 1240, 1242, 1249, 1255, 2556, 2579-2651, 3019
Pawtucket, R.I. Church of Saint Theresa of the Child Jesus, 2612
Pawtucket, R.I. Congregational Church, 2613-2614
Pawtucket, R.I. Fire Department, 1249
Pawtucket, R.I. First Baptist Church, 2615-2618
Pawtucket, R.I. Our Lady of Consolation Church, 2619
Pawtucket, R.I. Saint Joseph's Church, 2620
Pawtucket, R.I. Saint Maria Goretti Church, 2621

Pawtucket, R.I. Trinity Church, 2622
Pawtucket, R.I. Woodlawn Baptist Church, 2623-2624
Pawtucket Business Men's Association, 2594, 2626
Pawtucket-Central Falls Railroad Depot, 2598
Pawtucket Congregational Church, 2613-2614
Pawtucket Institution for Savings, 2627
Pawtucket Spinning Ring Company, 2635
Pawtucket Times (newspaper), 2629
Pawtuxet, place in Cranston and Warwick, 68, 70, 92, 95, 355, 576, 637, 785, 837, 1054
Pawtuxet Baptist Church, Cranston, 785, 1530, 1536
Pawtuxet Purchase, 506, 701, 900, 917
Pawtuxet River Valley, 38-39, 41, 186, 502-503, 608, 721, 1022
Paxton, Helen Thayer, 2575
Paxton, William, 3274
Payne, Abraham, 753
Payne, Charles H., 754
Peace, Nancy E., 755
Peace Dale, place in South Kingstown, 3808, 3831, 3842, 3847
Peace Dale Congregational Church, 3832
Peace societies, 368
Pearce, B. W., 2279
Pearce, Dorothy Joslin, 857
Peattie, Donald Culross, 756
Peck, George B., 757
Peck, Henry J., 3944
Peck, Reginald E., 4058
Peckham, Edward Lewis, 3275
Peckham, Stephen Farnum, 3275-3276
Peleg Arnold Tavern, North Smithfield, 2573
Pell, Claiborne De B., 758
Pell, Herbert, 2280-2281
Pembroke College, see Brown University--Pembroke College
Pendleton, Albert P., 4059-4061
Pendleton, William H., 3875
Pendleton House, Museum of Art, Rhode Island School of Design, 3175
Pennington, Edgar Legare, 759
People (newspaper), 2991
People's Evangelical Church, Providence, 3107
Pepper, John, 1899
Perfectionism, 1562
Perkins, Helen B., 1631
Perkins, Joseph, 3861
Perkins, Roy F., 1631
Perry, Amos, 760-762, 3277-3279
Perry, Calbraith Bourn, 763
Perry, Charles E., 1858
Perry, Charles M., 764, 1157
Perry, Elizabeth A., 1672
Perry, Harvey C., 4062
Perry, J. Tavenor, 2282
Perry, Joshua, 1277
Perry, Oliver Hazard, 2256, 2283
Perry, Thomas, Jr., 765
Perry family, 763
Perryville, place in South Kingstown
Pesaturo, Ubaldo U. M., 766
Peterson, Edward, 1193
Petroglyphs (inscribed rocks), 268-269, 480, 3982
Pettaconsett, place in Cranston
Pettaquamscutt Historical Society, Kingston, 1328-1329, 3854, 3876
Pettaquamscutt Purchase, 3816, 3854, 3868
Pettaquamscutt region, 1274, 3844

213

# Index

# Index

# Index

# Index

# Index

# Index

# Index

Union Library Asociation, Phenix, 4027
Union Station, Providence, 135
Union Village, place in North Smithfield
Unitarian churches, see Churches, Unitarian
United Baptist Church, Newport, 2242
United Brotherhood of Carpenters & Joiners of
    America. Carpenters Local Union, No. 94, 1088
United Colonies, Commissioners of, 1013
United Congregational Church, Little Compton,
    1769, 1775-1777
United Congregational Church, Newport, 1885,
    2243-2244, 2472
U.S. Army, 2078, 2215, 2338, 2489
U.S. Bobbin and Shuttle Company, 774
U.S. Coast Guard, 2447
U.S. Congress. House of Representatives, 1089
U.S. Custom House, Providence, 2689
U.S. Department of Transportation. Federal
    Railroad Administration. Northeast Corridor
    Improvement Project, 1091
U.S. Department of the Interior. Historic
    American Engineering Record, 1090
U.S. Department of the Interior. National Park
    Service. Cultural Resources Management
    Division, 3690
U.S. Naval Academy, Newport, 830
U.S. Naval Advanced Base Depot, Davisville, 2530
U.S. Naval Air Station, Quonset Point, 2523, 2530
U.S. Naval Hospital, Newport, 1894, 2448
U.S. Naval Torpedo Station, Newport, 1972, 2435
U.S. Naval Training Station, Newport, 2449, 2481
U.S. Naval War College, Newport, 1884, 1888,
    2016, 2022, 2099-2100, 2114, 2164, 2170, 2175,
    2216, 2273, 2306, 2347-2348, 2390-2391, 2424,
    2450-2451, 2458-2459, 2476
U.S. Naval Yeoman School, Newport, 2452
U.S. Navy, 131, 297, 718, 836, 1145, 2017, 2084,
    2108, 2216, 2283, 2520, 3214
U.S. Weather Bureau, 2538
U.S. Works Progress Administration, 195
United Train of Artillery, Providence, 3691
Universal Friend, see Wilkinson, Jemima
Universal Winding Machine, 1551
Universalist churches, see Churches, Universalist
Universities and colleges (see also Brown
    University; Providence College; University of
    Rhode Island), 830, 863, 1077, 1418, 2104,
    2724, 3215, 3313, 3472, 3536, 3656, 3794
University Grammar School, Providence, 3033
University Hall, Brown University, 2744, 2769,
    2774, 2973, 3026
University of Rhode Island, Kingston, 3806, 3812,
    3815, 3818, 3851, 3880, 3887, 3889, 3896,
    3898, 3905-3906, 3909
University of Rhode Island, Narragansett Bay
    campus, 1831, 2530
Updike, Daniel Berkeley, 2536
Updike, Wilkins, 1092-1093, 2537
Upholsterers, see Furniture (craft)
Upper classes, 617, 1128, 1189, 1712, 1875, 1915,
    1938, 1985, 1996, 2002, 2009, 2013, 2020,
    2085, 2093, 2156, 2264, 2453
Upper South Providence, place in Providence, 3381
Upton, Dell, 2676
Urban League of Rhode Island, 3131
Uroff, Margaret Dickie, 3692
Usquepaugh, place in Richmond and South
    Kingstown, 1313, 1341
Utter, G. Benjamin, 1094
Utter, George B., 1344

Valley Falls, place in Cumberland
Vampires, 578, 886
Van Hoesen, Henry Bartlett, 3693
Van Rensselaer, Mary (King), 2453
Van Rensselaer Lodge of Perfection, Freemasons,
    Newport, 2044
Van Slyck, Nicholas, 3691
Van Slyck, R. E. Nicholas, 3694
Van Wye, Eugene, 3695
Vanderbilt, Harold S., 2454
Vare, Glenna Collett, 1358
Varnum, James Mitchell, 149, 1570, 1598, 1604
Vars, N. B., 4072
Vars Homestead, Westerly, 4072
Vassall, William, 1421
Vaughan, Roger, 2455
Veeder, Paul L. II, 2456
Vehicles, 725, 729, 1678
Venava, Sully W., 2561
Vernon, Thomas, 2457
Vernon, place in Foster
Vernon House, Newport, 2086, 2397
Veterans, 2947-2948, 4028
Veterans of Foreign Wars. Sergeant David
    Langevin Post, No. 449, West Warwick, 4028
Victor, Stephen, 1095
Vikings, see Northmen
Villa Marina (historic house), Newport, 1988
Vinland (historic estate), Newport, 2485
Vinton, Francis, 1096
Visiglio, Geraldine, 4073
Vital records, 524, 3836, 3856
Vlahos, Michael, 2458-2459
Vollmert, Leslie J., 3522
Volpe, Fred S., 1097
Von Bulow, Claus, 2460
Vose, James Gardiner, 552, 3696-3697
Voting, see Elections; Suffrage
Voting rights, see Suffrage

Waddicor, Arthur, 1554-1555
Wade, Evelyn, 2731
Wade, Herbert T., 1098
Wade, Nathaniel, 1098
Wadleigh, John R., 2461
Wady, James, 1951
Wages, 3202
Wainwright, Nicholas B., 1792
Waite, John, 3860
Wakefield, place in South Kingstown, 3847, 3903
Wakefield, R.I. Church of the Ascension, 3899
Wakefield, R.I. Saint Francis of Assisi Church,
    3900
Wakefield Baptist Church, 3888
Wakefield Branch Company, 3901
Walden, George F., 1211, 1472
Walker, Cyrus, 3788
Walker, John, 2677
Walker Island, place in Bristol
Wallace, Robert W., 2462
Wallum Lake, place in Burrillville, 1433, 1442,
    1446
Walsh, David S., 1818
Walsh, Evelyn M., 1099
Walsh, Kenneth M., 1818
Walsh, Richard A., 3698
Walter, Dorothy C., 3699
Wampanoag Indians, 675, 1353, 3929, 3932-3933,
    3937, 3939, 3942, 3946-3947
Wannamoisett Country Club, East Providence,
    1631-1632

# Index

# Index

Wonson, Richard L., 1140
Wood, Horatio G., 2107
Wood, Anna Wharton, 2483
Wood, Cynthia, 3690
Wood, Squire Greene, 1512
Wood, W. LeRoy, 1633
Wood River Junction, place in Richmond, 3763
Wood River Valley, 1267, 1345
Wood River Valley Branch Railroad, 1339
Woodbridge, George, 2484
Woodbury, Augustus, 3452, 3536
Woodbury Union Church, Conimicut, 3968-3969
Woodlawn, place in Pawtucket
Woodlawn Baptist Church, Pawtucket, 2623-2624
Woods, Alva, 3749
Woods, Arlene, 2485
Woods, John Carter Brown, 2784, 3750
Woods, Michael, 2312
Woodville, place in Hopkinton and Richmond
Woodville, place in North Providence
Woodward, Carl Raymond, 1141, 2543, 3905-3909, 4001
Woodward, William McKenzie, 3518, 3521
Woolen manufacture, 1142, 1379
Woolsey, Sarah Chauncey, 1222
Woonasquatucket Valley, 1251
Woonsocket, R.I., 179, 554, 601, 1246, 3803, 4081-4125
Woonsocket, R.I. Church of the Holy Family, 4103-4105
Woonsocket, R.I. Church of the Precious Blood, 4106-4110
Woonsocket, R.I. Convent de Jésus-Marie, 4111
Woonsocket, R.I. Department of Planning and Development, 4112
Woonsocket, R.I. Fête-Saint-Jean-Baptiste, 1922, 4113
Woonsocket, R.I. Paroisse Notre Dame des Victoires, 4114
Woonsocket, R.I. Saint Anthony's Church, 4115-4116
Woonsocket, R.I. Saint Charles' Church, 4117-4118
Woonsocket, R.I. Saint Joseph's Church, 4119
Woonsocket, R.I. Saint Louis de Gonzague Church, 4120-4122
Woonsocket, R.I. Saint Michael's Ukranian-Catholic Church, 4123
Woonsocket, R.I. Woonsocket Senior High School, 4124
Woonsocket Commandery, No. 24, Knights Templars, 4085
Woonsocket Hill, place in North Smithfield
Woonsocket Hospital, 4125
Woonsocket Trust Company, 4088
Worcester, Janice, 3734
Worcester, Wayne, 1143

Word of God Prayer Community, Saint Patrick's Parish, Providence, 3501
World Series (baseball), 2804, 3079
World War Memorial, Providence, 3588
World War I (1914-1918), 467, 535, 651, 1813, 2759, 2766, 3588
World War II (1939-1945), 23, 526, 822, 971, 2459, 2520, 2530, 2535, 2549, 3780
Wormeley, Katharine Prescott, 2487
Worthington, W. Chesley, 1675, 3181, 3751
Worthington, William, 1607
Wren, Christopher, 2353
Wright, C. M., 2488
Wright, Catharine Morris, 1714
Wright, Marion I., 1144
Wright, Redwood, 2489
Wright, Russell, 1564, 1639, 1694, 1739, 2315, 3767, 3883
Wright, T., 1145
Wriston, Barbara, 3752-3753
Wroth, Lawrence Counselman, 1146, 3754-3756
Wulsin, Eugene, 1147
Wyman, Arthur Crawford, 1148
Wyman, Lillie B. C., 1148
Wyoming, place in Hopkinton, 1688
Wyss, Bob, 1556

Yacht racing (see also America's Cup races), 262, 2107, 2410
Yacht-building, 1374-1376, 1383, 1391-1394, 1419
Yachting, 262, 2655, 4075
Yankee (privateer), 1362, 1415, 1425
Yarnall, James L., 1223-1225
Yawcook Farm, Exeter, 1636
Yawgoog Pond, Hopkinton, 1701
Yeager, Henry J., 2491
Yeats, William Butler, 3515
Yellow fever, 3629, 3758
Yiddish language, 394
Yondorf, Wendy, 530
Young, Charles M., 3759
Young, Harold G., 1261
Young, Harold H., 1149
Young, John, 2492
Young Ladies' High School, Providence, 2697, 3146, 3760
Young Women's Christian Temperance Union, Providence, 2719

Zabriskie Memorial Church of Saint John the Evangelist, Newport, 1998, 2245-2246
Zeppelins, see Airships
Zinn, Max, 3116
Zooarchaeology, 2653
Zuccarelli, John G., 3761
Zurier, Melvin L., 1150-1151.